RELIGIONS

A BRIEF INTRODUCTION

Gurdwara
Sahib

The predominant forms of religions in the world today

ALASKA

GREENLAND

CANADA

ICELAND

UNITED KINGDOM

DENMARK

EIRE

NETH

BEL

SWIT

FRANCE

PORTUGAL

SPAIN

UNITED STATES OF AMERICA

NORTH ATLANTIC OCEAN

MEXICO

CUBA

BELIZE

HAITI

GUATEMALA

HONDURAS

EL SALVADOR

NICARAGUA

COSTA RICA

PANAMA

VENEZUELA

GUYANA

SURINAM

FRENCH GUIANA

COLOMBIA

ECUADOR

PERU

BRAZIL

BOLIVIA

PARAGUAY

CHILE

URUGUAY

ARGENTINA

SOUTH ATLANTIC OCEAN

WESTERN SAHARA

MOROCCO

ALGERIA

MAURITANIA

MALI

SENEGAL

THE GAMBIA

BURKINA

GUINEA-BISSAU

GUINEA

NIGER

SIERRA LEONE

IVORY COAST

GHANA

LIBERIA

TOGO

BENIN

EQUATORIAL GUINEA

Indigenous religions

Hinduism and Islam

Buddhism

China: Remnants of Confucianism, Buddhism, Taoism

Japan: Shinto, Buddhism, Sects

Christianity (Roman Catholicism, Protestantism, Eastern Orthodox)

Islam

Varied religions

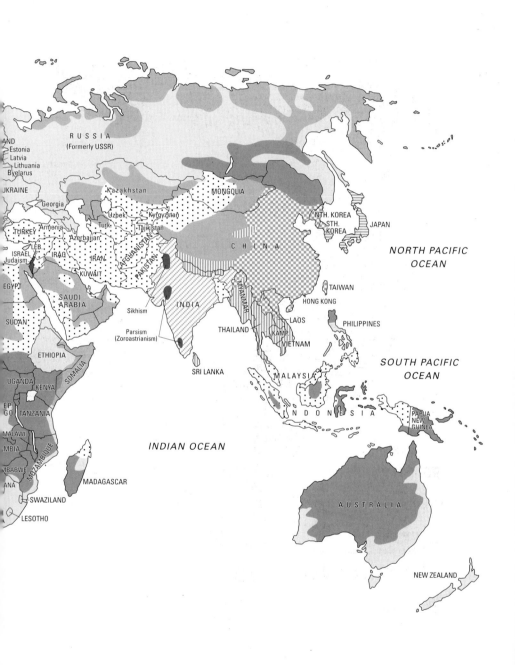

Unique FREE online study resource . . . the *Companion Website*™
www.prenhall.com/fisher

Prentice Hall's exclusive *Companion Website*™ that accompanies *Living Religions* offers unique tools and support that make it easy for students and instructors to integrate this online study guide with the text. The site is a comprehensive resource that is organized according to the chapters within the text and features a variety of learning and teaching modules:

For students:
- **Study Guide Modules** contain a variety of exercises and features designed to help with self-study.
- **Reference Modules** contain *Web Destinations* and *Net Search* options that provide the opportunity to quickly reach information on the web that relates to the content in the text.
- **Communication Modules** include tools such as *Live Chat* and *Message Boards* to facilitate online collaboration and communication.
- **Personalization Modules** include our enhanced **Help** feature that contains a test page for browsers and plug-ins.

For instructors:
- **Syllabus Manager**™ tool provides an easy-to-follow process for creating, posting, and revising a syllabus online that is accessible from any point within the companion website. This resource allows instructors and students to communicate both inside and outside of the classroom at the click of a button.

The Companion Website™ makes integrating the Internet into your course exciting and easy. Join us online at the address above and enter a new world of teaching and learning possibilities and opportunities.

LIVING RELIGIONS

A BRIEF INTRODUCTION

MARY PAT FISHER

SPECIALIST CONSULTANTS
Dr. Jeffrey Adams, St. Michael's College, Vermont
Dr. Jacob Olupona, University of California, Davis
Dr. Xinzhong Yao, University of Wales
Dr. Chatsumarn Kabilsingh, Thammasat University, Bangkok
Dr. Andrew Durwood Foster, Pacific School of Religion, Berkeley
Dr. Mehmet S. Aydin, Dokuz Eylul University, Izmir, Turkey
Dr. Jodh Singh, Punjabi University, Patiala
Dr. David Craig, University of Middlesex

200101

PRENTICE HALL
Upper Saddle River, N.J. 07458

f F

A Division of Pearson Education
Upper Saddle River, New Jersey 07458

This book is a brief edition of *Living Religions,* fourth edition
(Prentice Hall, 1999)

10 9 8 7 6 5 4 3 2 1

ISBN 0-13-061809-8

This book was designed and produced by
Laurence King Publishing Ltd.
71 Great Russell St., London WC1B 3BP
www.laurenceking.co.uk

Editor: Richard Mason
Cover designer: Karen Stafford
Typeset by Fakenham Photosetting, Norfolk, UK
Map: Eugene Fleury

Printed in China

Cover: Peter Davidson, *Upright Forms,* 1986. Acrylic on paper,
28 x 21 in. (71.7 x 52.7 cm.). Private Collection/Bridgeman Art Library.

CONTENTS

CHAPTER FOUR

BUDDHISM

page 75

CHAPTER FIVE

TAOISM AND CONFUCIANISM
page 103

CHAPTER SIX

SHINTO
page 125

CHAPTER SEVEN

JUDAISM
page 136

CHAPTER EIGHT

CHRISTIANITY
page 172

CHAPTER NINE

ISLAM
page 223

CHAPTER TEN

SIKHISM
page 256

CHAPTER ELEVEN

RELIGION AT THE TURN OF THE CENTURY
page 269

PREFACE

Religion is not a museum piece. At the dawn of the twenty-first century, it is a vibrant force in the lives of many people around the world, and many religions are presently experiencing a renaissance.

Living Religions: A Brief Introduction, which is a brief edition of *Living Religions*, fourth edition, remains a sympathetic approach to what is living and significant in the world's major religious traditions and in various new movements that are arising. This book provides a clear and straightforward account of the development, doctrines, and practices of the major faiths followed today. The emphasis throughout is on the personal consciousness of believers and their own accounts of their religion and its relevance in contemporary life.

Special features

The seven feature boxes on "Religion in Public Life" portray the spiritual roots of people who are making significant contributions to society. They include indigenous environmental activist Winona LaDuke, Hindu statesman and interfaith leader Dr. Karan Singh, His Holiness the Dalai Lama whose political efforts on behalf of Tibet are undergirded by Buddhist principles, social activist Dr. Janice Perlman whose Jewish roots have developed her compassion for marginalized people, Dr. Desmond Tutu and Dr. Farid Esack, who as a faithful Christian and a faithful Muslim, respectively, have played significant roles in South Africa's freedom movement and subsequent rebuilding, and His Holiness Baba Virsa Singh, who draws on the universal themes in Sikh tradition to encourage open-mindedness and altruism among Indian public figures.

The socio-political context of the contemporary practice of religions includes an exploration of Hindu nationalism, Buddhist social activism, Confucianism in today's China, Judaism in today's Israel, Islam and the development of nation-states, and Sikh politics. There is significant coverage of women in religion.

Personal interviews with followers of each faith provide first-person accounts of each religion as perceived from within the tradition. These are presented at length in boxes and also in excerpts woven throughout the text.

The book incorporates extensive quotations from primary sources to give a direct perception of the thinking and flavor of each tradition. Particularly memorable brief quotations are set off in boxes.

Three chapters in this book are quite unique. One is the first chapter, "The Religious Response," which explores perspectives on religion in general. These include sceptical materialistic views and psychological perspectives, as well as the point of view that religions are responses to a sacred Reality which cannot be physically perceived but which can perhaps be experienced inwardly. The chapter also includes an exploration of the role of myth and varying types of religious understanding, including contemporary tensions between absolutist and liberal interpretations.

The second chapter portrays the little-understood indigenous religions. I have tried to bypass misleading accounts of indigenous traditions written by outsiders, and to get at the heart of how real people experience their close-to-nature spiritual ways. As we face the possibility of ecological collapse and urban residents feel increasingly alienated from the natural world, it is especially important that these surviving followers of the ancient ways be heard correctly. The chapter includes contemporary efforts to revive the traditional knowledge and practices.

Chapter 11 explores the global religious scene at the turn of the twentieth century. It discusses some types of new religious movements of the late nineteenth and twentieth centuries and issues which have arisen with their development, such as opposition from previously established religions.

This chapter also surveys global trends found in all religions, including both an increase in "fundamentalist" rigidities and a softening of historical boundaries between people of different faiths. Included is a discussion of whether religions are basically similar or irreconcilably different in their claims to truth. There is also an examination of the evolving relationship between religion and materialism, the engagement of religions with social issues of our times, and the potential of religion for improving the future of humanity.

For the purpose of *Living Religions: A Brief Introduction*, I reluctantly took the decision to drop the chapter on Jainism rather than make further cuts to existing chapters. However, students can refer to *Living Religions*, fourth edition, for full coverage of this important religion.

Learning aids

The learning aids from *Living Religions*, fourth edition, have been retained. I have tried to present each tradition clearly and without a clutter of less important names and dates. Key terms, highlighted in bold or italics, are defined when they first appear and also in an extensive glossary. Because students are often unfamiliar with terms from other cultures, pronunciation guides for many of these terms appear in the glossary entries.

The history of the major religions is recapitulated in a time-line in the relevant chapter. The simultaneous development of all religions can be compared in the overall time-line on the end pages.

I assume that readers will want to delve further into the literature. At the end of each chapter, I offer an annotated list of books that might be particularly interesting and useful in deeper study of that religion.

Acknowledgements

In order to try to understand each religion from the inside, I have been traveling for many years to study and worship with devotees and teachers of all faiths, and to interview them about their experience of their tradition.

In preparing *Living Religions: A Brief Introduction*, I have worked directly with consultants who are authorities in specific traditions and who have offered detailed suggestions and resources. I have been blessed with extraordinarily capable and helpful consultants from around the world. They are Dr. Jeffrey Adams, St. Michael's College, Vermont; Dr. Jacob Olupona, University of California, Davis; Dr. Chatsumarn Kabilsingh, Thammasat University, Bangkok; Dr. Xinzhong Yao, University of Wales; Dr. Judith Plaskow, Manhattan College; Dr. Andrew Durwood Foster, Pacific School of Religion, Berkeley; Dr. Mehmet S. Aydin, Dokuz Eylul University, Izmir, Turkey; Dr. Jodh Singh, Punjabi University, Patiala, India; and Dr. David Craig, former head of Religious Programming for BBC World Service and now affiliated with the University of Middlesex. I am extremely grateful for their considerable help, for the assistance of the many scholars who have served as consultants to the previous editions and are acknowledged therein, and for the loving help of Robert Luyster, University of Connecticut, who served as special consultant and co-author to the initial edition of this textbook.

Reviewers offered extremely detailed constructive suggestions, and thus their help has been invaluable. They include: Professor Philip C. Schmitz, Eastern Michigan University; Dr. Christopher S. Queen, Harvard University; Dr. Ted J. Solomon, Drake University; Dr. Nancy A. Hardesty, Clemson University; Dr. Krishna Mallik, Bentley College; Dr. Guy L. Beck, College of Charleston; Dr. David Chappell, University of Hawaii at Manoa. Other people who have generously helped with source material for this edition include Madhuri Santanam Sondhi, Rev. Marcus Braybrooke, Marianne Fisher Vandiver, Edward Fisher, and Dr. G. S. Anand. Despite all this generous help, responsibility for the content of the book rests with me, and I welcome suggestions for its improvement from all scholars.

It is my great good fortune to have worked with two exceptionally talented editors in preparing this edition. One is my long-time editor, Melanie White of Calmann and King in London. Her quick and orderly mind has kept us organized, and her calm and friendly manner has kept the work pleasant, as always. The other is Richard Mason, a very experienced editor also with Calmann and King whose intelligent help has proved invaluable. I am very glad to be working with them both, and also with Kate Tuckett, who has swiftly handled the three-way communications among us.

Finally, I cannot adequately express my gratitude to my own revered teacher, Baba Virsa Singh of Gobind Sadan. Under his inspiration, both the common people and the great scholars of all religions are moving toward more profound understanding and practice of their own faiths and deeper appreciation of others' religions.

May God help us all in our search for truth and our efforts to become better human beings.

Mary Pat Fisher
Gobind Sadan Institute for Advanced Studies
in Comparative Religion, New Delhi

CHAPTER 1
THE RELIGIOUS RESPONSE

Before sunrise, members of a Muslim family rise in Malaysia, perform their purifying ablutions, spread their prayer rugs facing Mecca, and begin their prostrations and prayers to Allah. In a French cathedral, worshippers line up for their turn to have a priest place a wafer on their tongue, murmuring, "This is the body of Christ." In a South Indian village, a group of women reverently anoint a cylindrical stone with milk and fragrant sandalwood paste and place around it offerings of flowers. The monks of a Japanese Zen Buddhist monastery sit crosslegged and upright in utter silence, broken occasionally by the noise of the *kyosaku* bat falling on their shoulders. On a mountain in Mexico, men, women, and children who have been dancing without food or water for days greet an eagle flying overhead with a burst of whistling from the small wooden flutes they wear around their necks. By a stream in Iowa, a young woman sits with her eyes closed, praying to the universe that her life may serve some sacred purpose.

These and countless other moments in the lives of people around the world are threads of the tapestry we call "religion." The word is probably derived from the Latin, meaning "to tie back," "to tie again." Despite the rich diversity of its expressions, all of religion shares the goal of tying people back to something behind the surface of life—a greater reality which lies beyond, or invisibly infuses, the world that we can perceive with our five senses.

Attempts to connect with this greater reality have taken many forms. Many of them are organized institutions, such as Buddhism or Christianity, with leaders, sacred scriptures, and historical traditions. Others are private personal experiences of individuals who belong to no institutionalized religion but nonetheless have an inner life of prayer, meditation, or direct experience of an inexplicable presence.

In this introductory chapter, we will try to develop some understanding of religion in a generic sense before studying the characteristics of the particular group religions that are practiced today.

Why are There Religions?

Why is religion such a universal aspect of human life? Answers which have been offered to this question range from the highly sceptical to the totally faithful.

The **materialistic** point of view is that the supernatural is imaginary; only the material world exists. From this point of view, religions have been invented by humans.

An influential example of this perspective can be found in the work of the nineteenth-century philosopher Ludwig Feuerbach. He reasoned that there are no supernatural entities; deities are simply projections, objectifications of people's fears and desires. Following this line of reasoning, twentieth-century psychoanalyst Sigmund Freud described religion as a "universal obsessional neurosis"—a cosmic projection and replaying of the loving and fearful relationships that we had (and have) with our parents. From Freud's extremely sceptical point of view, religious belief is an illusion springing from people's infantile insecurity and neurotic guilt; as such it closely resembles mental illness.

Others believe that religions have been created or at least used to manipulate people. The nineteenth-century socialist philosopher Karl Marx argued that a culture's religion—as well as all other aspects of its social structure—springs from its economic framework. In Marx's view, religion is a tool for oppressing people, a mirror of an unjust economic structure:

> *Man makes religion: religion does not make man. . . . Religion is the sigh of the oppressed creature, the sentiment of a heartless world, and the soul of soulless conditions. It is the opium of the people. . . .*[1]

In contrast to analyses of religion which suggest that religion is bad for people, some psychologists argue that it is possible for religion to enhance a person's mental health and mature development. The twentieth-century psychoanalyst Erich Fromm suggested that humans have a normal need for a stable frame of reference, and that religion fulfils this need.

> *It appears that throughout the world man has always been seeking something beyond his own death, beyond his own problems, something that will be enduring, true and timeless. He has called it God, he has given it many names; and most of us believe in something of that kind, without ever actually experiencing it.*
>
> *Jiddu Krishnamurti*[2]

All religions help to uncover meaning in the midst of the mundane. The influential twentieth-century scholar of comparative religion, Mircea Eliade, wrote of the distinction between the *profane*—the everyday world of seemingly random, ordinary, and unimportant occurrences—and the **sacred**—the realm of the extraordinary and supernatural, the source of the universe and its values, which is charged with significance. Religions open pathways to the sacred by exploring the *transpersonal* dimension of life—the eternal and infinite, beyond limited human concerns.

Religions describe ideals which can radically transform people. Mahatma Gandhi was an extremely shy, fearful, self-conscious child. His transformation into one of the great political figures of our time occurred as he meditated single-mindedly on the great Hindu scripture, the

Bhagavad-Gita. Gandhi was particularly impressed by the second chapter, which he says was "inscribed on the tablet of my heart."[3] It reads, in part:

> *He is forever free who has broken*
> *Out of the ego-cage of I and mine*
> *To be united with the Lord of Love.*
> *This is the supreme state. Attain thou this*
> *And pass from death to immortality.[4]*

People long to gain strength for dealing with personal problems. Those who are suffering severe physical illness, privation, terror, or grief often turn to the divine for help. Agnes Collard, a Christian woman near death from four painful years of cancer, reported that her impending death was bringing her closer to God:

> *I don't know what or who He is, but I am almost sure He is there. I feel His presence, feel that He is close to me during the awful moments. And I feel love. I sometimes feel wrapped, cocooned in love.[5]*

Rather than seeking help from without, an alternative approach is to gain freedom from problems by changing our ways of thinking. Many contemplative spiritual traditions teach methods of turning within to discover and eradicate all attachments, desires, and resentments associated with the small self, revealing the purity of the eternal self. Once we have found it within, we begin to see it wherever we look. Kabir, a fifteenth-century Indian weaver who was inspired alike by Islam and Hinduism, described this state of spiritual bliss:

> *The blue sky opens out farther and farther,*
> *the daily sense of failure goes away,*
> *the damage I have done to myself fades,*
> *a million suns come forward with light,*
> *when I sit firmly in that world.[6]*

We may be struck by another religious impulse—appreciation for this extraordinary creation. For those who honor the miracle of life, each day is begun in gratitude. Brother David Steindl-Rast observes that gratitude is the basis of the spiritual life. Religions teach us that there is a "someone" or "something" to thank for all of this.

We look to religions for understanding, for answers to our many questions about life. Who are we? Why are we here? What happens after we die? Why is there suffering? Why is there evil? Is anybody up there listening? For those who find security in specific answers, some religions offer **dogma**—systems of doctrines proclaimed as absolutely true and accepted as such, even if they lie beyond the domain of one's personal experiences. Absolute faith provides some people with a sense of relief from anxieties, a secure feeling of rootedness, meaning, and orderliness. Religions may also provide rules for living, governing everything from diet to personal relationships. Such prescriptions are seen as earthly reflections of the order that prevails in the cosmos. Some religions, however, encourage people to explore the perennial questions by themselves, and to live in the uncertainties of not knowing intellectually, breaking through old concepts until nothing remains but truth itself.

Religious belief often springs from mystical experience—the overwhelming awareness that one has been touched by a reality that far transcends ordinary life. Those who have had such experiences find it hard to describe them, for what has touched them lies beyond the world of time and space to which our languages refer. These people usually know instantly and beyond a shadow of doubt that they have had a brush with spiritual reality. Having researched such experience, Nona Coxhead concluded:

> The 'flash of illumination' brings a state of glorious inspiration, exaltation, intense joy, a piercingly sweet realization that the whole of life is fundamentally right and that it knows what it's doing.[7]

The most beautiful and profound emotion that we can experience is the sensation of the mystical. It is the sower of all true science. He to whom this emotion is a stranger, who can no longer wonder and stand rapt in awe, is as good as dead. To know that what is impenetrable to us really exists, manifesting itself as the highest wisdom and the most radiant beauty which our dull faculties can comprehend only in their most primitive forms—this knowledge, this feeling is at the center of true religiousness. ... A human being is part of the whole. ... He experiences himself, his thoughts and feelings as something separated from the rest—a kind of optical delusion of his consciousness. ... Our task must be to free ourselves from this prison by widening our circle of compassion to embrace all living creatures, and the whole [of] nature in its beauty.

Albert Einstein[8]

Understandings of Ultimate Reality

Approached by different ways of knowing, by different people, from different times and different cultures, the sacred has many faces. The ultimate reality may be conceived as **immanent** (present in the world) or **transcendent** (existing above and outside of the material universe). Many people perceive the sacred as a personal Being, as Father, Mother, Teacher, Friend, Beloved, or as a specific deity. Religions based on one's relationship to the divine Being are called **theistic**. If the Being is worshipped as a singular form, the religion is **monotheistic**. If many attributes and forms of the Divine are emphasized, the religion may be labeled **polytheistic**. Religions which hold that beneath the multiplicity of apparent forms there is one underlying substance are called **monistic**.

Some people believe that the sacred reality is usually invisible but occasionally appears visibly in human **incarnations**, such as Christ or Krishna, or in special manifestations such as the flame Moses reportedly saw coming from the center of a bush but not consuming it. Or the deity which cannot be seen is described in human terms. Theologian Sallie McFague thus writes of God as Lover by imputing human feelings to God:

> *God as lover is the one who loves the world not with the fingertips but totally and passionately, taking pleasure in its variety and richness, finding it attractive and valuable, delighting in its fulfilment. God as lover is the moving power of love in the universe, the desire for unity with all the beloved.*[9]

Atheism is the non-belief in any deity. Following Karl Marx, many communist countries in the twentieth century discouraged or suppressed religious beliefs, attempting to replace them with secular faith in supposedly altruistic government. Atheism may also arise from within, in those whose experiences give them no reason to believe that there is anything more to life than the mundane.

Agnosticism is not the denial of the divine but the feeling, "I don't know whether it exists or not," or the belief that if it exists it is impossible for humans to know it. Ultimate reality may also be conceived in **nontheistic** terms. It may be experienced as a "changeless Unity," as "Suchness," or simply as "the Way." There may be no sense of a personal Creator God in such understandings.

These categories are not mutually exclusive, so attempts to apply the labels can sometimes confuse us rather than help us understand religions. Mystics may have deep personal encounters with the divine and yet find it so unspeakable that they say it is beyond human knowing. The eleventh-century Jewish scholar Maimonides asserted that:

> *the human mind cannot comprehend God. Only God can know Himself. The only form of comprehension of God we can have is to realize how futile it is to try to comprehend Him.*[10]

Jaap Sahib, the great hymn of praises of God by the Tenth Sikh Guru, Guru Gobind Singh, consists largely of the negative attributes of God.

> *Salutations to the One without colour or hue,*
> *Salutations to the One who hath no beginning.*
> *Salutations to the Impenetrable,*
> *Salutations to the Unfathomable ...*
> *O Lord, Thou art Formless and Peerless*
> *Beyond birth and physical elements. ...*
> *Salutations to the One beyond confines of religion. ...*
> *Beyond description and Garbless*
> *Thou art Nameless and Desireless.*
> *Thou art beyond thought and ever Mysterious.*[11]

Worship, Symbol, and Myth

No matter how believers conceive of the ultimate reality, it inspires their reverence. The outer forms of religions consist in large part of human attempts to express this reverence and perhaps enter the sacred state of communion with that which is worshipped.

Group ceremonies often include sharing of food, fire or candles, purifi-cation with water, flowers, fragrances, and offerings of some sort. Professor Antony Fernando of Sri Lanka explains:

Even the most illiterate person knows that in actual fact no god really picks up those offerings or is actually in need of them. What people offer is what they own. ... Sacrifices and offerings are a dramatic way of proclaiming that they are not the ultimate possessors of their life and also of articulating their determination to live duty-oriented lives and not desire-oriented lives.[12]

Deepest consciousness cannot speak the language of everyday life; what it knows can only be suggested in *symbols*—images borrowed from the material world which are similar to ineffable spiritual experiences. They appeal to the emotions and imagination rather than the rational mind. Many peoples have used similar images to represent similar sacred mean-ings. The sun, for example, is frequently honored as a symbol of the divine because of its radiance.

Myths are stories based on symbols. A primary function of religious myth is to establish models for human behavior. Stories about the heroic lives of the great founders and saints are held up as examples for molding one's own life. They also establish belief in a superhuman dimension to these lives. Great holy figures are often said to have been born of virgin mothers, for instance, for their seminal source is not human but rather the Invisible One. There are also myths of **cosmogony** (sacred accounts of the creation of the world) and of **eschatology** (beliefs concerning the pur-ported end of the world). These myths form a sacred belief structure which supports the laws, rituals, and institutions of the religion, as well as explaining the cosmic situation and the ways of the community.

It is now common to interpret such symbols and myths metaphorically rather than literally and to see them as serving functions for the society or the individual. For example, Joseph Campbell interpreted legends of the hero's journey (stories of separation, initiation, and return bearing truth to the people) as a form of psychological instruction for individuals:

It is the business of mythology to reveal the specific dangers and techniques of the dark interior way from tragedy to comedy. Hence the incidents are fantastic and "unreal": they represent psychological, not physical, triumphs. The passage of the mythological hero may be overground, [but] fundamentally it is inward—into depths where obscure resistances are overcome, and long lost, forgotten powers are revivified, to be made available for the transfiguration of the world.[13]

Absolutist and Liberal Interpretations

Within each faith people often have different ways of interpreting their tra-ditions. The **orthodox** stand by an historical form of their religion. They try to be strict followers of its established practices, laws, and creeds. Those who try to resist contemporary influences and affirm what they perceive as the historical core of their religion could be called **absolutists**. In our times, many people feel that their distinctive identity as individuals or as members of an established group is threatened by the sweeping social changes brought by modern industrial culture. The breakup of family relationships, loss of geographic rootedness, decay of clear behavioral codes, and loss of local control may be very unsettling. To find stable footing, some people may try to stand on selected religious doctrines or practices from the past. Religious leaders may encourage this trend toward rigidity by declaring themselves absolute authorities or by telling the people that their scriptures are literally, absolutely, and exclusively true.

The term **fundamentalism** is often applied to this selective insistence on parts of a religious tradition and to violence against people of other religions. This use of the term is misleading, for no religion is based on hatred of other people, and because those who are labeled "fundamentalists" may not be engaged in a return to the true basics of their religion. A Muslim "fundamentalist" who insists on the veiling of women, for instance, does not draw this doctrine from the foundation of Islam, the Holy Qur'an, but rather from historical cultural practice in some Muslim countries. A Sikh "fundamentalist" who concentrates on externals such as wearing a turban, sword, and steel bracelet overlooks the central insistence of the Sikh Gurus on the inner rather than outer practice of religion. A Hindu "fundamentalist" who objects to the presence of Christian missionaries working among the poor ignores one of the basic principles of ancient Indian religion, which is the tolerant assertion that there are many paths to the same universal truth. Rev. Valson Thampu, editor of the Indian journal *Traci*, writes that this selective type of religious extremism "absolutises what is spiritually or ethically superfluous in a religious tradition. True spiritual enthusiasm or zeal, on the other hand, stakes everything on being faithful to the spiritual essence."[14]

Angels Weep

Wherever there is slaughter of innocent men, women, and children for the mere reason that they belong to another race, color, or nationality, or were born into a faith which the majority of them could never quite comprehend and hardly ever practice in its true spirit; wherever the fair name of religion is used as a veneer to hide overweening political ambition and bottomless greed, wherever the glory of Allah is sought to be proclaimed through the barrel of a gun; wherever piety becomes synonymous with rapacity, and morality cowers under the blight of expediency and compromise, wherever it be—in Yugoslavia or Algeria, in Liberia, Chad, or the beautiful land of the Sudan, in Los Angeles or Abuija, in Kashmir or Conakary, in Colombo or Cotabatu—there God is banished and Satan is triumphant, there the angels weep and the soul of man cringes; there in the name of God humans are dehumanized; and there the grace and beauty of life lie ravished and undone.

Dr. Syed Z. Abedin, Director of the Institute for Muslim Minority Affairs.[15]

Those who are called religious **liberals** take a more flexible approach to religious tradition. They may see scriptures as products of a specific culture and time rather than the eternal voice of truth, and may interpret passages metaphorically rather than literally. If activists, they may advocate reforms in the ways their religion is officially understood and practiced. Those who are labeled **heretics** publicly assert controversial positions that are unacceptable to the orthodox establishment. **Mystics** are guided by their own spiritual experiences, which may coincide with any of the above positions.

The Negative Side of Organized Religion

Tragically, religions have often split rather than unified humanity, have oppressed rather than freed, have terrified rather than inspired.

Since the human needs that religions answer are so strong, those who hold religious power are in a position to dominate their followers. In fact, in many religions leaders are given this authority to guide people's spiritual lives, for their wisdom and special access to the sacred is valued. Because religions involve the unseen, the mysterious, these leaders' teachings may not be verifiable by everyday experience. They must more often be accepted on faith. While faith is one of the cornerstones of spirituality, it is possible to surrender to spiritual leaders who are misguided.

Religions try to help us make ethical choices in our lives, to develop a moral conscience. But in people who already have perfectionist or paranoid tendencies, the fear of sinning and being punished can be exaggerated to the point of neurosis or even psychosis by blaming, punishment-oriented religious teachings. If they try to leave their religion for the sake of their mental health, they may be haunted with guilt that they have done a terribly wrong thing. Religions thus have the potential for wreaking psychological havoc in their followers.

Because religions may have such a strong hold on their followers—by their fears, their desires, their deep beliefs—they are potential centers for political power. When church and state are one, the belief that the dominant national religion is the only true religion may be used to oppress those of other beliefs within the country.

Religion may also be used as a rallying point for wars against other nations, casting the desire for control as a holy motive. Throughout history, huge numbers of people have been killed in the name of eradicating "false" religions and replacing them with the "true" religion. Our spirituality has the potential for uniting us all in bonds of love, harmony, and mutual respect. But often it has served instead to divide us by creating barriers of hatred and intolerance.

As institutionalized religions spread their founders' teachings, there is the danger that more energy will go into preserving the outer form of the tradition than maintaining its inner spirit. When the founder dies, the movement's center may shift to people with managerial prowess, and those who turn the original inspirations into routine rituals and dogma.

Nonetheless, as we survey the various contemporary manifestations of the religious impulse, we will find people and groups—in all traditions—

who are keeping the spark of the divine alive today. To find them, we will attempt to drop the lens of seeing from the point of view of our own culture, and try instead to see religions as they see themselves. To use Mircea Eliade's term, we will be delving into the **phenomenology** of religion—its specifically sacred aspects—rather than trying to explain religions only in terms of other disciplines such as history, politics, economics, sociology, or psychology. The phenomenology of religion involves an appreciative—even loving—investigation of religious phenomena in order to comprehend their spiritual intention and meaning. We will also be striving for "thick description," a term used by the cultural anthropologist Clifford Geertz, not only reporting outward behaviors but also attempting to explain their meaning for believers within the faith. To take such a journey through many religions does not presuppose that we must forsake our own religious beliefs or our scepticism. But the journey is likely to broaden our perspective and thus bring us closer to understanding other members of our human family. Perhaps it will bring us closer to ultimate reality itself.

Suggested Reading

Campbell, Joseph, *The Hero with a Thousand Faces*, second edition, Princeton, New Jersey: Princeton University Press, 1968. Brilliant leaps across time and space to trace the hero's journey—seen as a spiritual quest—in all the world's mythologies and religions.

Campbell, Joseph with Bill Moyers, *The Power of Myth*, New York: Doubleday, 1988. More brilliant comparisons of the world's mythologies with deep insights into their common psychological and spiritual truths.

Carter, Robert E., ed., *God, The Self, and Nothingness—Reflections: Eastern and Western*, New York: Paragon House, 1990. Essays from major Eastern and Western scholars of religion on variant ways of experiencing and describing ultimate reality.

Otto, Rudolf, *The Idea of the Holy*, second edition, London: Oxford University Press, 1950. An important exploration of "non-rational" experiences of the divine.

Paden, William E., *Interpreting the Sacred: Ways of Viewing Religion*, Boston: Beacon Press, 1992. A gentle, readable introduction to the complexities of theoretical perspectives on religion.

Shinn, Larry D., ed., *In Search of the Divine: Some Unexpected Consequences of Interfaith Dialogue*, New York: Paragon House Publishers, 1987. Scholars from varied religions present a tapestry of understandings of the Sacred Reality.

CHAPTER 2

INDIGENOUS SACRED WAYS

"Everything is alive"

Here and there around the globe, pockets of people still follow local sacred ways handed down from their remote ancestors and adapted to contemporary circumstances. These are the traditional **indigenous** people—descendants of the original inhabitants of lands now controlled by political systems in which they have little influence.

Indigenous people comprise at least four percent of the world population. Some who follow the ancient spiritual traditions still live close to the earth in non-industrial small-scale cultures; many do not. But despite the disruption of their traditional lifestyles, many indigenous people maintain a sacred way of life that is distinctively different from all other religions. These enduring ways, which indigenous people may refer to as their Original Instructions on how to live, were almost lost under the onslaught of genocidal colonization, conversion pressures from global religions, mechanistic materialism, and destruction of their natural environments by the global economy of limitless consumption.

Much of the ancient visionary wisdom has disappeared. There are few traditionally trained elders left and few young people willing to undergo the lengthy and rigorous training necessary for spiritual leadership in these sacred ways. Nevertheless, in our time there is a renewal of interest in these traditions, fanning hope that what they offer will not be lost.

Barriers to Understanding

Outsiders have known or understood little of the indigenous sacred ways. When threatened with severe repression, many of these traditions have long been practiced only in secret. In Mesoamerica, the ancient teachings have remained hidden for five hundred years since the coming of the conquistadores, passed down within families as a secret oral tradition. The Buryats living near Lake Baykal in Russia were thought to have been converted to Buddhism and Christianity centuries ago; however, few attended the opening of a Buddhist temple after the fall of communism.

In parts of aboriginal Australia, the real teachings have been underground for two hundred years since white colonialists and Christian missionaries appeared. As aborigine Lorraine Mafi Williams explains:

> We have stacked away our religious, spiritual, cultural beliefs. When the missionaries came, we were told by our old people to be respectful, listen and be obedient, go to church, go to Sunday school, but do not adopt the Christian doctrine because it takes away our cultural, spiritual beliefs. So we've always stayed within God's laws in what we know.[1]

Not uncommonly, the newer global traditions have been blended with the older ways. For instance, Buddhism as it spread often adopted the existing customs, such as the recognition of local deities. Now many indigenous people practice one of the global religions while still retaining many of their traditional ways.

Until recently, those who attempted to ferret out the native sacred ways had little basis for understanding them. Many were anthropologists who approached spiritual behaviors from the non-spiritual perspective of Western science. Knowing that researchers from other cultures did not grasp the truth of their beliefs, the native peoples have at times given them information that was incorrect in order to protect the sanctity of their practices from the uninitiated.

Academic study of traditional ways is now becoming more sympathetic and self-critical, however, as is apparent in this statement by Gerhardus Cornelius Oosthuizen, a European researching African traditional religions:

> [The] Western worldview is closed, essentially complete and unchangeable, basically substantive and fundamentally non-mysterious; i.e. it is like a rigid programmed machine. ... This closed worldview is foreign to Africa, which is still deeply religious. ... This world is not closed, and not merely basically substantive, but it has great depth, it is unlimited in its qualitative varieties and is truly mysterious; this world is restless, a living and growing organism.[2]

Indigenous spirituality is a lifeway, a particular approach to all of life. It is not a separate experience, like meditating in the morning or going to church on Sunday. Rather, spirituality ideally pervades all moments, from reverence in gathering clay to make a pot, to respect within tribal council meetings. As an elder of the Huichol in Mexico puts it:

> Everything we do in life is for the glory of God. We praise him in the well-swept floor, the well-weeded field, the polished machete, the brilliant colors of the picture and embroidery. In these ways we prepare for a long life and pray for a good one.[3]

In most native cultures, spiritual lifeways are shared orally. Teachings are experienced rather than read from books. There are therefore no scriptures of the sort that other religions are built around (although there once existed some texts, such as the Mayan codices, which were destroyed by conquering groups). This characteristic helps to keep the indigenous sacred ways dynamic and flexible rather than fossilized. It also keeps the sacred experience fresh in the present. However, not until the latter part of the twentieth century did outside investigators begin to study the oral narratives as clues to the historical experiences of the individuals or groups.

Despite the hindrances to understanding of indigenous forms of spirituality, the doors to understanding are opening somewhat in our times. Firstly, the traditional elders are very concerned about the growing potential for planetary disaster. Some are beginning to share their basic values, if not their esoteric practices, in hopes of preventing industrial societies from destroying the earth. Secondly, those of other faiths are beginning to recognize the value and profundity of indigenous ways which were in the past viewed as abhorrent and suppressed by organized religions. Thirdly, many people who have not grown up in native cultures are attempting to embrace indigenous spiritual ways, finding their own traditions lacking in certain qualities for which they long, such as love for the earth.

But many native peoples are wary of this trend. They feel that their sacred ways are all they have left and worry that even these may be sold, stolen, and ruined.

Cultural Diversity

In this chapter we are considering the faith-ways of indigenous peoples as a whole. However, behind these generalizations lie many differences in social contexts, as well as in religious beliefs and practices. These traditions have evolved within materially as well as religiously diverse cultures. Some are descendants of civilizations with advanced urban technologies that were needed to support concentrated populations. When the Spanish conqueror Cortes took over Tenochtitlan (which now lies beneath Mexico City) in 1519, he found it a beautiful clean city with elaborate architecture, indoor plumbing, a highly accurate calendar, and advanced systems of mathematics and astronomy. The Tsalagi people had an advanced theocracy before the time of Christ. Former African kingdoms were highly culturally advanced with elaborate arts such as intricate bronze casting.

At the other extreme are those few cultures that still maintain a survival strategy of hunting and gathering. For example, some Australian aborigines continue to live as mobile foragers, though constricted to government-owned stations. A nomadic survival strategy necessitates simplicity in material goods; whatever can be gathered or built rather easily at the next camp need not be dragged along. But material simplicity is not a sign of spiritual poverty. The Australian aborigines have a complex cosmogony, or model of the origins of the universe and their purpose within it, as well as a working knowledge of their own bioregion.

Some traditional people live in their ancestral enclaves, somewhat sheltered from the pressures of modern industrial life, though not untouched by the outer world. Tribal peoples have lived deep in the forests and hills of India for thousands of years, utilizing the trees and plants for their food and medicines, although within the twentieth century their ancestral lands were taken over for "development" projects and encroached upon by groups which are more politically and economically powerful, rendering many of the 75 million Indian tribal people landless laborers. The Hopi

Nation has continuously occupied a high plateau area of the Southwestern United States for eight hundred to one thousand years; their sacred ritual calendar is tied to the yearly farming cycle.

Other indigenous people visit their sacred sites and ancestral shrines but live in more urban settings because of job opportunities. The people who participate in ceremonies in the Mexican countryside include subway personnel, journalists, and artists of native blood who live in Mexico City.

In addition to variations in lifestyles, indigenous traditions vary in their adaptations to dominant religions. Often native practices have become interwoven with those of global religions, such as Buddhism, Islam, and Christianity. In Southeast Asia, household Buddhist shrines are almost identical to the spirit houses in which the people still make offerings to honor the local spirits. The Dahomey tradition from West Africa was carried to Haiti by thousands of African slaves and called **Voodoo**, from *vodu*, one of the names for the chief non-human spirits. Forced by the European colonialists to adopt Christianity, worshippers of Voodoo secretly fused their old gods with their images of Catholic saints. While interaction with larger state societies or colonial powers has been extremely detrimental to indigenous peoples around the world, adaptation of the dominant religions has at times allowed the traditional people to survive.

Despite their different histories and economic patterns, indigenous sacred ways do tend to have some characteristics in common. Perhaps from ancient contact across land-bridges that no longer exist, there are linguistic similarities between the languages of the Tsalagi in the Americas, Tibetans, and the aboriginal Ainu of Japan.

Certain symbols and metaphors are repeated in the inspirational art and stories of many traditional cultures around the world, but the people's relationships to and concepts surrounding these symbols are not inevitably the same. Nevertheless, the following sections look at some recurring themes in the spiritual ways of diverse small-scale cultures.

The Circle of Right Relationships

For many indigenous peoples, everything in the cosmos is intimately interrelated. A symbol of unity among the parts of this sacred reality is a circle. This symbol is not used by all indigenous people; the Navajo, for instance, regard a completed circle as stifling and restrictive. However, many other indigenous people hold the circle sacred because it is infinite—it has no beginning, no end. Time is circular rather than linear, for it keeps coming back to the same place. Life revolves around the generational cycles of birth, youth, maturity, and physical death, the return of the seasons, the cyclical movements of the moon, sun, stars, and planets.

To maintain the natural balance of the circles of existence, most indigenous peoples have traditionally been taught that they must develop right relationships with everything that is. Their relatives include the unseen world of spirits, the land and weather, the people and creatures, and the power within.

Relationships with spirit

Many indigenous traditions worship a Supreme Being who they believe created the cosmos. This being is known by the Sioux as "Wakan tanka" or "Great Mysterious" or "Great Spirit."

African names for this One are attributes such as "All-powerful," "Creator," "the one who is met everywhere," "the one who exists by himself," or "the one who began the forest." The supreme being is often referred to by male pronouns, but in some groups the supreme being is a female, such as Ala, earth mother goddess of the Ibo. Many traditional languages make no distinction between male and female pronouns, and some see the divine as androgynous, a force arising from the interaction of male and female aspects of the universe.

Awareness of one's relationship to the Great Power is thought to be essential, but the power itself remains unseen and mysterious. An Eskimo mystic described his people's experience of:

> a power that we call Sila, which is not to be explained in simple words. A great spirit, supporting the world and the weather and all life on earth, a spirit so mighty that [what it says] to mankind is not through common words, but by storm and snow and rain and the fury of the sea; all the forces of nature that men fear. But Sila has also another way of [communicating]; by sunlight and calm of the sea, and little children innocently at play, themselves understanding nothing. ... When all is well, Sila sends no message to mankind, but withdraws into endless nothingness, apart.[4]

It cannot be said that indigenous concepts of and attitudes toward a Supreme Being are necessarily the same as that which Western monotheistic religions refer to as God or Allah. In African traditional religions, much more emphasis tends to be placed on the transcendent dimensions of everyday life, and doing what is spiritually necessary to keep life going normally. Many unseen powers are perceived to be at work in the material world. In various traditions, some of these are perceived without form, as mysterious and sacred presences. Others are perceived as having more definite, albeit invisible, forms and personalities. These may include deities with human-like personalities, the nature spirits of special local places such as venerable trees and mountains, animal spirit helpers, personified elemental forces, ancestors who still take an interest in their living relatives, special beings such as the spirit keepers of the four directions recognized by some Native Americans, or the *nagas*, known to the traditional people of Nepal as invisible serpentine spirits who control the circulation of water in the world and also within our bodies.

Ancestors may be extremely important. Traditional Africans understand that even the person is not an individual, but a composite of many souls—the spirits of one's parents and ancestors—resonating to their feelings. As Rev. William Kingsley Opoku, organizer of the African Council for Spiritual Churches, explains:

> Our ancestors are our saints. Christian missionaries who came here wanted us to pray to their saints, their dead people. But what about our saints? ...

If you are grateful to your ancestors, then you have blessings from your grandmother, your grandfather, who brought you forth. . . . Non-Africans came in and said we should not obey our ancestors, should not call upon them at all, because they are evil people. This has been a mental bondage, a terrible thing.[5]

Continued communication with the "living dead" is extremely important to traditional Africans. Food and drink are set out or poured for them, acknowledging that they are still in a sense living and engaged with the people's lives. Failure to keep in touch with the ancestors is a dangerous oversight which may bring misfortunes to the family.

The Dagara of Burkina Faso in West Africa are familiar with the *kontom-bili* who look like humans but are only about one foot tall, because of the humble way they express their spiritual power. Other West African groups, descendants of hierarchical ancient civilizations, recognize a great pantheon of deities, the **orisa** or *vodu*, each the object of special cult worship. The orisa are embodiments of the dynamic forces in life, such as Oya, goddess of death and change, experienced in tornadoes, lightning, winds, and fire; and Shango, a former king who is now honored as the stormy god of electricity and genius.

Kinship with all creation

In addition to the unseen powers, all aspects of the tangible world are imbued with spirit. Josiah Young III explains that in African traditional religion, both the visible and invisible realms are filled with spiritual forces:

The invisible connotes the numinous field of ancestors, spirits, divinities, and the Supreme Being, all of whom, in varying degrees, permeate the visible. Visible things, however, are not always what they seem. Pools, rocks, flora, and fauna may dissimulate invisible forces of which only the initiated are conscious.[6]

Within the spiritually-charged visible world, all things may be understood as spiritually interconnected. Everything is therefore experienced as family. The community is paramount, and it may extend beyond the living humans in the area. Many traditional peoples know the earth as their mother. The land one lives on is part of her body, loved, respected, and well-known. Oren Lyons, an elder of the Onondaga Nation Wolf Clan, speaks of this intimate relationship:

[The indigenous people's] knowledge is profound and comes from living in one place for untold generations. It comes from watching the sun rise in the east and set in the west from the same place over great sections of time. We are as familiar with the lands, rivers and great seas that surround us as we are with the faces of our mothers. Indeed we call the earth Etenoha, our mother, from whence all life springs. . . . We do not perceive our habitat as wild but as a place of great security and peace, full of life.[7]

Some striking feature of the natural environment of the area—such as a great mountain or canyon—may be perceived as the center from which the whole world was created. Such myths heighten the perceived sacredness of the land. Western Tibet's Mount Kailas, high in the Himalayas, is seen by the indigenous people of that area as the center of the earth, a ladder into the sky, a sacred space where the earthly and the supernatural meet.

In contrast to the industrial world's attempts to use and dominate the earth, native people say they consider themselves caretakers of their mother, the earth. They are now raising their voices against the destruction of the environment. Their prophecies warn of the potential for global disaster. Nepali shamans who have recently undertaken the difficult pilgrimage to Lake Mansarovar at the base of revered Mount Kailas report that the lake level is low and the *nagas* are unhappy. At the dawn of the twenty-first century, their prophecies indicate difficult times ahead unless we humans take better care of our planetary home. Some indigenous visionaries say they hear the earth crying. Contemporary Australian aboriginal elder Bill Neidjie speaks of feeling the earth's pain:

> *I feel it with my body,*
> *with my blood.*
> *Feeling all these trees,*
> *all this country . . .*
> *If you feel sore . . .*
> *headache, sore body*
> *that mean somebody killing tree or grass.*
> *You feel because your body in that tree or earth. . . .*
> *You might feel it for two or three years.*
> *You get weak . . .*
> *little bit, little bit . . .*
> *because tree going bit by bit . . .*
> *dying.*[8]

The earth abounds with living presences, in traditional worldviews. Rocks, bodies of water, and mountains—considered inanimate by other peoples—are personified as living beings by indigenous peoples. Before one can successfully climb a mountain, one must ask its permission. Visionaries can see the spirits of a body of water and many traditional cultures have recognized certain groves of trees as places where spirits live, and where specially trained priests and priestesses can communicate with them. As a Pit River Indian explained, "Everything is alive."

All creatures may be perceived as kin, endowed with consciousness and the power of the Great Spirit. Many native peoples have been raised with an "ecological" perspective: they know that all things depend on each other. They are taught that they have a reciprocal, rather than dominating, relationship with all beings. Hawaiian *kahuna* (shaman-priest) Kahu Kawai'i explains:

> *How you might feel toward a human being that you love is how you might*
> *feel toward a dry leaf on the ground and how you might feel toward the*
> *rain in the forest and the wind. There is such intimacy that goes on that*
> *everything speaks to you and everything responds to how you are in being—*
> *almost like a mirror reflecting your feelings.*[9]

Trees, animals, insects, and plants are all to be approached with caution and consideration. If one must cut down a tree or kill an animal, one must first explain one's intentions and ask forgiveness of the being. Scientific research now verifies that there can be a sort of communication between human and non-human species. Plants may actually grow better when loved and talked to; if a person even thinks of harming a plant, some polygraph tests show that the plant experiences a "fear" reaction.

Indigenous people feel that one who harms nature may himself be harmed in return. Tribal peoples of Madhya Pradesh in the jungles of central India will avoid killing a snake, for they feel that its partner would later come after them to seek revenge. When a Buryat cuts a tree to build a house, he must first offer milk, butter, rice, and alcohol to the spirits of the forest and ask their forgiveness, or he is likely to fall ill. In 1994, a half-French, half-Buryat businessman returned to Buryatia and started to build a guesthouse in a picturesque place, Svyatoy Nos, which had long been considered sacred to the god Huushan-baabay. When the businessman began cutting trees, he was warned by the traditional people that he would not be successful. Nonetheless, he proceeded and finished the guesthouse. Three months later, it burned down.

Respect is always due to all creatures, in the indigenous world view, but sometimes a degree of coercion is also necessary. In traditional Eskimo whale hunts by kayak through rough, icy seas, the odds were stacked so heavily in favor of the whale that it was necessary to use song and ritual to charm and befuddle the whale.

There are many stories of indigenous people's relationships with non-human creatures. Certain trees tell the healing specialists which herbs to use in curing the people. Australian aboriginal women are adept at forming hunting partnerships with dogs. Birds are thought to bring messages to the people from the spirit world. A Hopi elder said he spent three days and nights praying with a rattlesnake. "Of course he was nervous at first, but when I sang to him he recognized the warmth of my body and calmed down. We made good prayer together."[10]

Relationships with power

A second common theme is developing an appropriate relationship with spiritual energy.

All animals have power, because the Great Spirit dwells in all of them, even a tiny ant, a butterfly, a tree, a flower, a rock. The modern, white man's way keeps that power from us, dilutes it. To come to nature, feel its power, let it help you, one needs time and patience for that. ... You have so little time for contemplation. ... It lessens a person's life, all that grind, that hurrying and scurrying about.

Lame Deer, Lakota Nation[11]

In certain places and beings, the power of spirit is believed to be highly concentrated. It is referred to as *mana* by the people of the Pacific islands. This is the vital force that makes it possible to act with unusual strength, insight, and effectiveness.

Tlakaelel, a contemporary spiritual leader of the descendants of the Toltecs of Mexico, describes how a person might experience this power when looking into an obsidian mirror made to concentrate power:

> *When you reach the point that you can concentrate with all your will, inside there, you reach a point where you feel ecstasy. It's a very beautiful thing, and everything is light. Everything is vibrating with very small signals, like waves of music, very smooth. Everything shines with a blue light. And you feel a sweetness. Everything is covered with the sweetness, and there is peace. It's a sensation like an orgasm, but it can last a long time.*[12]

Sacred sites may be recognized by the power that believers feel there. Concentrated power spots were known to ancient as well as contemporary peoples of the earth. Some sacred sites have been used again and again by successive religions, either to capitalize on the energy or to co-opt the preceding religion. Chartres Cathedral in France, for instance, was built on an ancient ritual site. In New Zealand, the traditional Maori people know of the revivifying power of running water, such as waterfalls.

Because power can be built up through sacred practices, the ritual objects of spiritually developed persons may have concentrated power. Special stones and animal artifacts may also carry power. A person might be strengthened by the spiritual energy of the bear or the wolf by wearing sacred clothing made from its fur. Power can also come to one through visions or by being given a sacred pipe or the privilege of collecting objects into a personal sacred bundle.

In some cultures—such as the traditional peoples of the North American plains—women are thought to have a certain natural power; men have to work harder for it. Women's power is considered mysterious, dangerous, uncontrolled. It is said to be strongest during their menstrual period. In certain rituals in which both men and women participate, women's menstrual blood is often thought to diminish or weaken the ritual or the men's spiritual power. In most Native American nations that have sweat lodge ceremonies for ritual purification, menstruating women are not allowed to enter the lodge. Nevertheless, a few cultures such as the Ainu of Japan have prized menstrual blood as a potent offering returned to the earth.

Gaining power is both desirable and dangerous. If misused for personal ends, it becomes destructive and may turn against the person. To channel spiritual power properly, native people are taught that they must live within strict limits. Those who seek power or receive it unbidden are supposed to continually purify themselves of any selfish motives and dedicate their actions to the good of the whole. A pipe carrier must be ethically impeccable and must never turn away anyone who asks for help.

Spiritual Specialists

In a few of the remaining hunting and gathering tribes, religion is a relatively private matter. Each individual has direct access to the unseen. Although spirit is invisible, it is considered a part of the natural world. Anyone can interact with it spontaneously, without complex ceremony and without anyone else's aid.

More commonly, however, the world of spirit is thought to be dangerous, like a fire that can burn those who are unprepared for its power. Although everyone is expected to observe certain personal ways of worship, such as offering prayers before taking plant or animal life, many ways of interacting with spirit are thought to be best left to those who are specially trained for the roles. These specialists are gradually initiated into the secret knowledge that allows them to act as intermediaries between the seen and the unseen. They sacrifice themselves through ritual purification and emptying practices in order to be clean vessels for the sacred knowledge and the sacred role.

Storytellers and other sacred roles

One common role is that of storyteller. Because the traditions are oral rather than written, these people must memorize long and complex stories and songs so that the group's sacred traditions can be remembered and taught, generation after generation. It is very important to Australian aborigines that their children learn about the origin of the people and the local creatures, and that they understand the weather and the patterns of the stars. Songs about these matters may have a hundred verses or more. The orally transmitted epics of the indigenous Ainu of Japan are up to ten thousand "lines" long. Chants to the Yoruba orisa comprise 256 "volumes" of eight hundred long verses each.

What is held only in memory cannot be physically destroyed, but if a tribe is small and all its storytellers die, the knowledge is lost. This happened on a large scale during contacts with colonial powers, as native people were killed by war and imported diseases. Professor Wande Abimbola, who is trying to preserve the oral tradition of the Yoruba, has made thousands of tapes of the chants, but there must also be people who can understand and interpret them.

There are also bards who carry the energy of ancient traditions into new forms. Rather than memory, they cultivate the muse. In Africa, poets are considered "technicians of the sacred," conversing with a dangerous world of spirits. They are associated with the flow and rhythms of water. Players of the "talking drums" are highly valued as communicators with the spirits, ancestors, and Supreme Being.

"Tricksters" such as foxes often appear in the stories of indigenous traditions. They are paradoxical, transformative beings. Similarly, sacred clowns may endure the shame of behaving as fools during public rituals in order to teach the people through humor. Often they poke fun at the most sacred of rituals, keeping the people from taking themselves too seriously. A sacred fool, called *heyoka* by the Lakota, must be both innocent and very wise about human nature, and must have a visionary relationship with spirit as well.

> *Life is holiness and everyday humdrum, sadness and laughter, the mind and the belly all mixed together. The Great Spirit doesn't want us to sort them out neatly.*
>
> Leonard Crow Dog, Lakota medicine man[13]

A more coveted role is that of being a member of a secret society in which one can participate by initiation or invitation only. When serving in ceremonial capacities, members often wear special costumes to hide their human identities and help them take on the personas of spirits they are representing. In African religions, members of secret societies periodically appear as impersonators of animal spirits or of dead ancestors, helping to demonstrate that the dead are still watching the living, as awe-inspiring protectors of villages. The all-male Oro secret society in some Yoruba tribes uses this authority to enforce male domination; when Oro appears, "roaring" by swinging a piece of wood on a cord, women stay inside their huts.

Women also have their secret societies, whose activities are yet little known by outsiders. Among aboriginal peoples of Australia, the men's and women's groups initiate members into separate but interrelated roles for males and females. For instance, when boys are separated from the tribe for circumcision by the men's secret society, the women's secret society has its own separation rituals and may stage mock ritual fights with the men's society. Men's and women's rituals ultimately refer to the eternal **Dream Time**, in which there is no male–female differentiation.

Sacred dancers likewise make the unseen powers visible. Body movements are a language in themselves expressing the nature of the cosmos, a language which is understood through the stories and experiences of the community. Such actions keep the world of the ancestors alive in the consciousness of succeeding generations.

In some socially stratified societies there are also priests and priestesses. These are specially trained and dedicated people who carry out the rituals that ensure proper functioning of the natural world, and perhaps also communicate with particular spirits or deities. Though West African priests or priestesses may have part-time earthly occupations, they are expected to stay in a state of ritual purity and spend much of their time in communication with the spirit being to whom they are devoted, paying homage and asking the being what he or she wants the people to do. In West Africa, there are also mediums associated with the temples; they enter a state of trance or allow themselves to be possessed by gods or spirits in order to bring messages to the people.

Shamans

The most distinctive spiritual specialists among indigenous peoples are the **shamans**. They are called by many names, but the Siberian word "shaman" is used as a generic term by scholars for those who offer themselves as mystical intermediaries between the physical and the non-physical world for specific purposes, such as healing. Archaeological research has confirmed that shamanic methods are extremely ancient—at least twenty to thirty thousand years old. Ways of becoming a shaman and practicing shamanic arts are remarkably similar around the globe.

Shamans may be helpers to society, using their skills to benefit others. They are not to be confused with sorcerers, who practice black magic to harm others or promote their own selfish ends, interfering with the cosmic order. Spiritual power is neutral; its use depends on the practitioner. What Native Americans call "medicine power" does not originate in the medicine person. Black Elk explains:

> *Of course it was not I who cured. It was the power from the outer world,*
> *and the visions and ceremonies had only made me like a hole through which*
> *the power could come to the two-leggeds. If I thought that I was doing it*
> *myself, the hole would close up and no power could come through.*[14]

There are many kinds of medicine. One is the ability to heal physical, psychological, and spiritual problems. Techniques used include physical approaches to illness, such as therapeutic herbs, dietary recommendations, sweatbathing, massage, cauterization, and sucking out of toxins. But the treatments are given to the whole person—body, mind, and spirit, with special emphasis on healing relationships within the group—so there may also be metaphysical divination, prayer, chanting, and ceremonies in which group power is built up and spirit helpers are called in. If an intrusion of harmful power, such as the angry energy of another person, seems to be causing the problem, the medicine person may attempt to suck it out with the aid of spirit helpers and then dry vomit the invisible intrusion.

These shamanic healing methods, once dismissed as quackery, are now beginning to earn respect from the scientific medical establishment. Medicine people are permitted to attend indigenous patients in some hospitals, and in the United States, the National Institute of Mental Health has paid Navajo medicine men to teach young Indians the elaborate ceremonies that have often been more effective in curing the mental health problems of Navajos than has Western psychiatry.

In addition to healing, certain shamans are thought to have gifts such as talking with plants and animals, controlling the weather, seeing and communicating with the spirit world, and divination, prophesying by techniques such as reading patterns revealed by a casting of cowrie shells.

Shamans are contemplatives, Lame Deer explains:

> *The* wicasa wakan *[holy man] wants to be by himself. He wants to be*
> *away from the crowd, from everyday matters. He likes to meditate, leaning*
> *against a tree or rock, feeling the earth move beneath him, feeling the weight*
> *of that big flaming sky upon him. That way he can figure things out. Closing*
> *his eyes, he sees many things clearly. What you see with your eyes shut is*
> *what counts. . . . He listens to the voices of the* wama kaskan—*all those who*
> *move upon the earth, the animals. He is as one with them. From all living*

beings something flows into him all the time, and something flows from him.[15]

The role of shaman may be hereditary or it may be recognized as a special gift. Either way, training is rigorous. In order to work in a mystical state of ecstasy, moving between ordinary and non-ordinary realities, shamans must experience physical death and rebirth. Some have spontaneous near-death experiences. Uvavnuk, an Eskimo shaman, was spiritually initiated when she was struck by a lightning ball. After she revived, she had great power, which she dedicated to serving her people. Other potential shamans undergo rituals of purification, isolation, and bodily torment until they make contact with the spirit world.

For many shamans, initiation into the role is not a matter of their own choice. The spirit enters whom it will. Tsering, an aged Nepali *dhami* (shaman), relates:

We never wanted to become dhamis. *In fact, we tried hard to get the gods to leave us. We pleaded, performed worship ceremonies, even carried manure around with us to offend them, but nothing seemed to work. When calamities began to hit my family—when my brother died falling off the roof and our best horse drowned in the river—I realized I had no choice and had to make the initiatory journey to Kailas.*[16]

Once there, the new shamans had to plunge naked with unbound hair into the freezing Lake Mansarovar in order to commune with the spirits. Then on returning to their village, the deities who had possessed them insisted that they prove their spiritual connection by terrible feats such as drinking boiling oil. Thereafter, the shamans have been respected as authorities.

In addition to becoming familiar with death, a potential shaman must undergo lengthy training in shamanic techniques, the names and roles of the spirits, and secrets and myths of the tribe. Novices are taught both by older shamans and reportedly by the spirits themselves. If the spirits do not accept and teach the shaman, he or she is unable to carry the role.

The helping spirits that contact would-be shamans during the death-and-rebirth crisis become essential partners in the shaman's sacred work. Often it is a spirit animal who becomes the shaman's guardian spirit, giving him or her special powers. The shaman may even take on the persona of the animal while working. Many tribes feel that healing shamans need the powers of the bear; Lapp shamans metamorphosed into wolves, reindeer, bears, or fish.

Shamans also have the ability to enter parallel, spiritual realities at will in order to bring back knowledge, power, or help for those who need it. An altered state of consciousness is needed. Techniques for entering this state are the same around the world: drumming, rattling, singing, dancing, and in some cases hallucinogenic drugs. The effect of these influences is to open what the Huichol shamans of Mexico call the *Narieka*—the doorway of the heart, the channel for divine power, the point where human and spirit worlds meet. It is often experienced and represented artistically as a pattern of concentric circles.

Living Indigenous Sacred Ways

One of the remaining traditional shamans of Buryatia, Nadezhda Ananyevna Stepanova comes from a family of very powerful shamans. Her mother tried to prevent her becoming a shaman. Buddhist **lamas** had spread the impression that shamans were to be avoided, saying that they were ignorant, primitive servants of dark, lower spirits. Nadezhda explains:

"When I was twenty-six, I was told I would be a shaman, a great shaman. When I told Mother, she said, 'No, you won't.' She took a bottle, went to her native town, and then came back. 'Everything will be taken away; you won't become a shaman,' she said. I became seriously ill, and Mother was paralyzed. The doctors were surprised, but I understood then: We were both badly ill because she went against the gods.

Nobody could heal me. Then one seer said, 'You must cure.' I replied, 'I don't know anything about curing.' But a voice inside me said, 'If you don't become a shaman, you will die. You will be overrun by a lorry with a blue number.' I began to collect materials about medicine, about old rites. I was initiated by the men shaman of all the families, each praying to his god in a definite direction, for every god has his direction. I sat in the middle. Every shaman asked his gods to help me, to protect me, to give me power. The ritual was in early March. It was very frosty and windy, and I was only lightly dressed, but I wasn't cold at all. The wind didn't touch me. I sat motionless for about four hours, but I was not cold.

I began to cure. It is very difficult. The main thing to me is to help a person if I can. I pray to my gods, ask them for mercy, I ask them to pay them for mercy, I ask them to pay attention, to help. I feel the pain of those who come to me, and I want to relieve it. I have *yodo*—bark from a fir tree scratched by a bear; its smoke purifies. I perform rituals of bringing back the soul; often they work. My ancestors are very close to me; I see them as well as I see you.

Last year in the island Olechon in Lake Baikal, there was a great gathering of shamans from Tchita, Irkutsk, Ulan-Ude, Yakutiya, and Buryatia to pray to the great spirits of Baikal about the well-being and prosperity of the Buryat land. For a long time these spirits were forgotten by the people, and they fell asleep. They could not take an active part in the life of people; they could not help them any more. *Teylagan*, the prayer of the shamans for the whole Buryatia, was to awaken the great spirits.

It was a clear, clear sunny day, without a cloud. When the prayer began, it started to rain. It was a very good sign.

We had always prayed to the great spirits of this area. But when the Buddhists came, persecution began, and people prayed secretly, only for their families. They could not pray for the whole Buryat nation, and they did not. They forgot. Shamans were killed. Then the atheistic Soviet regime tried to make us forget the faith, and we forgot. The most terrible thing about them was that they wanted to make people forget everything, to live by the moment and forget their roots. And what is man without roots? Nothing. It is a loss of everything. That is why now nobody has compassion for anybody. Now we are reaping the fruit: robbery, drinking, drugs. This is our disaster. That is why we must pray to our own gods.[17]

The "journey" then experienced by shamans is typically into the Upperworld or the Lowerworld. To enter the latter, they descend mentally through an actual hole in the ground, such as a spring, a hollow tree, cave, animal burrow, or special ceremonial hole regarded as a navel of the earth. These entrances typically lead into tunnels which if followed open into bright landscapes. Reports of such experiences include not only what the journeyer saw but also realistic physical sensations, such as how the walls of the tunnel felt during the descent.

The shaman enters into the Lowerworld landscape, encounters beings there, and may bring something back if it is needed by the client. This may be a lost guardian spirit or a lost soul, brought back to revive a person in a coma. The shaman may be temporarily possessed by the spirit of departed relatives so that an afflicted patient may finally clear up unresolved tensions with them that are seen as causing illness. Often a river must be crossed as the boundary between the world of the living and the world of the dead. A kindly old man or woman may appear to assist this passage through the underworld. This global shamanic process is retained only in myths, such as the Orpheus story, in cultures that have subdued the indigenous ways.

Contemporary Rituals

Although the forces of life honored by traditional peoples are unseen, one can communicate with these forces in symbolic non-verbal ways, such as sprinkling cornmeal in thanks for the offerings of the earth or using pipe smoke to carry prayers up to the spirits. The people have also observed that life operates according to strict natural laws. Humans can help to maintain the harmony of the universe by their ritual observances.

In order to maintain the natural balance and to ensure success in the hunt or harvest, ceremonies must be performed with exactitude. There is a specific time for the telling of specific stories. Chona, a Tohono O'odham (Papago) medicine woman, told anthropologist Ruth Underhill:

> I should not have told you this [the origin of Coyote, who helped to put the world in order, with a few mistakes]. These things about the Beginning are holy. They should not be told in the hot time when the snakes are out. The snakes guard our secrets. If we tell what is forbidden, they bite.[18]

Paying attention to the proper forms brings clarity of attention and creates a sacred space in which many things can happen.

Group observances

Indigenous ways are community-centered. Through group rituals, traditional people not only honor the sacred but also affirm their bonds with each other and all of creation. Rituals often take people out of everyday consciousness and into awareness of the presence of the sacred. When participants return from such altered states, they typically experience a heightened group consciousness that powerfully binds individuals together as a community.

Each group has its own special ways of ritual dedication to the spirits of life, but they tend to follow certain patterns everywhere. Some honor major points in the human life cycle, such as birth, naming, puberty, marriage, and death. These rites of passage assist people in the transition from one state to another and help them become aware of their meaningful contribution to life. When a Hopi baby is twenty days old, it is presented at dawn to the rays of Father Sun for the first time and officially given a name. Its face is ritually cleansed with sacred cornmeal, a ceremony that will be repeated at death for the journey to the Underworld.

There are also collective rituals to support the group's survival strategies. In farming communities these include ways of asking for rain, of insuring the growth of crops, and of giving thanks for the harvest. Dhyani Ywahoo explains, "When Native American people sing for the rain, the rain comes—because those singers have made a decision that they and the water and the air and the Earth are one."[19]

Ritual dramas about the beginnings and sacred history of the people engage performers and spectators on an emotional level through the use of special costumes, body paint, music, masks, and perhaps sacred locations. These dramas provide a sense of orderly interface among humans, the land, and the spiritual world. They also dramatize mysticism, drawing the people toward direct contact with the spirit world. Those who have sacred visions and dreams are supposed to share them with others, and often this is done through dramatization.

According to legend, the Plains Indians were given the sacred pipe by White Buffalo Calf Woman as a tool for communicating with the mysteries and understanding the ways of life. The bowl of the pipe represents the female aspect of the Great Spirit, the stem the male aspect. When they are ritually joined, the power of the spirit is thought to be present as the pipe is passed around the circle for collective communion with each other and with the divine.

Groups also gather for ritual purification and spiritual renewal of individuals. Indigenous peoples of the Americas "smudge" sites and possessions, cleansing them with smoke from special herbs, such as sage and sweetgrass. Many groups make an igloo-shaped "sweat lodge" into which hot stones are carried. People huddle together in the dark around the stone pit. When water is poured on the stones, intensely hot steam sears bodies and lungs. Everyone prays earnestly. Leonard Crow Dog says of the *inipi* (sweat lodge):

> The *inipi* is probably our oldest ceremony because it is built around the simplest, basic, life-giving things: the fire that comes from the sun, warmth without which there can be no life; inyan wakan, or tunka, the rock that was there when the earth began, that will still be there at the end of time; the earth, the mother womb; the water that all creatures need; our green brother, the sage; and encircled by all these, man, basic man, naked as he was born, feeling the weight, the spirit of endless generations before him, feeling himself part of the earth, nature's child, not her master.[20]

Pilgrimages to sacred sites are often communal. Buryats gather on top of

Erde, the mountain where the spirit of the earth lives, and all join hands to encircle it, playing games; a great energy is said to appear in the huge circle. The Huichol Indians of the mountains of western Mexico make a yearly journey to a desert they call Wirikuta, the Sacred Land of the Sun. They feel that creation began in this place. And like their ancestors, they gather their yearly supply of peyote cactus at this sacred site. Peyote has the power to alter consciousness: it is their "little deer," a spirit who helps them to communicate with the spirit world.

Sacrificing oneself for the sake of the whole is highly valued in most indigenous traditions. In the Americas a powerful ceremony for this purpose is the sun dance. Among the Oglala Lakota, participants may dance for four days without food or water, looking at the sun and praying for blessings for the people. In diverse forms, sun dances are now performed at many sites each spring and summer, most of them on the midwestern and northern plains of North America. In theory, only those who have had visions that they should perform the dance should do so.

When indigenous groups are broken up by external forces, they lose the cohesive power of these group rituals. Africans taken to the New World as slaves lost not only their own individual identity but also their membership in tight-knit groups. In an attempt to re-establish a communal sense of shared spiritual traditions among African-Americans, Professor Maulana Ron Karenga created a contemporary celebration, *Kwanzaa*, based on indigenous African "first fruits" harvest festivals. Using symbolic objects to help create a special atmosphere (such as candles, corn, fruits and vegetables, and a "unity cup," all called by their Swahili names), families and groups of families meet from December 26 to January 1 to explore their growth over the past year. They look at their own experiences of the Seven Principles—unity, self-determination, collective work, family-centeredness, purpose, creativity with limited resources, and confidence—and reward each other for progress by giving gifts.

Individual observances

In indigenous sacred ways, it is considered important for each person to experience a personal connection with the spirits. The people acknowledge and work with the spirits in many everyday ways. For instance, when searching for herbs, a person is not to take the first plant found; an offering is made to it, with the prayer that its relatives will understand one's needs. Guardian spirits and visions are sought by all the people, not just specialists such as shamans. The shaman may have more spirit helpers and more power, but visionary experiences and opportunities for worship are available to all. Indigenous traditions have therefore been called "democratized shamanism."

Temples to the spirits may exist, but one can also worship them anywhere. Wande Abimbola observes:

> Big temples aren't necessary to worship the orisa, even though there are
> temples for most orisa in Africa. If you are a devotee of Ifa, you can carry the

objects of Ifa in your pocket. If you want to make an offering to Ogun, put any piece of iron on the floor and make an offering to it. It's just like a Christian would carry a Bible or maybe a cross.[21]

To open themselves for contact with the spirit world, individuals in many indigenous cultures undergo a **vision quest**. After ritual purification, they are sent alone to a sacred spot to cry to the spirits to reveal something of their purpose in life and help them in their journey. This may also be done before undertaking a sacred mission, such as the sun dance. Indigenous Mexican leader Tlakaelel describes the vision quest as he observes it:

You stay on a mountain, desert, or in a cave, isolated, naked, with only your sacred things, the things that you have gained, in the years of preparation— your eagle feathers, your pipe, your copal [tree bark used as incense]. You are left alone four days and four nights without food and water. During this time when you are looking for your vision, many things happen. You see things move. You see animals that come close to you. Sometimes you might see someone that you care about a lot, and they're bringing water. You feel like you're dying of thirst, but there are limits around you, protection with hundreds of tobacco ties. You do not leave this circle, and this vision will disappear when they come to offer the water or sometimes they will just drop it on the ground. Or someone comes and helps you with their strength and gives you messages.[22]

In the traditional sacred ways, one is not supposed to ask for a vision for selfish personal reasons. The point of this individual ordeal, which is designed to be physically and emotionally stressful, is to ask how one can help the people and the planet.

Contemporary Issues

Sadly, traditional spiritual wisdom has been largely obliterated in many parts of the world by those who wanted to take the people's lands or save their souls with some other path to the divine. Under the slogan "Kill the Indian and save the man," the American founder of the boarding school system for native children took them away from their families at a young age and transformed their cultural identity, presenting the native ways as inferior and distancing them from normal participation in the traditional sacred life.

A similar policy of attempted acculturation of Australian aboriginal children was conducted between the 1880s and 1960s. Taken away from their parents by force, the "Stolen Generation" were often abused or used as slaves. Five children of Eliza Saunders were taken away by social workers while she and her husband were looking for employment. She recalls, "You walk miles and miles and find they're not there. It's like your child has been killed." One of her children, the Green Party politician Charmaine Clarke, managed to run away from foster care after eleven years and rejoin her mother, but she says of her missing family history, "When myself and my brothers and sisters go home, we five have to sit there quite mute and just listen, observe. Because we were never there."[23] In 1998, Australian citizens attempted to apologize for this "attempted genocide," with some 300,000 signatures in Sorry Books and hundreds of emotional multi-racial ceremonies in churches, schools, and cities across Australia.

In Africa, despite changing social contexts, traditional religion is still strong among some groups, such as the Yoruba, whose priest-diviners are still respected, and to whom the orisa contacted in trance still reveal the nearness and importance of the invisible forces. However, in contemporary urban African areas, the traditional interest in the flow of the past into the present, with value placed on the intensity of present experience, has been rapidly replaced by a Westernized view of time, in which one is perpetually anxious about the future. This shift has led to severe psychological disorientation and social and political instability. Those whose spiritual cultures have been merged with world religions such as Islam, Buddhism, or Christianity are now examining the relationship of their earlier tradition to the intercultural missionary traditions. African scholars have noted, for instance, that to put God in the forefront, as Christians do, does violence to the greater social importance of ancestor spirits in African traditional religions.

Indigenous peoples have also been recent victims of well-meaning but disastrous development projects. In Zimbabwe, for example, thousands of traditional self-sufficient Vaduma people were displaced from their ancestral lands, when the lands were flooded to create a huge artificial lake for irrigating an area hundreds of kilometers away. Jameson Kurasha of the University of Zimbabwe describes the effects on the Vaduma:

> When the "idea" of development was imposed on them, families were separated by a massive stretch of water. Now the Murinye Mugabe families are alienated from each other. They are now peoples without a tangible past to guide and unite them because their past (i.e. ancestors) are either buried or washed away by the lake. They are basically a people without a home to point to. The separation has left a cultural damage that will never be restored.[24]

Modern development schemes—as well as outright plunder of natural resources for profit—are being called into question by land-based traditional peoples around the world and attempts have begun to revive the ancient wisdom by acknowledging its validity. In India, officials in the ministry of environment and forests are now acknowledging that the remaining sacred groves of the indigenous people are essential bastions of biodiversity and should not be destroyed. The remaining sacred groves, such as those used for ceremonial feeding of snakes, are treasure-houses of biodiversity and of plants used in healing. In such areas, it is often the shamans who teach the tribal people the importance of protecting the vegetation.

Some indigenous people feel that their traditional sacred ways are not only valid, but actually essential for the future of the world. They see these understandings as antidotes to mechanistic, dehumanizing, environmentally destructive ways of life. Rather than regarding their ancient way as inferior, intact groups such as the Kogi of the high Colombian rainforest feel they are the Elder Brothers of all humanity, responsible for keeping the balance of the universe and re-educating their Younger Brothers who have become distracted by desire for material gain.

Winona LaDuke

As the narrator of Winona LaDuke's semi-fictional novel, *Last Standing Woman*, puts it, her clanspeople have a special destiny:

> *In times past, they were warriors, the ogichidaa, those who defended the people. Sometimes we still are. We are what we are intended to be when we have those three things that guide our direction*—our name, our clan, and our religion.[25]

Winona herself is a prime example. She is continually in the news as a fighter on behalf of the future of the earth and its disadvantaged peoples. When in 1996 she ran as the Green Party candidate for Vice-President of the U.S., she campaigned for reforms oriented toward long-term survival:

> *I am interested in reframing the debate on the issues of this society, the distribution of power and wealth, abuse of power, the rights of the natural world, the environment, and the need to consider an amendment to the U.S. Constitution in which all decisions made today would be considered in light of the impact on the seventh generation from now.*[26]

Winona now lives on her father's traditional tribal lands in northern Minnesota in the White Earth Reservation. She is trying to re-establish an economic base which will allow her Anishinaabe people to return to their land and to have the legal right to control its use. The land is of spiritual as well as economic importance to her people.

The project she has initiated has already repurchased over 1,300 acres of former tribal lands. The lands include burial grounds with undisturbed birch and sugar maple

forests, and a 715-acre area encompassing two lakes, nesting sites for waterfowl, wild rice, and many medicinal plants. The latter area is earmarked to teach Anishinaabe children their own traditional cultural practices, and also to demonstrate their value for planetary survival.

Winona, a Harvard-educated journalist, lives in a lakeside log cabin on the reservation with her two children, trying to teach them traditional beliefs. She has no fear of fighting against large-scale vested interests. In 1994 she chained herself to a paper company's gates to protest their clearance of forests including thousand-year-old trees to make phone books. The publicity led other companies to cancel their contracts with that paper company.

An Anishinaabe tribal prophecy indicates that the people of the seventh fire—the current period—will look around and discover the things which they had lost. With loss of the land had come loss of traditional spiritual principles. At the end of *Last Standing Woman*, the narrator speaks in the year 2018, describing her culture which has rediscovered its spiritual traditions:

> *To understand our relationship to the whole and our role on the path of life. We also understand our responsibility. We only take what we need, and we leave the rest. We always give thanks for what we are given. What carries us through is the relationship we have to the Creation and the courage we are able to gather from the experience of our aanikoobijigan, our ancestors, and our oshkaabewisag, our helpers.*[27]

Personal visions and ancient prophecies about the dangers of a lifestyle that ignores the earth and the spiritual dimensions of life are leading native elders around the world to gather internationally and raise their voices together. They assert indigenous spiritual insights and observations about the state of the planet, political matters, and contemporary lifestyle issues. At such gatherings it is often the voices of the native elders which help to ground the lofty abstractions in sacred reality. The indigenous delegates to the 1993 Parliament of World Religions in Chicago noted that:

> *One hundred years ago during the 1893 Parliament of World Religions, the profoundly religious Original Peoples of the Western Hemisphere were not invited. We are still here and still struggling to be heard for the sake of our Mother Earth and our children.*[28]

Many people have said that indigenous peoples are myths of the past, ruins that have died. But the indigenous community is not a vestige of the past, nor is it a myth. It is full of vitality and has a course and a future. It has much wisdom and richness to contribute. They have not killed us and they will not kill us now. We are stepping forth to say, "No, we are here. We live."
                                        Rigoberta Menchú of the K'iché Maya[29]

Suggested Reading

Beck, Peggy V. and Walters, Anna L., *The Sacred: Ways of Knowledge, Sources of Life*, Tsaile (Navajo Nation), Arizona: Navajo Community College Press, 1977. A fine and very genuine survey of indigenous sacred ways, particularly those of North America.

Berger, Julian, *The Gaia Atlas of First Peoples: A Future for the Indigenous World*, New York: Anchor Books, 1990. An illustrated survey of contemporary survival issues facing the original inhabitants of many lands, with particular reference to threats to their environment from invading cultures.

Brown, Joseph Epes, *The Sacred Pipe*, 1953, New York: Penguin Books, 1971. Detailed accounts of the sacred rites of the Oglala Sioux by Black Elk, a respected holy man.

Gleason, Judith, *Oya: In Praise of the Goddess*, Boston: Shambhala Publications, 1987. A complex exploration of the Yoruba goddess which gives some insight into African traditions.

Lame Deer, John and Richard Erdoes, *Lame Deer: Seeker of Visions*, New York: Pocket Books, 1976. Fascinating first-hand accounts of the life of a rebel visionary who tried to maintain the old ways.

Olupona, Jacob K., *African Traditional Religions in Contemporary Society*, New York: Paragon House, 1991. A rich collection of papers by African scholars affirming and analyzing the contemporary characteristics and impacts of indigenous African sacred ways.

Zuesse, Evan M., *Ritual Cosmos: The Sanctification of Life in African Religions*, Athens, Ohio: Ohio University Press, 1979. A perceptive attempt to explain the essential differences between African traditional religions and Western monotheistic traditions, with detailed examples of African efforts to sanctify and find meaning in everyday life.

CHAPTER 3

HINDUISM

"With mind absorbed and heart melted in love"

In the Indian subcontinent there has developed a complex variety of religious paths. All those that honor the ancient scriptures called the **Vedas** are commonly grouped together under the term "Hinduism." This label is derived from a name applied by foreigners to the people living in the region of the Indus River. The indigenous term for the Veda-based traditions in the entire Indian region is **Sanatana Dharma** ("eternal religion"). Sanatana, "eternal" or "ageless," reflects the belief that this religion has always existed. Dharma is often translated as "religion," but its meaning encompasses matters of duty, natural law, social welfare, ethics, health, and transcendental realization. Dharma is thus a holistic approach to social coherence and the good of all, corresponding to order in the cosmos.

The spiritual expressions of Sanatana Dharma range from extreme asceticism to extreme sensuality, from the heights of personal devotion to a deity to the heights of abstract philosophy, from metaphysical proclamations of the oneness behind the material world to worship of images representing a multiplicity of deities. According to tradition, there are actually three hundred thirty-three million deities in India. The feeling is that the Divine has countless faces, and all are divine.

The extreme variations within Sanatana Dharma are reflections of its great age. Few of the myriad religious paths that have arisen over the millennia have been lost. They continue to co-exist in present-day India. Some scholars of religion argue that these ways are so varied that there is no central tradition which can be called "Hinduism." The term appeared in the nineteenth century under colonial British rule as a category for census-taking, to encompass all Indians who did not belong to any other named religion, such as Jainism, Buddhism, Islam, or Christianity. Both Western scholars and Indians then adopted the term and applied it retroactively to include a great variety of scriptures and spiritual practices.

> *Truth is one; sages call it by various names.*   *Rig Veda*

One avenue into understanding this mosaic of beliefs and practices is to trace the supposed chronological development of major patterns which exist today. However, in villages, where the majority of Indians live, worship of deities is quite diverse and does not necessarily follow the more reified and philosophical Brahmanic tradition which is typically referred to as "Hinduism." The Brahmanic tradition tends to be upper class, educated, and male-dominated. Even in this Brahmanic tradition, historians of religion and devotees of its various forms have widely variant ideas about the historical origin of its threads. The archaeological evidence is fragmented, and Indians have not traditionally emphasized chronology. Reports of actual events and people are interwoven with mythology.

Harappan Civilization

Many of the threads of Sanatana Dharma may have existed in the religions practiced by the aboriginal Dravidian peoples of India. There were also advanced urban centers in the Indus Valley from about 2500 BCE or even earlier until 1500 BCE. Major fortified cities have been found by archaeologists at Harappa, Mohenjo-Daro, and Dholavira; the culture they represent is labeled "Harappan."

Archaeologists have found little conclusive evidence of temples in the Harappan cities, but the people clearly lavished great care on their plumbing and irrigation systems. The major structure at Mohenjo-Daro, called the Great Bath, is a large lined tank with steps leading down into it, surrounded by an open courtyard; an adjoining structure has what appear to be private bathing rooms. Historians speculate from this evidence that the early Indus people placed a religious sort of emphasis on hygiene and/or ritual purification.

They also seem to have venerated life-giving power. Although few pieces of ritual art remain, seals have been found depicting an ascetic male figure in cross-legged yogic posture. He has an erect phallus, wears a great horned headdress, and is surrounded by strong animals such as bulls and tigers. There were also many stone **lingams**, natural elongated oval stones or sculptures up to two feet tall. Both the seals and the lingams suggest that the early Indus people knew about meditation practices and were worshippers of a deity who bore the attributes of the later god **Siva**,[1] who is still one of the major forms of the Divine worshipped today.

Even more prominent among the artefacts are terracotta figurines that seem to honor a great goddess. Sacred pots, like those still used in South Indian village ceremonies honoring the goddess, may have been associated then, as now, with the feminine as the receptacle of the primeval stuff of life. There is also considerable evidence of worship of local deities by stone altars placed beneath sacred trees. Each tree is still popularly believed to be the home of a tree spirit, and many are honored with offerings.

Vedic Religion

Western historians developed the Aryan Invasion Theory that the highly organized cultures of the Indus Valley and the villages in other parts of the subcontinent were gradually overrun by nomadic invaders from outside India. The theory argues that the **Vedas**, the sublime religious texts often referred to as the foundations of Sanatana Dharma, were the product of the invaders, and not of indigenous Indians. These invaders were identified as **Aryans**, who were among the Indo-European tribes thought to have migrated outward from the steppes of southern Russia during the second millennium BCE. The material culture of these patriarchal tribes was relatively simple—although they had powerful means of making war, such as horse-drawn chariots, composite bows, and a warrior class—and they were probably illiterate. The Vedas sing the praises of the Indian subcontinent, and do not refer to any other homeland. The Harappan urban centers do seem to have declined, but there is no clear evidence why they did so.

Today the Aryan Invasion Theory is hotly contested by scholars and by Hindu nationalists who refuse to believe that their religion is foreign-born. There may have been considerable mixing between indigenous Dravidian people and those who composed the Vedas in **Sanskrit**, the ancient language whose origins are also not definitely established. If the Aryan Invasion Theory is not true, many ideas about the origins and evolution of Sanatana Dharma which have been prevalent among historians of religion for the last 150 years must be re-examined. The relationship between the Harappan civilization and the religion of the Vedas is still unclear. And the Vedas themselves are the foundation of upper-caste Brahmanic Hinduism, but not necessarily of all forms of Sanatana Dharma.

Although their origins and antiquity are still unknown, the Vedas themselves can be examined. They are a revered collection of ancient sacred hymns comprising four parts which appear to have developed over time. The earliest are the *Samhitas*, hymns of praise in worship of deities. Then appeared the **Brahmanas**, directions about performances of the ritual sacrifices to the deities. Some people went to the forests to meditate as recluses; their writings form the third part of the Vedas—the *Aranyakas*, or "forest treatises." The latest of the Vedas are the **Upanishads**, consisting of teaching from highly-realized spiritual masters.

These sacred teachings seem to have been written down by the middle of the first millennium BCE, though the Indian people and some scholars feel that they are far older. We know that the Vedas are much older than their earliest written forms; they were originally transmitted orally from teacher to student and may then have been written down over a period of eight or nine hundred years.

According to orthodox Hindus, the Vedas are the breath of the eternal, as "heard" by the ancient sages, or **rishis**, and later compiled by Vyasa. The scriptures are thought to transcend human time and are thus as relevant today as they were thousands of years ago.

The oldest of the known Vedic scriptures—and among the oldest of the world's existing scriptures—is the *Rig Veda*. This praises and implores the blessings of the **devas**—the controlling forces in the cosmos, deities who consecrate every part of life. The major devas included Indra (god of thunder and bringer of welcome rains), Agni (god of fire), Soma (associated with a sacred drink), and Ushas (goddess of dawn). The devas included both opaque earth gods and transparent deities of the sky and celestial realms. But behind all the myriad aspects of divinity, the sages perceived

HINDUISM

WESTERN HISTORIANS' STANDARD VIEW		INDIAN TRADITION
	6000 **BCE**	Vedas heard by rishis, carried orally c.8000–6000
	5000	
	4000	
	3000	Beginning of Kali Yuga: Vishnu incarnates as Vyasa, who writes down the Vedas c.3102
Harappan civilization c.2500–1500 Aryan invasions of north India c.2000–900	**2000**	
Early Vedas first written down c.1500	**1000**	
Brahmanas written down c.900–700 Upanishads recorded c.600–400 Jainism: Mahavira's life c.599–527 Buddhism: Buddha's life c.563–483 Ramayana (present form) 400 BCE–200 CE Mahabharata (present form) 400 BCE–400 CE Patanjali systematizes *Yoga Sutras* by 200 BCE	**500**	
	CE	Yoga practices are ancient, indigenous
Code of Manu compiled before 100 CE Tantras written down c.300		Tantras are as old as the Upanishads
Bhakti movement flourishes c.600–1800 Muslim invasions begin 711 Shankara (c.788–820 or earlier) reorganizes Vedanta *Bhagavata Purana* written down c.800–900	**500**	
	1000	
	1500	
Mughal Empire 1556–1707		
Brahmo Samaj revitalization 1828 Ramakrishna's life 1836–1886 Mahatma Gandhi's life 1869–1948 Arya Samaj reform 1875	**1800**	
British rule of India 1857–1947	**1900**	
Independence, partition of India and Pakistan 1947		
Demolition of Babri mosque 1992	**2000**	

one unseen Reality. This Reality, beyond human understanding, ceaselessly creates and sustains everything that exists, encompassing all time, space, and causation.

Fire sacrifices and the cosmic order

Vedic worship centered around the fire sacrifice. Communities seem to have gathered around a fire placing offerings in it to be conveyed to the gods by **Agni**, the god of fire. The Vedic hymns sung to Agni are spiritually complex invocations of the power of truth against darkness. Metaphysically, fire represents the "forceful heat, flaming will, . . . and burning brightness" of the divine, according to the twentieth-century seer Sri Aurobindo.[2]

Over time elaborate fire sacrifice rituals were created, controlled by **Brahmins** (priests). Specified verbal formulas, sacred chants, and sacred actions were to be used by the priests to invoke the breath behind all of existence. This universal breath was later called **Brahman**, the Absolute, the Supreme Reality. The verbal formulas were called **mantras**; their sound was believed to evoke the reality they named. The language used was Sanskrit. It was considered a re-creation of the actual sound-forms of objects, actions, and qualities, as heard by ancient sages in deep meditation.

The fire rituals were apparently held in the open air. The most auspicious places for their performance were at the confluence of two rivers. The junction of the sacred Ganges (Ganga) and Jumna (Yamuna) rivers was considered extremely holy. The feeling that special blessings are available there continues today; the confluence is still a major pilgrimage spot.

Offerings to Agni usually consisted of clarified butter oil (ghee), grains, **soma**, and sometimes animals. Soma was a drink apparently made of a specific plant that grew in mountainous, windy places; its juice seemed to confer great vigor.

The Vedic principle of sacrifice was based on the idea that generous offerings to a deity will be rewarded by some specific result. This attitude toward giving has remained in Indian culture. Ritual fire offerings are still central to Hindu worship. Hospitality to human guests is also a duty. To turn someone away from your door without feeding him is considered a great sin, for the person could be the deity incarnate. Even today, there are huge ceremonies for making offerings to a deity and feeding the public. Professional beggars take advantage of belief in sacrifice by suggesting that those who give to them will be blessed. But the most important sacrifices are considered to be inner sacrifices—giving one's entire self over to the Supreme Reality.

In the *Rig Veda*, the sacrifical aspects of Vedic religion are linked metaphorically with the orignal personal sacrifice by which the universe was created. **Purusha**, the primal Being, was dismembered by the gods. His mind became the moon, his eyes the sun, his breath the wind, and so forth. The power that preserves the unity of all these parts of the cosmos, maintains harmony in society, and keeps human personalities well integrated is called *rta*. Earthly sacrifices were designed to preserve this order. If the sacrifices were offered correctly, the gods would be guided by the people's requests.

Castes and social duties

Because the sacrifices were a reciprocal communion with the gods, priests who performed the public sacrifices had to be carefully trained and maintain high standards of ritual purity. Those so trained—the Brahmins—comprised a special occupational group. According to Vedic religion, the orderly working of society included a clear division of labor among four major occupational groups, which later became entrenched as **castes**. The Brahmins were the priests and philosophers, specialists in the life of the spirit. They had even higher status than the next group, later called *kshatriyas*. These were the nobility of feudal India: kings, warriors, and vassals. Their general function was to guard and preserve the society; they were expected to be courageous and majestic. *Vaishyas* were the economic specialists: farmers and merchants. The *shudra* caste were the manual laborers and artisans. Some of the shudras carried on work such as removing human wastes and corpses and sweeping streets which made their bodies and clothing abhorrent to others. In time they were considered "untouchable."

Over time, Vedic religion was increasingly controlled by the Brahmins, and contact between castes was limited. Caste membership became hereditary. The caste system became as important as the Vedas themselves in defining Hinduism until its social injustices were attacked in the nineteenth century. One of its opponents was the courageous leader Mahatma Gandhi, who renamed the lowest caste *harijans*, "the children of God." In 1948 the stigma of "untouchability" was legally abolished, though many caste distinctions still linger in modern India. Marriage across caste lines, for instance, is still often disapproved in India. If a boy and girl—one of whom is from the lowest caste—fall in love, sometimes the families from both sides will kill them rather than allow their marriage, to prevent disgrace or retribution.

Despite its abuses, the division of labor represented by the caste system is part of Sanatana Dharma's strong emphasis on social duties and sacrifice of individual desires for the sake of social order. Dharma's purpose is to uplift people from worldly concerns and to encourage them to behave according to higher laws. The Vedas, other scriptures, and historical customs have all conditioned the Indian people to accept their social roles. These were set out in a major document known as the Code of Manu, compiled by 100 CE. In it are laws governing all aspects of life, including the proper conduct of rulers, dietary restrictions, marriage laws, daily rituals, purification rites, social laws, and ethical guidance. It prescribes hospitality to guests and the cultivation of such virtues as contemplation, truthfulness, compassion, non-attachment, generosity, pleasant dealings with people, and self-control. The Code of Manu also specifies the reciprocal duties of men and women. Women are expected to be dependent on men at all times; men are to revere women in their household settings. Of ancient origin, such dharmic laws still have a strong impact in Indian culture.

Philosophy of the Upanishads

Of the four parts of the Vedas, the Upanishads are thought to have developed last, around 600 to 400 BCE. They represent the mystical insights of rishis who sought ultimate reality through their meditations in the forest. Many people consider them the cream of Indian thought, among the highest spiritual literature ever written. They were not taught to the masses but rather were reserved for advanced seekers of spiritual truth.

CONTEMPLATION OF THE LUMINOUS SELF   The word "Upanishad" embraces the idea of the devoted disciple sitting down by the teacher to receive private spiritual instruction about the highest reality, loosening all doubts and destroying all ignorance. Emphasis is placed not on outward ritual performances, as in the earlier Vedic religion, but on inner experience as the path to realization and immortality.

The rishis explain that the bodily senses are made for looking outward; the eyes, ears, nose, tongue, and skin are enticed by sensory pleasures. But ultimately these are fleeting, impermanent. They pass away and then one dies, never having experienced what is of greater value because it is infinite, everlasting. What is real and lasting, they found, can only be discovered by turning away from worldly things. They taught their pupils to turn their attention inside, and thus discover a transcendent reality from within. This unseen but all-pervading reality they called Brahman, the Unknowable: "Him the eye does not see, nor the tongue express, nor the mind grasp."[3]

From Brahman spring the multiplicity of forms, including humans. The joyous discovery of the rishis was that they could find Brahman as the subtle self or soul (**Atman**) within themselves. One of the rishis explained this relationship thus:

In the beginning there was Existence alone—One only, without a second. He, the One, thought to himself: Let me be many, let me grow forth. Thus out of himself he projected the universe, and having projected out of himself the universe, he entered into every being. All that is has its self in him alone. Of all things he is the subtle essence. He is the truth. He is the Self. And that, ... THAT ART THOU.

Chandogya Upanishad[4]

The rishis declared that when one discovers the inner self, Atman, and thus also its source, Brahman, the self merges into its transcendent source, and one experiences unspeakable peace.

REINCARNATION   In addition to these profound descriptions of contemplation of the Absolute, the Upanishads express several doctrines that are central to all forms of Sanatana Dharma. One is the idea of **reincarnation**. In answer to the universal question, "What happens after we die?" the rishis taught that the soul leaves the dead body and enters a new one. One takes birth again and again in countless bodies—perhaps as an animal or some other life form—but the self remains the same. Birth as a human being is a precious and rare opportunity for the soul to advance toward its ultimate goal of liberation from rebirth and merging with the Absolute Reality.

KARMA   An important related concept is that of **karma**. It means action, and also the consequences of action. Every act we make, and even every thought and every desire we have, shape our future experiences. Our life is what we have made it. And we ourselves are shaped by what we have done. Not only do we reap in this life the good or evil we have sown; they also follow us after physical death, affecting our next incarnation.

The ultimate goal, however, is not creation of good lives by good deeds, but a clean escape from the karma-run wheel of birth, death, and rebirth, which is called **samsara**. To escape from samsara is to achieve **moksha**, or liberation from the limitations of space, time, and matter through realization of the immortal Absolute. Many lifetimes of upward-striving incarnations are required to reach this transcendence of earthly miseries.

Bhakti in the epics and Puranas

It is difficult to pray to the impersonal Absolute, for it is formless and is not totally distinct from oneself. More personal worship of a divine Being can be inferred from the artefacts of ancient India. It probably persisted during the Vedic period and was later given written expression. Eventually **bhakti**—intense devotion to a personal manifestation of Brahman—became the heart of Hinduism as the majority of people now experience it.

Although there are many devotional passages in the Upanishads, personal love for a deity flowered in the spiritual literature that followed the Vedas. After 500 BCE (according to Western scholarship), long heroic narratives and poems popularized spiritual knowledge and devotion through national myths and legends.

In contrast to the rather abstract depictions of the Divine Principle in the Upanishads, these writings represent the Supreme as a person, or rather as various human-like deities. As T. M. P. Mahadevan explains:

> The Hindu mind is averse to assigning an unalterable or rigidly fixed form or name to the Deity. Hence it is that in Hinduism we have innumerable god-forms and countless divine names. And, it is a truth that is recognized by all Hindus that obeisance offered to any of these forms and names reaches the one supreme God.[5]

Two great epics, the **Ramayana** and the **Mahabharata**, present the Supreme usually as **Vishnu**, who intervenes on earth during critical periods in the cosmic cycles. In the inconceivable vastness of time as reckoned by Hindu thought, each world cycle lasts 4,320,000 years and is divided into four ages, or **yugas**.

Dharma—moral order in the world—is natural in the first age. The second age is like a cow standing on three legs; people must be taught their proper roles in society. During the darker third age, revealed values are no longer recognized, people lose their altruism and willingness for self-denial, and there are no more saints. The final age, **Kali Yuga**, is as imbalanced as a cow trying to stand on one leg. The world is at its worst, with egotism, ignorance, recklessness, and war rampant. According to Hindu time reckoning, we are now living in a Kali Yuga period which began in 3102 BCE. Such an age is described thus:

> *When society reaches a stage where property confers rank, wealth becomes the only source of virtue, passion the sole bond of union between husband and wife, falsehood the source of success in life, sex the only means of enjoyment, and when outer trappings are confused with inner religion....*[6]

Each of these lengthy cycles witnesses the same turns of events. The balance inexorably shifts from the true dharma to dissolution and then back to the dharma as the gods are again victorious over the anti-gods. The scriptures describe many ways that the Supreme has incarnated in the world when dharma is decaying, to help restore virtue and defeat evil.

THE RAMAYANA   The epics deal with this eternal play of good and evil, symbolized by battles involving the human incarnations of Vishnu. Along the way, they teach examples of the virtuous life, which is a life of responsibilities to others defined by one's social roles. One is first a daughter, son, sister, brother, wife, husband, mother, father, or friend in relationship to others, and only secondarily an individual.

The *Ramayana*, a long poetic narrative in the Sanskrit language thought to have been compiled between approximately 400 BCE and 200 CE, is much beloved, and is acted out with great pageantry throughout India every year. It depicts the duties of relationships, portraying ideal characters such as the ideal servant, the ideal brother, the ideal wife, the ideal king. In the story, Vishnu incarnates as the virtuous prince Rama in order to kill Ravana, the ten-headed demon king of Sri Lanka. Rama is heir to his father's throne, but the mother of his stepbrother compels the king to banish Rama into the forest for fourteen years. Rama, a model of morality, goes willingly, observing that a son's duty is to obey his parents implicitly, even when their commands seem wrong. He is accompanied into the ascetic life by his wife Sita, the model of wifely devotion in a patriarchal society.

Eventually Sita is kidnapped by Ravana, who woos her unsuccessfully in his island kingdom and guards her with all manner of terrible demons. Although Rama is powerful, he and his half-brother Lakshman need the help of the monkeys and bears in the battle to get Sita back. Hanuman the monkey becomes the hero of the story. He symbolizes the power of faith and devotion to overcome our human frailties. In his love for the Lord he can do anything.

The bloody battle ends in single-handed combat between Ravana and Rama. Rama blesses a sacred arrow with Vedic mantras and sends it straight into Ravana's heart. After Rama's kingship is restored, he asks Sita to prove her purity in order to preserve the integrity of his rule from the people's suspicions. After many ordeals, according to one traditional version of the *Ramayana*, she utters these final words, becomes a field of radiance, and disappears into the ground:

O Lord of my being, I realize you in me and me in you. Our relationship is eternal. Through this body assumed by me, my service to you and your progeny is complete now. I dissolve this body to its original state.

Mother Earth, you gave form to me. I have made use of it as I ought to. In recognition of its purity may you kindly absorb it into your womb.[7]

Indian arts are intended to be interpreted on many levels. One way of interpreting the *Ramayana* is to see all the characters as parts of ourself. Rama, for instance, is the innate principle of goodness, while Ravana is our dark side, or ego—that which tends to greed, jealousy, and selfishness. Sita represents our devotion to the Supreme. If our good side loses its Sita, we will see evil all around, like the demons whom Rama had to confront. To restore our devotional connection with Brahman, we must kill the ego.

THE MAHABHARATA   The other famous Hindu epic is the *Mahabharata*, a Sanskrit poem of over one hundred thousand verses. Perhaps partly historical, it may have been composed between 400 BCE and 400 CE. The plot concerns the struggle between the sons of a royal family for control of a kingdom near what is now Delhi. The story teaches the importance of sons, the duties of kingship, the benefits of ascetic practice and righteous action, and the qualities of the gods. In contrast to the idealized characters in the *Ramayana*, the *Mahabharata* shows all sides of human nature, including greed, lust, intrigue, and desire for power. It is thought to be relevant for all times and all peoples. A serial dramatization of the *Mahabharata* has drawn huge television audiences in contemporary India, and many people replay the episodes on home videotape. Throughout its episodes, the *Mahabharata* teaches one primary ethic: that the happiness of others is essential to one's own happiness.

The eighteenth book of the *Mahabharata*, which may have originally been an independent mystical poem, is the *Bhagavad-Gita* ("Song of the Supreme Exalted One"). Krishna, revered as a glorious manifestation of the Supreme, appears as the charioteer of Arjuna, who is preparing to fight on the virtuous side of a battle that will pit brothers against brothers. The battle provides the occasion for a treatise about the conflict between our earthly duties and our spiritual aspirations.

Before they plunge into battle, Krishna instructs Arjuna in the arts of self-transcendence and realization of the eternal.

Lord Krishna says those who do everything for love of the Supreme transcend the notion of duty. Everything they do is offered to the Supreme, "without desire for gain and free from egoism and lethargy."[8] Thus they feel peace, freedom from earthly entanglements, and unassailable happiness.

Over time, instructions pertaining to "that very ancient science of the relationship with the Supreme"[9] became lost, so Krishna has taken human form again and again to teach the true religion:

Whenever and wherever there is a decline in religious practice … and a predominant rise of irreligion—at that time I descend Myself.

To deliver the pious and to annihilate the miscreants, as well as to re-establish the principles of religion, I advent Myself millennium after millennium.[10]

Krishna says that everything springs from his being:

> *There is no truth superior to Me. Everything rests upon Me, as pearls are strung on a thread. . . .*
>   *I am the taste of water, the light of the sun and the moon, the syllable* om *in Vedic mantras; I am the sound in ether and ability in man. . . .*
>   *All states of being—goodness, passion or ignorance—are manifested by My energy.*[11]

This Supreme Godhead is not apparent to most mortals. The Lord can only be known by those who love him, and for them it is easy, for they remember him at all times: "Whatever you do, whatever you eat, whatever you offer or give away, and whatever austerities you perform—do that . . . as an offering to Me." Any small act of devotion offered in love for Krishna becomes a way to him.

KRISHNA OF THE PURANAS   The **Puranas**, poetic Sanskrit texts which narrate the myths of ancient times, were probably compiled between 500 and 1500 CE. Bhakti—the way of devotion so beloved by the masses in India, and said to be the best path for Kali Yuga—is evident in the *Tales of the Lord* (*Bhagavata Purana*) to an even greater extent than in the *Mahabharata*. Most Western Indologists think it was written about the ninth or tenth century CE, but according to Indian tradition it was one of the works written down at the beginning of Kali Yuga by the sage Vyasa, describing the Supreme as a Person to be adored.

This material universe we know is only one of millions of material universes. Each is like a bubble in the eternal spiritual sky, arising from the pores of the body of Vishnu, and these bubbles are created and destroyed as Vishnu breathes out and in. This cosmic conception is so vast that it is impossible for the mind to grasp it. It is much easier to comprehend and adore Krishna in his incarnation as a cowherding boy. Whereas he was a wise teacher in the *Bhagavad-Gita,* Krishna of the Puranas is a much-loved child raised by cowherds in an area called Vrindavan on the Jumna River. This area was actually home to a cowherding tribe, but whether the stories about Krishna have any historical basis is unclear.

The mythology is rich in earthly pleasures. The boy Krishna mischievously steals balls of butter from the neighbors and wanders garlanded with flowers through the forest, happily playing his flute. Between episodes of carefree bravery in vanquishing demons that threaten the people, he playfully steals the hearts of the *gopis*, the cowherd girls, many of them married. His favorite is the lovely Radha, but through his magical ways, each thinks that he dances with her alone. He is physically beautiful.

Eventually Krishna is called away on a heroic mission, never returning to the *gopis*. Their grief at his leaving, their loving remembrances of his graceful presence, and their intense longing for him serve as models for the bhakti path—the way of extreme devotion. In Hindu thought, the emotional longing of the lover for the beloved is one of the most powerful vehicles for concentration on the Supreme Lord.

Spiritual Disciplines

Another ancient and persistent thread of Sanatana Dharma is spiritual discipline. The process of attaining spiritual realization or liberation is thought to take at least a lifetime, and probably many lifetimes. Birth as a human being is prized as a chance to advance toward spiritual perfection.

In the past, spiritual training was usually available to upper-caste males only; women and shudras were excluded. It was preceded by an initiation ceremony in which the boy received the **sacred thread**, a cord to be worn over the left shoulder. Traditionally, after years of being a student, and then a married householder, having fulfilled his worldly obligations, a man could withdraw from these pursuits and turn to meditation and spiritual study. Eventually he might withdraw totally from society and become a **sannyasin**.

Some sannyasins take up residence in comfortable temples; others wander alone with only a water jar, a walking staff, and a begging bowl as possessions. Some wandering sannyasins wear no clothes. In silence, the sannyasin is supposed to concentrate on practices that will finally release him from samsara into cosmic consciousness.

The majority of contemporary Hindu males do not follow this path to its sannyasin conclusion in old age, but many Hindus still become sannyasins. Some of them have renounced the world at a younger age and joined a monastic order, living in an **ashram**, or retreat community that has developed around a guru.

The guru

Those who choose the path of study and renunciation often place themselves at the feet of a spiritual teacher, or **guru**. Gurus do not declare themselves as teachers; people are drawn to them because they have achieved spiritual status to which the seekers aspire. Gurus are often regarded as enlightened or "fully realized" men or women. They give advice, example, and encouragement to those seeking enlightenment or realization.

For instance, Ramana Maharshi, who died in 1951, lived on a holy mountain in South India, so absorbed in Ultimate Consciousness that he neither talked nor ate and had to be force-fed by another holy man. But the needs of those who gathered around him drew out his compassion and wisdom, and he spontaneously counseled them in their spiritual needs. His glance alone was said to have illuminated many who visited him.

When seekers find their guru, they love and honor him or her as their spiritual parent. They often bend to touch the feet or hem of the robe of the guru, partly out of humility and partly because great power is thought to emanate from the guru's feet. Humbling oneself before the guru— becoming like an empty receptacle—is considered necessary in order to receive the teaching.

Yogic practices

Spiritual seekers are generally encouraged to engage in disciplines that clear the mind and support a state of serene, detached awareness. The practices for increasing balance, purity, wisdom, and peacefulness of mind are known collectively as **yoga**. According to a modern classification system, there are four main yogic paths, suited to different kinds of human personalities—*raja, jnana, karma,* and *bhakti.*

RAJA YOGA   The physical and psychic practices of raja yoga are thought to be extremely ancient. Some believe that the **sadhanas**, or practices, were known as long ago as the Neolithic Age and were practiced in the great Indus Valley culture. By 200 BCE, a yogi named Patanjali (or perhaps a series of people taking the same name) had described a coherent system for attaining the highest consciousness.

Yogis say that it is easier to calm a wild tiger than it is to quiet the mind, which is like a drunken monkey that has been bitten by a scorpion. The problem is that the mind is our vehicle for knowing the Self. If the mirror of the mind is disturbed, it reflects the disturbance rather than the pure light within. The goal of yogic practices is to make the mind absolutely calm and clear.

Included in the yogic path described by Patanjali are **asanas**. These are physical postures used to cleanse the body and develop the mind's ability to concentrate. Regulated breathing exercises are also used to calm the nerves and increase the body's supply of **prana**, or invisible life energy. Breath is thought to be the key to controlling the flow of this energy within the subtle energy field surrounding and permeating the physical body. Its major pathway is through a series of **chakras**, or subtle energy centers along the spine. Ideally, opening of the highest chakras leads to the bliss of union with the Sublime. In its fully open state, the crown chakra is depicted as a thousand-petaled lotus, effulgent with light.

In addition to these practices using the body and breath, Indian thought has long embraced the idea that repetition of certain sounds has sacred effects. It is said that some ancient yogic adepts could discern subtle sounds and that mantras (sacred formulas) express an aspect of the Divine in the form of sound vibration.

Indians liken the mind to the trunk of an elephant, always straying restlessly here and there. If an elephant is given a small stick to hold in its trunk, it will hold it steadily, losing interest in other objects. Just so, the mantra gives the restless mind something to hold, quieting it by focusing awareness in one place. If chanted with devoted concentration, the mantra may also invoke the presence and blessings of the deity.

Many forms of music have also been developed in India to elevate one's attunement. Concerts may go on for hours if the musicians are spiritually absorbed. The most cherished sound vibrations are the "unheard, unstruck" divine sounds which cannot be heard with our outer ears.

Another way of steadying and elevating the mind is concentration on some visual form—a candle flame, the picture of a saint or guru, the **OM** symbol, or **yantras**. A yantra is a linear image with complex cosmic symbolism. Large yantras are also created as designs of colorful grains for ritual invocations of specific deities.

One-pointed concentration ideally leads to a state of meditation. In meditation, all worldly thoughts have dissipated. Instead of ordinary thinking, the clear light of awareness allows insights to arise spontaneously as flashes of illumination. There may also be phenomena such as colored lights, visions, waves of ecstasy, or visits from supernatural beings. The mind, heart, and body may gradually be transformed.

The ultimate goal of yogic meditation is **samadhi**: a super-conscious state of union with the Absolute. Swami Sivananda attempts to describe it:

> *Words and language are imperfect to describe this exalted state. . . . Mind, intellect and the senses cease functioning. . . . It is a state of eternal Bliss and eternal Wisdom. All dualities vanish* in toto. *. . . The individual soul becomes that which he contemplates.*[12]

JNANA YOGA   Another yogic path employs the rational mind rather than trying to transcend it by concentration practices. This is **jnana yoga**—"the way of wisdom." In this path, ignorance is considered the root of all problems. Our basic ignorance is our idea of our selves as being separate from the Absolute. One method is continually to ask, "Who am I?" The seeker discovers that the one who asks the question is not the body, not the senses, not the pranic body, not the mind, but something eternal beyond all these. The guru Ramana Maharshi explains:

> *After negating all of the above-mentioned as "not this," "not this," that Awareness which alone remains—that I am. . . . The thought "Who am I?" will destroy all other thoughts, and, like the stick used for stirring the burning pyre, it will itself in the end get destroyed. Then, there will arise Self-realization.*[13]

In the jnana path, the seeker must also develop spiritual virtues (calmness, restraint, renunciation, resignation, concentration, and faith) and have an intense longing for liberation. Finally one graduates from theoretical knowledge of the self to direct experience of it. The ultimate wisdom is spiritual insight rather than intellectual knowledge.

> *Spiritual knowledge is the only thing that can destroy our miseries for ever; any other knowledge removes wants only for a time.*
>
> *Swami Vivekananda*[14]

KARMA YOGA   In contrast to these ascetic and contemplative practices, another way is that of helpful action in the world. **Karma yoga** is service rendered without any interest in its effects and without any personal sense of giving. The yogi knows that it is the Absolute who performs all actions, and that all actions are gifts to the Absolute. This consciousness leads to liberation from the self in the very midst of work. Krishna explains these principles in the *Bhagavad-Gita*:

> *The steadily devoted soul attains unadulterated peace because he offers the results of all activities to Me; whereas a person who is not in harmony with the Divine, who is greedy for the fruits of his labor, becomes entangled.*[15]

BHAKTI YOGA   The final type of spiritual path is the one embraced by most Indian followers of Sanatana Dharma. It is the path of devotion, bhakti yoga. "Bhakti" means "to share," to share a relationship with the Supreme. The relationship is that of intense love. Bhakta Nam Dev described this deep love in sweet metaphors:

> Thy Name is beautiful, Thy form is beautiful, and very beautiful is Thy love, Oh my Omnipresent Lord.
> As rain is dear to the earth, as the fragrance of flowers is dear to the black bee, and as the mango is dear to the cuckoo, so is the Lord to my soul.
> As the sun is dear to the sheldrake, and the lake of Man Sarowar to the swan, and as the husband is dear to the wife, so is God to my soul.
> As milk is dear to the baby and as the torrent of rain to the mouth of the sparrow-hawk who drinks nothing but raindrops, and as water is dear to the fish, so is the Lord to my soul.[16]

A vision of a deity is what the bhakta hopes for. Mirabai, a fifteenth-century Rajput princess, was married to a ruler at a young age, but from her childhood she had been utterly devoted to Krishna. When she continued to spend all her time in devotions to Krishna, her infuriated husband tried to poison her. It is said that Mirabai drank the poison while laughingly dancing in ecstasy before Krishna; in Krishna's presence the poison seemed like nectar to her and did her no harm. Such is the devotion of the fully devoted bhakta that the Beloved One is said to respond and to be a real presence in the bhakta's life.

Ramakrishna explains why the bhakti way is more appropriate for most people:

> How very few can obtain this Union [Samadhi] and free themselves from this "I"? It is very rarely possible. Talk as much as you want, isolate yourself continuously, still this "I" will always return to you. Cut down the poplar tree today, and you will find tomorrow it forms new shoots. When you ultimately find that this "I" cannot be destroyed, let it remain as "I" the servant.[17]

Major Theistic Cults

After a period when Brahmanic ritual and philosophy dominated Sanatana Dharma, the bhakti approach came to prominence around 600 CE. It opened spiritual expression to both shudras and women, and has been the primary path of the masses ever since. It may also have been the initial way of the people, for devotion to personal deities is thought to predate Vedic religion.

Of all the deities worshipped by Hindus, there are three major groupings: **Vaishnavites**, who worship the God Vishnu, **Saivites** who worship the god Siva, and **Saktas** who worship a goddess. Each devotee has his or her own "chosen deity," but will honor others as well.

Ultimately, many Hindus rest their faith in one genderless deity with

AN INTERVIEW WITH SARALA CHAKRABARTY

Living Hinduism

Sarala Chakrabarty, a Calcutta grandmother, has undertaken spiritual studies with a guru in the Ramakrishna tradition. Her love for the Supreme, in many forms, is highly personal.

"In our Hindu religion, we worship God in some form. God is infinite, but we cannot imagine the infinite. We must have some finite person—whom I love like friend, like father, like son, like lover. We make a relation with God like this. When I think he is my lover, I can always think of him. When I think he is my father, when I am in trouble, I pray to him, ask him to save me.

And I always pray to the Holy Mother [Ramakrishna's spiritual bride and successor, Sarada Devi]. When I have a problem, Mother will save me. She has given word when she was leaving her body (you say 'dying')—she said, 'I am blessing all who have come, who are coming, who have not come yet but are coming, blessings for all.' Only Mother can say this—so big heart, so much affection for us.

I feel something. Somebody is standing behind me. I feel always the hands on my shoulders, guarding me. Everybody is protected by God, everyone. I am not his only child. But I think God is only mine.

I want everything from God. God does not want anything from me. He wants bhakti—devotion. A mother wants nothing from a child but love. She says only, 'Pray to me, call me, and I will do everything for you.' When I am traveling I say to Her, 'I am talking to you,' and this is done.

As we love God, God loves us. Our Lord Krishna says Love is the rope. It ties God and pulls him down to you.

I have a very powerful guru, a swami of the Ramakrishna Mission, who has passed on. He gave me a mantra, and it gives me very much peace. When I chant, I cannot leave it. Time is over, somebody is calling, I have to cook, I have to work—then I get up and still I am chanting in my mind. After bedding, I worship and chant. After that I realize I am pleased, I am quiet. There is no trouble in body and mind. I am very happy, very blissful. Whatever that problem is, all goes away."

three basic aspects: creating, preserving, and destroying. The latter activity is seen as a merciful act that allows the continuation of the cosmic cycles.

Saktas

An estimated fifty million Hindus worship some form of the goddess. As we have seen, worship of the feminine aspect of the Divine probably dates back to the pre-Vedic ancient peoples of the Indian subcontinent. Her power is called **sakti**. Lushly erotic, sensual imagery is frequently used to symbolize her abundant creativity.

The feminine principle is worshipped in many forms. At the village level, especially in South India, local deities are most typically worshipped as goddesses. They may not be perceived as taking human-like forms; rather, their presence may be represented by stones, trees, or small shrines without images. These local goddesses are intimately concerned with village affairs, unlike the more distant great goddesses of the upper class, access to whose temples was traditionally forbidden to those of low caste.

The great goddesses have been worshipped both in the plural and in the singular, in which case one goddess is seen as representing the totality of Deity—eternal creator, preserver, and destroyer. The great goddess **Durga** is often represented as a beautiful woman with a gentle face but ten arms holding weapons with which she vanquishes the demons who threaten the dharma; she rides a lion. She is the blazing splendor of God incarnate, the ultimate light and power in benevolent female form.

Kali, by contrast, is the divine in its fierce form. She may be portrayed as a hag or depicted dripping with blood, carrying a sword and a severed head, and wearing a girdle of severed hands and a necklace of skulls symbolizing her aspect as the destroyer of evil. With her merciful sword she cuts away all personal impediments to realization of truth, for those who sincerely desire to serve the Supreme. At the same time, she opens her arms to those who love her. Some of them worship her with blood offerings.

Fearsome to evil doers, but loving and compassionate as a mother to devotees, Kali wears a mask of ugliness. The divine reality is a wholeness encompassing both the pleasant and the unpleasant, creation and destruction. Sanskrit scholar Leela Arjunwadkar observes that there is a deeply sensed unity among all beings in classical Indian literature:

> That is why we find all types of characters in Sanskrit literature—human beings, gods and goddesses, rivers, demons, trees, serpents, celestial nymphs, etc., and their share in the same emotional life is the umbilical cord that binds all to Mother Nature.[18]

From ancient times, worship of the divine female has been associated with worship of nature, particularly great trees and rivers. The Ganges River is considered especially sacred, an extremely powerful female presence, and her waters which flow down from the Himalayas are thought to be extraordinarily purifying. Pilgrims reverently bathe in Mother Ganga's waters and corpses or the cremated ashes of the dead are placed in the river so that their sins will be washed away.

Sacred texts called **Tantras** instruct worshippers how to honor the feminine Divine. Sakti worship has also been incorporated into worship of the gods. Each is thought to have a female consort, often portrayed in close physical embrace signifying the eternal unity of male and female principles in the oneness of the Divine. Here the female is often conceived as the life-animating force; the transcendent male aspect is inactive until joined with the productive female energy.

Worship of the goddess in India and Nepal continues to exist side by side with social attempts to limit and confine women's power. This ambivalence is ancient. On the one hand, the female is highly venerated in Hinduism, compared to many other religions. Traditionally, women are thought to make major contributions to the good earthly life, consisting of dharma (order in society), marital wealth (by bearing sons in a patriarchal society), and the aesthetics of sensual pleasure. Women are auspicious beings,

mythologically associated with wealth, beauty, and grace. As sexual partners to men, they help activate the life-force. No ceremonial sacrifice is
complete unless the wife participates as well as the husband.

In the ideal marriage, husband and wife are spiritual partners. Marriage
is a vehicle for spiritual discipline, service, and advancement toward a spiritual goal, rather than a means of self-gratification. Men and women are
thought to complement each other, although the ideal of liberation has traditionally been intended largely for the male.

Women were not traditionally encouraged to seek liberation through
their own spiritual practices; their role is usually linked to that of their
husband, who takes the position of their god and their guru. For many
centuries, there was even the hope that a widow would choose to be cremated alive with her dead husband in order to remain united with him
after death.

In early Vedic times, women were relatively free and honored members of Indian society, participating equally in important spiritual rituals.
By the time the British took control of India in the nineteenth century,
however, wives had become virtual slaves of the husband's family. With
expectations that the girl will take a large dowry to the boy's family in a
marriage arrangement, having girls is such an economic burden that
many female babies are intentionally aborted or killed at birth. There are
also cases today of women being beaten or killed by the husband's family
after their dowry has been handed over. Nevertheless many women in
contemporary India have been well-educated, and many have attained
high political positions.

Saivites

Siva is a personal, many-faceted manifestation of the attributeless supreme
deity. In older systems he is one of the three major aspects of deity: Brahma
(Creator), Vishnu (Preserver), and Siva (Destroyer). Saivites nevertheless
worship him as the totality, with many aspects. As Swami Sivasiva Palani,
Saivite editor of *Hinduism Today*, explains: "Siva is the unmanifest; he is creator, preserver, destroyer, personal Lord, friend, primal Soul"; and he is the
"all-pervasive underlying energy, the more or less impersonal love and light
that flows through all things."[19] Siva is often depicted dancing above the
body of the demon he has killed, reconciling darkness and light, good and
evil, creation and destruction, rest and activity in the eternal dance of life.

Siva is also the god of yogis, for he symbolizes asceticism. He is often
shown in austere meditation on Mount Kailas, clad only in a tiger skin,
with a snake around his neck. The latter signifies his conquest of the ego.
In one prominent story, it is Siva who swallows the poison which threat-
ens the whole world with darkness, neutralizing the poison by the power
of his meditation.

Siva has various saktis or feminine consorts, including Durga. He is often
shown with his devoted spouse **Parvati**. Through their union cosmic
energy flows freely, seeding and liberating the universe. Nevertheless, they
are seen mystically as eternally chaste. Siva and his sakti are also expressed

as two aspects of a single being. Some sculptors portray Siva as androgy-nous, with both masculine and feminine physical traits. This unity is often expressed abstractly, as lingam within **yoni**, a symbol of the female vulva.

Lingams are naturally-occurring or sculpted cylindrical forms honored since antiquity in India (and apparently in other cultures as well, as far away as Hawaii). Those shaped by nature, such as stones polished by cer-tain rivers, are most highly valued, with rare natural crystal lingams con-sidered especially precious. Tens of thousands of devotees each year undergo dangerous pilgrimages to certain high mountain caves to venerate large lingams naturally formed of ice. Most Siva-worshippers see the lingam as a nearly amorphous, "formless" symbol for the unmanifest, tran-scendent nature of Siva—that which is beyond time, space, cause, and form—whereas the yoni represents the manifest aspect of Sivaness.

Siva and his family were the subject of an extraordinary event which happened in temples in many parts of India, as well as in Hindu temples in other parts of the world. On September 21, 1995, statues devoted to these deities began drinking milk from spoons, cups, and even buckets of milk offered by devotees. Crowds queued up at temples to see if the Divine would accept their offering. Scientists suggested explanations such as mass hysteria or capillary action in the stone, but the phenomenon, which lasted only one day, was fully convincing to many who experienced it.

Vaishnavites

Vishnu is beloved as the tender, merciful Deity. In one myth a sage was sent to determine who was the greatest of the gods by trying their tempers. The first two, Brahma and Siva, he insulted and was soundly abused in return. When he found Vishnu, the god was sleeping. Knowing of Vishnu's good-naturedness, the sage increased the insult by kicking him awake. Instead of reacting angrily, Vishnu tenderly massaged the sage's foot, con-cerned that he might have hurt it. The sage exclaimed, "This god is the mightiest, since he overpowers all by goodness and generosity!"

Vishnu has been worshipped since Vedic times and came to be regarded as the Supreme as a Person. According to ideas appearing by the fourth century CE, Vishnu is considered to have appeared in many earthly incar-nations, some of them animal forms. Most beloved of his purported incar-nations have been Rama, subject of the *Ramayana*, and Krishna. However, many people still revere Krishna without reference to Vishnu.

Popular devotion to Krishna takes many forms, depending on the relationship the devotee feels toward Krishna. If Krishna is regarded as the transcendent Supreme Lord, the worshipper humbly lowers himself or herself. If Krishna is seen as master, the devotee is his servant. If Krishna is loved as a child, the devotee takes the role of loving parent. If Krishna is the divine friend, this is also the position taken by the devo-tee. And if Krishna is the beloved, the devotee is his lover. The latter relationship was popularized by the ecstatic sixteenth-century Bengali saint and sage Sri Caitanya, who adored Krishna as the flute-playing lover. Following Sri Caitanya, the devotee makes himself (if a male) like

a loving female in order to experience the bliss of Lord Krishna's presence. It is this form of Hindu devotion that was carried to America in
1965, and then spread to other countries. Its followers are known as Hare
Krishnas.

Major Philosophical Systems

Although the majority of followers of Sanatana Dharma are bhaktas, the
spiritual wisdom of India has also expressed itself in elaborate intellectual
systems of philosophy. All have deep roots in the Vedas and other scriptures but also in direct personal experiences of the truth through meditation. All hold ethics to be central to orderly social life. They attribute
suffering to the law of karma, thereby suggesting incentives to more ethical behavior. All hold that the ultimate cause of suffering is people's ignorance of their true nature, the Self, which is omniscient, omnipotent,
omnipresent, perfect, and eternal. Prominent among these systems are
Samkhya and Advaita **Vedanta**.

Samkhya

The Samkhya system, though undatable, is thought to be the oldest in
India, of pre-Vedic origin. Samkhya philosophy holds that there are two
states of reality. One is the Purusha, the Self which is eternally wise, pure,
and free, beyond change, beyond cause. The other is **Prakriti**, the cause of
the material universe. All our suffering stems from our false confusion of
Prakriti with Purusha, the eternal Self. A **dualistic** understanding of life is
essential, according to this system, if we are to distinguish the ultimate
transcendent reality of Purusha from the temporal appearances of Prakriti,
which bring us happiness but also misery and delusion.

An illuminating story is told about Indra, who was once king of the gods.
He was forced by the other devas to descend to earth in the body of a boar.
Once there, he began to enjoy the life, wallowing in the mud, mating, and
siring baby pigs. The devas were aghast; they came down to try to convince
him to return, but Indra had forgotten his kingly state and insisted on remaining as a boar. Unable to talk him out of his delusion, the devas tried killing his
babies; he was distraught but simply mated to have more piglets. Then the
devas killed his mate. Indra grieved his loss but stayed in the mud. They
finally had to kill him as well to bring him back to his senses. His soul could
then see the body of the boar it had been inhabiting and was glad to return
to heaven. The moral is that we, too, are like gods who forget the heights
from which we came, so intent are we on the joys and sorrows of earthly life.

Advaita Vedanta

Whereas Samkhya is a dualistic system, Advaita ("non-dualist") Vedanta is
generally monistic, positing a single reality. It is based on the Upanishads.
Shankara reorganized the teachings many centuries later, probably
between the eighth and ninth centuries CE.

Whereas one view of the Upanishads is that the human self (Atman) is an emanation of Brahman, Shankara insisted that the Atman and Brahman are actually one. According to Shankara, our material life is an illusion. It is like a momentary wave arising from the ocean, which is the only reality. Ignorance consists in thinking that the waves are different from the ocean. The absolute spirit, Brahman, is the essence of everything, and it has no beginning and no end. It is the eternal ocean of bliss within which forms are born and die.

Maya is the power by which the Absolute veils itself, the illusion that the world as we perceive it is real. Shankara uses the metaphor of a coil of rope that, at dusk, is mistaken for a snake. The physical world, like the rope, does actually exist but we superimpose our memories and subjective thoughts upon it. Moreover, he says, only that which never changes is truly real. Everything else is changing, impermanent.

Popular Forms of Worship

Having evolved in so many directions for thousands of years, Sanatana Dharma today is rich in personal and public opportunities for serving and celebrating the Supreme in many forms.

Devotions and rituals

There are sixteen rites prescribed in the ancient scriptures to purify and sanctify the person in his or her journey through life, including rites at the time of conception, the braiding of the pregnant mother's hair, birth, name-giving, first leaving the family house, beginning of solid foods, starting education, investing boys with a sacred thread, starting studies of Vedas, marriage, and death. The goal is to continually elevate the person above his or her basically animal nature.

Pilgrimages to holy places and sacred rivers are also thought to be special opportunities for personal purification and spiritual elevation. Millions of pilgrims yearly undertake strenuous climbs to remote mountain sites that are thought to be blessed by the divine. One of the major pilgrimage sites is Amarnath cave. At 3,380 meters altitude in the Himalayas of Kashmir, ice has formed a giant stalagmite which is highly revered as a Siva lingam. Pilgrims may have been trekking to this holy place in the high Himalayas for up to three thousand years. The 45-kilometer footpath is so dangerous that 250 people were killed by freak storms and landslides in 1996, but in subsequent years, tens of thousands of devotees continue to undertake the pilgrimage.

Nearly every home in India has a shrine with pictures or small statues of various deities, and many have a special prayer room set aside for their daily worship. For **puja**, or worship, ritual purity is emphasized; the time for prayer and offerings to the deities is after the morning bath or after one has washed in the evening. Typically, a small oil lamp and a smoldering stick of incense are waved in a circle before the deities' images. If the devotee has a guru, a picture of him or her is usually part of the shrine.

Public worship is usually performed by *pujaris*, or Brahmin priests, who are trained in Vedic practices and in proper recitation of Sanskrit texts. They take fees for this service, in an informal system which is not without abuses. The sacred presence is made tangible through devotions employing all the senses. Siva-lingams may be anointed with precious substances, such as ghee (clarified butter oil), honey, or sandalwood paste, with offerings of rose water and flowers. In a temple, devotees may have the great blessing of receiving **darsan** (visual contact with the Divine) through the eyes of the images. One hears the sounds of mantras and ringing bells. Incense and flowers fill the area with uplifting fragrances. **Prasad**, food that has been sanctified by being offered to the deities and/or one's guru, is distributed to devotees, who eat it as sacred and spiritually charged.

In temples, the deity image is treated as if it were a living king or queen. Fine-haired whisks are waved before it, purifying the area for its presence. Aesthetically pleasing meals are presented on the deity's own dishes at appropriate intervals; fruits must be perfect, without any blemishes. In the morning, the image is ritually bathed and dressed in sumptuous clothes for the day; at night, it may be put to rest in bedclothes. For festivals, the deity is carefully paraded through the streets. The great Jagganath festival held only once every twelve years in Puri was attended by some one and a half million devotees in 1996, all clambering for darsan of the deity, pulled in a massive sixteen-wheeled chariot.

For the devout, loving service to the Divine makes it real and present. To many Hindus the statue is not just a symbol of the deity; the deity may be experienced through the statue, reciprocating the devotee's attentions.

Orthodox Brahmins observe many days of fasting and prayer, corresponding to auspicious points in the lunar and solar cycles or times of danger, such as the four months of the monsoon season. The ancient practice of astrology is so highly regarded that many couples are now choosing birth by Caesarean section for the purpose of selecting the most auspicious moment for their child's birth.

Festivals

Sanatana Dharma honors the Divine in so many forms that almost every day a religious celebration is being held in some part of India. Sixteen religious holidays are honored by the central government so that everyone can leave work to join in the throngs of worshippers. These are calculated partially on a lunar calendar, so dates vary from year to year. Most Hindu festivals express spirituality in its happiest aspects. The humorous abandon of the merry-makers attracts the gods to overcome evils.

On a mid-winter night, people happily celebrate *Lohari* by building a bonfire and throwing popcorn, peanuts, and sesame candies into it. The feeling is that one is symbolically throwing away one's evils, and at the same time invoking blessings for the year to come. In particular, families who have given birth to a male child during the past year perform this ceremony for his auspicious future.

Holi is the riotously joyful celebration of the death of winter and the return of colorful spring. In northern Indian areas where Vaishnavism is strong, the holiday is associated with Krishna, for as an infant he is said to have killed a demon employed by the king of winter. In some areas, the two-day craziness is dedicated to Kama, the god of sexual love. Whatever the excuse, bands of people take to the streets throwing brightly-colored powder or paint on anyone they meet. At the end of this uninhibited gaiety, everyone hugs and old grudges are dropped as the new year begins.

In July or August a special day, *Naga Panchami*, is devoted to the *nagas*, or snakes. Snakes were considered powerful gods by the indigenous peoples, and the tradition persists. In South Indian villages, where they are especially honored, thousands of live snakes are caught and exhibited by brave handlers. Worshippers sprinkle vermilion and rice on the hoods of cobras, considered especially sacred. On Naga Panchami, farmers abstain from ploughing to avoid disrupting any snake-holes.

In August or September, Vaishnavites celebrate Krishna's birthday (*Janmashtami*). At his birthplace, Mathura, Krishna's devotees fast and keep a vigil until midnight, retelling stories of his life. In some places Krishna's image is placed in a cradle and lovingly rocked by devotees. Elsewhere, pots of milk, curds, and butter—playfully stolen by young Krishna—are strung high above the ground to be seized by young men who form human pyramids to get to their prize.

At the end of the summer, it is Ganesh who is honored, especially in west and South India, during *Ganesh Chaturti*. Special potters make elaborate clay images of the jovial elephant-headed remover of obstacles, son of Parvati, who formed him as a boy from the residue of her bathing tub and set him to stand guard while she bathed. Since he wouldn't let Siva in, her angry spouse smashed the boy's head into a thousand pieces. Parvati demanded that the boy be restored to life with a new head, but the first one found was that of a baby elephant. To soothe Parvati's distress at the peculiarity of the transplant, Siva granted Ganesh the power of removing obstacles. The elephant-headed god is now the first to be invoked in all rituals. After ten days of being sung to and offered sweets, the Ganesh images are carried to a body of water and bidden farewell with prayers for an easy year.

In different parts of India, the first nine or ten days of the lunar month corresponding to September or October are dedicated either to the *Durga Puja* (in which elaborate images of the many-armed goddess celebrate her powers to vanquish the demonic forces) or to *Dussehra* (in which huge effigies of the wicked Ravana and his helpers may be burned, re-enacting the climax of the *Ramayana* and the triumph of Rama, his brother Lakshman, and the beloved monkey Hanuman). The theme is the same: the triumph of good over evil.

Twenty days later is *Divali*, the happy four-day festival of lights. Variously explained as the return of Rama after his exile, the puja of Lakshmi (goddess of wealth, who visits only clean homes), and the New Year of Indian calendars, it is a time for tidying business establishments and financial records, cleaning and illuminating houses after the mess of the monsoon season, wearing new clothes, gambling, feasting, honoring clay images of Lakshmi and Ganesh, and setting off fireworks.

Initially more solemn is *Mahashivaratri*, in which a day of fasting and a night of keeping vigil to earn merit with Siva are followed by gaiety and eating. During the ascetic part of the observance, many pilgrims go to sacred rivers or special tanks of water for ritual bathing. Siva lingams and statues are venerated, and the faithful chant and tell stories of Siva to keep each other awake.

Every few years, millions of Hindus of all persuasions gather for the immense *Kumbha Mela*. It is held alternately at four sacred spots where drops of the holy nectar of immortality are said to have fallen. On one day in 2001, in what has been recorded as the largest ever gathering of human beings for a single purpose, over twenty million people amassed at the point near Allahabad where the Jumna River meets the sacred Ganges. There they took a purifying bath in the frigid waters on auspicious dates, as determined by astrologers. Among the Kumbha Mela pilgrims are huge processions of ascetic **sadhus** from various orders, many of whom leave their retreats only for this festival. The sadhus gather to discuss religious matters and also social problems, sometimes leading to revisions of the codes of conduct governing Hindu society. Many of the lay pilgrims are poor people who undergo great hardships to reach the site.

Hinduism in the Modern World

Hinduism did not develop in India in isolation from other religions and national influences. Groups continually flowed into the subcontinent from outside. Muslims began taking over certain areas beginning in the eighth century CE; during the sixteenth and seventeenth centuries a large area was ruled by the Muslim Mogul emperors.

When the Mughal Empire collapsed, European colonialists moved in. Ultimately the British dominated and in 1857 India was placed under direct British rule. Christian missionaries set about to correct abuses they perceived in certain Hindu practices, such as widow-burning and the caste system. But they also taught those who were being educated in their schools that Hinduism was "intellectually incoherent and ethically unsound."[20] Some Indians believed them and drifted away from their ancient tradition.

To counteract Western influences, Mahatma ("Great Soul") Gandhi (who died in 1948) encouraged grassroots nationalism, emphasizing that the people's strength lay in awareness of spiritual truth and in non-violent resistance to military-industrial oppression. He claimed that these qualities were the essence of all religions, including Hinduism, which he considered the universal religion.

In addition to being made a focus for political unity, Hinduism itself was revitalized by a number of major figures. One of these was Ramakrishna, who lived from 1836 to 1886. He was a devotee of the Divine Mother in the form of Kali. Eschewing ritual, he communicated with her through intense love. He practiced Tantric disciplines and the *bhavanas* (types of loving relationships). These brought him spiritual powers, spiritual insight, and reportedly a visible brilliance, but he longed only to be a vehicle for pure devotion.

Ramakrishna worshipped the Divine through many Hindu paths, as well as Islam and Christianity, and found the same One in them all. Intoxicated with the One, he had continual visions of the Divine Mother and ecstatically worshipped her in unorthodox, uninhibited ways. For instance, once he fed a cat some food that was supposed to be a temple offering for the Divine Mother, for she revealed herself to him in everything, including the cat. He also placed his spiritual bride, Sarada Devi, in the chair reserved for the Deity, honoring her as the Great Goddess.

The pure devotion and universal spiritual wisdom Ramakrishna embodied inspired what is now known as the Ramakrishna Movement, or the Vedanta Society. A famous disciple named Vivekananda (1863–1902) carried the eternal message of Sanatana Dharma to the world beyond India, and excited so much interest in the West that Hinduism became a global religion. He also reintroduced Indians to the profundities of their great traditions.

Within India Hinduism was also influenced by reform movements such as Brahmo Samaj and Arya Samaj. The former defended Hindu mysticism and bhakti devotion to an immanent Deity. The latter advocated a return to what it saw as the purity of the Vedas, rejecting image worship, devotion to a multiplicity of deities, priestly privileges, and popular rituals. Though different, both movements were designed to convince intellectuals of the validity of "true" Hinduism.

> *Do not care for doctrines, do not care for dogmas, or sects, or churches, or temples; they count for little compared with the essence of existence in each [person], which is spirituality. . . . Earn that first, acquire that, and criticise no one, for all doctrines and creeds have some good in them.*
>
> *Ramakrishna*[21]

Global Hinduism

Hinduism is also experiencing vibrant growth beyond the Indian subcontinent, partly among expatriates and partly among converts from other faiths. For the past hundred years, many self-proclaimed gurus left India to develop followings in other countries. Some were discovered to be fraudulent, with scandalous private behavior or motives of wealth and power. Despite increased Western wariness of gurus, some of the exported movements have continued to grow.

Many non-Indians discovered Sanatana Dharma by reading *Autobiography of a Yogi*, by Paramahansa Yogananda (1893–1952). The book, which has been translated into eighteen languages, describes his intriguing spiritual experiences with Indian gurus and also explains principles of Sanatana Dharma in loving fashion. Yogananda travelled to the United States and began a movement, the California-based *Self-Realization Fellowship*, which has survived his death and is still growing under the supervision of Western disciples, with centers, temples, and living communities in forty-six countries.

Another still-flourishing example is the Netherlands-based *Transcendental Meditation* (TM) movement begun by Maharishi Mahesh Yogi in the 1960s. For a fee, he and his disciples teach people secret mantras and assert that repeating the mantra for twenty minutes twice each day will bring great personal benefits. These range from enhanced athletic prowess to increased satisfaction with life. By paying more money, advanced practitioners can also learn how to "fly." That is, they take short hops into the air while sitting crosslegged. The organization claims a success rate of sixty-five percent in ending drug and alcohol addiction. Its "flying" practitioners are sent to cities to mediate intensely and thus lower the crime rates in the area, according to research published by the TM organization.

Another rather unlikely success story continues to unfold in *ISKCON*, the International Society for Krishna Consciousness. In 1965, the Indian guru A. C. Bhaktivedanta Swami Prabhupada arrived in the United States, carrying the asceticism and bhakti devotion of Sri Caitanya's tradition of Krishna worship from India to the heart of Western materialistic culture. Adopting the dress and diet of Hindu monks and nuns, his followers lived in temple communities. Their days began at 4 a.m. with meditation, worship, chanting of the names of Krishna and Ram, and scriptural study, with the aim of turning from a material life of sense gratification to one of transcendent spiritual happiness. During the day, they chanted and danced in the streets to introduce others to the bliss of Krishna, distributed literature (especially Swami Prabhupada's illustrated and esteemed translation of the *Bhagavad-Gita*), attracted new devotees, and raised funds.

Despite schisms and scandals, the movement has continued since Swami Prabhupada's death, and is growing in strength in various countries, particularly in India and Eastern Europe. Exposure of scandals such as the physical, emotional, and sexual abuse of children in ISKCON schools has prompted new reform efforts within the movement. At present there are approximately one million ISKCON followers worldwide.

Hindu exclusivism vs. universalism

There is a highly ecumenical spirit of tolerance in many of the ways that Sanatana Dharma is being shared with the world. The international Vedanta Society and the Ramakrishna Movement, for instance, emphasize these central principles:

> *Truth or God is One.*
> *Our real nature is divine.*
> *The purpose of our life is to realize the One in our own soul.*
> *There are innumerable spiritual paths, all leading to this realization of divinity.*[22]

At the same time, inter-religious disharmony is being fanned in India by those using the name of religion for divisive, power-amassing political purposes. Late in 1992, Hindu mobs stormed and destroyed the Babri Masjid, a Muslim mosque built in the sixteenth century by the Muslim emperor Babar in Ayodhya on the site where his army had torn down a temple

Dr. Karan Singh

Globally active in an extraordinary number of public posts and projects, Dr. Karan Singh is also one of the world's most respected spokesmen for Hinduism. He was born wealthy, as heir to the Maharaja of Jammu and Kashmir, but has never retired from a life of intense public service. In fact, he turned over his entire princely inheritance to the service of the people of India and converted his palace into a museum and library.

A brilliant orator, Dr. Karan Singh quotes extensively from the Vedas in his talks and says he has been deeply influenced by them—in particular, the Upanishads.

The Upanishads are the high-water mark of Hindu philosophy. They are texts of tremendous wisdom and power. They represent some of the deepest truths with regard to the all-pervasiveness of the Divine. One is the concept that every individual encapsulates a spark of the Divine, the atman. There is also the concept of the human race as an extended family. Then there is the concept that "The truth is one; the wise call it by many names." That is the ultimate unity of all religions. We also have the concept of the welfare of the many, the happiness of the many.

Busy though he is, Dr. Karan Singh always takes time daily to perform his private *puja* (worship ceremonies). He is a worshipper of Lord Siva. Before Lord Siva, he also worships the goddess.

As part of my daily routine, I have my own puja. I do it in the morning, again at night before going to bed, and in the course of the day. Ours is not a religion where you go once a week to a church and that's it. Hinduism is supposed to be

something which permeates your entire consciousness. Therefore these puja sessions are supposed to be ways of reminding yourself of the Divinity.

Despite his personal devotion to Lord Siva, Dr. Karan Singh emphasizes that Hinduism supports acceptance of all manifestations of the divine, and therefore all religions.

The exclusivism or monopolistic tendencies in religions who claim that they have the sole agency in the sphere of the divine is not acceptable in this day and age. We have got to accept the fact that there are multiple paths to the Divine. We have to not only accept them—we have to respect whoever is travelling on his or her path. That has come to me particularly from the Vedanta tradition.

Although Dr. Karan Singh has often been deeply involved in government, he is free from the taint of corruption and scandal which mars so many political careers. He attributes his clear reputation partly to the fact that the was born into "favourable financial circumstances," and also to his religious upbringing:

Not being corrupt is part of the basic religious teachings around the world. We are brought up on the stories of Raja Harish Chandra, who gave up everything for the sake of truth, and Sri Rama, who gave up everything for the sake of his father's word, and so on. Those sort of mythological stories based on truth and the quest for truth are very strong in wisdom. And if you are pursuing the path of truth, then I presume that automatically rules out your being corrupt.[23]

thought to mark Lord Rama's birthplace. The extensive Hindu–Muslim violence that ensued throughout India revealed deep communal antipathies strengthened by fundamentalist Hindu organizations. One of these is the RSS—Rashtriya Svayamsevak Sangh—which arose early in the twentieth century, espousing Hindu renewal. It gave expression to the ideals of V. D. Savarkar, who wrote of an ancient Hindu nation and "Hindu-ness," excluding Muslims and Christians as aliens.

Political affiliates of the RSS with a "Hindu agenda"—particularly the BJP (Bharatiya Janata Party)—have become very powerful in Indian politics. Its religious affiliate—the Vishva Hindu Parishad (VHP)—is pushing ahead controversial plans to build a new temple to Lord Ram in Ayodhya as a symbol of restoration of the rule of Ram, a legendary time when Hindu virtues were maintained by a perfect ruler.

The VHP is also trying to woo Christian converts back to Hinduism and is actively opposing Christianity in India. In recent years, Christian nuns in India have been raped, priests killed, Bibles burned, and churches and Christian schools destroyed, apparently by Hindu extremists. Some "untouchable" Hindus have converted to Christianity, Buddhism, or Islam because those religions do not make caste distinctions.

Hindu political exclusivism is meeting with mixed reactions within Sanatana Dharma. Politics aside, there is a growing interest in the spiritual foundations of Sanatana Dharma, both in India and abroad. In the current "Hindu renaissance," many large new temples are being built around the world, encouraging Indian expatriates to return to public forms of worship.

Despite a current tendency toward nationalistic, exclusivist interpretations of Sanatana Dharma, the Indian Supreme court has formally defined Hindu beliefs in a way that affirms universality. According to the Court's definition, to be a Hindu means:

1 Acceptance and reverence for the Vedas as the foundation of Hindu philosophy;
2 A spirit of tolerance, and willingness to understand and appreciate others' points of view, recognizing that truth has many sides;
3 Acceptance of the belief that vast cosmic periods of creation, maintenance, and dissolution continuously recur;
4 Acceptance of belief in reincarnation;
5 Recognition that paths to truth and salvation are many;
6 Recognition that there may be numerous gods and goddesses to worship, without necessarily believing in worship through idols;
7 Unlike other religions, absence of belief in a specific set of philosophic concepts.[24]

Finally, Hindu scholar and statesman Karan Singh observes that the vast understandings of the ancient Vedas will always make them relevant to the human condition:

We, who are children of the past and the future, of earth and heaven, of light and darkness, of the Human and the divine, at once evanescent and eternal, of the world and beyond it, within time and in eternity, yet have the capacity to comprehend our condition, to rise above our terrestrial limitations, and, finally, to transcend the throbbing abyss of space and time itself. This, in essence, is the message of Hinduism.[25]

Suggested Reading

The Bhagavad-Gita, available in numerous translations. Central teachings about how to realize the immortal soul.

Eck, Diana, *Darsan: Seeing the Divine Image in India,* second edition, Chambersburg, Pennsylvania: Anima Books, 1985. A lively explanation of deity images and how the people of India respond to them.

Feuerstein, Georg, Subhash Kak, and David Frawley, *In Search of the Cradle of Civilization,* Wheaton, Illinois: Quest Books, 1995. Survey of contemporary scholarship about ancient India which questions the Aryan Invasion Theory and common conclusions which have been based on this theory, such as the idea that the Aryans wrote the Vedas.

Jayakar, Pupul, *The Earth Mother,* New Delhi: Penguin Books, 1989. Explorations of ways of worshipping the Goddess in rural India.

Lopez, Donald S., Jr., ed., *Religions of India in Practice,* Princeton, New Jersey: Princeton University Press, 1995. An interesting anthology of popular texts with contemporary rather than stereotypical understandings, primarily from Hinduism but also including Buddhist, Jain, and Sikh material.

Sahi, Jyoti, *The Child and the Serpent,* London: Routledge and Kegan Paul, 1980. An artist's attempt to rediscover the inner meanings of traditional visual symbols by living in the villages of South India.

Singh, Karan, *Essays on Hinduism,* New Delhi: Ratna Sagar, 1987 and 1990. An excellent and concise introduction of the many facets of Hinduism, interpreted in modern terms.

Sondhi, Madhuri Santanam, *Modernity, Morality and the Mahatma,* New Delhi: Haranand Publications, 1997. A brilliant analysis of Indian responses to the challenges of modernity, including the contribution of many religious figures.

Sontheimer, Gunther-Dietz, and Hermann Kulke, *Hinduism Reconsidered,* New Delhi: Manohar, 1997. Provocative articles by Indian and Western scholars on controversial new ways of interpreting many facets of Sanatana Dharma.

CHAPTER 4

BUDDHISM

*"He will deliver by the boat of knowledge
the distressed world"*

The man who came to be known as the Buddha preached an alternative to the ritual-bound Brahmanism of sixth-century BCE India. The Buddha taught about earthly suffering and its cure. Many religions offer comforting supernatural solutions to the difficulties of earthly life. In its early forms, Buddhism was quite different: it held that our salvation from suffering lies only in our own efforts. The Buddha taught that in understanding how we create suffering for ourselves we can become free.

We might imagine that the discomfort of having to face ourselves and take responsibility for our own liberation would be an unappealing path that would attract few followers. But the way of the Buddha spread from his native India throughout East Asia, becoming the dominant religion in many Eastern countries. In the process, it took on devotional and mystical qualities from earlier local traditions, with various deity-like buddhas to whom one could appeal for help. And now, more than two and a half thousand years after the Buddha's death, the religion that he founded is also attracting considerable interest in the West.

The Life of the Buddha

What we know about the Buddha himself is sketchy. His prolific teachings were probably not collected in written form until at least four hundred years after his death. In the meantime they were apparently held, and added to, as an oral tradition chanted from memory by monks, groups of whom were responsible for remembering specific parts of the teachings. Only a few factual details of the Buddha's own life have been retained. While stories from the life of the Buddha are abundant in authorized Buddhist texts, most of what is usually taught about the life of the Buddha is rich in symbolic meanings but not verifiable as historical fact.

The one who became the Buddha (a title that means "Enlightened One") was born about 563 BCE. His father was apparently a wealthy landowner serving as one of the chiefs of a kshatriya clan, the Shakyas. They lived in the foothills of the Himalayas and could probably see these great mountains looming in the distance.

The birth legends describe a miraculous conception in which the Future Buddha came to his mother in the form of a white elephant and entered her right side. He had been born many times before and was drawn to earth once again by his compassion for all suffering beings. Stories also tell of the Brahmins' interpretation of his mother's dream (and of marks on the baby himself): a son would be born whose greatness would lead to his either becoming king of all India or one who retires from earthly life to become an enlightened being, sharing his own awakening with the world.

The heralded birth occurred in Lumbini, a garden retreat which is now in Nepal. The boy was named Siddhartha*, "wish-fulfiller," or "he who has reached his goal." His family name, Gautama, honored an ancient Hindu sage whom the family claimed as ancestor or spiritual guide. It is said that Siddhartha's father, wanting his son to succeed him as a king, tried to make the boy's earthly life so pleasant that he would not choose to retire from it. Siddhartha later described a life of fine clothes, white umbrellas for shade, perfumes, cosmetics, a mansion for each season, the company of female musicians, and a harem of dancing girls. He was also trained in martial arts and married to at least one wife, who bore a son.

In the midst of this life of ease, Siddhartha was apparently unconvinced of its value. He was struck by the stark fact that despite its temporary pleasures, life always leads to decay and death. According to the legend, the gods arranged for him to see the "Four Sights" that his father had carefully tried to hide from him: a bent old man, a sick person, a dead person, and a monk seeking eternal rather than temporal pleasure. Seeing the first three sights, he was reportedly dismayed by the impermanence of life and the existence of suffering, old age, and death; the sight of the monk suggested the possibility of a life of renunciation. Increasingly dissatisfied with the futility of sensual delights, at the age of twenty-nine Prince Siddhartha renounced his wealth and position as heir to the throne, left his wife and baby, shaved his head, and donned the coarse robe of a wandering ascetic.

Many Indian sannyasins were already leading the homeless life of poverty considered appropriate for seekers of spiritual truth. Although the future Buddha would later develop a new religion that departed significantly from Brahmanic Hindu beliefs, he initially tried the traditional methods. He headed southeast to study with a famous Brahmin teacher who had many followers. Although Siddhartha is said to have achieved the mental state of No-thing-ness under his teachings, he resumed his search, apparently feeling that a still higher state of realization lay beyond. His next Brahmin teacher helped him to realize an even higher level. But again he moved on, not satisfied that he had reached his ultimate goal: the way of total liberation from suffering. He sought out temple priests but was

---

*Buddhist terms have come to us both in **Pali**, an Indian dialect first used for preserving the Buddha's teachings (the Buddha himself probably spoke a different ancient dialect), and in Sanskrit, the language of Indian sacred literature. For instance, the Pali *sutta* (aphorism) is equivalent to the Sanskrit **sutra**. In this chapter Sanskrit will be used, as it is more familiar to Westerners, except in the section on Theravada, which uses the Pali.

disturbed by their animal sacrifices to the gods, which Siddhartha considered cruel. Before leaving them, he tried to teach them that it was hypocritical and futile to try to atone for misdeeds by destroying life.

Still searching, Siddhartha found five pupils of his second teacher living as ascetics in the forest. Admiring their efforts to subdue the senses, he decided to try their practices himself as an experiment in liberation. For six years he outdid them in extreme self-denial techniques: nakedness, exposure to great heat and cold, breath retention, a bed of brambles, severe fasting. Finally he acknowledged that this extreme ascetic path had not led to enlightenment.

Siddhartha then shifted his practice to a Middle Way of neither self-indulgence nor self-denial. To the disillusionment of the five ascetics, who left him, he revived his failing health by accepting food once more and taking reasonable care of his body. Placing his faith in clarity of mind, he began a period of reflection. On the night of the full moon in the sixth lunar month, as he sat in deep meditation beneath a sacred fig tree at Gaya, he finally experienced Supreme Enlightenment.

After passing through four states of serene contemplation, he first recalled all his previous lives. Then he had a realization of the wheel of deaths and rebirths, in which past good or bad deeds are reflected in the next life. Finally, he realized the cause of suffering and the means for ending it. After this supreme experience, it is said that he radiated light. The realization made Siddhartha an enlightened being, a *Buddha*. According to the legend, he was tempted by Mara, the personification of evil, to keep his insights to himself, for they were too complex and profound for ordinary people to understand. But the Buddha, as he now knew himself, compassionately determined to set the wheel of teaching in motion, even if only for the sake of a few who would understand.

The first people with whom the Buddha shared the essence of his insights were the five ascetics who had abandoned him, thinking he had given up. In his famous Deer Park sermon at Sarnath, he taught them what became the essence of Buddhism: the Four Noble Truths about suffering and the Eightfold Path for liberation from suffering. Soon convinced, they became the first disciples of the new path.

The Buddha continued to teach the **dharma** (Pali: *dhamma*)—which in his system means the truths of reality, and the right conduct for each person's state of evolution—for forty-five years. As he walked through the northern Indian countryside, still as a voluntarily poor teacher with a begging bowl, he gave sermons to people of all sects and classes. Some, including his son, became **bhikshus** (Pali: *bhikkhus*), monks emulating his life of poverty and spiritual dedication; others adopted his teachings but continued as householders.

The **sangha**—the order of Buddha's disciples—was free from the caste system; people from all levels of society became Buddhists. His stepmother and his wife became *bhikshunis* (Pali: *bhikkhunis*), members of the order of nuns that the Buddha founded. After the death of his father the king, the Buddha's stepmother had requested permission to start an order of Buddhist nuns. The Buddha refused. Then she and 500 women from the court reportedly shaved their heads, put on yellow robes, and followed him on foot, making the same request. At last he agreed. His reluctance is today a matter of much speculation. In patriarchal Indian society, for women to leave their homes and become itinerant mendicants would likely have been perceived as socially disruptive, as well as being difficult for women of the court. According to Hindu social codes, a woman could not lead a religious life and could only achieve spiritual salvation through devotion to her husband. By contrast, the Buddha asserted that women were equally capable as men of achieving enlightenment.

The circumstances of the Buddha's death at the age of eighty bespeak his selfless desire to spare humankind from suffering. His last meal, served by a blacksmith, inadvertently included some poisonous mushrooms. Severely ill and recognizing his impending death, the Buddha nevertheless pushed on to his next teaching stop at Kusinara, converting a young man along the way. He sent word back to the blacksmith that he must not feel remorse or blame himself for the meal, for his offering of food brought him great merit.

When he reached his destination, he lay down on a stone couch, at which point, it is said, the trees above rained blossoms down upon him. As his monks came to pay their last respects, he urged them to tend to their own spiritual development:

> You must be your own lamps, be your own refuges. . . . A monk becomes his
> own lamp and refuge by continually looking on his body, feelings,
> perceptions, moods, and ideas in such a manner that he conquers the
> cravings and depressions of ordinary men and is always strenuous, self-
> possessed, and collected in mind.[1]

He designated no successor, no one to lead the order. But it survived and spread because, as his closest helper, Ananda, explained, before his passing away, the Buddha had made it clear that his followers should take the dharma and discipline as their support. They should study the dharma, put it into practice, and if outsiders criticized it, they should be able to defend it.

The Dharma

Buddhism is often described as a nontheistic religion. There is no personal God who creates everything and to whom prayers can be directed. The Buddhists at the 1993 Chicago Parliament of the World's Religions found it necessary to explain to people of other religions that they do not worship Buddha:

> Shakyamuni Buddha, the founder of Buddhism, was not God or a god. He
> was a human being who attained full Enlightenment through meditation
> and showed us the path of spiritual awakening and freedom. Therefore,
> Buddhism is not a religion of God. Buddhism is a religion of wisdom,
> enlightenment and compassion. Like the worshippers of God who believe
> that salvation is available to all through confession of sin and a life of
> prayer, we Buddhists believe that salvation and enlightenment are available

*to all through removal of defilements and delusion and a life of meditation.
However, unlike those who believe in God who is separate from us,
Buddhists believe that Buddha which means "one who is awake and
enlightened" is inherent in us all as Buddhanature or Buddhamind.*[2]

Unlike other Indian sages, the Buddha did not focus on descriptions of
ultimate reality, the nature of the soul, life after death, or the origin of the
universe. He said that curiosity about such matters was like a man who,
upon being wounded by a poisoned arrow, refused to have it pulled out
until he was told the caste and origin of his assailant, his name, his height,
the color of his skin, and all details about the bow and arrow. In the meantime, he died.

*Being religious and following Dhamma has nothing to do with the dogma
that the world is eternal; and it has nothing to do with the other dogma that
the world is not eternal. For whether the world is eternal or otherwise,
birth, old age, death, sorrow, pain, misery, grief, and despair exist. I am
concerned with the extinction of these.*[3]

The Buddha spoke of his teachings as a raft to take us to the farther
shore, rather than a description of the shore or something to be carried
around once we get there. The basic planks of this raft are insights into the
truths of existence and the path to liberation; **nirvana** (Pali: *nibbana*) is the
farther shore, the goal of spiritual effort.

The basic facts of existence

In his very first sermon, the "Deer Park" sermon preached to the five ascetics, the Buddha set forth the *"Four Noble Truths"* around which all his later
teachings revolved. These were:

1 Life inevitably involves suffering, is imperfect and unsatisfactory.
2 Suffering originates in our desires.
3 Suffering will cease if all desires cease.
4 There is a way to realize this state: the Noble Eightfold Path.

The Buddha is therefore neither pessimistic nor optimistic about our
human condition. Sri Lankan monk and scholar Walpola Rahula speaks of
the Buddha as being "the wise and scientific doctor for the ills of the
world."[4]

To look at the diagnosis and treatment of our human condition one step
at a time, the Buddha's First Noble Truth is the existence of **dukkha**,
which means suffering or frustration. We all experience grief, unfulfilled
desires, sickness, old age, physical pain, mental anguish, and death. We
may be happy for a while, but happiness is not permanent. Even our identity is impermanent. There is no continual "I." What we regard as our self
is simply an ever-changing bundle of fleeting feelings, sense impressions,
ideas, and evanescent physical matter. One moment's identity leads to the
next like one candle being lit from another.

The Second Noble Truth is that dukkha has its origin in desire—desire for sensory pleasures, for fame and fortune, for things to stay as they are or become different than they are—and in attachment to ideas. The reason that desire leads us to suffering, the Buddha taught, is that we do not understand the nature of things, of that which we desire. Everything is actually impermanent, changing all the time. We seek to grasp and hold life as we want it to be, but we cannot, since everything is in constant flux.

What a Buddhist strives for instead is the recognition of dukkha, **anicca** (impermanence), and **anatta** (the revolutionary and unique doctrine that there is no separate, permanent, or immortal self. Rather, a human being is an energy process composed of momentary energy flashes, interconnected with all other beings and with the universe as energy processes). This realization of anatta is spiritually valuable because it reduces attachment to one's mind, body, and selfish desires. Suffering is also useful to us because it helps us to see things as they really are. Our attention is drawn to the fact that everything changes and passes away, moment by moment; there are only momentary configurations within a continual process of change. Once we have grasped these basic facts of life, we can be free in this life, and free from another rebirth.

The Third Noble Truth is that dukkha can cease if desire ceases. Thus illusion ends and ultimate reality, or nirvana, is revealed. One lives happily and fully in the present moment, free from self-centeredness and full of compassion for others. One can serve them purely, for in this state there is no thought of oneself.

The Fourth Noble Truth is that only through a life of morality, concentration, and wisdom—which the Buddha set forth as the Noble Eightfold Path—can desire and therefore suffering be extinguished.

The Eightfold Path of liberation

The Buddha set forth a systematic approach by which dedicated humans could pull themselves out of suffering and achieve the final goal of liberation. The *Eightfold Path* offers ways to burn up all past demerits, avoid accumulating new demerits, and build up merit for a favorable rebirth. Perfection of the path means final escape from the cycle of death and rebirth, into the peace of nirvana.

One factor is *right understanding*—comprehending reality correctly through deep realization of the Four Noble Truths. Initially this means seeing through illusions, such as the idea that a little more wealth could bring happiness. Gradually one learns to question old assumptions in the light of the Four Noble Truths. Everything we do and say is governed by the mind. The Buddha said that if our mind is defiled and untrained, suffering will follow us just as a chariot follows the horse. If we think and act from a purified, trained mind, happiness will always follow us.

A second aspect of the Eightfold Path is *right thought or motives*. The Buddha encourages us to uncover any "unwholesome" emotional roots behind our thinking, such as a desire to hide our imperfections or avoid contact with others. As we discover and weed out such emotional blocks, our thought becomes free from the limitations of self-centeredness—relaxed, clear, and open.

BUDDHISM

	600 **BCE**	Life of Gautama Buddha c.563–483 BCE
	400	King Asoka begins spreading Buddhism outward from India c. 258 BCE
Development of Theravada Buddhism c.200 BCE–c.200 CE	**200**	Perfection of Wisdom scriptures originally developed c.100 BCE– c.300 CE
Buddhism transmitted to China and then East Asia c.50 CE	**CE**	Pali Canon written down in Ceylon (Sri Lanka) c.80 BCE
Development of Mahayana Buddhism 1st C CE	**200**	Nagarjuna expounds concept of voidness c.200s CE
	400	
Peak of Chinese Buddhism 589–845		Buddhism enters Japan c.550
Songtsan declares Buddhism the national religion of Tibet 600s	**600**	
Persecution of Buddhism begins in China 845	**800**	
	1000	Life of Milarepa 1079–1153
Ch'an Buddhism of China carried to Japan as Zen 13th C	**1200**	Life of Nichiren 1222–1282
Buddhism declines in northern India 13th C		
Buddhism declines in southern India 15th C	**1400**	
	1600	
	1800	
	2000	Communist Chinese repress Buddhism in Tibet 1959

A third factor is *right speech*. The Buddha cautions us to relinquish our propensity to vain talk, gossip, tale-bearing, harsh words, and lying, and to use communication instead in the service of truth and harmony. He also advises us to speak in a positive manner to our own minds—to say to ourselves, "May you be well and happy today."

A fourth factor, *right action*, begins for the layperson with observing the five basic precepts for moral conduct: avoid destroying life, stealing, sexual misconduct, lying, and intoxicants. Beyond these, we are to base our actions on clear understanding. "Evil deeds," said the Buddha, are those "done from motives of partiality, enmity, stupidity, and fear."[5]

Fifth is *right livelihood*—being sure that one's way of making a living does not violate the five precepts. One's trade should not harm others or disrupt social harmony.

Right effort, a sixth factor in the Eightfold Path, bespeaks continual striving to cut off "unwholesome states," past, present, and future. This is not a way for the lazy.

A seventh factor, *right mindfulness*, is particularly characteristic of Buddhism, for the way to liberation is said to be through the mind. We are urged to be aware in every moment. In **The Dhammapada**, short verses about the way of truth, said to have been uttered by the Buddha, there appears this pithy injunction:

Check your mind.
Be on your guard.
Pull yourself out
as an elephant from mud.[6]

The eighth factor, *right meditation*, applies mental discipline to the quieting of the mind itself. "It is subtle, invisible, treacherous,"[7] explains the Buddha. Skillful means are therefore needed to see and transcend its restless nature. When the mind is fully stilled, it becomes a quiet pool in which the true nature of everything is clearly reflected.

Try to be mindful, and let things take their natural course. Then your mind will become still in any surroundings, like a clear forest pool. All kinds of wonderful, rare animals will come to drink at the pool, and you will clearly see the nature of all things. You will see many strange and wonderful things come and go, but you will be still. This is the happiness of the Buddha.

Achaan Chah, meditation master, Wat Pa Pong, Thailand[8]

The wheel of birth and death

Buddhist teachings about rebirth are slightly different from those of Hindu orthodoxy, for there is no eternal soul to be reborn. In Buddhism, one changing state of being sets another into motion. The central cause in this process is karma (Pali: *kamma*)—our acts of will. These influence the level at which that process we think of as "me" is reborn. The impressions of our good and bad actions help to create our personality moment-by-moment. When we die, this process continues, passing on the flame to a new life on a plane that reflects our past karma.

There are thirty-one planes of existence, interpreted as psychological metaphors by some Buddhists. Whether metaphors or metaphysical realities, these include hells, "hungry ghosts" (beings tormented with unsatisfied desires), animals, humans, and gods. Like the lower levels, the gods are imperfect and impermanent. Round and round we go, life after life, caught in this cycle of samsara (worldly phenomena), repeatedly experiencing aging, decay, suffering, death, and painful rebirth, unless we are freed into nirvana, which is beyond all the cause-and-effect-run planes of existence.

Nirvana

About the goal of Buddhist practice, nirvana, the Buddha had relatively little to say. The word itself refers to the extinguishing of a flame from lack of fuel. The only way to end the cycle in which desire feeds the wheel of suffering is to end all cravings and lead a passion-free existence which has no karmic consequences. Thence one enters a condition of what the Buddha called "quietude of heart."[9] "Where there is nothing," he said, "where naught is grasped, there is the Isle of No-beyond. Nirvana do I call it—the utter extinction of aging and dying,"[10] "the unborn, . . . undying, . . . unsorrowing, . . . stainless, the uttermost security from bonds."[11]

For the **arhant** (Pali: *arhat, arahat*), saint, who has found nirvana in this life:

> *No suffering for him*
> *who is free from sorrow*
> *free from the fetters of life*
> *free in everything he does.*
> *He has reached the end of his road. . . .*
>
> *peaceful his thinking, peaceful his speech,*
> *peaceful his deed, tranquil his mind.*[12]

What happens when such a being dies? One enters a deathless, peaceful, unchanging state that cannot be described. Individuality disappears and one enters the realm of ultimate truth, about which the Buddha was silent. Why? At one point he picked up a handful of leaves from the forest floor and asked his disciples which were more numerous, the leaves in his hand or those in the surrounding forest. When they replied, "Very few in your hand, lord; many more in the grove," he said:

> *Exactly. So you see, friends, the things that I know and have not revealed are more than the truths I know and have revealed. And why have I not revealed them? Because, friends, there is no profit in them; because they are not helpful to holiness; because they do not lead from disgust to cessation and peace, because they do not lead from knowledge to wisdom and Nirvana.*[13]

Buddhism South and North

As soon as he had attracted a small group of disciples, the Buddha sent them out to help teach the dharma. This missionary effort spread in all directions. Two hundred years after the Buddha died, a great Indian king, Asoka, developed appreciation of many religions. Under his leadership Buddhism was carried throughout the kingdom and outward to other countries as well, beginning its development as a global religion. After Asoka's death, Brahmins reasserted their political influence and Buddhists were persecuted in parts of India. By the time of the twelfth-century Muslim invasions of India, Buddhism had nearly died out and never became the dominant religion in the Buddha's homeland.

Many Buddhist sects have developed as the Buddha's teachings have been expanded upon and adapted to local cultures in different areas. There are two primary divisions. The remaining form that tries to adhere closely to what it considers the original teachings is called **Theravada**, or "Way of the Elders." It is prevalent in the Southeast Asian countries such as Sri Lanka, Myanmar (Burma), Thailand, Kampuchea (Cambodia), and Laos and is therefore geographically referred to as the Southern School. The other major grouping is the Northern School, dominant in Nepal, Tibet, China, Korea, Mongolia, and Japan. Those of this group call it **Mahayana**, the "Greater Vehicle," because they feel that theirs is a bigger raft that can carry more people across the sea of samsara than the stark teachings of the Theravadins, which they call the **Hinayana**, or "Lesser Vehicle." Both groups are in general agreement about the Four Noble Truths, the Eightfold Path, and the teachings about karma and nirvana described above.

Theravada: the path of mindfulness

Theravada is a conservative and traditional Buddhist way. Theravadin Buddhists study the early scriptures in Pali, honor the monastic life of renunciation, and follow mindfulness meditation teachings. These characteristics are more obvious among the intellectuals and monastics; the common people are more devotional in their practices.

THE PALI CANON   Buddhists who follow the Theravada tradition study a large collection of ancient scriptures preserved in the Pali language of ancient India. This ancient **canon**, or authoritative collection of writings, is called the *Pali Canon*. It is also referred to as the *Tipitaka*, the "Three Baskets." This label derives from the old practice of storing palm-leaf manuscripts in wicker baskets; thus, the "Three Baskets" are three collections of sacred writings. The teachings were collected immediately after the Buddha's death by a council of five hundred Elders, monks who had studied directly with him. From memory, the Venerable Ananda recited his discourses and another close disciple rehearsed the discipline of the order. Then the Elders agreed upon a definitive body of the Buddha's teachings which were carried orally until the first century BCE, when they were written down on palm leaves and stored in baskets.

In addition to the Tipitaka, Theravadins also honor other non-canonical Pali works, such as later commentaries and then commentaries-on-the-commentaries. The 547 lively Jataka Tales appear in the commentaries as explanations of the context of the pithy sayings found in the discourses. These folk tales are said to have been told by the Buddha and to represent scenes from his own previous births, but they are also used to demonstrate Buddhist virtues, such as wisdom and compassion.

THE TRIPLE GEM   Like all Buddhists, those of the Southern School soften the discipline of the mind with devotion to the **Triple Gem**: Buddha (the Enlightened One), Dhamma (the doctrine he taught, ultimate reality), and sangha (the order of his disciples). To become a Buddhist, and then afterwards to reassert the basis of one's faith, a person "takes refuge" in these three jewels by reciting the Pali formula, *Buddham saranam gacchami* ("I go to the Buddha for refuge"), *dhammam saranam gacchami* ("I go to the dhamma for refuge"), *Sangham saranam gacchami* ("I go to the sangha for refuge").

One takes refuge in the Buddha not by praying to him for help but by paying homage to him as supreme teacher and inspiring model.

The dhamma is like a medicine, but it will not cure our suffering unless we take it.

The sangha is the order of bhikkhus and bhikkhunis who have renounced the world in order to follow, preserve, and share the dhamma. The Buddha established one of the world's first monastic orders, and this core remains strong in Theravada. There are presently about half a million Theravadin monks in Southeast Asia. To simplify their wordly lives and devote themselves to studying and teaching the dhamma, monks must shave their heads, dress in simple robes, own only a few basic material items, eat no solid foods after noon, practice celibacy, and depend upon the laity for their food, clothing, and medical supplies. Early every morning they set forth with begging bowl, and the laypeople regard it as a merit-making opportunity to offer food to them. In this interdependent system, the monks reciprocate by offering spiritual guidance, chanted blessings, and various social services, including secular advice and education. Monks offer discourses on the dhamma in monasteries or in private homes.

Buddhist monasteries are at the center of village life, rather than separated from it. The monasteries are open, and people come and go. The monks hold a revered social position as models of self-control, kindness, and intelligence. In Thailand it is common for young men to take temporary vows of monkhood—often for the duration of the rainy season when little farmwork can be done. They wear the saffron robes, set forth with shaven heads and begging bowls, and receive religious instruction while they practice a life of simplicity.

By contrast, there has traditionally been little social support for bhikkhunis, or Buddhist nuns, in Southeast Asia. Provisions were made during the time of the Buddha for women monastics to live in the same monasteries as men, with the same lifestyle, but the order of fully ordained nuns disappeared completely in Theravadin countries about a thousand years ago. Many of the early Buddhist scriptures take an egalitarian position toward women's capacity for wisdom and attainment of nibbana, but spiritual power was kept in the hands of monks. Nuns were by rules of the order forever subservient to the monks, seniority notwithstanding, so there was little opportunity for them to grow into positions of leadership.

Over time, some of the monks and the texts they edited apparently became actively misogynist. Even today a Thai Buddhist monk is not allowed to come into direct contact with a woman, with the idea that women are hindrances to monks' spiritual development. Feminist scholars object to this interpretation. Thai Buddhist Dr. Chatsumarn Kabilsingh, for instance, asserts:

> *Newly ordained monks who have not had much experience with practice and are very weak in their mental resolve may be easily swayed by sensual impulses, of which women are the major attraction. Even if no women are present, some monks still create problems for themselves by images of women they have in their minds. Women are not responsible for the sexual behavior or imaginings of men; the monks themselves must cope with their own sensual desires. Enlightened ones are well-fortified against such mental states and are able to transcend gender differences. The Buddha himself found no need to avoid women, because women no longer appeared to him as sexual objects. He was well-balanced and in control of his mental processes.[14]*

There are now attempts to revive fully ordained orders of nuns in Theravadin countries. In 1998 a landmark occurred: the full ordination of 135 nuns from many countries in Bodh Gaya. According to the code of discipline, ordination of nuns is only possible if both ordained monks and nuns are present. The lack of ordained nuns had been used by conservative senior monks as a way of blocking women's ordinations. But in China, Taiwan, Japan, and Korea, women's orders had continued, and thus Master Hsing Yun, founder of a Taiwanese Buddhist order, was able to bring the requisite participants to Bodh Gaya and perform the ordinations, 980 years after the bhikkhuni order had become extinct in India and Sri Lanka.

VIPASSANA MEDITATION   In addition to trying to preserve what are thought to be the Buddha's original teachings, Theravada is the purveyor of mindfulness meditation techniques. **Vipassana** literally means "insight" but the meditation methods used to develop insight begin by increasing one's attentiveness to every detail as a way of calming, focusing, and watching the mind. As taught by the Burmese meditation master Mahasi Sayadaw, the beginning vipassana practice is simply to watch oneself breathing in and out, with the attention focused on the rise and fall of the abdomen. To keep the mind concentrated on this movement, rather than dragged this way and that by unconscious, conditioned responses, one continually makes concise mental notes of what is happening: "rising," "falling." Inevitably other mental functions will arise in the restless mind. As they do, one simply notes what they are—"imagining," "wandering," "remembering"—and then returns the attention to the rising and falling of the breath. Body sensations will appear, too, and one handles them the same way, noting "itching," "tight," "tired." Periods of sitting meditation are alternated with periods of walking meditation, in which one notes the exact movements of the body in great detail: "lifting," "moving," "placing."

This same mindfulness is carried over into every activity of the day. If ecstatic states or visions arise, the meditator is told simply to note them and let them pass away without attachment. In the same way, emotions that arise are simply observed, accepted, and allowed to pass away, rather than labeled "good" or "bad." By contrast, says dharma teacher Joko Beck, we usually get stuck in our emotions:

> Everyone's fascinated by their emotions because we think that's who we are. We're afraid that if we let our attachment to them go, we'll be nobody. Which of course we are! When you wander into your ideas, your hopes, your dreams, turn back—not just once but ten thousand times if need be, a million times if need be.[15]

The truths of existence as set forth by the Buddha—dukkha (suffering), anicca (impermanence), anatta (no eternal self)—will become apparent during this process, and the mind becomes calm, clear, attentive, and flexible, detached from likes and dislikes. Thus it is free.

THE LAITY   Although meditators from all over the world are now traveling to Southeast Asia to study with the masters of meditation, their demanding discipline is embraced by relatively few Theravadins. Not all monasteries are meditation centers. Most laypeople's religious lives are more devotional than intellectual. Traditional teaching in Theravada emphasizes development of morality, concentration, and wisdom leading to freedom, but popular Buddhism as it is practiced in Southeast Asia tends to shift the emphasis to giving alms and observing the Three Refuges.

Even within the relatively austere Theravada path there have arisen a number of ways of worship. One is the veneration of relics thought to be from the Buddha. These are placed in **stupas**, architectural mounds reaching into the sky, perhaps derived from the indigenous spiritual traditions. A tiny bone chip believed to be a relic from the Buddha, for instance, is enshrined at Doi Suthep temple in Chiang Mai in Thailand. Thousands of pilgrims climb the 290 steps to the temple today, praying for blessings by acts such as pressing squares of gold leaf onto an image of the Buddha, lighting three sticks of incense to honor the Triple Gem, lighting candles, and offering flowers to the Buddha images.

Loving images of the Buddha proliferate in the temples and roadside shrines. These physical images of the Buddha give a sense of his protective, guiding presence even though according to Theravadin orthodoxy the Buddha no longer exists as an individual, having entered nibbana. Even the monks are regarded as magical protectors of sorts, and the faithful can request chantings of blessings for protection.

Mahayana: the path of compassion and metaphysics

Further Buddhist practices and teachings appeared in a wide range of

AN INTERVIEW WITH KOMKAI CHAROENSUK

Living Buddhism

In Thailand, over ninety-three percent of the population is Buddhist, and there are historically close ties between State and sangha. The pressures of rapid modernization, consumerism, and economic troubles are beginning to erode traditional values in this society where people had been happy and free, perhaps partly because of their Buddhist faith.

Komkai Charoensuk is a cheerful, matter-of-fact Bangkok grandmother who practices meditation and studies with monks and nuns. She says, "I'm just beginning to become a good Buddhist. We have meditation courses every month at our center in Bangkok. The course I have been taking is a ten-day course, and I have taken it over twenty times. Now I'm going to take a thirty-day course in India. My daughter and my son-in-law are happy with my going. My daughter is going to buy an airplane ticket for me, and her husband is going to help me with the hotel expenses. I'm going there with six other people, including a professor in engineering and a woman physician. All of them are younger than I. I hope my meditation there will be of great benefit to me because of its continuity in practice. We'll be sitting in a cell by ourself for thirty days, getting up at 4 o'clock and starting our meditation at 4:30. Most of the day we are working in our cell. Then in the evening from 7 to 8:30 p.m. we come to listen to the discourse on tapes in the hall together with other students, but no talking is encouraged at all. Noble silence all day, all the time.

Otherwise, I practice meditation, but not continuously. It needs a lot of patience and great attention. Not time. The present moment—that's the most important thing we must know.

When somebody else is angry and starts to curse us, it is very easy for us to feel that we are hurt by them. But we can try to find out what is the cause of their suffering, their anger. The longer you keep the pain in yourself, the worse it will become. You stay angry, angry, and angry. That's the way that you are hurting yourself. And it's foolish to hurt one's own heart or one's mind. But we need a lot of practice before we can overcome these sorts of things.

We don't want to start and end and come back and start and end again and come back and start again. We don't want to be born again and suffer, another time be happy, another time suffer. You laugh and you cry, and you laugh and you cry all your life. That's why we want to go to nirvana: no more happiness, no more unhappiness. And then when anyone scolds you, you are smiling, you understand why they are scolding you. You understand everything. Nobody can hurt you."

scriptures dating from the first century BCE. These innovations in thought and practice became grouped together and called *Mahayana*, the Great Vehicle. Rather than emphasizing a distinction between monastics and common people, these new scriptures take a more liberal approach designed to encompass everyone. They honor the scriptures in the Pali Canon but claim to be more advanced teachings of the Buddha.

The Mahayana sutras (scriptures) emphasize the importance of religious experience. The dharma is not embodied only in scriptures; for the Mahayanist it is the source of a conversion experience that awakens the quest for enlightenment as the greatest value in life.

Each school, and there are many branches within Mahayana, offers a special set of methods, or "skillful means," for awakening. They are quite varied, in contrast to the relative uniformity of Theravada, but most Mahayana traditions have a few characteristics in common.

BODHISATTVAS An early Mahayana scripture, the Lotus Sutra, defended its innovations beyond the Pali Canon by claiming that the earlier teachings were merely skillful means for those with lower capacities. They were ideally to be replaced by the true dharma of the Lotus. The idea is that the Buddha geared his teaching to his audience, and that his teachings were at different levels of completeness depending on the readiness of his audience to hear the full truth.

In contrast to the earlier goal of individual liberation from suffering by those who were capable, the Lotus Sutra claimed that a higher goal was to become like the Buddha by seeking enlightenment for the sake of saving others. In fact, it asserted that we are called not just to individual liberation but to Buddhahood itself. The Lotus Sutra says that all beings have the capacity for Buddhahood and are destined to attain it eventually. Members of the new Mahayana communities called themselves **Bodhisattvas**, beings dedicated to attaining enlightenment. Both monastics and laity took the Bodhisattva vow to become enlightened.

Today Mahayana Buddhists often express this commitment in the Four Great Bodhisattva Vows compiled in China in the sixth century CE by Tien-t'ai Chih-i (founder of the Tendai School of Mahayana Buddhism):

Beings are infinite in number, I vow to save them all;
The obstructive passions are endless in number, I vow to end them all;
The teachings for saving others are countless, I vow to learn them all;
Buddhahood is the supreme achievement, I vow to attain it.

As His Holiness the Fourteenth Dalai Lama says:

The motivation to achieve Buddhahood in order to save all sentient beings is really a marvelous determination. That person becomes very courageous, warm-hearted, and useful in society.[16]

Bodhisattvahood is not just an ideal for earthly conduct; numerous heavenly Bodhisattvas are available to hear the pleas of those who are suffering. The heavenly Bodhisattvas are seen as aspects of the eternal Buddha. Each has a specific attribute, such as wisdom or compassion, and worshippers can pray to them for help.

The most popular Bodhisattva in East Asia is Kuan-yin (Japanese: Kannon), who symbolizes compassion and refuses help to no one. Kuan-yin is typically represented as female, often as the giver or protector of babies. An image with a baby has become especially popular in East Asia as a refuge for aborted fetuses and their mothers.

THE THREE BODIES OF BUDDHA   In Theravada, Buddha is an historical figure who no longer exists but who left his dharma as a guide. By contrast, Mahayana regards the Buddha as a universal principle. Metaphysically, Buddha is said to be an eternal presence in the universe with three aspects, or "bodies": the pure universal consciousness in which the Buddha is identical with absolute reality; the body of bliss, that radiant celestial aspect of Buddhahood that communicates the dharma to Bodhisattvas; and the body of transformation, by which the Buddha principle becomes human to help liberate humanity. It was in this third body that the Buddha appeared for a time on the earth as the historical figure Siddhartha Gautama of the Shakyas. He is called *Shakyamuni Buddha* (Shakya sage) by Mahayanists to distinguish him from other Buddhas.

Whereas Theravada is nontheistic, Mahayana has thus elevated Buddhahood to almost theistic status. The common people therefore recognize a multitude of Buddhas and Bodhisattvas to whom they can pray for help. But some Mahayanists interpret teachings about the Bodhisattvas and the three bodies of the Buddha symbolically rather than literally, as metaphors for aspects of consciousness within the mysteries of the cosmos.

EMPTINESS   Many schools within Mahayana also affirm, along with Theravadins, that there is an eternal reality, the transcendent "Suchness," Truth, or Law by which the universe is governed. In the Udana scripture from the Pali Canon, the Buddha stated, "O monks, there is an unborn, undying, unchanging, uncreated. If it were not so, there would be no point to life, or to training."

Some of the most complex and paradoxical of Mahayana teachings concern the concept of **sunyata**, meaning voidness or emptiness. They were elaborated by the Indian philosopher Nagarjuna around the second and third century CE on the basis of the earlier Perfection of Wisdom scriptures. According to Nagarjuna, all earthly things arise and pass away, as a process of events dependent on other events, having no independent origin and no eternal reality. The world of phenomena—samsara—is therefore empty of inherent existence. Nirvana is also empty in the sense that it is a thought construct, not an eternal reality that can be acquired. In the paradoxical analyses of voidness, even ultimate reality is called sunyata because it transcends all thought constructs. In the Perfection of Wisdom scriptures, the student to whom the lengthy teachings on sunyata are given is at last asked if he has understood them. "In truth, nothing has been taught," he declares.

The Perfection of Wisdom scriptures that celebrate the liberating experience of emptiness are foundational texts for most of Mahayana. What is distinctive and startling about Mahayana is the application of the idea of emptiness to all things, even including the teachings of the Buddha. In the popular Heart Sutra that is used liturgically throughout East Asia, the core doctrines of traditional Buddhism are systematically shattered: Bodhisattva Kuan-yin sees that the five aggregates of a person (form, sensation, perception, reaction, and consciousness) are each empty of absolute self-nature; they exist only relative to other aggregates. With this realization, the

Bodhisattva becomes free of all suffering. Next, birth and death, purity and defilement, increase and decrease are seen as empty; the six sense objects, the six sense organs, and the six sense awarenesses are seen to be empty; the Wheel of Life is seen as empty; the Four Noble Truths and Eightfold Path are seen as empty. Even knowledge and attainment are proclaimed to be empty. With this "perfection of wisdom," there are no obstacles, and therefore no fear, and going beyond delusions one attains nirvana, having emptied Buddhism of its central objects. The Heart Sutra replaces the doctrines with a mantra which it proclaims as supreme: *Gate, Gate, paragate, parasamgate, bodhi, svaha!* ("Gone, gone, gone beyond, gone to the other shore. O enlightenment, all hail!"). As Professor David Chappell observes,

> The systematic emptying of the central doctrines of the tradition is unparalleled in religious history. (Imagine a Christian saying that the Ten Commandments and Lord's Prayer and Apostles' Creed are empty!) And yet, insight into the impermanence of all things, and their connectedness, gives Mahayana a self-critical profundity and an inclusive acceptance of diversity, which provides balance in the midst of movement, and peace in the midst of compassion.[17]

Vajrayana: indestructible way to unity

Of the many branches of Mahayana Buddhism, perhaps the most prolific in creating elaborations is **Vajrayana**. It developed in the Tibetan area, but has also historically been practiced in Nepal, Bhutan, Sikkim, and Mongolia, and its practice is increasingly centered in the Tibetan diaspora and the United States.

Prior to the introduction of Buddhism from India, the mountainous Tibetan region may have been home to a shamanistic religion called Bon (pronounced "pern"). In the seventh century CE a particularly powerful king of Tibet, Songtsan, became interested in the religion that surrounded his isolated kingdom. He sent a group of students to study Buddhism in India, but they all died in the searing heat of the plains. Only one member of a second group survived the arduous trip across the Himalayas, returning with many Sanskrit texts. After some of these works were translated into Tibetan, Songtsan declared Buddhism the national religion and encouraged Buddhist virtues in his subjects.

The Bon shamans are said to have kept trying to sabotage this threat to their power until a tantric adept, Padmasambhava, was invited to the country from Kashmir in the eighth century CE. Along the way, it is said, he subdued and converted the local Bon deities. He—and perhaps his consort, Yeshe Tsogyel—developed Tibetan Buddhism by combining elements of the Bon ways and esoteric tantric practices with Mahayana Buddhism. Many of the Bon gods and goddesses were adopted as lower-grade tantric guardian deities, but animal sacrifice was replaced with symbolic forms of worship and black magic gave way to inner purification practices. When people interpreted tantric teachings literally, indulging freely in alcohol and perhaps sex in the name of spirituality, another teacher named Atisha from the great center of Buddhist learning at Nalanda, India, was called in to set things right.

Under Atisha, Tibetan Buddhism became a complex path with three stages, said to have been prescribed by the Lord Buddha. While the Buddha did not develop them to their current state, he is said to have supported the idea of different levels of teachings for the less and more evolved. The first of these is called Hinayana by the Tibetans: quieting of the mind and relinquishing of attachments through meditation practices. The second is Mahayana: training in compassion and loving-kindness. The third is the advanced esoteric path called Vajrayana ("the diamond vehicle") or **Tantrayana**, said to be the speeded-up path that allows enlightenment within a single lifetime. It includes extremely rigorous practices derived from the tantric yoga of India. Adepts in this path attempt to construct an indestructible "diamond-body" that will allow them physically to sustain entries into the energies of higher levels of consciousness.

The "Hinayana" part of this process is similar to vipassana meditation. Meditators are advised to watch their emotions rising and falling, without attachment to them, without judgment. But whereas Theravadins doing this practice tend to emphasize revulsion over the emptiness of samsara, Tibetans use the center of emotions as a source of energy. Lama Tarthang Tulku explains:

With an attitude of acceptance, even our negative emotions have the potential to increase our energy and strength. . . . Concentrate on the center of the feeling; penetrate into that space. There is a density of energy in that center that is clear and distinct. This energy has great power, and can transmit great clarity. Our consciousness can go into the emotion, contacting this pure energy so that our tension breaks. With gentleness and self-understanding we control this energy.[18]

After then developing tranquillity, freedom, and loving-kindness, as encouraged in Mahayana Buddhism, dedicated Vajrayana aspirants are guided through a series of tantric practices by gurus. The highest of these are lamas, who are revered as teachers. Some are considered as incarnate Bodhisattvas and carefully trained from a young age for their role as those who have realized the Supreme Truth and can help others advance toward it. As in Hinduism, submission to the guru in gratitude for the teachings is the only way to receive them.

Initiates are given practices in **deity yoga**: meditating on one of the many deities who embody various manifestations of energy in the universe. These radiant forms are themselves illusory, like the moon's image on water. But meditating on them is considered a way of reflecting on and thus bringing forth one's own true nature. Some of the deities are wrathful, such as Mahakala, defender of dharma. Buddhists understand that wrathful acts without hatred are sometimes socially necessary to protect truth and justice.

The highest form of Vajrayana is the use of the subtle vital energies of the body to transform the mind. A very high state of consciousness is produced after lengthy practice in which the "gross mind" is neutralized and

His Holiness the Dalai Lama

Surely one of the best-known and most-loved spiritual leaders in the world, His Holiness the fourteenth Dalai Lama is a striking example of Buddhist peace and compassion. Wherever he goes, he greets everyone with evident delight. His example is all the more powerful because he is the leader in exile of Tibet, a small nation which knew extreme oppression and suffering during the twentieth century.

The simplicity of His Holiness' words and bearing give no evidence of his intellectual power. His Holiness was only a peasant child of two in 1937 when he was located and carefully identified as the reincarnation of the thirteenth Dalai Lama. He was formally installed as the fourteenth Dalai Lama when he was only four and a half years old, thus becoming the spiritual and temporal ruler of Tibet. He was raised and rigorously educated in Lhasa in the Potala. One of the world's largest buildings, it then contained huge ceremonial halls, thirty-five chapels, meditation cells, the government storehouses, national treasures, all records of Tibetan history and culture in seven thousand huge volumes, plus two thousand illuminated volumes of the Buddhist scriptures.

A rigorous grounding in religion, maintains the Dalai Lama, brings steadiness of mind in the face of any misfortunes. He says,

Humanitarianism and true love for all beings can only stem from an awareness of the content of religion. By whatever name religion may be known, its understanding and practice are the essence of a peaceful mind and therefore of a peaceful world.[19]

The Dalai Lama's equanimity of mind must have been sorely challenged by the Chinese invasion and oppression of his small country. In 1959, when he escaped from Tibet to lessen the potential for bloodshed during a widespread popular revolt against the Chinese, Tibet was home to over six thousand monasteries. Only twelve of them were still intact by 1980. It is said that at least one million Tibetans have died as a direct result of the Chinese occupation, and the violence against the religion, the culture, and the people of Tibet continues today as Chinese settlers fill the country.

In the face of the military power of the Chinese, and armed with Buddhist precepts, the Dalai Lama has tried to steer his people away from violent response to violence. He explains:

The best way to solve problems is through human understanding, mutual respect. On one side make some concessions; on the other side take serious consideration about the problem. There may not be complete satisfaction, but something happens. At least future danger is avoided. Non-violence is very safe.[20]

While slowly, patiently trying to influence world opinion so that the "weak" voice of Tibet will not be extinguished by Chinese might, the Dalai Lama has established an entire government in exile in Dharamsala, India, in the Himalayas. In his effort to keep the voice of Tibet alive, he has also emerged as a great moral leader in the world. His quintessentially Buddhist message to people of all religions is that only through kindness and compassion toward each other and the cultivation of inner peace shall we all survive.

the "subtle mind" manifests powerfully, "riding" on what Tibetans call "the clear light of bliss." This innermost subtle mind of clear light is considered the only aspect of existence that is eternal. Once it is uncovered, one is said to be capable of attaining Buddhahood in a single lifetime.

The practices used to transform the mind also have as side-effects such abilities as levitation, clairvoyance, meditating continuously without sleep, and warming the body from within while sitting naked in the snow. Milarepa, the famous Tibetan poet-saint whose enlightenment was won through great austerities, once sang this song:

> Blissful within, I don't entertain
> The notion "I'm suffering,"
> When incessant rain is pouring outside.
>
> Even on peaks of white snow mountains
> Amidst swirling snow and sleet
> Driven by new year's wintry winds
> This cotton robe burns like fire.[21]

Tibetans have suffered persecution by the communist Chinese, who over-ran the country in 1951, destroying ancient monasteries and scriptures and killing an estimated one-sixth of the people over decades of occupation. Hundreds of thousands of Tibetans have escaped into exile. Among them is the highest of the lamas—the beloved fourteenth Dalai Lama, spiritual and political leader of the people. His speaking appearances around the world have been a major factor in the contemporary revival of interest in Buddhism.

Despite persecution, religious fervor and ceremony still pervade every aspect of Tibetan life, from house-raising to ardent pilgrimages. Monks and laypeople alike meditate on **thang-kas** and **mandalas**, visual aids to concentration and illumination which portray a Buddha or Bodhisattva surrounded by deities in a diagram symbolically representing the universe. Both also chant mantras. A favorite one is the phrase associated with the beloved Tibetan Bodhisattva of mercy, Avalokitesvara: *Om mani padme hum.* It evokes awareness of the "jewel in the lotus of the heart," that beautiful treasure lying hidden within each of us. Because some emphasis is placed on the number of repetitions, mantras are written out thousands of times and spun in prayer wheels or placed on prayer flags which continue the repetition of the mantra as they blow in the wind.

Zen: the great way of enlightenment

Buddhism was transmitted from India to China around 50 CE and thence to Korea, Japan, and Vietnam, absorbing elements of Taoism along the way. Then, according to tradition, in the fifth century, Bodhidharma, a successor to the Buddha, traveled from South China to a monastery in northern China. There he reportedly spent nine years in silent meditation, "facing the wall." On this experiential foundation, he became the first patriarch of the radical path that came to be called *Ch'an Buddhism*, from the Sanskrit *dhyana*, the yogic stage of meditation. Although this traditional account of its origins and founder is not fully accepted by scholars as absolute fact, it is known that this way was transmitted to Japan, where its name became **Zen**.

Zen claims to preserve the essence of the Buddha's teachings through direct experience, triggered by mind-to-mind transmission of the dharma. It dismissed scriptures, Buddhas, and Bodhisattvas in favor of training for direct intuition of cosmic unity, known as the **Buddha-nature** or the Void.

A central way of directly experiencing the underlying unity is **zazen**, "sitting meditation." "To sit," said the Sixth Zen Patriarch, "means to obtain absolute freedom and not to allow any thought to be caused by external objects. To meditate means to realize the imperturbability of one's original nature."[22]

The Great Way is not difficult
for those who have no preferences.
When love and hate are both absent
everything becomes clear and undisguised.
Make the smallest distinction, however,
and heaven and earth are set infinitely apart.   *Sengtsan*[23]

Prescriptions for the manner of sitting are quite rigorous: one must take a specific upright posture and then not move during the meditation period, to avoid distracting the mind. Skillful means are then applied to make the mind one-pointed and clear. One beginning practice is simply to watch and count each inhalation and exhalation from one to ten, starting over from one if anything other than awareness of the breath enters the mind. Although this explanation sounds simple, the mind is so restless that many people must work for months before finally getting to ten without having to start over. Getting to ten is not really the goal; the goal is the process itself, the process of recognizing what comes up in the mind and gently letting it go without attachment or preferences.

As one sits in zazen, undisturbed by phenomena, as soon as one becomes inwardly calm, the natural mind is revealed in its original purity. This "original mind" is spacious and free, like an open sky. Thoughts and sensations may float through it like clouds, but they arise and then disappear, leaving no trace. What remains is reality, "True Thusness." In some Zen schools, this perception of thusness comes in a sudden burst of enlightenment, or **kensho**.

When the mind is calmed, action becomes spontaneous and natural. Zen practitioners are taught to have great confidence in their natural functioning, for it arises from our essential Buddha-nature.

On the other hand, the Zen tradition links spontaneity with intense, disciplined concentration. In the art of calligraphy, the perfect spontaneous brushstroke—executed with the whole body, in a single breath—is the outcome of years of attentive practice. Giving ourselves fully to the moment, to be aware only of pouring tea when pouring tea, is a simplicity of beingness that most of us have to learn. Then whatever we give ourself to fully, be it painting, or serving tea, or simply breathing, reveals the Thusness of life, its unconditioned reality.

Another tool used in one Zen tradition is the *koan*. Here the attention is focused ardently on a question that boggles the mind, such as "What is the sound of one hand clapping?" or "What is your face before your parents' birth?" As Roshi [venerable teacher] Philip Kapleau observes, "Koans deliberately throw sand into the eyes of the intellect to force us to open our Mind's eye and see the world and everything in it undistorted by our concepts and judgments." To concentrate on a koan, one must look closely at it without thinking about it, experiencing it directly. Beyond abstractions, Roshi Kapleau explains, "The import of every koan is the same: that the world is one interdependent Whole and that each separate one of us is that Whole."[24]

The aim of Zen practice is enlightenment, or **satori**. One directly experiences the unity of all existence, often in a sudden recognition that nothing is separate from oneself. As one Zen master put it:

> *The moon's the same old moon,*
> *The flowers exactly as they were,*
> *Yet I've become the thingness*
> *Of all the things I see!*[25]

All aspects of life become at the same time utterly precious, and utterly empty, "nothing special." This paradox can only be sensed with the mystically expanded consciousness; it cannot be grasped intellectually.

Pure Land: calling on Amida Buddha

Zen is essentially an inner awareness in which great attention is given to every action; it has little appeal for the laity. Other forms developed in India and the Far East have much greater popular appeal. One of the major trends is known as **Pure Land** Buddhism. At times of great social upheaval (for instance, when the old Japanese feudal aristocracy was falling apart), it was widely thought that people had become so degenerate that it was nearly impossible for them to attain enlightenment through their own efforts. Instead, many turned to **Amida** Buddha, the Buddha of Boundless Light, to save them. Amida (first worshipped in India under the Sanskrit name Amitabha) was believed to have been an ancient prince who vowed to attain enlightenment. When he did, he used his virtue to prepare a special place of bliss, the Pure Land, for all those who called on his name.

Japan had an ancient tradition of worshipping mountains as the realm to which the dead ascend and from which deities descend to earth. The originally abstract Indian Buddhists' concept of the "Pure Land" far to the west to which devotees return after death was transformed in Japan into concrete images. They depicted Amida Buddha riding on clouds billowing over the mountains, coming to welcome his dying devotees.

The results of loving trust in Amida Buddha were described very vividly by the monk Genshin. After graphic depictions of the eight hells, such as the burning vat in which people are cooked like beans, he describes the ineffable pleasures of being reborn into the Pure Land upon death:

Rings, bracelets, a crown of jewels, and other ornaments in countless
profusion adorn his body. And when he looks upon the light radiating from
the Buddha, he obtains pure vision, and because of his experiences in former
lives, he hears the sounds of all things. And no matter what color he may see
or what sound he may hear, it is a thing of marvel.[26]

Many interpret these passages literally, anticipating that if they are sufficiently faithful they will enjoy a beautiful life after death. But some understand the Pure Land as a state to be achieved in this life; a metaphor for the
mystical experience of enlightenment, in which one's former identity
"dies" and one is reborn into an expanded state of consciousness.

Nichiren: salvation through the Lotus Sutra

A thirteenth-century Japanese fisherman's son, who named himself
Nichiren, stressed the importance of striving to reform not only ourselves but
also society. He blamed the political struggles of the time on false Buddhist
paths, including the Pure Land focus on the next life rather than this one. For
Nichiren, the highest truths of Buddhism were embodied in the Lotus Sutra,
a large compilation of parables, verses, and descriptions of innumerable forms
of beings who support the teachings of the World-Honored One, the Buddha.
Nichiren gave particular attention to two of these beings: the Bodhisattva of
Superb Action, who staunchly devotes himself to spreading the Perfect Truth,
even in evil times, and the Bodhisattva Ever-Abused, who is persecuted
because of his insistence on revering everyone with unshaken conviction
that each person is potentially a Buddha. Nichiren himself was repeatedly
abused by authorities but persisted in his efforts to reform Buddhism in Japan
and then spread its purified essence, the Bodhisattva ideal, to the world.

The phrase chanted by Nichiren and his followers, *"Namu myoho*
rengekyo," refers to faith in the entire Lotus Sutra. Today it is chanted by
Nichiren monks and nuns by the hour, slowly revealing its depths as it
works inwardly, beyond thought. In our time, some in the Nichiren tradition undertake long peace walks, such as one sponsored by Nipponzan
Myohoji in 1995. People walked from Auschwitz in Poland to Hiroshima
and Nagasaki in Japan, to commemorate the fiftieth anniversary of the end
of World War II with a plea for nonviolence and respect for all of life. They
beat small hand drums while chanting *"Namu myoho rengekyo,"* and hope to
contribute to world peace by truly bowing to the Buddha in each person,
even if they encounter abuse. As the Most Venerable Nichidatsu Fujii, who
passed away in 1985 at the age of one hundred and influenced Gandhi's
doctrine of nonviolence, has explained:

We do not believe that people are good because we see that they are good, but
by believing that people are good we eliminate our own fear and thus we
can intimately associate with them.[27]

The chanting of *"Namu myoho rengekyo"* has also caused seventy Peace
Pagodas to arise thus far in Japan, England, Austria, India, and the United
States, in fulfillment of the prophecy in the Lotus Sutra that wherever this

Scripture of the Lotus Blossom of the Fine Dharma is preached, a beautiful stupa will spontaneously emerge as a physical reminder of the Buddha's "supernatural penetrations." These pagodas are built with donated materials and labor by people of all faiths who support the belief expressed by Nichidatsu Fujii, in hopes of world peace.

Another new offshoot of Nichiren's movement is *Soka Gakkai*, based in Japan but claiming over twenty million members around the world. Its founder, Daisaku Ikeda, called for a peaceful world revolution through transformation of individual consciousness. Soka Gakkai has also sponsored an important political party in Japan, Komeito. The order emphasizes chanting of *"Namu myoho rengekyo"* for earthly happiness. According to a pamphlet distributed by the group:

> *One who chants is able to gain the power and wisdom to live with confidence, overcome any problem, and develop a happy future. . . . Such benefits include better jobs, places to live and cars to drive. Buddhism maintains that all realms are essential to happiness.[28]*

This focus on material benefits may be a selective interpretation of classical Buddhism, which seems to have emphasized detachment from earthly concerns. But Soka Gakkai's strategy is to help people gain earthly power first and then lead them toward higher goals. As its leaders explain, "When enough people passionately embrace the viewpoint that life is sacred and inviolable, peace will ensue."[29]

Yet another branch of Buddhism inspired by the Lotus Sutra is *Rissho Kosei-kai*, founded in the 1930s by Rev. Nikkyo Niwano and Myoko Naganuma to spread the message of the Lotus Sutra in practical ways to encourage happiness and peace. Members meet to discuss ways of applying the Buddha's teachings to specific problems in their own lives. The organization asserts that "The Eternal Buddha, invisible but present everywhere, is the great life-force of the universe, which sustains each of us."[30]

Buddhism in the West

Images of the Buddha are now enshrined around the world, for what began in India has gradually spread to the West as well as the East. Much of this transmission occurred in the twentieth century, when the United States became a vibrant center of Buddhism. Scholars are studying Buddhist traditions in great depth at many universities, and many people are trying to learn Buddhist meditation practices.

A number of the highest Tibetan lamas, forced out of Tibet, have established spiritual communities in the United States, complete with altars full of sacred Tibetan artefacts. The majority of the five million Buddhists in the United States follow Tibetan Buddhism. Some have traveled to the Dalai Lama's community in exile in India to be personally given the complex *kalachakra* initiation by the Dalai Lama. Many Americans who have adopted Tibetan Buddhism have become its voice in the West, helping with translation work and establishing flourishing publishing houses. Hence in the last two decades, many books have appeared in English on Tibetan Buddhist traditions.

Intensive vipassana retreats of up to three months are carried out in centers such as the Insight Meditation Society in rural Barre, Massachusetts. Theravadin teachers from Southeast Asia and Europe make frequent appearances to conduct retreats, and American teachers undertake rigorous training in Southeast Asia under traditional meditation masters. In addition to numerous Zen centers where Westerners who have undergone training in the East serve as teachers to lay practitioners of meditation, there are a number of Zen monasteries giving solid training in zazen and offering a monastic lifestyle as a permanent or temporary alternative to life in the world.

Many Buddhist centers in the United States are led by women, in contrast to the cultural suppression of females in the East. Leading women in American Buddhism have deeply imbibed traditional Buddhist teachings and are explaining them to Westerners in fresh, contemporary ways.

The American monk Venerable Sumedho, classically trained in Theravada Buddhism in Thailand, has established monastic forest communities and meditation centers in England, Switzerland, Italy, and the United States. They include a center for nuns.

The Vietnamese monk Venerable Master Thich Nhat Hanh now lives in exile in France, where he conducts retreats for women and men in his Plum Village community. When he travels internationally, large audiences are inspired by his teachings. He speaks simply, using homely examples, and emphasizes bringing the awareness fostered by meditation into daily life, rather than making spirituality a separate aspect of one's life.

When we walk in the meditation hall, we make careful steps, very slowly. But when we go to the airport, we are quite another person. We walk very differently, less mindfully. How can we practice at the airport and in the market? That is engaged Buddhism.[31]

Buddhism has often been embraced by Westerners because of their longing for the peace of meditation. In the midst of a chaotic materialistic life, there is a desire to discover emptiness, to let the identity with self fall away, or to become familiar with the mind's tricks in the still simplicity of a **zendo**, a Zen meditation hall. Many psychotherapists are studying Buddhism for its insights into the mind and human suffering. Richard Clarke, who is both a Zen teacher and a psychotherapist, feels that a discipline such as Zen should be part of the training of therapists:

Emptiness is . . . the source of infinite compassion in working with people: to really feel a person without any agenda, to be spacious to that person, to will that they be the way they are. When a person experiences that in someone's presence, then they can drop away those things that they've invented to present themselves with. Those faces, those armors, those forms of the self become unnecessary.[32]

The growing interest in Buddhism in the West is helping to revitalize Buddhism in Asia. As Asia entered the modern world, many of its peoples lost interest in their traditional religions, which became superficial re-enactments of ceremonial practices. But as Westerners themselves are taking strong interest in Buddhism, those who have grown up as Buddhists are reassessing their religion and finding new depths in it. There are now many laypeople interested in studying meditation, and their teachers include women who conduct special meditation retreats.

Buddhist women from West and East have joined hands to hold international gatherings to enhance the role of women in Buddhism. The international Association of Buddhist Women, Sakyadhita or "Daughters of the Buddha," established in Bodh Gaya in 1987, continues to work to improve conditions for women's Buddhist practice and education, full ordination of women, and training of women as teachers of Buddhism.

Socially Engaged Buddhism

An emerging focus in contemporary Buddhist practice is the relevance of Buddhism to social problems. Contrary to popular assumptions, the Buddha did not advise people to permanently leave society to seek their own enlightenment. Sri Lankan Buddhist monk Walpola Rahula explains:

> It may perhaps be useful in some cases for a person to live in retirement for a time in order to improve his or her mind and character, as preliminary moral, spiritual, and intellectual training, to be strong enough to come out later and help others. But if someone lives an entire life in solitude, thinking only of their own happiness and salvation, without caring for their fellow beings, this surely is not in keeping with the Buddha's teaching which is based on love, compassion, and service to others.[33]

The Buddha's teachings on retraining and purifying the mind are far better known than his social commentaries, but he did make many pronouncements about how social suffering is to be corrected. No holy wars have been conducted in his name, for he preached non-violence:

> Hatred is never appeased by hatred. It is appeased by love. This is an eternal law. Just as a mother would protect her only child, even at the risk of her own life, even so let one cultivate a boundless heart towards all beings. Let one's thoughts of boundless love pervade the whole world. . . .[34]

Buddhists have therefore often been non-violent social activists, protesting and trying to correct injustice, oppression, famine, cruelty to animals, nuclear testing, warfare, and environmental devastation. E. F. Schumacher preached what he called "Buddhist economics," to restore willingness to live simply, generously, and humanely with each other. Venerable Maha Ghosananda of Cambodia has led numerous long marches to promote peace in his country, particularly on the eve of elections.

Buddhism was returned to its native India after some one thousand years' absence by the bold action of a converted Buddhist activist, Dr. B. R. Ambedkar (1891–1956). Born an untouchable Hindu, he became the first law minister of India after its independence from Britain in 1947. He was the chief architect of India's new democratic constitution, and built into it many provisions designed to end the oppression of the traditional Hindu caste system. In his personal search for a religion offering freedom and dignity to all human beings, he chose Buddhism. And when he publicly converted shortly before his death in 1956, he carried with him almost half a million untouchables. Despite this mass conversion, he openly questioned and changed certain Buddhist teachings. Among them were the Second Noble Truth that suffering results from desires and ignorance. He felt that such a concept may prevent recognition that some people are victims of oppression rather than their own faults, and thus may prevent action to end social injustices. Another traditional Buddhist ideal he challenged was the emphasis on renunciation and meditation rather than active social engagement, helping the people. His slogan was "Educate, Agitate, and Organize." Decades after his death, some contemporary engaged Buddhists are following a path similar to the one he took, though his emphasis on agitation is not fully accepted within Buddhist circles.

In Sri Lanka, a Buddhist schoolteacher has started the Sarvodaya Shramadana Sangamaya movement which has now spread to five thousand villages. It engages people in working together to eliminate social decadence and poverty, through developing schools, nutrition programs, roads, and irrigation canals, and propagating the Four Noble Truths and the Eightfold Path. Sri Lanka's 70 percent Buddhist majority is now engaged in ethnic war with its Hindu minority. Old ethnic tensions have become politicized, turning this former paradise into a battlefield. But in the midst of the violence, the Buddhist monks of the Sarvodaya movement continue to work with Hindus and Christians as well as Buddhists, attempting to promote harmony and rural development. The founder, Dr. A. T. Ariyaratne, encourages people to look at their own egotism, distrust, greed, and competitiveness and to recognize that these are the cause of their suffering and inability to work together for progress.

Sulak Sivaraksa, founder of the International Network of Engaged Buddhists, explains that socially engaged Buddhism does not mean promoting Buddhism per se:

> The presence of Buddhism in society does not mean having a lot of schools, hospitals, cultural institutions, or political parties run by Buddhists. It means that the schools, hospitals, cultural institutions, and political parties are permeated with and administered with humanism, love, tolerance, and enlightenment, characteristics which Buddhism attributes to an opening up, development, and formation of human nature. This is the true spirit of non-violence.[35]

Not to respond to the suffering around us is a sign of an insane civilization. Buddhism is thus as relevant today, and its insights as necessary, as in the sixth century, when Siddhartha Gautama renounced the life of a prince to save all sentient beings from suffering.

Suggested Reading

Conze, Edward, Horner, I. B., Snellgrove, David, and Waley, Arthur, ed. and trans., *Buddhist Texts through the Ages*, Oxford, England: Oneworld Publications, 1995. A fine collection of Buddhist scriptures translated from the Pali, Sanskrit, Chinese, Tibetan, and Japanese.

de Bary, William Theodore, ed., *The Buddhist Tradition in India, China, and Japan*, New York: Modern Library, 1969. An excellent survey with useful commentaries and selections from Buddhist scriptures.

Eppsteiner, Fred, ed., *The Path of Compassion: Writings on Socially Engaged Buddhism*, Berkeley, California: Parallax Press, 1988. A highly readable and relevant collection of essays by leading contemporary Buddhist teachers about the ways in which Buddhism can be applied to social problems.

Fremantle, Francesca, and Trungpa, Chogyam, trans., *The Tibetan Book of the Dead*, Boston and London: Shambhala Publications, 1975. The classic Tibetan Buddhist scripture on the projections of the mind and the practices of deity yoga to attain enlightenment.

Gross, Rita M., *Buddhism after Patriarchy*, Albany, New York: State University of New York Press, 1993. A feminist reconstruction of Buddhist history, revealing its core of gender equality but later overlays of sexism, plus analysis of key Buddhist concepts from a feminist point of view.

Lal, P., trans., *The Dhammapada*, New York: Farrar, Straus and Giroux, 1967. A basic book attributed to the Buddha that covers the essentials of the dharma in memorable, pithy verses.

Levine, Stephen, *A Gradual Awakening*, Garden City, New York: Doubleday, 1979 and London: Rider and Company, 1980. Gentle, poetic presentation of vipassana techniques in their relevance to contemporary life.

Lopez, Donald S., Jr., ed., *Buddhism in Practice*, Princeton: Princeton University Press, 1995. Annotated translation of original sources dealing with Buddhist practice around the world, organized around the Triple Jewels of Buddha, dharma, and sangha.

Rahula, Walpola Sri, *What the Buddha Taught*, New York: Grove Press, 1974. The classic introduction to Buddhist teachings—an accurate and clear guide through the complexities of Buddhist thought and practice, with representative texts.

Sivaraksa, Sulak, *Seeds of Peace: A Buddhist Vision for Renewing Society*, Berkeley, California: Parallax Press, 1992. A renowned Thai social activist examines the "politics of greed" and issues involved in transformation of society, from the point of view of Buddhist ideals.

Suzuki, Shunryu, *Zen Mind, Beginner's Mind*, New York and Tokyo: Weatherhill, 1970. A beautiful book leading one gracefully and seemingly simply through the paradoxes of Zen.

CHAPTER 5

TAOISM AND CONFUCIANISM

The unity of opposites

While India was giving birth to Hinduism and Buddhism, three other major religions were developing in East Asia. Taoism and Confucianism grew largely in China, and later spread to Japan and Korea; Shinto was distinctively Japanese. These religions have remained associated primarily with their homelands. In this chapter we will explore the two that developed in China from similar roots but with different emphases: Taoism and Confucianism. Buddhism also spread to East Asia and its practice has often been mixed with the native traditions.

In East Asia, religions that will be treated as separate entities in this chapter and the next, on Shinto, are in fact more subtly blended and practiced. Taoism and Confucianism, though they may seem quite opposite to each other, co-exist as complementary value systems in East Asian societies, and a person's thought and actions may encompass both streams. Twentieth-century political shifts in China, however, have made it difficult to pin-point or predict the continued existence of religious ways there.

Ancient Traditions

Indigenous spiritual ways permeate all later religious developments in China, Korea, and Japan. One major feature is the veneration of ancestors. The spirits of deceased ancestors remain very closely bonded to their living descendants for some time. Respect must be paid to them—especially the family's founding ancestor and those recently deceased—through funerals, mourning rites, and then continuing sacrifices. The sacred rituals are called **li**. They are essential because the ancestors will help their descendants, if treated with proper respect, or cause trouble if ignored.

Kings sought their ancestors' help through the medium of oracle bones. These were shells or bones onto which the divining specialist scratched questions the king wanted the ancestors to answer. Touching the bones with a hot poker made them crack, forming patterns which the diviner interpreted as useful answers from the ancestors. On the other hand, ghosts who have been ignored or ill-treated during their lifetime can cause so much mischief, according to old Chinese beliefs, that many

TAOISM		CONFUCIANISM
	Legendary Yellow Emperor	
Ancient traditions **TAOISM**	**Shang Dynasty (c.1751–1123 BCE)**	Ancient traditions **CONFUCIANISM**
Lao-tzu (6th C BCE? 300 BCE?) Chuang-tzu (c.365–290 BCE)	**Chou Dynasty (c.1122–221 BCE)**	Confucius (c.551–479 BCE) Mencius (c.390–305 BCE) Hsun-tzu (c.340–245 BCE)
Immortality movements Queen Mother of the West cult	**Chin Dynasty (221–206 BCE)**	Confucian scholars suppressed, books burned
Early religious Taoist sects Heavenly Master tradition begins	**Han Dynasty (206 BCE–220 CE)**	Confucian Classics used as basis of civil service exams *I Ching* elaborated
Mutual influences between Taoism and Buddhism Taoist Canon first compiled (748)	**T'ang Dynasty (618–907)**	Buddhism reaches peak, then is persecuted Confucianism makes comeback
Tai-chi chuan appears Northern Taoist sects flourish	**Sung Dynasty (960–1280)**	Neo-Confucianism Chu-hsi (1130–1200 CE)
Last imperial dynasty overthrown	**1911**	Imperial dynasty overthrown De-established as state ideology
National Association of Taoism (White Clouds Temple, Beijing)	**1949+**	Chairman Mao's red book replaces Confucian Classics
Temple and books destroyed	**1966–1976 Cultural Revolution**	Temples and books destroyed
	1989	Scholars' requests refused at Tienanmen Square
Taoist sects, temples re-established; First Taoist Grand Ritual; popular faith and practices	**1990s**	Confucian Classics reintroduced in schools; Confucius's birthday celebrated; International Association of Confucians established

efforts were made to thwart them, including evil-deflecting charms, gongs, and firecrackers, appeals through mediums, spirit-walls to keep them from entering doorways, exorcisms, prayers, incense, and fasts.

To the early Chinese and in continuing popular belief, the world is full of invisible spirits. In addition to ancestors, there are charismatic humans who have died but are still available to help the people.

As is understood in indigenous religions everywhere, the world is also full of nature spirits. Plants, animals, rivers, stones, mountains, stars—all parts of the natural world may be inhabited by sentient life, often personified and honored as deities. From early times, Chinese people made offerings to these beings and sought their aid with personal problems, sometimes through the mediumship of a shaman who can communicate with the spirit world.

According to Chinese belief which can be traced back at least to the earliest historical dynasty, the Shang (c. 1751 to 1111 BCE), there also exists a great spiritual being referred to as *Shang Ti*, the Lord-on-High, ruler of the universe, the supreme ancestor of the Chinese. Deities governing aspects of the cosmos and the local environment are subordinate to him. This deity is conceived of as being masculine and closely involved in human affairs, though not as a Creator God.

During the Chou dynasty (c. 1123–221 BCE) which overthrew the Shang, the rulers developed the idea of the *"Mandate of Heaven"* which justified their rule. This Mandate is the self-existing moral law of virtue, the supreme reality. According to the Chou rulers, human destiny is determined by virtuous deeds. Rulers have a moral duty to maintain the welfare of the people and a spiritual duty to conduct respectful ceremonies for the highest heavenly beings.

In addition to ancestors, spirits, Shang Ti, and Heaven, there has long existed in China a belief that the cosmos is a manifestation of an impersonal self-generating force called **ch'i**. This force has two aspects whose interplay causes the ever-changing phenomena of the universe. **Yin** is the dark, receptive, "female" aspect; **yang** is the bright, assertive, "male" aspect. Wisdom lies in recognizing their ever-shifting, but balanced patterns and moving with them. This creative rhythm of the universe is called the **Tao**, or "way."

To harmonize with the ancestors and gods, and yin and yang, the ancients devised many forms of divination. One system was eventually written down as the *I Ching*, or *Book of Changes*. It is a common source for both Taoism and Confucianism and is regarded as a classic text in both traditions. The *I Ching* was highly elaborated with commentaries by scholars beginning in the Han dynasty (206 BCE–220 CE). To use this subtle system, one respectfully purifies the divining objects—such as yarrow stalks or coins which symbolize yin and yang—asks a question, casts the objects six times, and then consults the *I Ching* for symbolic interpretaton of the yin–yang combinations.

By studying and systematizing the ways of humans and of nature, the ancient Chinese tried to order their actions so that they might steer a coherent course within the changing cosmos. They recognized that any extreme action will produce its opposite as a balancing reaction and thus they strived for a middle way of subtle discretion and moderation. From these ancient roots gradually developed two contrasting ways of harmonizing with the cosmos—the more mystically religious ways which are collectively called Taoism, and the more political and moral ways known as Confucianism. Like yin and yang, they interpenetrate and complement each other, and are themselves evolving dynamically.

Taoism—The Way of Nature and Immortality

Taoism is as full of paradoxes as the Buddhist tradition it influenced: Ch'an or Zen Buddhism. It has been adored by Westerners who seek a carefree, natural way of life as an escape from the industrial rat race. Yet beneath its words of the simple life in harmony with nature is a tradition of great mental and physical discipline. As it has developed over time, Taoism includes both efforts to align oneself with the unnamable original force— the Tao—and ceremonial worship of deities from the Jade Emperor to the kitchen god. Some Taoist scriptures counsel indifference about birth and death; others teach ways of attaining physical immortality. These variations developed within an ancient tradition that had no name until it had to distinguish itself from Confucianism. "Taoism" is actually a label invented by scholars and awkwardly stretched to cover both a philosophical tradition and an assortment of religious sects whose relationship to the former is complex, but which probably developed at least in part from the early philosophical texts and practices. Religious Taoism itself is often an amalgam, with the Taoist way of natural life and meditation as its base, plus Confucian virtues, Buddhist-like rituals, and immortality as its final goal.

Teachings of Taoist sages

Aside from its general basis in ancient Chinese ways, the specific origin of Taoist philosophy and practices is unclear. In China, tradition attributes the publicizing of these ways to the Yellow Emperor, who supposedly ruled from 2697 to 2597 BCE. He was said to have studied with an ancient sage and to have developed meditation, health, and military practices based on what he learned. After ruling for one hundred years, he ascended to heaven on a dragon's back and became one of the immortals.

The philosophical basis of Taoism is expounded in the famous scripture, the *Tao-te Ching* ("The Classic of the Way and the Power"). It is second only to the Bible in number of Western translations, for its ideas are not only fascinating but also elusive for translators working from the terse ancient Chinese characters and confronting variations in existing copies of the Chinese text.

Even the supposed author of the *Tao-te Ching* is obscure. According to tradition, the book was dictated by Lao-tzu (or Lao-tse), a curator of the royal library of the Chou dynasty, to a border guard as he left society for the mountains at the reported age of 160. The guard recognized Lao-tzu as a sage and begged him to leave behind a record of his wisdom. Lao-tzu reportedly complied by inscribing the five thousand characters now known as the *Tao-te Ching*. This is traditionally said to have happened during the sixth century BCE, with Lao-tzu purportedly fifty-three years older than

Confucius. But some historians date the existent version of the *Tao-te Ching* at c. 300 BCE and claim it was a reaction to Confucianism. Some think the *Tao-te Ching* was an oral tradition derived from the teachings of several sages and question whether Lao-tzu ever existed.

The book's central philosophy is that one can best harmonize with the natural flow of life by being receptive and quiet. These teachings were elaborated more emphatically and humorously by a sage named Chuang-tzu (c. 365–290 BCE). He, too, was a minor government official for a while but left political involvement for a hermit's life of freedom and solitude. Unlike Lao-tzu, whose philosophy was addressed to those in leadership positions, Chuang-tzu asserted that the best way to live in a chaotic, absurd civilization is to become detached from it.

FLOWING WITH TAO   At the heart of Taoist teachings is Tao, the "unnamable," the "eternally real."[1] Contemporary Master Da Liu asserts that Tao is so ingrained in Chinese understanding that it is a basic concept that cannot be defined, like "goodness." Moreover, Tao is a mystical reality that cannot be grasped by the mind. The *Tao-te Ching* says:

> *The Tao that can be told of*
> *Is not the Absolute Tao,*
> *The Names that can be given*
> *Are not Absolute Names.*
> *The Nameless is the origin of Heaven and Earth;*
> *The Named is the Mother of All Things . . .*
> *These two (the Secret and its manifestations)*
> *Are (in their nature) the same; . . .*
> *They may both be called the Cosmic Mystery:*
> *Reaching from the Mystery into the Deeper Mystery*
> *Is the Gate to the Secret of All Life.[2]*

Chapter 25 of the *Tao-te Ching* is more explicit about the Unnamable:

> *There is a thing confusedly formed,*
> *Born before heaven and earth.*
> *Silent and void*
> *It stands alone and does not change,*
> *Goes round and does not weary.*
> *It is capable of being the mother of the world.*
> *I know not its name*
> *So I style it "the way."*
> *I give it the makeshift name of "the great."[3]*

Although we cannot describe the Tao, we can live in harmony with it. There are several basic principles for the life in harmony with Tao. One is to experience the transcendent unity of all things, rather than separation. Everything has its own nature and function, says Chuang-tzu. But disfigured or beautiful, small or large, they are all one in Tao. Taoism is concerned with direct experience of the universe, accepting things as they are, not setting standards of morality, not labeling things as "good" or "bad." Chuang-tzu asserts that herein lies true spirituality:

*Such a man can ride the clouds and mist, mount the sun and moon, and
wander beyond the four seas. Life and death do not affect him. How much
less will he be concerned with good and evil!*[4]

In addition to experiencing oneness, the Taoist sage takes a low profile
in the world. He or she is like a valley, allowing everything needed to flow
into his or her life, or like a stream. Flowing water is a Taoist model for
being. It bypasses and gently wears away obstacles rather than fruitlessly
attacking them, effortlessly nourishes the "ten thousand things" of material
life, works without struggling, leaves all accomplishments behind without
possessing them. Lao-tzu observes:

Water is the softest thing on earth,
Yet its silken gentleness
Will easily wear away the hardest stone.

Everyone knows this;
Few use it in their daily lives.
Those of Tao yield and overcome.[5]

This is the uniquely Taoist paradox of **wu-wei**—"doing nothing," or
taking no action contrary to nature. Wu-wei is spontaneous, creative
activity proceeding from the Tao, action without ego-assertion, letting the
Tao in nature take its course. Chuang-tzu uses the analogy of a butcher
whose knife always stays sharp because he lets his hand be guided by the
natural makeup of the carcass, finding the spaces between the bones where
a slight movement of the blade will glide through without resistance. Even
when difficulties arise, the sage does not panic and take unnecessary action.

The result of wu-wei is non-interference. Much of Lao-tzu's teaching is
directed at rulers, that they might guide society without interfering with its
natural course. Nothing is evil, but things may be out of balance. The world
is naturally in harmony; Tao is our original nature. But according to tradition, the Golden Age of Tao declined as humans departed from the Way.
"Civilization," with its intellectual attempts to improve on things and its
rigid views of morality, actually leads to world chaos, the Taoists warn.
How much better, Lao-tzu advises, to accept not-knowing, moving freely
in the moment with the changing universe.

Thirdly, philosophical Taoism places great value on withdrawal from the
madding crowd to a contemplative life in nature. From the love of nature
and the teaching of following the natural way developed a unique science
known as **feng-shui** or geomancy. By observing the contours of the land
and the flows of wind and water, specialists in feng-shui could reportedly
determine the best places for the harmonious placement of a temple,
dwelling place, or grave.

Whether in a peaceful or chaotic environment, the Taoist seeks to find
the still center, save energy for those times when action is needed, and take
a humble, quiet approach to life. Things of importance to the worldly are
seen as having little value. Chuang-tzu even goes to some lengths to point
out that it is the useless who survive; the tree which is good for nothing
does not get chopped down.

> Sweet music and highly seasoned food
> Entertain for a while,
> But the clear, tasteless water from the well
> Gives life and energy without exhaustion.   *Lao-tzu*[6]

Immortals Taoism

Under the umbrella of what scholars call "Taoism" lie not only philosophical Taoism but also religious sects which developed from the second century CE. They are sometimes known collectively as Hsien ("Immortals") Taoism. The sects are characterized by belief in numerous gods and ancestral spirits, magic-making, ritual, and the aid of priests. Practices such as alchemy, faith-healing, sorcery, and the use of power objects seem to have existed from ancient times in China, but their conversion into institutionalized and distinctive social movements with detailed rituals, clergy, and revealed texts dates from the second century CE. At that time, the Han dynasty was declining amidst famine and war. An array of revelations and prophecies predicted the end of the age and finally led to the rise of religious/political organizations. For example, in 184 CE hundreds of thousands of followers of a leader who was known as a faith healer and advocate of egalitarian ideas rebelled in eight of China's twelve provinces; their rebellion took ten months to suppress.

Simultaneously, in western China, Chang Tao Ling had a vision of Lao-tzu as the heavenly Lord Lao. He advocated similar practices of healing by faith and developed a quasi-military organization of religious officials. After thirty years of dominance in their region, they abandoned political goals to focus on spiritual practices. Once Chang Tao Ling ascended to the heavens, they referred to him as the first Celestial Master. The older Han religion had involved demons and exorcism, belief in an afterlife, and a God of Destinies who granted fortune or misfortune based on heavenly records of good and bad deeds. These roles were now ascribed to a pantheon of celestial deities, who in turn were controlled by the new Celestial Master priesthood led by Chang's family.

After the sack of the northern capitals early in the fourth century, the Celestial Masters and other aristocrats fled south and established themselves on Dragon-Tiger Mountain in southeast China. Today the 64th patriarch in the lineage lives in Taiwan, although practices are being revived on Dragon-Tiger Mountain in mainland China.

In approximately 365 CE another aristocratic family in exile in southern China began receiving revelations from a deceased member, Lady Wei, which were recorded in exquisite calligraphy and transmitted to only a few advanced disciples. This elite group of celibates residing on Mount Mao called their practices "Highest Purity Taoism." They looked down on the Celestial Master tradition and its sexual rituals as crude, and they avoided village rituals and commoners. Instead, they focused on personal immortality through meditations for purifying the body with divine energies so as "to rise up to heaven in broad daylight." Highest Purity Taoism texts and influence continue to be revered today as the elite tradition of Taoism.

The assimilation of Buddhism into Chinese culture added a great medley of new meditation practices, divine beings, rituals, scriptures, heavens, and hells to Chinese cosmology. Various Taoist movements freely borrowed from these resources. During the last eight hundred years, the most successful tradition has been "Complete Perfection Taoism." It unites Taoist inner alchemy with Ch'an Buddhist meditation and Confucian social morality, harmonizing the three religions. Actively monastic, it focuses on meditation and non-attachment to the world. Today its major center is the White Cloud Monastery in Beijing, the headquarters of the government-approved Chinese Taoism Association. Complete Perfection is also the foundation for most Hong Kong Taoist temples and martial arts groups.

The many revealed scriptures of Taoist movements were occasionally compiled and canonized by the court. The present Taoist canon was compiled in 1445 CE. Containing over one thousand sophisticated scriptures, it has only recently begun to be studied by non-Taoist scholars. It includes a wealth of firsthand accounts by mystical practitioners—poems of their visionary shamanistic journeys, encounters with deities, advanced meditation practices, descriptions of the perfected human being, methods and elixirs for ascending to heavenly realms and achieving immortality, and descriptions of the Immortals and the heavenly bureaucracies. Since ancient times, one of the most revered celestial beings has been the Queen Mother of the West. She guards the elixir of life and is the most wondrous incarnation of yin energy. The Taoist canon also includes the writings of some female Taoist sages who undertook the great rigors of Taoist meditation practices and reportedly mastered its processes of inner transformation. In her mystical poetry, the twelfth-century female sage Sun Bu-er describes the ultimate realization:

> All things finished.
> You sit still in a little niche.
> The light body rides on violet energy,
> The tranquil nature washes in a pure pond.
> Original energy is unified, yin and yang are one;
> The spirit is the same as the universe.[7]

SPIRITUAL ALCHEMY   Flowing with Tao is easy and natural. But paradoxically, it is based on masterful spiritual discipline. Lao-tzu describes what mastery entailed:

> The ancient Masters were profound and subtle.
> Their wisdom was unfathomable. . . .
> They were careful
> as someone crossing an iced-over stream.
> Alert as a warrior in enemy territory.
> Courteous as a guest.
> Fluid as melting ice.
> Shapable as a block of wood.

Receptive as a valley.
Clear as a glass of water.[8]

The mastery to which Taoist writers refer may be the result of powerful unknown ascetic practices traditionally passed down secretly from teacher to pupil. These teachers lived in the mountains; great Taoist teachers are said to be still hidden in the remote mountains of China and Korea.

The aim of the ascetic practices is to use the energy available to the body in order to intuitively perceive the order of the universe. Within our body is the spiritual micro-universe of the "three treasures" necessary for the preservation of life: generative force (*ching*), vital life force (*ch'i*), and personal spirit or mind (*shen*). Using breath and the subtle energy channels in the body, the practitioner builds a reservoir of ching energy in the "cauldron" several inches below the navel, whence it rises up the spine as a vapor, transmuted into ch'i energy. Ch'i is in turn transmuted into shen in an upper cauldron in the head (an area similar to the Third Eye of Indian yogic practice), drops down to illuminate the heart center, and then descends to an inner area of the lower cauldron. There it forms what is called the Immortal Fetus, which adepts can reportedly raise through the Heavenly Gate at the top of the head and thus leave their physical body for various purposes, including preparation for life after death. In addition, the adept learns to draw the ch'i of the macro-universe of heaven and earth into the micro-universe of the body, unifying and harmonizing inner and outer, heaven and earth.

THE LURE OF IMMORTALITY   It is unclear whether Taoist texts are to be taken allegorically or literally. Literal readings have long lured those desiring physical longevity or spiritual immortality to discover Taoist secrets. Chuang-tzu had counseled indifference to birth and death: "The Master came because it was time. He left because he followed the natural flow. Be content with the moment, and be willing to follow the flow."[9] Lao-tzu referred enigmatically to immortality or long life realized through spiritual death of the individual self, the body and mind transmuted into selfless vehicles for the eternal. However, as Professor Huai-Chin Han puts it, people who are interested in Taoist practices:

> *usually forget the highest principles, or the basis of philosophical theory behind the cultivation of Tao and the opening of the ch'i routes for longevity. ... Longevity consists of maintaining one's health, slowing down the ageing process, living without illness and pain, and dying peacefully without bothering other people. Immortality does not mean indefinite physical longevity; it indicates the eternal spiritual life.*[10]

A quiet contemplative life in natural surroundings, with sexual abstinence, peaceful mind, health-maintaining herbs, practices to strengthen the inner organs and open the meridians (subtle energy pathways known to Chinese doctors), and ch'i-kung breath practices to transmute vital energy into spiritual energy, does seem to bring a marked tendency to longevity. Chinese literature and folk knowledge contain many references to venerable sages thought to be centuries old. They live hidden in the mountains, away from society, and are said to be somewhat translucent. Their age is difficult to verify. The Chinese sage Li Ch'ing Yuen claimed that he was two hundred and fifty years old, shortly before he died early in the twentieth century, apparently from the effects of being exposed to "civilization." The most famous of the legendary long-lived are the Eight Immortals, humans who were said to have gained immortality, each with his or her own special magical power.

Another way of flowing with Tao, and thereby living long and effectively, is the body-centered practice of **T'ai-chi chuan**. Of unknown origin, it appeared in China by the tenth century as a martial art and is still practiced daily by many Chinese at dawn and dusk for their health. It looks like slow swimming in the air, with continual circular movement through a series of dance-like postures. They are ideally manifestations of the unobstructed flow of ch'i through the body. According to the *T'ai-chi Ch'uan Classics*, "In any action the entire body should be light and agile and all of its parts connected like pearls on a thread."[11] Ch'i is cultivated internally but not expressed externally as power. In combat, the practitioner of T'ai-chi is advised to "yield at your opponent's slightest pressure and adhere to him at his slightest retreat,"[12] using mental alertness to subtle changes rather than muscular strength in order to gain the advantage.

T'ai-chi is also a physical way of becoming one with the eternal interlocking of yin and yang, and of movement and stillness. T'ai-chi master Al Chung-liang Huang says:

> *Think of the contrasting energies moving together and in union, in harmony, interlocking, like a white fish and a black fish mating. If you identify with only one side of the duality, then you become unbalanced. . . . Movement and stillness become one. One is not a static point. One is a moving one, one is a changing one, one is everything. One is also that stillness suspended, flowing, settling, in motion.[13]*

Despite the development of these techniques for body–mind harmony with Tao, the desire for shortcuts to longevity has persisted from ancient times to the present. From aristocrats to peasants, the Chinese people sought to prolong life through the advice and potions of Taoist alchemists. Some of them have been frauds; others have taken the allegorical references to spiritual alchemy literally, trying to compound actual chemical formulas to make the body immortal. These efforts persist.

Popular Taoism today

In addition to philosophical and religious Taoist movements, popular Taoist-related rituals and beliefs are in current practice both within communist mainland China and in Chinese communities elsewhere. Since approximately 1000 CE, the Chinese peoples have practiced rituals associated with a period of testing and purification of the soul after death. Either Taoist or Buddhist priests may be hired by private families to perform rituals to help the deceased appear before the Ten Hell Judges, as well as to join in communal rituals of grave-cleaning in April and of universal liberation and feeding of hungry ghosts in August. Every temple has a side shrine to T'u-ti Kung, Lord of the Earth, who can transport offerings to deceased loved ones at any time. Written prayers and paper money are burned to send them to the other world.

New revelations and scriptures continue to be produced in new temples in Taiwan. They are identified as "precious scrolls" emanating from deities such as the Golden Mother of the Celestial Pool. It is believed that in the past the Divine Mother sent Buddha and Lao-tzu as messengers, but that now the crisis of the present world requires her direct intervention.

Popular religion also follows the ancient practice of worshipping certain people as divine, appointed to heavenly office after they died. There are many examples, such as a virtuous daughter of the Lin family who saved members of her own family and others in distress during the Sung dynasty. Now she is worshipped as Tien-hou, the Holy Mother in Heaven, especially in coastal regions. The reverence that is still shown to the twentieth-century liberator of China, Mao tse-Tung, who died in 1976, likewise reflects the Chinese pattern of recognizing certain humans as possessing divine power to help and save the people.

Historically, whenever the central Chinese government has been strong, it has tended to demand total allegiance to itself as a divine authority and to challenge or suppress competing religious groups. The emperors of ancient China either claimed divine origin or referred to themselves as the Sons of Heaven appointed from on high. Confucian scholars were suppressed and their books were burned by the Ch'in dynasty (221–206 BCE), shamans were forbidden during the Han dynasty, Buddhists were persecuted during the T'ang dynasty, the T'ai-p'ing rebellion of the nineteenth century attempted to purge China of Taoism and Buddhism, and during the Cultural Revolution of 1966 to 1976, zealous young Red Guards destroyed Taoist, Buddhist, and Confucian temples and books. However, during the economic liberalization of the late twentieth century in mainland China, in spite of an atheistic communist ideology, temples have been maintained as historic sites, pilgrimages to temples in natural sites and religious tourism have been encouraged, and an explosion of temple building has occurred.

Domestic rituals continue in every home, such as the farewell party to the god of the kitchen at the end of the lunar year (often in late January). In hopes that the god of the kitchen, who sits in the corner watching what the family does, will speak well of them in his annual report to the Jade Emperor, god of the present, families offer sweets, incense, and paper horses, with the prayer, "When you go to heaven you should report only good things, and when you come down from heaven you should protect us and bring peace and safety to us."[14]

Confucianism—The Practice of Virtue

The sixth century BCE was a period of great spiritual and intellectual flourishing in many cultures. It roughly coincided with the life of the Buddha and perhaps of Lao-tzu, the Persian empire, the Golden Age of Athens, the great Hebrew prophets, and in China with the life of another outstanding figure. Westerners call him Confucius and his teaching Confucianism. His family name was K'ung; the Chinese honored him as K'ung Fu-tzu ("Master K'ung") and called his teaching **Juchiao** ("the teaching of the scholars"). It did not begin with Confucius. Rather, it is based on the ancient Chinese beliefs in the Lord on High, the Mandate of Heaven, ancestor worship, spirits, and the efficacy of rituals. Confucius developed from these roots a school of thought which emphasizes the cultivation of moral virtues and the interaction between human rulers and Heaven, with political involvement as the way to transforming the world.

This philosophy became highly influential in China and still permeates the society despite great political changes. It exists not only as a school of thought but also as the practice of religious ethics, as a political ideology, and as the link between the state and the Mandate of Heaven.

For two thousand years, Taoism, Buddhism, and Confucianism have coexisted in China. Both Taoism and Buddhism emphasize the ever-changing nature of things in the cosmos, whereas Confucianism focuses on ways of developing a just and orderly society.

Professor Yu Yingshi explains that Taoism and Confucianism can coexist because in Chinese tradition there are no major divisions between mind and matter, utopian ideals and everyday life:

> For Chinese, the transcendental world, the world of the spirit,
> interpenetrates with the everyday world though it is not considered identical
> to it. If we use the tao to represent the transcendental world and the
> Confucian ideal of human relationships to represent the human world, we
> can see how they interface. The tao creates the character of these human
> relations. For these relations to exist as such, they must follow the tao, they
> cannot depart from the tao for a moment. These two worlds operate on the
> cusp of interpenetration, neither dependent on or independent of the other.
> So mundane human relationships are, from the very beginning, endowed
> with a transcendental character.[15]

Master K'ung's life

Young K'ung Ch'iu was born in approximately 551 BCE, during the Chou dynasty, into a family whose ancestors had been prominent in the previous dynasty. They had lost their position through political struggles, and Ch'iu's father, a soldier, died when the boy was only three years old. Although young Ch'iu was determined to be a scholar, the family's financial straits necessitated his taking such humble work as overseeing granaries and livestock. He married at the age of nineteen and had at least two children.

Ch'iu's mother died when he was twenty-three, sending him into three years of mourning. During this period he lived ascetically and studied ancient ceremonial rites (li) and imperial institutions. When he returned to social interaction, he gained some renown as a teacher of li and of the arts of governing.

It was a period of political chaos, with the stability of the early Chou dynasty having given way to disorder. As central power weakened, feudal lords held more power than kings of the central court, ministers assassinated their rulers, and sons killed their fathers. Confucius felt that a return to classical rites and standards of virtue was the only way out of the chaos, and he earnestly but unsuccessfully sought rulers who would adopt his ideas.

Confucius turned to a different approach: training young men to be wise and altruistic public servants. He proposed that the most effective strategy was for the rulers to perform classical rites and music properly so that they would remain of visibly high moral character and thus inspire the common people to be virtuous. He thus revived and instructed his students in the "Six Classics" of China's cultural heritage: the *I Ching*, poetry, history, rituals, music and dance, and the Spring and Autumn Annals of events in his state, Lu. According to tradition, it was Confucius who edited older documents pertaining to these six areas and who put them into the form now known as the Confucian Classics. There are now only five; the treatises on music were either destroyed or never existed. Of his role, Confucius claimed only: "I am a transmitter and not a creator. I believe in and have a passion for the ancients."[16]

Confucius's work and teachings were considered relatively insignificant during his lifetime. After his death in 479 BCE, interstate warfare increased, ancient family loyalties were replaced by large and impersonal armies, and personal virtues were replaced by laws and state control. After the brutal reunification of China by the Ch'in and Han dynasties, however, rulership required a more cultured class of bureaucrats who could embody the virtues advocated by Confucius. In the second century BCE the Confucian Classics thus became the basis of the civil service examinations for the scholar-officials who were to serve in the government. The life of the gentleman-scholar devoted to proper government became the highest professed ideal. Eventually temples were devoted to the worship of Confucius himself as the model for unselfish public service, human kindness, and scholarship. However, the official state use of the Confucian Classics can be seen as a political device to give the government a veneer of civility.

The Confucian virtues

Foremost among the virtues that Confucius felt could save society was **jen**. Translations of this central term include innate goodness, love, benevolence, perfect virtue, humaneness, and human-heartedness. In Chapter IV of the *Analects*, Confucius describes the rare person who is utterly devoted to jen as one who is not motivated by personal profit but by what is moral, is concerned with self-improvement rather than public recognition, is ever mindful of parents, speaks cautiously but acts quickly, and regards human nature as basically good.

The prime example of jen should be the ruler. Rulers were required to rule not by physical force but by the example of personal virtue:

> *Confucius said: If a ruler himself is upright, all will go well without orders. But if he himself is not upright, even though he gives orders they will not be obeyed. ... One who governs by virtue is comparable to the polar star, which remains in its place while all the stars turn towards it."*[17]

Asked to define the essentials of strong government, Confucius listed adequate troops, adequate food, and the people's trust. But of these, the only true necessity is that the people have faith in their rulers. To earn this faith, the ruling class should "cultivate themselves," leading lives of virtue and decorum. They should continually adhere to jen, always reaching upward, cherishing what is right, rather than reaching downward for material gain.

The Chinese character for jen is a combination of "two" and "person," conveying the idea of relationship. Those relationships emphasized by Confucius are the interactions between father and son, older and younger siblings, husband and wife, older and younger friend, ruler and subject. In these relationships, the first is considered superior to the second. Each relationship is nonetheless based on distinct but mutual obligations and responsibilities. This web of human relationships supports the individual like a series of concentric circles.

At the top, the ruler models himself on Heaven, serving as a parent to the people and linking them to the larger cosmic order through ritual ceremonies. In Confucius's ideal world, there is a reciprocal hierarchy in which each knows his place and respects those above him. As the *Great Learning* states it, peace begins with the moral cultivation of the individual and order in the family. This peace extends outward to society, government, and the universe itself like circular ripples in a pond.

The heart of moral rectification is filial piety to one's parents. According to Confucian doctrine, there are three grades of filial piety: the lowest is to support one's parents, the second is not to bring humiliation to one's parents and ancestors, and the highest is to glorify them. In the ancient *Book of Rites*, as revived by Confucius, deference to one's parents is scrupulously defined. For instance, a husband and wife should go to visit their parents and parents-in-law, whereupon:

> On getting to where they are, with bated breath and gentle voice, they
> should ask if their clothes are (too) warm or (too) cold, whether they are ill
> or pained, or uncomfortable in any part; and if they be so, they should
> proceed reverently to stroke and scratch the place. They should in the same
> way, going before or following after, help and support their parents in
> quitting or entering (the apartment). In bringing in the basin for them to
> wash, the younger will carry the stand and the elder the water; they will beg
> to be allowed to pour out the water, and when the washing is concluded,
> they will hand the towel. They will ask whether they want anything, and
> then respectfully bring it. All this they will do with an appearance of
> pleasure to make their parents feel at ease.[18]

Confucius also supported the ancient Chinese custom of ancestor veneration as the highest achievement of filial piety.

Confucius said relatively little about the supernatural, preferring to focus on the here-and-now: "While you are not able to serve men, how can you serve the ghosts and spirits?"[19] He made a virtue of li (the rites honoring ancestors and deities), but with the cryptic suggestion that one make the sacrifices "as if" the spirits were present. According to some interpreters, he encouraged the rites as a way of establishing earthly harmony through reverent, ethical behavior. The rites should not be empty gestures; he recommended that they be outwardly simple and inwardly grounded in jen.

Although Confucius did not speak much about an unseen Reality, he asserted that li are the earthly expressions of the natural cosmic order. Li involves right conduct in terms of the five basic relationships essential for a stable society: kindness in the father and filial piety in the son; gentility in the older brother and respect in the younger; righteous behavior in the husband and obedience in the wife; humane consideration in the older friend and deference in the younger friend; and benevolence in rulers and loyalty in subjects.

Everything should be done with a sense of propriety. Continually eulogizing the typical gentleman of China's ancient high civilization as the model, Confucius used examples such as the way of passing someone in mourning. Even if the mourner were a close friend, the gentleman would assume a solemn expression and "lean forward with his hands on the crossbar of his carriage to show respect; he would act in a similar manner towards a person carrying official documents."[20] Even in humble surroundings, the proprieties should be observed: "Even when a meal consisted only of coarse rice and vegetable broth, [the gentleman] invariably made an offering from them and invariably did so solemnly."[21]

Divergent followers of Confucius

The Confucian tradition has been added to by many later commentators. Two of the most significant were Mencius and Hsun Tzu, who differed in their approach.

A little over a hundred years after Confucius died, the "Second Sage" Meng Tzu (commonly latinized as Mencius) was born. During his lifetime (c. 390–305 BCE) Chinese society became even more chaotic. Like his predecessor, the Second Sage tried to share his wisdom with embattled rulers, but to no avail. He, too, took up teaching, based on stabilizing aspects of the earlier feudal system.

Mencius's major additions to the Confucian tradition were his belief in the goodness of human nature and his focus on the virtue of **yi**, or righteous conduct. Mencius emphasized the moral duty of rulers to govern by the principle of humanity and the good of the people. If rulers are guided by profit motives, this self-centered motivation will be reflected in all subordinates and social chaos will ensue. On the other hand, "When a commiserating government is conducted from a commiserating heart, one can rule the whole empire as if one were turning it in one's palm."[22] This is a natural way, says Mencius, for people are naturally good: "The tendency of human nature to do good is like that of water to flow downward."[23] Heaven could be counted on to empower the righteous.

Another follower quite disagreed with this assessment. This was Hsun Tzu, who seems to have been born when Mencius was an old man. Hsun Tzu argued that human nature is naturally evil and that Heaven is impersonal, operating according to natural laws rather than intervening on the side of good government or responding to human wishes ("Heaven does not suspend the winter because men dislike cold"[24]). Humans must hold up their own end. Their natural tendency, however, is to envy, to hate, and to desire personal gain and sensual pleasure. The only way to constrain these tendencies is to teach and legally enforce the rules of li and yi. Though naturally flawed, humans can gradually attain sagehood by persistent study, patience, and good works and thereby form a cooperative triad with Heaven and earth.

Hsun Tzu's careful reasoning provided a basis for the new legalistic structure of government. The idealism of Mencius was revived much later as a Chinese response to Buddhism and became required for the civil service examinations from the thirteenth to the twentieth centuries. However, their points of agreement are basic to Confucianism: the appropriate practice of virtue is of great value; humans can attain this through self-cultivation; and study and emulation of the ancient sages are the path to harmony in the individual, family, state, and world.

The state cult

Since ancient times, as we have seen, rulers have been regarded as the link between earth and Heaven. This understanding persisted in Chinese society, but Confucius and his followers had elaborated the idea that the ruler must be virtuous for this relationship to work. During the Han dynasty (206 BCE to 220 CE) Confucius's teachings were at last honored by the state. The Han scholar Tung Chung-shu set up an educational system based on the Confucian Classics that lasted until the twentieth century. He used Confucian ideals to unite the people behind the ruler, who himself was required to be subject to Heaven.

It was during this period that civil service examinations based on the Confucian classics were first established as a means of attaining government positions. The Confucian Classics were established as the Five Classics and the Four Books as the standard textbooks for education during the Sung dynasty by the Neo-Confucian scholar, Chu Hsi (1130–1200 CE). His *Reflections on Things at Hand* gave a metaphysical basis for Confucianism: the individual is intimately linked with all of the cosmos, "forming one body with all things." According to Chang Tsai's *Western Inscription*:

> *Heaven is my father and earth is my mother and even such a small creature as I finds an intimate place in their midst. Therefore, that which extends throughout the universe I regard as my body and that which directs the universe I regard as my nature. All people are my brothers and sisters and all things are my companions.[25]*

By becoming more humane one can help to transform not only oneself but also society and even the cosmos. The Neo-Confucianists thus stressed the importance of meditation and dedication to becoming a "noble person."

Women were encouraged to offer themselves in total sacrifice to others. Confucian women had previously been expected to take a subordinate role in the family and in society, but equally to be strong, disciplined, and capable in their relationships with their husbands and sons. In Neo-Confucianism, such virtues were subsumed under an ideal of self-sacrifice.

Although Confucius had counseled restrained use of li, Neo-Confucianism also included an increased emphasis on sacrifice, as practiced since ancient times and set forth in the traditional *Book of Rites* and *Etiquette and Ritual*. These rites were thought to preserve harmony between humans, Heaven, and earth. At the family level, offerings were made to propitiate the family ancestors. Government officials were responsible for ritual sacrifices to beings such as the gods of fire, literature, cities, mountains, waters, the polar star, sun, moon, and former rulers, as well as spirits of the earth and sky.

The most important ceremonies were performed by the emperor, to give thanks and ask blessings from heaven, earth, gods of the land and agriculture, and the dynastic ancestors. Of these, the highest ritual was the elaborate annual sacrifice to Shang Ti at the white marble Altar of Heaven by the emperor. He was considered Son of Heaven, the "high priest of the world." Both he and his retinue prepared themselves by three days of fasting and keeping vigil. In a highly reverent atmosphere, he then sacrificed a bull, offered precious jade, and sang prayers of gratitude to the Supreme, such as this one:

> *With reverence we spread out these precious stones and silk, and, as swallows rejoicing in the spring, praise Thy abundant love. ... Men and creatures are emparadised, O Ti, in Thy love. All living things are indebted to Thy goodness, but who knows whence his blessings come to him? It is Thou alone, O Lord, who art the true parent of all things.*[26]

Confucianism under communism

The performance of rituals was a time-consuming major part of government jobs, carried out on behalf of the people. But as China gradually opened to the West in recent centuries, a reaction set in against these older ways, and the last of the imperial dynasties was overthrown in 1911. Although worship of Confucius continued, in the 1920s Republic, science and social progress were glorified by radical intellectuals of the New Culture movement who were opposed to all the old systems. Under the communist regime established in 1949, communism took the place of religion, attempting to transform the society by secular means. Party Chairman Mao tse-Tung was venerated almost as a god, with the little red book of quotations from Chairman Mao replacing the Confucian Classics.

During the Cultural Revolution (1966–76), Confucianism was attacked as one of the "Four Olds"—old ideas, culture, customs, and habits. The Cultural Revolution attempted to destroy the hierarchical structure that Confucianism had idealized and to prevent the intellectual elite from ruling over the masses. Contrary to the Confucian virtue of filial piety, young people even denounced their parents at public trials, and scholars were made objects of derision. An estimated one million people were attacked. Some were killed, some committed suicide, and millions suffered.

Mao said that he had hated Confucius from his childhood. What he so disliked was the intellectual emphasis on study of the Classics and on rituals. But in some respects, Confucian morality continued to form the basis of Chinese ethics. Mao particularly emphasized the (Confucian) virtues of selfless service to the people and of self-improvement for the public good:

All our cadres, whatever their rank, are servants of the people, and whatever we do is to serve the people. How then can we be reluctant to discard any of our bad traits?[27]

For decades, communist China prided itself on being the most law-abiding country in the world. The streets were safe, and tourists found that if they could not understand the currency, they could trust taxi drivers to take the exact amount, and no more, from their open wallets. But recently there has been a rise in crime and official corruption. The society has changed abruptly since China opened its doors to the West in 1978, undermining traditional Confucian virtues. The government blames the influx of materialistic values, from indiscriminating embrace of the underside of Western culture and the rapid shift toward a free market economy. In early 1989, Zhao Ziyang, then Communist Party leader, urged officials to maintain Confucian discipline (without naming it that) in the midst of the changes: "The Party can by no means allow its members to barter away their principles for money and power."[28] But when the people picked up this cry, aging leaders chose brutally to suppress popular calls for greater democracy and an end to official corruption; they did so in the name of another Confucian value: order in society.

For their part, the intellectuals of the democracy movement had tried to do things in the proper way but were caught on the horns of the poignant Chinese dilemma. Under Confucian ethics, it has been the continuing responsibility of scholars to morally cultivate themselves and properly remonstrate with their rulers, to play the role of upright censors. On the other hand, scholars had to remain loyal to the ruler, for they were subjects and observing one's subservient position as a subject preserved the security of the state. The leaders of the democracy movement tried to deal with this potential conflict by ritualized, respectful action: they formally walked up the steps of the Great Hall of the People in Tiananmen Square to present their written requests to those in power. But they were ignored and brutally suppressed.

Again, in 1995, forty-five of China's most distinguished scholars and scientists delivered a petition to the government urging freedom of thought and accountability of the government to the public, in order to end socially corrosive corruption. Some observers speculate that slow transformations will bring a new form of Confucian tradition. Already, interest in Confucian thought is increasing among intellectuals. Conferences have recently been held on the mainland in China and also in Taiwan and Singapore to discuss Confucianism. Today it is being analyzed not as an historical artefact but as a tradition which is relevant to modern life. Even though it may not be practiced in the same ways as before, it may nonetheless contribute significantly to cultural identity,

Living Confucianism

Ann-ping Chin grew up in Taiwan, the daughter of parents from the northern part of mainland China. She teaches Confucianism and Taoism at Wesleyan University and has visited China five times to do research on the continuing changes in that society.

"Lots of things are changing in China. First of all, the economic boom is changing women's perceptions of themselves and of their family. For instance, if a woman is determined to have a profession of her own, in this huge marketplace of China this implies that she would become involved in a private enterprise or begin one herself. If she does that, this means that she would have to consider child-rearing as secondary.

Divorce is very common. Family units are breaking up and children have less security—there are all the problems that we associate with divorce in the West. The woman simply says, 'Look— I'm going to leave or you leave.'

Making money is now the most important thing for the Chinese. From an initial impression, perhaps you can say that the fundamental Confucian values are disappearing. Through more than two thousand years of Chinese history, both in traditional Confucian teachings and in Taoist teachings as well, you find a tremendous deprecation of the idea of making money—of taking advantage or making a profit, be it in money or in human relationships. Now unless you have the determination to make money, you are not considered a true man in Chinese society.

On the other hand, I would say that the very basic relationships of parents and children, and of friends to friends are still very strong. The Chinese have given up their relationship with the ruler; that's really a joke. The relationship between husband and wife is much more complicated. Men love the idea of having a very devoted wife. They know that is perhaps impossible, but they still yearn for it. And they still value the traditional qualities that you find in the biographies of virtuous women.

Other values have been abandoned. I'm very disturbed and saddened, pained, by what is happening to the Chinese scholars. They cannot go out and do private enterprise, for they are scholars. They get paid a very pathetic amount of money each month, not enough to make ends meet. Scholars have always been really respected even though people didn't understand them. But now there isn't even that respect since the society is placing so much emphasis on making money.

My parents both came from very scholarly backgrounds. They passed down to us the traditions without the formalities, without the rigidities, so we were extremely fortunate. I think my father passed down to us his love of students, his love of teaching, and of the very special relationship between teachers and disciples. It's not obedience—rather, it's a concern that the disciple expresses toward the teacher.

My father's character had a profound effect on me. He always tried to do the right thing. And to do the right thing sometimes can be so difficult. This was the only way that he could live—to always try to do the right thing, whether it was for a friend, or for us, for my mom, for his own parents, or for strangers. He would never compromise that."

economic progress, social harmony, and a personal sense of the meaning of human life.

Confucianism may inform capitalistic behavior as well as Marxist communism. There is now talk of "Capitalist Confucianism"—business conducted according to Confucian ethics such as humanity, trustworthiness, sincerity, and altruism. As Professor Xinzhong Yao explains,

Free choice is the foundation of modern society, and the pre-condition of market economy. However, freedom without responsibility would result in the collapse of the social network and in the conflict between individuals and between individuals and society, and would lead to the sacrifice of the future in order to satisfy short-term needs. This has become a serious challenge to human wisdom and to human integrity. In this respect, Confucianism can make a contribution to a new moral sense, a new ecological view and a new code for the global village.[29]

Confucian values are also being reappraised as a significant addition to holistic education. In them is imbedded the motivation to improve oneself and become a responsible and ethical member of one's family and society. The Neo-Confucians developed multi-stage learning programs for the life-long process of self-improvement. Confucianism has always promoted education as the only means to social reform, and further encourages a sense of voluntary service to the community.

In the moral and spiritual vacuum left after the demise of fervent Maoism, Confucianism may also help restore a sense of holy purpose to people's lives. The traditional feeling was that the Mandate of Heaven gives transcendent meaning to human life. Professor Tu Wei-ming, a modern Neo-Confucian, explains:

We are the guardians of the good earth, the trustees of the Mandate of Heaven that enjoins us to make our bodies healthy, our hearts sensitive, our minds alert, our souls refined, and our spirits brilliant. . . . We serve Heaven with common sense, the lack of which nowadays has brought us to the brink of self-destruction. Since we help Heaven to realize itself though our self-discovery and self-understanding in day-to-day living, the ultimate meaning of life is found in our ordinary, human existence.[30]

Chinese authorities have recently reintroduced the teaching of Confucius in elementary schools throughout the country as a vehicle for encouraging social morality. After a gap of more than half a century, the Confucian-based civil service examinations are being partially reintroduced in the selection of public servants. Earlier castigated as "feudal institutions," Confucian academies are being described as fine centers for learning. Chinese authorities are also reviving aspects of the religious cult, such as observance of the birthday of Confucius, perhaps mostly for the sake of tourism. But believers such as members of the Confucian Academy in Hong Kong take such observances seriously. In rural areas, observance of Confucian virtues has remained rather steady through time.

Confucianism in East Asia

Countries near China which have historically been influenced by China politically and culturally also show signs of having been influenced by Confucian values. The city-state of Singapore has since 1978 sponsored an annual courtesy campaign to inspire virtuous behavior in the midst of fast-paced modern life. In 1997, the focus of the campaign was courteous use of mobile phones and pagers. It was politely suggested that one should turn them off in theaters, places of worship, and public functions to avoid disturbing others.

In Korea, where few people now consider themselves adherents of Confucianism as a religion, lectures and special events are being sponsored by hundreds of local Confucian institutes to promote Confucian teachings. In some cases, Confucianism is associated with particular clans in East Asia, and thus with political favoritism. Some of the Korean institutes are politically conservative, opposing women's efforts to revise family laws. The Korean Overseas Information Service advocates a flexible, liberal version of the tradition, open to other cultures and to all religions but still providing a firm foundation for social order:

> *Confucianism can present contemporary Koreans with a set of practical standards of conduct in the form of rituals and etiquette. Extensive introduction of Western modes of behavior led to the confusion and adulteration of Korea's native behavior pattern. Civility and propriety in speech and deportment enhance the dignity of man. Rites and conduct befitting to a civilized people should be refined and adjusted to the conditions of the time. . . . Korea should, through its Confucian heritage, sustain the tradition of propriety and modesty and defend the intrinsically moral nature of man from submergence in economic and materialistic considerations.*[31]

Various Confucian organizations have developed in Hong Kong, Taiwan, and other parts of East Asia which are attempting to restore religious versions of Confucianism, such as the worship of Confucius himself or study of the Confucian Classics in Sunday schools.

Confucian thought has also played a significant role in Japan. It entered Japan during the seventh century when Chinese political thought and religious ideas first began to have significant influence there. It left its mark on the first constitution of Japan, on the arrangement of government bureaucracy, and in the educational system. From the seventeenth to nineteenth century, Confucianism began to spread more widely among the people of Japan because of its adoption as an educational philosophy in public and private schools. Confucian moral teachings became the basis for establishing proper relationships in the family and in Japanese society.

Both Confucianism and Shinto were manipulated by the military during the pre-war period to inculcate a nationalist expansionist ideology. More in keeping with the original motives of Confucianism, some scholars have observed that Japan's notably effective modernization during the twentieth century is partly due to values derived from Confucianism. These values include a high regard for diligence, consensus, education, moral self-cultivation, frugality, and loyalty.

Suggested Reading

Chang, Wing-Tsit, *A Sourcebook in Chinese Philosophy*, Princeton: Princeton University Press, 1963. A large and helpful anthology of Confucian, Taoist, and Buddhist texts.

de Bary, William Theodore, Chan, Wing-tsit, and Watson, Burton, eds., *Sources of Chinese Tradition*, New York: Columbia University Press, 1960. Useful commentaries and extensive texts from Confucian and Taoist schools.

I Ching, translated into German by Richard Wilhelm and thence into English by Cary Baynes, third edition, Princeton, New Jersey: Princeton University Press, 1967. Insights into the multiple possibilities of the interplay of yin and yang in our lives.

Kohn, Livia, *The Taoist Experience*, Albany, New York: State University of New York Press, 1993. Interesting translations of ancient and more recent texts covering the various aspects of Taoism.

Schipper, Kristofer M., *The Taoist Body*, trans. Karen Duvall, Berkeley: University of California Press, 1992. Explores integration of religious and philosophical Taoism within the Celestial Masters movement, from the Han dynasty to contemporary Taiwan.

Tao-te Ching, attributed to Lao-tzu, available in numerous translations, including the English translation by D. C. Lau, London: Penguin Books, 1963.

Taylor, Rodney, *The Religious Dimensions of Confucianism*, Albany: State University of New York Press, 1990. A collection of essays dealing with the central question of whether Confucianism is a religion.

Thompson, Laurence G., *Chinese Religion: An Introduction*, fifth edition, Belmont, California: Wadsworth, 1996. The many strands of Chinese religions are here clearly sorted out for introductory study.

Tu Wei-ming, *Confucian Thought: Selfhood as Creative Transformation*, Albany: State University of New York Press, 1985. A collection of Tu's seminal essays on his concern that Confucian humanity be understood as a living tradition with something distinctive to contribute to contemporary discussions in philosophy and comparative religions.

Watson, Burton, *Chuang Tzu: Basic Writings*, New York: Columbia University Press, 1964. An engaging translation of major writings by Chuang Tzu, with an introduction that is particularly helpful in dealing with this paradoxical material.

Welch, Holmes H. (with Anna Seidel), ed., *Facets of Taoism*, New Haven: Yale University Press, 1979. A collection of essays that shows the diversity of Taoist movements up to the present.

CHAPTER 6
SHINTO
The way of the kami

Japan has embraced and adapted many religions that originated in other countries, but it also developed its own unique path: Shinto. It is an organized version of the indigenous religion of the country, closely tied to nature and the unseen world. Of those modern Japanese who are religious, many combine practices from several religions, for each offers something different. Confucianism informs organizations and ethics, Buddhism and Christianity offer ways of understanding suffering and the afterlife, traditional veneration of ancestors links the living to their family history, and Shinto harmonizes people with the natural world.

The Essence of Shinto

Shinto has no founder, no orthodox canon of sacred literature, and no explicit code of ethical requirements. It is so deep-seated and ancient that the symbolic meanings of many of its elaborate rituals have been forgotten by those who practice them. It seems to have begun as the local religion of agricultural communities and had no name until Buddhism was imported in the sixth century CE. To distinguish the indigenous Japanese way from the foreign one, the former was labeled "shin" (divine being) "do" (way). During one period it was used by the central government to inspire nationalism, but since the forced separation of church and state after World War II Shinto has quietly returned to its roots. They can be described through three central aspects of the path: affinity with natural beauty, harmony with the spirits, and purification rituals.

Kinship with nature

Before industrial pollution and urbanization, Japan was a country of exquisite natural beauty, and to a certain extent, it still is. The islands marry mountains to sea, and the interiors are laced with streams, waterfalls, and lush forests. Even the agriculture is beautiful, with flowering fruit trees and terraced fields. The people lived so harmoniously with this environment that they had no separate word for "nature" until they began importing modern Western ideas late in the nineteenth century.

Living close to nature, the people experienced life as a continual process of change and renewal. They organized their lives around the turn of the seasons, honoring the roles of the sun, moon, and lightning in their rice farming. Mount Fuji, greatest of the volcanic peaks that formed the islands, was honored as the sacred embodiment of the divine creativity that had thrust the land up from the sea. It has never been called Mount Fuji by the Japanese, but rather *Fuji-san*, indicating a friendship and intimacy with the mountain. The sparkling ocean and rising sun so visible along the extensive coastlines were loved as earthly expressions of the sacred purity, brightness, and awesome power at the heart of life.

> *To be fully alive is to have an aesthetic perception of life because a major part of the world's goodness lies in its often unspeakable beauty.*
> Rev. Yukitaka Yamamoto, Shinto priest [1]

Although industrialization and urbanization have blighted some of the natural landscape, the sensitivity to natural beauty survives in small-scale arts. In traditional rock gardening, flower arranging, the tea ceremony, and poetry, Japanese artists continue to honor the simple and natural. If a rock is placed just right in a garden, it seems alive, radiating its natural essence. In a tea ceremony, great attention is paid to each natural sensual delight, from the purity of water poured from a wooden ladle to the genuineness of the clay vessels. These arts are often linked with Zen Buddhism, but the sensitivities seem to derive from the ancient Japanese ways.

Honoring the kami

Surrounded by nature's beauty and power, the Japanese people found the divine all around them. In Shinto, the sacred is both immanent and transcendent. In Japanese mythology, the divine originated as one essence:

> *In primeval ages, before the earth was formed, amorphous matter floated freely about like oil upon water. In time there arose in its midst a thing like a sprouting reedshoot, and from this a deity came forth of its own.* [2]

This deity gave birth to many **kami**, or spirits, two of whom—the Amatsu Kami—were told to organize the material world. Standing on the Floating Bridge of Heaven, they stirred the ocean with a jeweled spear. When they pulled it out of the water, it dripped brine back into the ocean, where it coagulated into eight islands, with mountains, rivers, plants, and trees (these may be interpreted either as Japan or the whole world). To rule this earthly kingdom they created the Kami Amaterasu, Goddess of the Sun. Through their union, the Amatsu Kami also gave birth to the ancestors of the people of Japan. All of the natural world—land, trees, mountains, waters, animals, people—is thus joined in kinship as the spiritual creation of the kami.

Although the word "kami" (a way of pronouncing the character "shin") is usually translated as "god" or "spirit," these translations are not exact. Kami can be either singular or plural, for the word refers to a single essence manifesting in many places. Rather than evoking an image, like the Hindu or Mahayana Buddhist deities, kami refers to a quality. It means that which evokes wonder and awe in us. The kami harmonize heaven and earth and also guide the solar system and the cosmos. It/they tend to reside in beautiful or powerful places, such as mountains, certain trees, unusual rocks, waterfalls, whirlpools, and animals. In addition, it/they manifest as wind, rain, thunder, or lightning. Kami also appear in abstract forms, such as the creativity of growth and reproduction. In general, explains Sakamiki Shunzo, kami include:

> all things whatsoever which deserve to be dreaded and revered for the extraordinary and preeminent powers which they possess. ... [Kami] need not be eminent for surpassing nobleness, goodness, or serviceableness alone. Malignant and uncanny beings are also called kami, if only they are the objects of general dread.[3]

Shrines

Recognizing the presence of kami, humans have built shrines to honor it/them. There are even now approximately eighty thousand Shinto shrines in Japan. Shrines may be as small as bee-hives or elaborate temple complexes covering thousands of acres. Some honor kami protecting the area; some honor kami with special responsibilities, such as protecting crops from insects. The shrines are situated on sites thought to have been chosen by the kami for their sacred atmosphere. At one time, every community had its own guardian kami.

It is thought that the earliest Shinto places of worship were sacred trees or groves, perhaps with some enclosure to demarcate the sacred area. Shrine complexes which developed later also have some way of indicating where sacred space begins: tall gate-frames known as *torii*, walls, or streams with bridges which must be crossed to enter the holy precinct of the kami. Water is a purifying influence, and basins of water are also provided for washing one's mouth and hands. Statues of guardian lions further protect the kami from evil intrusions, as do ropes with pendants hanging down.

In temple compounds, one first comes to a public hall of worship, behind which is an offering hall where priests conduct rites. Beyond that is the sacred sanctuary of the kami, which is entered only by the high priest. Here the spirit of the kami is invited to come down to dwell within a special natural object or perhaps a mirror which reflects the revered light of brightness and purity, considered the natural order of the universe. If there is a spiritually powerful site already present—a waterfall, a crevice in a rock, a hot spring, a sacred tree—the spirit of the kami may dwell there. Some shrines are completely empty at the center. In any case, the eyes of the worshippers do not fall on the holy of holies; their worship is imageless. As Kishimoto Hideo explains,

> A faithful believer would come to the simple hall of a Shinto sanctuary, which is located in a grove with a quiet and holy atmosphere. He may stand quite a while in front of the sanctuary, clap his hands, bow deeply, and try

to feel the deity in his heart. . . . Seldom do the believers know the individual name of the deity whom they are worshipping. They do not care about that. . . . The more important point for them is whether or not they feel the existence of the deity directly in their hearts.[4]

The kami of a place may be experienced as energies. They are not necessarily pictured as forms, and at times Shintoism has been strongly iconoclastic (opposed to images of the divine). In the eighteenth century, for instance, a famous Shinto scholar wrote:

Never make an image in order to represent the Deity. To worship a deity is directly to establish a felt relation of our heart to the living Divinity through sincerity or truthfulness on our part. If we, however, try to establish a relation between Deity and man indirectly by means of an image, the image will itself stand in the way and prevent us from realizing our religious purpose to accomplish direct communion with the Deity. So an image made by mortal hands is of no use in Shinto worship.[5]

Ceremonies

To properly encourage the spirit of the kami to dwell in the holy sanctuary, long and complex ceremonies are needed. In some temples, it takes ten years for the priests to learn them. The priesthood was traditionally hereditary. One temple has drawn its priests from the same four families for over a hundred generations. Not uncommonly, the clergy are women priestesses. Neither priests nor priestesses live as ascetics; it is common for them to be married, and they are not traditionally expected to meditate. Rather, they are specialists in the arts of maintaining the connection between the kami and the people.

Everything has symbolic importance, even when people do not remember quite what it is, so rites are conducted with great care. The correct kind of wood, cloth, and clay in temple furnishings, the nine articles held by priests during ceremonies (such as branch, gourd, sword, and bow), the bowing, the sharp clapping of hands, beating of drums, the waving of a stick with paper strips—everything is established by tradition and performed with precision. Traditionally, there are no personal prayers to the kami for specific kinds of help, but rather a reverent recognition of the close relationship between the kami, the ancestors, the people, and nature. When people have made a pilgrimage to a special shrine, they often take back spiritual mementos of their communion with the kami, such as a paper symbol of the temple encased within a brocade bag.

Followers of the way of the kami may also make daily offerings to the kami in their home. Their place of worship usually consists of a high shelf on which rests a miniature shrine, with only a mirror inside. The daily home ritual may begin with greeting the sun in the east with clapping and a prayer for protection for the household. Then offerings are placed before the shrine: rice for health, water for cleansing and preservation of life, and salt for the harmonious seasoning of life. When a new house is to be built, the blessings of the kami are ceremonially requested.

To acknowledge and follow the kami is to bring our life into harmony with nature, Shintoists feel. The word used for this concept is **kannagara**, which is the same word used for the movements of the sun, moon, stars, and planets. Yukitaka Yamamoto, 96th Chief Priest of the Tsubaki Grand Shrine, says kannagara could be translated as "Natural Religion":

> *Natural Religion is the spontaneous awareness of the Divine that can be found in any culture. . . . The Spirit of Great Nature may be a flower, may be the beauty of the mountains, the pure snow, the soft rains or the gentle breeze.* Kannagara *means being in communion with these forms of beauty and so with the highest level of experiences of life. When people respond to the silent and provocative beauty of the natural order, they are aware of* kannagara. *When they respond in life in a similar way, by following ways "according to the kami," they are expressing* kannagara *in their lives. They are living according to the natural flow of the universe and will benefit and develop by so doing.*[6]

Purification

In traditional Shinto, there is no concept of sin. The world is beautiful and full of helpful spirits. Sexuality per se is not sinful; the world was created by mating deities, and people have traditionally bathed together communally in Japan. However, there is a great problem of ritual impurity that may offend the kami and bring on calamities such as drought, famine, or war.

The quality of impurity or misfortune is called **tsumi**. It can arise through defilement by corpses or menstruation, by unkind interaction between humans, between humans and the environment, or through natural catastrophes. In contrast to repentance required by religions that emphasize sin, tsumi requires purification. Followers of the way of the kami have various means of removing tsumi. One is paying attention to problems as they arise:

> *To live free of obstructing mists, problems of the morning should be solved in the morning and those of the evening should be solved by evening. Wisdom and knowledge should be applied like the sharpness of an axe to the blinding effect of the mists of obstruction. Then may the kami purify the world and free it of tsumi.*[7]

The kami of the high mountain rapids will carry the tsumi to the sea, where the whirlpool kami will swallow it and the wind kami will blow it to the netherworld, where kami of that place absorb and remove it.

> *After this has been completed, the heavenly kami, the earthly kami and the myriad of kami can recognise man as purified and everything can return to its original brightness, beauty and purity as before since all tsumi has wholly vanished from the world.*[8]

People may also be purified spontaneously by a kind of grace that washes over them, often in nature, bringing them into awareness of unity with the universe. Hitoshi Iwasaki, a young Shinto priest, says that he likes to look at the stars at night in the mountains where the air is clear:

When I am watching the thoroughly clear light of the stars, I get a pure feeling, like my mind being washed. I rejoice to think this is a spiritual Misogi [purification ritual]. . . . Master Mirihei Ueshiba, the founder of Aikido, is said to have looked upon the stars one night, suddenly realized he was united with the universe, and burst into tears, covering his face with his hands. We human beings, not only human beings but everything existing in this world, are one of the cells which form this great universe.[9]

In addition to these personal ways of cleansing, there are ritual forms of purification. One is **oharai**, a ceremony commonly performed by Shinto priests which includes the waving of a piece of wood from a sacred tree, to which are attached white streamers. This ceremony is today performed on cars and new buildings. A version used to soothe a kami who is upset by an impurity was called for in 1978 when there was a rash of suicides in a Tokyo housing complex by residents jumping off roofs.

Before people enter a Shinto shrine, they will splash water on their hands and face and rinse their mouth to purify themselves in order to approach the kami. Water is also used for purification in powerful ascetic practices, such as **misogi**, which involves standing under a waterfall. Sprinkling of salt on the ground or on ritual participants is also regarded as purifying.

Such ritual practices all have inner meaningfulness. At Tsubaki Grand Shrine in Japan, priests purify more than two hundred new cars every weekend, and the same practice has been adopted at Tsubaki Shrine in California. There, Rev. Tetsuji Ochiai explains to new car owners whose cars are being ritually purified that they themselves must also practice mental purification for the sake of traffic safety. Just as they attended the ceremony for their car with a calm mind, they should be calm as they drive. Thus, even though the ceremony is not guaranteed to protect them from accidents, it will help them to concentrate their energy on safe driving.

Festivals

In addition to elaborate regular ceremonies, Shintoism is associated with numerous special festivals throughout the year and throughout a person's life. They begin four months before the birth of a baby, when the soul is thought to enter the fetus. Then, thirty-two or thirty-three days after the infant's birth, its parents take it to the family's temple for initiation by the deity. In a traditional family, many milestones—such as coming of age at thirteen, or first arranging one's hair as a woman at age sixteen, marriage, turning sixty-one, seventy-seven, or eighty-eight—are also celebrated with a certain spiritual awareness and ritualism.

The seasonal festivals are reminders to the people that they are descendants of the kami. This means remembering to live in gratitude for all that they have received. Festivals became exuberant affairs in which the people and the kami join in celebrating life. Many have an agricultural basis, ensuring good crops and then giving thanks for them. Often the local kami is carried about the streets in a portable shrine.

Among the many local and national Japanese festivals with Shinto roots, one of the biggest is New Year's. It begins in December with ceremonial housecleaning, the placing of bamboo and pine "trees" at doorways of everything from homes to offices and bars to welcome the kami, and dressing in traditional kimonos. On December 31, there is a national day of purification. On New Year's day, people may go out to see the first sunrise of the year and will try to visit a shrine as well as friends and relatives.

Many ceremonies honor those reaching a certain age. For instance, on January 15, those who are twenty years old are recognized as full-fledged adults, and on November 15, children who are three, five, or seven years old (considered delicate ages) are taken to a shrine to ask for the protection of the kami. On February 3, the end of winter, people throw beans to toss out bad fortune and invite good, and at shrines the priests shoot arrows to break the power of misfortune. A month-long spring festival is held from March to April, with purification rites and prayers for a successful planting season. The month of June is devoted to rites to protect crops from insects, blights, and bad weather. Fall brings thanksgiving rites for the harvest, with the first fruits offered to the kami and then great celebrating in the streets.

Buddhist and Confucian Influences

Over time, the essence of Shinto has been blended with other religions imported into Japan. The two religions with which Shinto has been most blended are Buddhism, first introduced into Japan in the sixth century CE, and Confucianism, which has been an intimate part of Japanese culture since its earliest contact with Chinese influences.

Buddhism is still practiced side-by-side with Shinto. The fact that their theologies differ so significantly has been accepted by the people as covering different kinds of situations. The Japanese often go to Shinto shrines for life-affirming events, such as conception, birth, and marriage, and to Buddhist temples for death rites. Shingon Buddhist monks tried long ago to convince the Japanese that the Shinto kami were actually Buddhist deities. The two religions were therefore closely interwoven in some people's minds until the Meiji government extricated its version of Shinto from Buddhism in the nineteenth century. But the parallel worship of the two paths continues, with some villages having stone monuments to the kami and statues of Nichiren placed next to each other.

As for Confucianism, seventeenth-century Japanese Confucian scholars attempted to free themselves from Buddhism and to tie the Chinese beliefs they were importing to the ancient Japanese ways. The Neo-Confucianists' alliance with Shinto to throw off the yoke of Buddhism actually revived Shinto itself and made the ancient, somewhat formless tradition more self-conscious. Scholars began to study and interpret its teachings. The combination of Confucian emphasis on hierarchy and Shinto devotion helped pave the way for the establishment in 1868 of the powerful Meiji monarchy.

State Shinto

The Meiji regime distinguished Shinto from Buddhism and took steps to promote Shinto as the spiritual basis for the government. Shinto, amplifying the

Japanese traditions of ancestor veneration, had long taught that the emperor was the offspring of Amaterasu, the Sun Goddess. *Naobi no Mitma* ("Divine Spirit of Rectification"), written in the eighteenth century, expressed this ideal:

> *This great imperial land, Japan, is the august country where the divine ancestral goddess Amaterasu Omikami was born, a superb country. . . . Amaterasu deigned to entrust the country with the words, "So long as time endures, for ten thousand autumns, this land shall be ruled by my descendants."*
>
> *According to her divine pleasure, this land was decreed to be the country of the imperial descendants . . . so that even now, without deviation from the divine age, the land might continue in tranquility and in accord with the will of the kami, a country ruled in peace.[10]*

It had been customary for the imperial family to visit the shrine to the Sun Goddess at Ise to consult the supreme kami on matters of importance. But the emperor Meiji carried this tradition much farther. He decreed that the way of the kami should govern the nation. The way, as it was then interpreted, was labeled *State Shinto*. It was administered by government officials rather than bona fide Shinto priests, whose objections were silenced, and many of the ancient spiritual rituals were suppressed. State Shinto became the tool of militaristic nationalists as a way to enlist popular support for guarding the throne and expanding the empire.

By the time that Japan was defeated in World War II, the emperor Hirohito, Meiji's grandson, may have been little more than a ceremonial figurehead. But he had been held up as a god, not to be seen or touched by ordinary people. At the end of the war he officially declared himself human. The traditional spiritual Shinto, however, was left with the stigma built up by State Shinto.

Traditional Shinto also spawned new religious **sects** which had their roots in Shinto beliefs and practices of communicating with the kami. These new sects were also labeled "Sect Shinto" by the Meiji regime. One of these new sects, called *Oomoto*, developed from revelations given to Madame Nao Deguchi when she was reportedly possessed by a previously little-known kami in 1892. The revelations criticized the "beastly" state of humanity, with:

> *the stronger preying on the weaker. . . . If allowed to go on in this way, society will soon lose the last vestiges of harmony and order. Therefore, by a manifestation of Divine Power, the Greater World shall undergo reconstruction, and change into an entirely new creation. . . . The Greater World shall burst into bloom as plum blossoms at winter's end.[11]*

The Oomoto movement survived persecution by the Meiji regime. It has denied that it is a Shinto sect and now has a universalist approach, recognizing founders of other religions as kami. Its leaders travel around the world encouraging self-examination, environmental restoration, and global religious cooperation.

AN INTERVIEW WITH HITOSHI IWASAKI

Living Shinto

Hitoshi Iwasaki is a young Shinto priest struggling to educate himself in the suppressed ancient ways of his people. He has officiated at the Shinto shrine in Stockton, California, and at its parent shrine in Japan, Tsubaki Grand Shrine in the Mie Prefecture, where a fine waterfall is used for purification practices.

"We Japanese are very fortunate. We are grateful for every natural phenomenon and we worship the mountain, we worship the river, we worship the sea, we worship the big rocks, waterholes, winds.

Unfortunately, after World War II, we were prohibited from teaching the Shinto religion in schools. We never learned about Shinto at school. Many young Japanese know the story of Jesus Christ, but nothing about Shinto. The government is not against Shinto. [The silence comes from] newspapers, the media, and the teachers' union, because they were established just after World War II. They have a very left-wing attitude [and associate Shinto with State Shinto]. Ordinary Japanese people don't link Shinto with politics nowadays, but the teachers' union and newspapers never give credence to religion, Shinto, or Japanese old customs.

Against this kind of atmosphere, we learned in the school that everything in Japan was bad. Shinto and Japanese customs were bad. Many young people are losing Japanese customs. But I went to Ise Shrine University, where I learned that Shinto is not just State Shinto. Some young people like me study Japanese things and they become super-patriots. That's the problem. There is no middle, just super-left or super-right.

I learned Shinto partly by learning aikido. The founder was a very spiritual person who studied in one of the Shinto churches. In Shinto we don't have services, we don't preach, we don't do anything for people who want to be saved. But I want to introduce the idea of Shinto to the people of the United States and young Japanese and I can do it through aikido. I think I learned the way of nature through aikido practice. We are born as a child of kami, which means we are part of the universe, like a tree. People practice aikido not to fight but to be a friend, to unite.

In Japan some people are going to Shinto. They were all doing Zen before, but Zen is very difficult. In waterfall purification there is no choice, just standing under the waterfall.

My friend, a Shinto priest, went to the Middle East, in complete desert. He says it was difficult to explain Shinto there. For them, nature is the enemy. They have to fight nature.

In Japan we have water everywhere. Now the big rivers and streams are polluted. But people come to the shrines. People gather because this is a sacred place from ancient times where people have come to pray. And other people want to go where people are gathered, so some of the shrines become vacation places, surrounded by souvenir shops. Many come to Shinto shrines and pray Buddhist prayers. Why not? Buddha is one of the kami. Everything has kami."

Shinto Today

In general, Shintoism is an indigenous Japanese faith, and it remains so. Outside Japan, it is a common faith only in Hawaii and Brazil, because many Japanese have settled there. Shintoism has not been a proselytizing religion (that is, it does not seek to convert others).

Within Japan, reaction to the horrors of the war and desire for modernization threatened to leave Shinto in the shadows of the past. After World War II, the Japanese Teachers Association began teaching rejection of patriotism, of the imperial family, of Japanese history, and also of traditional Shintoism. The Japanese national flag—a red circle on a white background—became a symbol of the past, although its symbolism transcends history. The red circle signifies the rising sun and the white background purity, righteousness, and national loyalty, Shinto values which are not necessarily militaristic. As Hitoshi Iwasaki notes (see Interview), for a time it was difficult for young people to learn about Shintoism. But the shrines remain and are visited by over eighty million Japanese at New Year. People often visit more as tourists than as believers, but many say they experience a sense of spiritual renewal when they visit a shrine. Long-established households still have their kami shelf, often next to the Buddhist family altar. In Japan, Shinto also survives as the basis for the seasonal holidays.

Despite the fact that Japan is now one of the most technologically advanced countries in the world, with business its primary focus, there still seems to be a place for communion with the intangible kami that, in Shinto belief, permeate all of life. Rapid and extreme urbanization and industrialization in twentieth-century Japan also brought extremes of pollution and disease. Minamata disease, for example, has since mid-century brought paralysis and painful suffering in an area of southern Japan where a chemical factory had been dumping mercury into the bay, contaminating the fish eaten by the residents. In another area of southern Japan, iron and steel factories had so polluted the air that children developed severe respiratory diseases and the sky was never blue. However, citizens' groups—many of them led by concerned mothers—are intervening to protest the despoliation of the environment and of human health and to urge a new appreciation of the natural beauty of the islands. Such actions can perhaps be seen as practical applications of Shinto sentiments.

Some Shintoists now explain their path as a universal natural religion, rather than an exclusively Japanese phenomenon, and try to explain the way of harmony with the kami to interested non-Japanese, without striving for conversions. A Shinto shrine has been built in California, offering ritual ways of experiencing one's connection with nature and learning to see the divine in the midst of life.

Within Japan, the Association of Shinto Shrines feels that it can play a role in helping people to remember the natural world. The Association recently stated:

> [Traditionally] the Japanese viewed nature not as an adversary to be
> subdued, but rather as a sacred space overflowing with the blessings of the

kami, and toward which they were to act with restraint. . . . While the Japanese have loathed environmental destruction, the advance of civilization centered on science and technology, and the rush toward economic prosperity has created a tidal wave of modernization that has frequently resulted in the loss of that traditional attitude handed down from ancestors. . . . By reconsidering the role of the sacred groves possessed by the some eighty thousand shrines in Japan, we hope to heighten Japanese consciousness, and expand the circle of active involvement in environmental preservation.[12]

Suggested Reading

Bocking, Brian, *A Popular Dictionary of Shinto*, Richmond, Surrey: Curzon Press, 1996. Thorough discussions of ancient and contemporary facets of Shinto, including shrines, festivals, kami, new religious movements, historical events, and key figures.

Hebert, Jean, *Shinto: At the Fountain-head of Japan*, New York: Stein and Day, 1967. A classic survey of the intricacies of Shinto practice.

Hori, Ichiro, *Folk Religion in Japan*, Chicago and London: University of Chicago Press, 1968. A lively study of Japanese folk traditions such as shamanism and mountain worship which contributed to Shinto.

Kitagawa, Joseph M., *On Understanding Japanese Religion*, Princeton, New Jersey and Guildford, Surrey: Princeton University Press, 1987. A scholarly history including Shinto and "new religions."

Mason, J. W. T., *The Meaning of Shinto: The Primaeval Foundation of Creative Spirit in Modern Japan*, Port Washington, New York: Kennikat Press, Inc., 1967.

Moore, Charles A., ed., *The Japanese Mind: Essentials of Japanese Philosophy and Culture*, Honolulu: University of Hawaii Press, 1967, 1971. A valuable collection of essays covering Shinto and Buddhism as well as secular aspects of Japanese lifeways.

Picken, Stuart D. B., *Essentials of Shinto: An Analytical Guide to Principal Teachings*. Westport, Connecticut and London: Greenwood Press, 1994. A clear introduction by a minister of the Church of Scotland who is also a misogi practitioner.

Smith, Robert J., *Ancestor Worship in Contemporary Japan*, Stanford, California: Stanford University Press, 1974. A sociological study of the continuing tradition of venerating family ancestors in contemporary Japan, including historical chapters which are of help in understanding the roots of State Shinto.

Yamamoto, Yukitaka, *Way of the Kami*, Stockton, California: Tsubaki American Publications, 1987. A highly accessible introduction to Shinto, seen as a universal natural way.

CHAPTER 7

JUDAISM

A Covenant with God

Judaism, which has no single founder, no central leader or group making theological decisions, is the tradition associated with the Jewish people. This family can be defined either as a religious group or an ethnic group.

In religious terms, Jews are those who experience their long and often difficult history as a continuing dialogue with God. According to one tradition, God offered to share the divine law with seventy nations, but the semi-nomadic tribes of Israel were the only people in the world to answer God's call, to enter into a living covenant with their creator. Jews feel that this call is still available to all peoples. In a religious sense, "Israel" refers to all those who answer the call, who strive to obey the one God, through the **Torah**, or "teaching," given to the patriarchs, Moses, and the prophets.

As a nation, "Israel" is a people who have been repeatedly dispersed and oppressed. After the horrors of the Holocaust, some Jews founded a homeland in the land of Israel where their ancestors had once walked. Other Jews live around the world. Many who consider themselves Jews have been born into a Jewish ethnic identity but do not feel or practice a strong connection to Jewish religious traditions.

A History of the Jewish People

The Jewish sense of history begins with the stories recounted in the Hebrew Bible or **Tanakh** (which Christians call "the Old Testament"). Biblical history begins with the creation of the world by a supreme deity, or God, and progresses through the patriarchs, matriarchs, and Moses who spoke with God and led the people according to God's commandments, and the prophets who heard God's warnings to those who strayed from the commandments. But Jewish history does not end where the stories of the Tanakh end, about the second century BCE. After the holy center of Judaism, the Temple of Jerusalem, was captured and destroyed by the Romans in 70 CE, Jewish history is that of a dispersed people, finding unity in their evolving teachings and traditional practices, which were eventually codified in the great compendium of Jewish law and lore, the **Talmud**.

Biblical stories

Although knowledge of the early history of the children of Israel is based largely on the narratives of the Tanakh, scholars are uncertain of the historical accuracy of the accounts. Some of the people, events, and genealogies set forth cannot be verified by other evidence. It may be that the Israelites were too small and loosely organized a group to be noted by historians of other cultures. No mention of Israel appears in other sources until about 1230 BCE, but biblical narratives and genealogies place Abraham, said to be the first patriarch of the Israelites, at about 1700 to 1900 BCE.

Jews hold the **Pentateuch**, the "five books of Moses" which appear at the beginning of the Tanakh, as the most sacred part of the scriptures. Traditionalists believe that these books were divinely revealed to Moses and written down by him as a single document. Some contemporary biblical researchers disagree. They speculate that these books were oral traditions reworked and set down later by several different sources with the intent of interpreting the formation of Israel from a religious point of view, as the results of God's actions in human history.

Although the accuracy of many of the stories has not yet been independently documented, they are of great spiritual significance in Christianity and Islam as well as Judaism. They are also politically important, for with the Talmud they later gave a scattered people a sense of group identity.

FROM CREATION TO THE GOD OF ABRAHAM The Hebrew scriptures begin with a sweeping poetic account of the creation of heaven and earth by God in six days, from the time of "the earth being unformed and void, with darkness over the surface of the deep and a wind from (or: the spirit of) God sweeping over the water."[1] After creating the material universe, God created man and woman in the divine "image" or "likeness," placing them as masters of the earth, rulers of "the fish of the sea, the birds of the sky, and all the living things that creep on the earth."[2] In this account, God is portrayed as a transcendent Creator, without origins, gender, or form, a being utterly different from what has been created. Since Hebrew has no gender-neutral pronouns, God is generally—though not always—described in male singular terms. This creation story (in Genesis 1 and 2:1–4) is attributed by scholars to the "priestly source," thought to be editors writing after the exile of the Jews to Babylon in 586 BCE.

A second, probably earlier, version of the creation story follows, beginning in Genesis 2:4. Instead of presenting woman as the equal of man, it portrays her as an offshoot of Adam, the first man; she was formed from one of Adam's ribs to keep him company. This version has commonly been interpreted as blaming woman for the troubles of humanity, although this reading is not supported in the Hebrew manuscripts. According to the legend of Adam and Eve, originally God placed the first two humans in a garden paradise. The woman Eve ("mother of all the living") was promised wisdom by a serpent (later often interpreted as a symbol of Satan) to tempt her to taste the fruit of the tree of knowledge of good and evil, against

JUDAISM

	2000 **BCE**	Abraham, the first patriarch, 1900–1700 BCE?
	1500	
Moses leads the Israelites out of bondage in Egypt c.13th or 12th C BCE	**1200**	David, King of Judah and Israel 1010–970 BCE?
	1000	King Solomon builds the first Temple 961–931 BCE
	800	
	600	First Temple destroyed; Jews exiled to Babylon 586 BCE
		Second Temple built 515 BCE
	400	Torah established c.430 BCE: Ezra the Scribe
	200	
		Hillel the Elder 30 BCE–10 CE
Development of rabbinic tradition 1st–4th C	**CE**	
	200	Jerusalem falls to the Romans 70 CE
		Jewish Canon fixed c.90
		Mishnah compiled c.200
	500	Babylonian Talmud completed mid-6th C
	800	
	1000	
		Maimonides 1135–1204
	1200	
	1400	Ghettos of Italy and German 1555 onward
The Inquisition begins 1480		
Mass expulsion of Jews from Spain 1492	**1600**	
The Baal Shem Tov 1700–1760		
The Enlightenment in Europe 1800s	**1800**	
		Nuremberg laws strip Jews or rights 1935
The Holocaust 1940–1945	**2000**	Death camps established 1942
The Six-Day War 1967		Israel declared an independent state 1948

God's command. She gave some to Adam as well. According to the legend, this ended their innocence. God cursed the serpent and the land and banished them from their garden; their lives were no longer paradisiacal nor were they immortal, for they no longer had access to the "tree of life."

The theme of exile reappears continually in the Hebrew Bible, and in later Jewish history the people are rendered homeless again and again. The biblical narratives emphasize that the people risk God's displeasure every time they stray from God's commands. They are repeatedly exiled from their spiritual home and continually seek to return to it.

A more optimistic interpretation developed later, however. This was the feeling that the Jewish people were spread throughout the world by God's will, for a sacred purpose: to be good citizens of whatever land they reside in, and to help raise the imperfect world back up to the condition of perfection in which God had created it. Israel would only find its way home when all of creation was lifted up. The rabbinic tradition which began in the first century CE and has shaped Jewish theology into the modern period emphasized that the way out of exile was through wisdom and righteous living. Ethical commandments have their origin in God and, if followed, will lead humanity back to a life in harmony with God.

Again and again, however, according to the scriptural stories, the people disobey God's will. One of the legends recounted concerns Noah, the sole righteous man of his generation. According to the narrator, who attributes thoughts and emotions to God, God despairs of the general wickedness of humans, regrets having created them, and sends a great flood "to destroy all flesh under the sky."[3] But with Noah, God establishes a covenant and gives directions for the building of an ark which saves Noah's family and two of each of God's creatures. God promises never again to destroy the created world or interfere with the established natural order, with the rainbow as a sign of this covenant "between me and all flesh that is on earth."[4]

God does, however, continue to intervene in history, according to the narrators. Ten generations after the legend of Noah, the narrative focuses on Abraham, Isaac, and Jacob (the "patriarchs"), and their wives, Sarah, Rebecca, Leah, and Rachel (the "matriarchs"). According to the biblical narratives, Abraham, born in Ur (now in Iraq), was called by God to journey to Canaan. With his household, he left the land of his father and also the religion of his father, whom oral tradition describes as not only a worshipper of the old gods but also a maker of statues devoted to them.

Abraham is held up as an example of obedience to God's commands. Without hesitation, he is said to undergo *circumcision* (cutting away of the foreskin of the penis) as an initiatory rite, a sign of the covenant in which God agrees to be the divine protector of Abraham and his descendants.

After Abraham has a son, Ishmael, by the Egyptian slave woman Hagar, God blesses the one-hundred-year-old Abraham's ninety-year-old wife Sarah, saying that she will become the "mother of nations: the kings of many people shall spring from her" (Genesis 17:16). According to the biblical account, Sarah does indeed give birth to a son, Isaac, and then insists that Ishmael and Hagar be banished to the wilderness. God supports this demand, assuring Abraham that he will be father of two nations—one line through Isaac (to become the Israelites) and one through Ishmael (whom Arabs consider their ancestor).

God then tests Abraham by asking him to sacrifice his son Isaac. When the patriarch prepares to comply, the Lord stops him, satisfied that "now I know that you fear God."[5] The Hebrew word *yirah*, usually translated as "fear" of God, also implies "awe of God's greatness," or what Rabbi Lawrence Kushner calls "trembling in the presence of ultimate holiness."[6]

As is common in the growth of any new religion, elements of the older faiths of the area were incorporated into or adapted to the new one. However, the ultimate thrust of Judaism was rejection of the gods of surrounding peoples. The Israelites came to see themselves as having been chosen by a single divine Patron. In their patriarchal culture, this God was perceived as a ruler in a close relationship to the people, like a parent to children, or a sovereign to vassals.

ISRAEL'S BIRTH IN STRUGGLE   It is unclear who the people of the biblical narratives were. Some scholars think the word "Hebrew" is derived from the term *habiru*, used for the low-class landless people who lived as outlaws and were often hired as mercenaries. Others point to *'ibri*, meaning "children of Eber," an ethnic term. But because of frequent moving and inter-marrying, the Israelites were actually of mixed ethnic stock, including Hebrew, Aramean, and Canaanite.

According to the genealogies set forth in the Pentateuch, the people who became known as Israelites were the offspring of Israel (first called Jacob), grandson of Abraham. Jacob received the new name after wrestling all night with a being who turned out to be an angel of God. "Israel" means "the one who struggled with God."

This story in which a human being struggles and finally is reborn at a higher level of spirituality has been taken as a metaphor for the spiritual evolution of the people Israel. As a result of the struggle, Israel the patriarch receives not only a new name but also the promise that many nations will be born from him. The nation Israel—"the smallest of peoples"[7]—is perceived as the spiritual center for the world to grow toward God. This is its destiny, though Jews do not feel that it has yet been fulfilled.

EGYPT: BONDAGE AND EXODUS   Jacob/Israel is said to have had one daughter and twelve sons by his two wives and their two maidservants. The twelve sons became the heads of the twelve tribes of Israel. The whole group left Canaan for Goshen in Egypt during a famine. Exodus, the second book of the Tanakh, opens about four centuries later with a statement that the descendants of Israel had become numerous. To keep them from becoming too powerful, the reigning Pharaoh ordered that they be turned into slaves for massive construction projects. To further curb the population, the Pharaoh ordered midwives to kill all boy babies born to the Israelite women.

One who escaped this fate was Moses, an Israelite of the tribe of Levi who was raised in the palace by the Pharaoh's own daughter. He is said to have fled the country after killing an Egyptian overseer who was beating an Israelite worker. While he lived in exile in Midian, the oppression of the Israelites in Egypt grew worse and worse.

According to the scriptural book of Exodus, Moses was chosen by God to defy the Pharaoh and lead the people out of bondage, out of Egypt. On Mount Sinai, an angel of God appeared to him from within a bush blazing with fire but not consumed by it. God called to him out of the bush and yet cautioned, "Do not come closer. Remove your sandals from your feet, for the place on which you stand is holy ground."[8] When God told Moses to go rescue "My people, the Israelites, from Egypt,"[9] Moses demurred, but God insisted, "I will be with you."[10] And when Moses asked how to explain to the Israelites who sent him to rescue them, God said:

> Thus you shall say to the Israelites, "Ehyeh [I Am] sent me to you. . . . The LORD, the God of your fathers, the God of Abraham, the God of Isaac, and the God of Jacob, has sent me to you."[11]

The word given in this translation as "LORD" is considered too sacred to be pronounced. In the Hebrew scriptures it is rendered only in consonants as YHWH or YHVH; the pronunciation of the vowels is not known.

With his brother Aaron to act as spokesperson, Moses did indeed return to Egypt. Many chapters of Exodus recount miracles used to convince the Pharaoh to let the people go into the wilderness to worship their God. These signs included a rod that turned into a serpent, plagues of locusts, flies, and frogs, animal diseases, a terrible storm, lasting darkness, and finally the killing by the Lord of all firstborn children and creatures. The Israelites were spared this fate, marking their doors with the blood of a slaughtered lamb so that the Lord would pass over them. At this, the Pharaoh at last let the Israelites go. The redemption from bondage by the special protection of the Lord has served ever since as a central theme in Judaism.

According to the scriptural account, the Lord's presence led the Israelites, manifesting as a pillar of cloud by day and a pillar of fire by night. The armies of the Pharaoh pursued them until Moses stretched his staff toward the sea and God caused an east wind to blow all night, dividing the waters so that the Israelites could pass through safely on a dry seabed. As the Egyptians tried to follow, God told Moses again to hold out his arm over the sea, and the walls of water came crashing down on them, drowning every one.

FROM THE WILDERNESS TO CANAAN   According to the Pentateuch, God told Moses that he would lead the people back to Canaan. First, however, it was necessary to travel to the holy Mount Sinai to re-establish the covenant between God and the people. The Lord is said to have descended to its summit in a terrifying show of lightning, thunder, fire, smoke, and trumpeting. God is said to have then given the people through Moses a set of rules for righteous living, later called the Torah. Among them are the Ten Commandments. God also gave a set of social norms, prescribed religious feasts, and detailed instructions for the construction of a portable tabernacle with a holy ark, the **Ark of the Covenant**, in which to keep the stone tablets on which God inscribed the commandments.

During the forty-day period while Moses was on the mountain receiving these instructions, the people who had just agreed to a holy covenant with God became disturbed and impatient. The biblical account says that under Aaron's reluctant supervision, they melted down their gold jewelry and cast it into the form of a golden calf, practicing what the authors of the biblical narratives considered idol-worship, which had been explicitly forbidden by God. Moses is said to have been so outraged by their idolatry that he smashed the stone tablets and destroyed the idol. He ordered the only people still siding with YHWH, the Levites, to slay three thousand of those who had strayed.

After another forty-day meeting with God on the summit of Mount Sinai, Moses again returned with stone tablets on which God had inscribed the commandments. Moses' face was said to be so radiant from his encounter with God that he had to veil it. Aaron and his sons were invested as priests, the tabernacle was constructed as directed, and the people set off for the land of Canaan, with the Presence of the Lord filling the tabernacle.

Even with the powerful presence of the Ark they carried, the Israelites had to wander forty years through the desert before they could re-enter the promised land, fertile Canaan, which at that time belonged to other peoples. The long sojourn in the wilderness is a familiar metaphor in the spiritual search. Faith is continually tested by difficulties. But even in the wilderness, the Israelites' God did not forsake them. Every day they found their daily bread scattered on the ground, in the form of an unknown food which they named *manna*.

Through what was described as the miraculous help of God, they fought many battles against the tribes of Canaan. Archaeological evidence indicates that every Canaanite town was destroyed from one to four times between the thirteenth and eleventh centuries BCE, though the identity of the conquerors is not known. The editors of the scriptures clearly considered the Canaanite religion spiritually invalid and morally inferior to their own. But the Israelites' attention to their God was not absolute. According to the scriptures, whenever they turned away from YHWH, forgetting or worshipping other gods, surrounding peoples found them easy prey.

THE FIRST TEMPLE OF JERUSALEM   David, the second King of Israel, is remembered as Israel's greatest king. An obscure shepherd, David was chosen by the prophet Samuel to be anointed on the head and beard with oil, for thus were future kings found and divinely acknowledged. David was summoned to the court of the first Israelite king, Saul, to play soothing music whenever an evil spirit seized the king. David also bore the king's arms. When Saul and his son were killed in battle, David was made king. By defeating or allying with surrounding nations, David created the beginnings of a secure, prosperous Israelite empire. He made the captured city of Jerusalem its capital and brought the Ark of the Covenant there.

Under the reign of King Solomon (son of David), a great Temple was built in Jerusalem. It was to be a permanent home for the Ark of the Covenant, which was housed in the innermost sanctum, and a place for making the burnt offerings of animals, grain, and oil to the divine. There already existed an ancient practice among pre-Israelite peoples of using high places for altars where sacrifices were made to the gods. After centuries of wandering worship, the Israelites now had a central, stationary place where God would be most present to them. God is said to have appeared to Solomon after the fourteen-day Temple dedication ceremony and pledged, "I consecrate this House which you have built and I set My name there forever. My eyes and My heart shall ever be there."[12]

Solomon also accumulated great personal wealth, at the expense of the people, and built altars to the gods of his wives, who came from other nations. This so angered the Lord, according to the scriptures, that he divided the kingdom after Solomon's death. An internal revolt of the ten northern tribes established a new kingdom of Israel, which was independent of Jerusalem and the dynasty of David. The southern kingdom, continuing in its allegiance to the house of David and retaining Jerusalem as its capital, renamed itself Judah, after David's tribe.

Prophets such as Elijah warned the people against worshipping gods other than the Lord, and exhorted them to end their evil ways. Over the centuries, these prophets were men and women who had undergone transformational ordeals which made them instruments for the word of God. The "early prophets" such as Elijah focused on the sin of idolatry; the "later prophets" warned that social injustice and moral corruption would be the ruin of the Jewish state.

By the reign of King Hoshea of Israel, the kingdom was so corrupt and idolatrous that, in the scriptural interpretation, God permitted the strong kingdom of Assyria to overtake what was left of the small country. To sustain the population needs for its empire-building and keep Israel from rising again as a nation, Assyria carried off most of the Israelites to exile among the **Gentiles** (non-Jewish people). Most of the Israelites became dispersed within Assyria; these people are known as the "Ten Lost Tribes of Israel." This destruction of the northern kingdom took place in 722 BCE, and is attested in Assyrian annals.

Judah maintained its independence, declining and warned of impending doom by its prophets, until King Nebuchadnezzar of Babylonia (which by 605 BCE had taken over the Assyrian empire) captured Jerusalem. In 586 BCE the walls of Jerusalem were battered down, and its buildings put to the torch by the Babylonians. The great Temple was emptied of its sacred treasures, the altar dismantled, and the building destroyed. Many Judaeans were taken to exile in Babylonia, where they were thenceforth known as "Jews," since they were from Judah.

The prophets interpreted these events as reasonable punishment by God for Judah's idolatry. Nevertheless, Isaiah and a later anonymous prophet prophesied that God would soon usher in a new era of peace and justice among all peoples, from his holy temple in Jerusalem.

I never could forget you.
See, I have engraved you
On the palms of My hands ...   *Isaiah 49: 15–16*

Return to Jerusalem

After fifty years of exile in Babylon, a small group of devoted Jews, probably fewer than fifty thousand, returned to their holy city. They were allowed to do so by the Persian king Cyrus. He authorized the rebuilding of the Temple in Jerusalem, which was completed in 515 BCE.

The second Temple became the central symbol to a scattered Jewish nation, most of whom did not return to Jerusalem from Babylon, which was now their home (and were thenceforth said to be living in the *Diaspora*, from the Greek word for "disperse").

A new emphasis on Temple rites developed, with an hereditary priesthood tracing its ancestry to Aaron. The priestly class, under the leadership of Ezra, a priest and a scribe, also undertook to revise the stories of the people, editing the Pentateuch to reveal the hand of God.

The Torah was now established as the spiritual and secular foundation of the dispersed nation. In approximately 430 BCE, Ezra the scribe set the precedent of reading for hours from the Torah scrolls in a public square. These "five books of Moses" were accepted as a sacred covenant.

As the Jews lived under foreign rule—Persian, Greek, Parthian, and then Roman—Judaism became somewhat open to cross-cultural religious borrowings. Concepts of Satan, the hierarchy of angels, reward or punishment in an afterlife, and final resurrection of the body on the Day of Judgment are thought by some scholars to have made their way into Jewish belief from the Zoroastrianism of the Persian Empire, for these beliefs were absent from earlier Judaic religion. However, they were not uniformly accepted. Greek lifestyle and thought were introduced into the Middle East by Alexander the Great in the fourth century BCE. The rationalistic, humanistic influences of Hellenism led many wealthy and intellectual Jews, including the priests in Jerusalem, to adopt a Hellenistic attitude of scepticism rather than unquestioning belief.

Tension between traditionalists and those embracing Greek ways came to a head during the reign of Antiochus IV Epiphanes, the 175–164 BCE ruler of Syria, the nation which then held political sovereignty over the land of Israel. Antiochus seems to have tried to achieve political unity by forcing a single Hellenistic culture on all his subjects, abolishing the Torah as the Jewish constitution, burning copies of the Torah, and killing families who circumcised their sons. The Maccabean rebellion, a revolt led by the Hasmon family of priests, called in Hebrew the Maccabees ("Hammers"), won a degree of independence for Judaea in 164 BCE. The successful rebellion led by the Maccabees established a new kingdom, once again called Israel, once again centered around Jerusalem, and ruled by the Hasmonean family. This kingdom lasted only until its conquest by the Roman general Pompey in 63 BCE, and was the last independent Jewish nation until the twentieth century.

Under the Hasmonean kings, three main groups of Jews formed in Judaea. One was the **Sadducees**, priests and wealthy businesspeople, conservatives intent on preserving the letter of the law. The **Pharisees** were more liberal citizens from all classes who sought to study the applications of Torah to everyday life. A third group was uncompromising in their piety and their disgust with what they considered a corrupted priesthood. Some of them retreated to a fortified compound at Qumran, near the Dead Sea, where they joined or formed the **Essenes**. Their leader was "the Teacher of Righteousness," a priest, reformer, and mystic whose name was not uttered. The library of this Essene community, now known as the Dead Sea Scrolls, was discovered near Qumran at the northwest end of the Dead Sea in 1947. From these two-thousand-year-old texts, we now know that the Essenes emphasized discipline, communal living, obedience, study, and spiritual preparation for the Day of Judgment they anticipated, the New Age when the "sons of light" would be victorious over the "sons of darkness."

Eventually the conflicts between the Sadducees and the Pharisees erupted into civil war. The Roman general Pompey was called in from Syria in 63 BCE to arbitrate the dispute, but he took over the country instead. There followed four centuries of oppressive Roman rule of Judaea, with the colonized Jews heavily taxed.

Under Roman rule, a popular belief grew among Jews that a **Messiah** would come at last to rescue the people from their sufferings. For example, a vision had reportedly been given to Daniel when the Jews were in exile in Babylon. Daniel foresaw that one "like a human being" (or "son of man") would come on heavenly clouds, and on him the white-haired, fiery-throned "Ancient of Days" would confer "everlasting dominion" over all people, a kingship "that shall not be destroyed."[13] By the first century CE, expectations had developed that through this Messiah, God would gather the chosen people and not only free them from oppression but also reinstate Jewish political sovereignty in the land of Israel. Then all nations would recognize that Israel's God is the God of all the world. The messianic end of the age, or end of the world, would be heralded by a period of great oppression and wickedness. Many felt that this time was surely at hand. There were some who felt that Jesus was the long-awaited Messiah.

Spurred by anti-Roman militias called **Zealots**, the Jews rose up in armed rebellion against Rome in 66 CE. The rebellion was suppressed. After heroic resistance, the Jewish defenders were slaughtered in the holy walled city of Jerusalem in 70 CE. The Roman legions destroyed the Jewish Temple in Jerusalem, leaving only a course of foundation stones still standing. This Temple has never been rebuilt; the foundation stones, called the western wall, have been a place of Jewish pilgrimage and prayer for twenty centuries. The Essene movement was apparently annihilated in this uprising.

A second disastrous revolt followed in 132–135 CE. Jerusalem was reduced to ruins, along with all Judaean towns. Those remaining Jews who had not been executed were forbidden to read the Torah, observe the Sabbath, or circumcise their sons. None were allowed to enter Jerusalem when it was rebuilt as the Roman city Aelia Capitolina, except on the anniversary of the destruction of the Temple, when they could pay to lean against all that remained of it—the western wall—and lament the loss of their sacred home. Judaea was renamed Palestine after the ancient Philistines. Judaism no longer had a physical heart or a geographic center.

Rabbinic Judaism

Judaism could have died then, as its people scattered throughout the Mediterranean countries and western Asia. One of the groups who survived the destruction of Judaea were the **rabbis**, inheritors of the Pharisee tradition. They are the founders of rabbinic Judaism, which has defined the major forms of Jewish practice over the last two thousand years. Another was the messianic movement that had formed up around Jesus of Nazareth, later known as Christianity. Between them they have kept the teachings of the Tanakh vibrantly alive.

The rabbis were teachers, religious decision-makers, and creators of liturgical prayer. No longer were there priests or Temple for offering sacrifices. The substitute for animal sacrifice was liturgical prayer and ethical behavior. Without the Jerusalem Temple, the community itself gained new importance. The people met in **synagogues**, which simply means "meeting places," to read the Torah and to worship communally, praying simply and directly to God. Synagogue services did not involve animal sacrifices, but rather prayer, song, and readings from the Torah. A *minyan*—a quorum of ten adult males—had to be present for community worship.

Everyone was taught the basics of the Torah as a matter of course, but many men also occupied themselves with deep study of the scriptures, from the age of five or six. Women were excluded or exempted from formal Torah study. Women's family responsibilities at home were considered primary for them; elsewhere they were to be subordinate to men. Literacy was highly valued for men, and this characteristic persisted through the centuries even in the midst of largely illiterate societies. It is said that in the afterlife one can see the Jewish sages still bent over their books studying. This is Paradise.

The revealed scriptures were closed; what remained was to interpret them as indications of God's word and will in history. This process continues to the present, giving Judaism a continually evolving quality in tandem with unalterable roots in the ancient books of Moses. Centering the religion in books and teachings rather than in a geographical location or a politically vulnerable priesthood has enabled the dispersed community to retain a sense of unity across time and space, as well as a common heritage of law, language, and practice.

The rabbis set themselves the task of thoroughly interpreting the Hebrew scriptures. Their process of study, called **midrash**, yielded two types of interpretation: legal decisions, called **halakhah** ("proper conduct"), and non-legal teachings, called **haggadah** (folklore, sociological and historical knowledge, theological arguments, ritual traditions, sermons, and mystical teachings).

In addition to delving into the meanings of the written Torah, the rabbis undertook to apply the biblical teachings to their contemporary lives, in very different cultural circumstances than those of the ancients, and to interpret scripture in ways acceptable to contemporary values. The model for this delicate task of living interpretation had been set by Hillel the Elder, who taught from about 30 BCE to 10 CE, probably overlapping with the life of Jesus. He was known as a humble and pious scholar who stressed loving relationships, good deeds, and charity toward the less-advantaged. He also established a valuable set of rules for flexible interpretation of Torah.

> *What is hateful to you, do not do to your neighbor:*
> *that is the entire Torah;*
> *the rest is commentary;*
> *go and learn it.*   *Hillel the Elder*[14]

This process of midrash yielded a vast body of legal and spiritual literature, known in Jewish tradition as the oral Torah. According to rabbinical tradition, God gave Moses two versions of the Torah at Sinai: the *written Torah*, which appears in the five books of Moses, and the *oral Torah*, a larger set of teachings which was memorized and passed down through the generations all the way to the early rabbis. After the fixing of the Jewish canon—the scriptures admitted to the Tanakh, in about 90 CE—the rabbinical schools set out to systematize all the commentaries and the oral tradition, which was continually evolving on the basis of expanded and updated understandings of the original oral Torah. In about 200 CE, Judah the Prince completed a terse edition of legal teachings of the oral Torah which was thenceforth known as the **Mishnah**.

The Mishnah became the basic study text for rabbinic academies in Judaea and Babylonia, and after several centuries, the Mishnah together with the rabbis' commentaries on it were organized into the Talmud. This is a vast compendium of law, midrash, and argument. It does not have a beginning, middle, and end in any traditional sense. It records disagreements among rabbis and sometimes leaves them standing. Drawing on "prooftexts" from the Torah, the rabbis came to different and often inventive conclusions.

Midrash is still open-ended, for significant commentaries and commentaries upon commentaries have continued to arise over the centuries. No single voice has dominated this continual study of the Torah and its interpretations. Rabbis often disagreed in their interpretations. These disagreements, sometimes between rabbis from different centuries, are presented together. This continual interweaving of historical commentaries, as if all Jewry were present at a single marathon Torah-study event, has been a significant unifying factor for the far-flung, often persecuted Jewish population of the world.

In the hearty process of exegesis, the rabbis have actually introduced new ideas into Judaism, while claiming that they were merely revealing what already existed in the scriptures. Notions of the soul are not found in the Tanakh, but they do appear in the Talmud and midrash. The way in which God is referred to and perceived also changes. In the early biblical narratives, the Lord appears to the patriarchs and Moses in dramatic forms, such as the burning bush and the smoking mountain. Later, the prophets are visited by angelic messengers and sometimes hear a divine inner voice speaking to them. In the rabbinical tradition God is presented in even more transcendent, less anthropomorphic ways. God's presence in the world, in relationship to the people, is called the **Shekhinah**, a feminine noun which often represents the nurturing aspect of God.

According to midrash, the Shekhinah came to the earth at creation but as a result of human wickedness she withdrew to the heavens, to be brought down by human acts of faithfulness, charity, and loving-kindness. God spoke to Moses from a burning thorn-bush, rather than some more lofty object, to demonstrate that there is no place where the Shekhinah cannot dwell.

It is noteworthy that despite the subordination of women to men in traditional Jewish legal codes, there are also directives regarding men's responsibility to women, and in general the responsibility of rulers and privileged members of society to insure legal justice for people of all classes and to provide for the material well-being of the lower classes, widows, orphans, and resident aliens. Accordingly, Jews have often been prominent in movements for social justice.

Judaism in the Middle Ages

In the early centuries of the Common Era, the Jewish population of the land of Israel declined. Many Jews established themselves beyond the boundaries of Rome among the Zoroastrian Persians in Mesopotamia. The city of Babylon, which already had a sizeable Jewish population dating back to the biblical exile, became the major center of Jewish intellectual activity, a position it would hold well into the tenth century. The authoritative Babylonian Talmud received its final editing in the middle of the sixth century CE.

Even when the Talmud was complete, the rabbinic enterprise continued. The administrators of the two great Babylonian rabbinic academies were often appealed to with difficult questions from far-flung Jewish communities. The questions and their answers, which were considered binding on all Jews, became a new and enduring form of legal writing, *Responsa* literature, which continues up to the present.

The Babylonian Jewish community continued to flourish after the Muslim conquests of the late seventh century, and when Baghdad became the capital city of the great Abassid empire in the eighth century, Jewish life concentrated around that city as well. Jews were treated relatively well under Islamic rule. Like Christians, they were recognized as a "People of the Book," and were allowed to maintain their religious traditions and run their communities autonomously as long as they paid a substantial head tax in acknowledgment of their subordinate status. Throughout the Islamic Middle East, many Jews were prosperous merchants, professionals, and craftsmen. In the early Middle Ages, in fact, Jews tended to dominate international trade because of their facility with languages and their ability to find supportive co-religionists in virtually any community.

Life under Islamic rule was also intellectually exciting for the Jewish community, which had rapidly adopted Arabic as its spoken language. During its early centuries, Islam was far advanced beyond Christian Europe in its explorations of science, medicine, philosophy, poetry, and the fine arts. Jews living in Muslim countries benefited from an atmosphere of cultural creativity and toleration, and themselves developed Jewish religious philosophy and Hebrew secular poetry. Many Jews were well-known physicians. Muslim Spain, in particular, where some Jews rose to high political position in Muslim courts, is renowned for its outstanding Hebrew poets and major philosophical and scientific Jewish writers.

From time to time, however, Jews were threatened by intolerant Muslim rulers and were forced to flee to other territories. The great scholar and physician Maimonides was forced to leave his ancestral home of Cordoba, Spain in the mid-twelfth century; he and his family eventually settled in Egypt. Considered one of the greatest of all Jewish intellectuals, Maimonides is particularly famous for his synthesis between reason and faith. In writings such as his *Guide of the Perplexed* he spoke on behalf of the rationality that had characterized Judaism since the dawning of the rabbinic age:

> *What is man's singular function here on earth? It is, simply, to contemplate abstract intellectual matters and to discover truth ... And the highest intellectual contemplation that man can develop is the knowledge of God and his unity.*[15]

Jews who lived in Christian countries were less exposed to the intellectual energy so vibrant in the Islamic world between the seventh and twelfth centuries. Christian Europe in those centuries was primarily a feudal agricultural society in which literacy mainly belonged to the Church. Jews, who were primarily merchants, were among the few town dwellers, and generally lived under charters of protection from the ruler of the area. In France and Germany, Jewish intellectual life flourished, but Christians assumed the financial functions. Jews became expendable, and throughout the later Middle Ages there is a steady pattern of expulsions of Jews from countries in which they had long lived.

The ultimate event of this kind was the expulsion of the Jews from Spain in 1492, when tens of thousands of Jews were forced to leave a country in which they had lived for over a thousand years. Others chose to convert to Christianity rather than to leave their homeland even though staying in Spain as *conversos* (converted Jews) would expose them to the dreaded Inquisition, which had been established in Spain in 1483. The Inquisition represented the Roman Catholic Church, and its mission was to discover perceived heretics within the Christian community. It had no power over Jews, but it did have jurisdiction over the large numbers of Jews who had converted to Christianity, whether voluntarily or by force, and who might be practicing their religion in secret. The Inquisition, which had the power to torture the accused and to execute the convicted, continued to function in Spain and in Spanish territories, including those in the New World, well into the eighteenth century.

There was further deterioration of Jewish life in Western Europe in the sixteenth and seventeenth centuries. After 1555, those Jews who still remained in some cities of Italy and Germany were forced to live in **ghettos**, special Jewish-only quarters often walled in and locked at night and during Christian holy days, to limit mixing between Christians and Jews. Despite the constriction and crowding, Jewish leaders ran the ghettos

according to talmudic law, providing for the needs of the poor, and foster-
ing Jewish study and scholarship.

During the later Middle Ages, Poland had become a haven for the
expelled Jews of Western Europe. They rapidly grew in numbers, finding
in their new home an enclave of peace and prosperity. By the sixteenth
century Eastern Europe had become the major European center of Jewish
life and scholarship. Jews lived an intensely religious life in villages and
towns that were almost completely Jewish, speaking Yiddish, a distinctive
Jewish language based on the medieval German they had spoken. In 1648,
the situation changed drastically with the revolt against Polish rule by
the peasants of the Ukraine. Associating Jewry with their Roman Catholic
Polish oppressors, the Russian Orthodox Cossacks led terrible massacres
against the Jews, followed by even more killing as Poland collapsed.

The eighteenth-century European movement called the Enlightenment
brought better conditions for the Jews in Western Europe. It played down
tradition and authority in favor of tolerance, reason, and material progress.
In such a rational atmosphere, restrictions on Jews began to decrease. The
French Revolution brought equality for the masses, including Jews living
in France, and in the course of the nineteenth century this trend slowly
spread to other European nations. Ghettos were torn down and some Jews
even ascended to positions of prominence in Western European society.
The Rothschild family, for instance, became international financiers, bene-
factors, and patrons of the arts.

Kabbalah and Hasidism

Mystical yearning has always been a part of Jewish tradition. The fervent
experience of and love for God is an undercurrent in several writings of the
biblical prophets, and is incorporated into the Talmud as well. Some mystical writings are found outside the biblical canon, in the extra-biblical collections of texts known as the *Apocrypha* and the *Pseudepigrapha*. The
apocryphal Book of Enoch describes the ascent to God as a journey
through seven heavenly spheres to an audience with the King of the celestial court. The core mystical encounter with indescribable sanctity is based
on the vision of the prophet Isaiah (Isaiah 6), and includes the chant of the
heavenly court, *"Kadosh, Kadosh, Kadosh"* ("Holy, Holy, Holy"), which is
included in all Jewish communal prayer.

In the Middle Ages, Jewish mystical traditions, known as **Kabbalah**,
began to be put into writing. The most important of these books is the
Zohar ("Way of Splendor"). The Zohar is a massive and complex offering of
stories, explanations of the esoteric levels of the Torah, and descriptions of
visionary practice and experiences. It depicts the world we perceive with
our senses as but a lower reflection of a splendid higher world. Mystics held
the Hebrew Bible in great esteem, but felt that it was not to be interpreted
literally. During the sixteenth century Kabbalah's most influential leader
was Isaac Luria. He explained creation as the beaming of the divine light
into ten special vessels, some of which were shattered by the impact
because they contained lower forces that could not bear the intensity of the

light. The breaking of the vessels spewed forth particles of evil as well as fragments of light into the world. According to Lurianic teachings, only the coming of the Messiah will bring *tikkun* ("correction" or "repair" of this situation), ending chaos and evil in the world. Humans have a great responsibility to prepare by regathering the "sparks of holiness" in the unclean realms to repair the holy vessels. To this end, Luria asked his followers to follow strict ascetic purification practices, prayer, observance of the commandments of the Torah, and chanting of sacred formulas.

Lurianic Kabbalism resurfaced in a very different form in the eighteenth century as **Hasidism**, the path of ecstatic piety. It developed in Ukraine and Poland, where Jews were subject to legal limitations, poverty-stricken, and fearing for their lives from riots and murders. The rabbis had little to offer them, retreating into academic debates about legal aspects of the Torah.

Into this grim setting came the Baal Shem Tov (1700–1760), a beloved healer and Hasidic teacher offering a joyful version of Jewish holiness. To him, Torah study and obedience to the letter of the law were not superior to deep-felt, pure-hearted prayer; everyone is capable of the highest enlightenment. He asserted that the divine could be found everywhere, in the present, thereby de-emphasizing the perennial waiting for a future Messiah. "Leave sorrow and sadness," he cried; "man must live in joy and contentment, always rejoicing in his lot."[16] Followers of the Baal Shem Tov worshipped through joyous songs and ecstatic, swaying prayer, and found God in the midst of the ghetto.

> *As the hand held before the eye conceals the greatest mountain, so the little earthly life hides from the glance the enormous lights and mysteries of which the world is full, and he who can draw it away from before his eyes, as one draws away a hand, beholds the great shining of the inner worlds.*
> *attributed to Reb Nachman of Bratzlav*

Soon an estimated half of all Eastern European Jews were followers of the Hasidic path. Spread of the teachings is credited to Dov Ber, who emphasized the importance of the **tzaddik**, or enlightened saint and teacher, called *rebb*e (or Reb) when ordained as a Hasidic spiritual guide. Ber urged Hasidim to take spiritual shelter with a tzaddik, whose prayers and wisdom would be more powerful than their own because of the tzaddik's personal relationship with God. This idea stirred enormous opposition from non-Hasidic leaders who believed that each Jew should be his or her own tzaddik. While the position of tzaddik became hereditary and was sometimes subject to exploitation by less-than-holy lineage carriers, such charismatic leadership remains a central element and perhaps one of the enduring attractions of modern Hasidism. The religious fervor associated with Hasidism clearly continues as an influence within Judaism.

American Judaism

Substantial Jewish immigration to the United States began in the mid-nineteenth century. By 1880, there were 250,000 Jews in the country, mostly of middle-class German background. Between 1881 and the early 1920s, additional Jewish immigration to the United States totalled two million, mainly Jews from Eastern Europe. This exodus was prompted by virulent anti-semitism in Russia, and endemic Jewish poverty in both Russia and eastern provinces of Austria–Hungary. If these Eastern European immigrants were religious, they tended to be extremely orthodox; if they were political, their politics were far to the left; socially, they tended to be craftsmen and laborers.

Today, the United States, with approximately six million Jews, has the largest Jewish population in the world. It continues to be a highly diverse and highly acculturated population.

Holocaust

For many Jews the defining event of the twentieth century was the Holocaust, the murder of almost six million European Jews by the Nazi leadership of Germany during the Second World War. These Jews constituted over a third of the Jewish people in the world and half of all Jews in Europe. The Holocaust is the overwhelmingly tragic event of Jewish history, and an indelible marker for all time of the depths of twentieth-century inhumanity and evil.

Anti-semitism, or prejudice against Jews, was part of Greco–Roman culture and had been present in Europe since the Roman Empire first adopted Christianity as its state religion in the fourth century CE. New and virulent strains of this disease appeared in Western Europe at the end of the nineteenth century. Racist theories spread that those of "pure" Nordic blood were genetically ideal, while Jews were a dangerous "mongrel" race.

Reactionary anti-Jewish feelings also resurfaced late in the nineteenth century in Russia and Eastern Europe, where Jews were growing in wealth and presence in higher educational circles. Jews were increasingly associated with left-wing movements pushing for social change, even though many Jewish socialists were non-observant Jews. Leon Trotsky, for example, was religiously indifferent but of Jewish ancestry. His leadership in the violent Bolshevik Revolution and the Red Army brought terrible reprisals, called *pogroms*, against Jewish communities by the White Russians in the civil war. Up to seventy thousand Jews were killed by unrestrained rioting mobs. After the Bolshevik Revolution, continuing social chaos in Russia led to massacres of an estimated quarter of a million Jews.

In the aftermath of Germany's defeat in World War I, and the desperate economic conditions that followed, Adolf Hitler's Nazi Party bolstered its popular support by blaming the Jews for all of Germany's problems. Germany, they claimed, could not regain its health until all Jews were stripped of their positions in German life or driven out of the country, eliminated for the sake of "racial hygiene."

Seeing the writing on the wall, many Jews, including eminent professionals, managed to emigrate, leaving their homes, their livelihood, and most of their possessions behind. Others stayed, hoping that the terrifying signs would be short-lived.

Beginning in 1935, German and then Austrian Jews were deprived of their legal and economic rights by the Nuremberg Laws. Jewish businesses were forcibly taken over by "Aryans." Polish Jews living in Germany were rounded up into trucks and conveyed to the Polish border, where Polish officials refused to take them in.

By 1939, 300,000 of Germany's 500,000 Jews, together with another 150,000 from Austria, had fled. Few countries, however, would allow them to enter. The United States government's attempts to arrange for systematic emigration were abandoned when Germany invaded Poland and then in rapid succession Denmark, Norway, Belgium, Holland, and France, thereby placing several million more Jews under Nazi control. Immediately, systematic oppression began, with orders to all Polish Jews to move into the towns, where walled ghettos were then created to confine them. Since all other jobs were taken away from them, they could do only menial labor.

Along the Russian front, special "Action Groups" were assigned to slaughter Jews, gypsies, and commissars as the German troops advanced, and to incite the local militia to do the same. One cannot comprehend the numbers of men, women, and children killed in these mass murders—34,000 at Babi Yar, 26,000 at Odessa, 32,000 at Vilna.

By 1942, large-scale death camps had been set up by the Nazis to facilitate the "Final Solution"—total extermination of all Jews in Europe, a population the Nazis estimated at eleven million. From the ghettos Jews were transported by cattle cars (in which many suffocated to death) from all over Europe to concentration camps. There they were starved, worked to death as slaves, tortured, "experimented" on, and/or shipped to extermination camps. Industrial-scale gas chambers were found to be the most efficient means of killing and also an impersonal way to get around the increasing unwillingness of German military personnel, as well as Polish and Russian prisoners of war, to kill so many Jewish men, women, and children.

No modern Jewish thinker can ignore the challenge which the Holocaust poses to traditional Jewish beliefs of an omnipotent and caring God. But Elie Wiesel, a survivor of the Nazi death camp at Auschwitz (in Poland), feels that the painful memories must be continually rekindled. He says that we cannot turn away from the questions about how it could happen, for genocidal actions are being undertaken against other minority groups in our times as well. As Wiesel points out:

> According to Jewish tradition, the death of one innocent person tarnishes the cosmos. Other people's tragedies are our tragedies. We must study the past, the horrors of the past and the melancholy of the past, if we are to be sensitive in the present. [In this] there are eternities of distress—the terrifying power of evil over innocence—but also some strength in the resolve of the victim never to become a killer.[17]

Zionism

Zionism is the Jewish movement dedicated to the establishment of a politically viable, internationally recognized Jewish state in the biblical land of

Israel. While political Zionism was a reaction to increasing anti-semitism in the late nineteenth century, it is a movement with deep roots in Judaism and Jewish culture. The desire to end the centuries-long exile from Zion (the site of the Jerusalem Temples) was a central theme in all of Jewish prayer and in many religious customs. Jewish messianism is focused around a descendant of King David who will return his united people to the land of Israel, where Jewish sovereignty will be eternally re-established in an atmosphere of universal peace.

Zionism became an organized international political movement under the leadership of the Viennese journalist Theodor Herzl. He believed that the Jews could never defend themselves against anti-semitism until they had their own nation. Herzl worked to provide political guarantees for Jewish settlement and to offer institutional support through the formation of various Zionist organizations. Simultaneously, pioneers, mainly secular Jews from Eastern Europe, began establishing a Jewish presence on the land of Palestine. The 1917 Balfour Declaration stated Britain's support for limited Jewish settlement in Palestine following World War I, when Britain expected to take over control of the region. While most Jews worldwide also applauded this Zionist victory, not all supported the movement. Most Reform Jews of that time believed the destiny of Jews was to be lived out among the Gentiles, where the Enlightenment had fueled hopes of a freer future and where Jews hoped they could be recognized as legitimate citizens of the countries in which they lived. Some support for Zionism came from traditional Orthodox Jews, but not all of the traditional community embraced the idea. Many felt it was God who had punished the people for their unfaithfulness by sending them away from the promised land; only God could end the exile.

By a United Nations decision in 1947, Palestine was partitioned into two areas, one to be governed by Jews and the other by Arabs. Political tensions between the two groups have been violently expressed again and again in the area. Israel declared the Law of Return, which welcomed all Jews who chose to resettle in their homeland, and continues to resettle Jews to this day. Israel established itself as a sovereign state in 1948, yet it still faces the hostility of many of its Arab neighbors and the large Palestinian population of the territories occupied in 1967. Many Jews are unhappy with the bitterness of the relations between two peoples who have so much in common. Some feel that Israel's Jews must not forget their own history of oppression and must maintain their compassion for the oppressed people among them.

In addition to pressures from neighbors, tensions exist within Israel. Jewish settlers have come to Israel from many divergent backgrounds. Those who are of Eastern European origin—the Ashkenazi who founded the state—tend to regard themselves as superior to Jewish settlers from other areas, such as Africa, Asia, and the Middle East. Ultra-Orthodox religious authorities insist upon strict observance of religious rituals, assert considerable control over education and politics in the nation, and claim that converts consecrated by Reform and Conservative rabbis in the United States are not really Jews at all. The Orthodox rabbis generally favor hard-line political policies in Israel. However, they do not represent the majority of Israeli citizens in religious terms, for only an estimated 15 percent of Israelis claim to live completely according to religious laws. The majority are non-Orthodox or secular, not religiously observant at all. There is also internal dissension over relationships with the Palestinian minority within Israel. By contrast with those who sympathize with the Palestinians' situation, some Jewish factions believe that the land has been promised to them by God and should never be given into Arab hands. A peaceful resolution of the conflicts in West Asia remains elusive.

Torah

It is difficult to outline the tenets of the Jewish faith. As we have seen, Jewish spiritual understanding has changed repeatedly through history. Rationalists and mystics have often differed. Since the nineteenth century, there has been disagreement between liberal and traditional Jews, to be discussed at the end of the chapter.

Nevertheless, there are certain major themes that can be extricated from the vast history and literature of Judaism. Jewish teachings are known as Torah. In its narrowest sense, Torah refers to the Five Books of Moses. On the next level, it means the entire Hebrew Bible and the Talmud, the written and the oral law. For some, "Torah" can refer to all sacred Jewish literature and observance. At the highest level, Torah is God's will, God's wisdom.

The One God

The central Jewish belief is monotheism. It has been stated in different ways in response to different cultural settings. But the central theme is that there is one Creator God, the "cause of all existent things."[18]

God is everywhere, even in the darkness, as David sings in Psalms:

Where can I escape from Your spirit?
Where can I flee from Your presence?
If I ascend to Heaven, You are there:
if I descend to Sheol [the underworld],
You are there too.

If I take wing with the dawn
to come to rest on the western
*   horizon,*
even there Your hand will be
*   guiding me,*
Your right hand will be
*   holding me fast.*
*   Psalm 139:7–14*

This metaphysical understanding of God's oneness is difficult to explain in linear language, which refers to the individual objects perceived by the senses. As the eleventh-century Spanish poet and mystical philosopher Ibn Gabirol put it, "None can penetrate ... the mystery of Thy unfathomable unity."[19]

One of the most elegant attempts to "explain" God's oneness has been offered by the great twentieth-century thinker Abraham Joshua Heschel. He links the idea of unity to eternity, explaining that in eternity, "past and future are not apart; here is everywhere, and now goes on forever." Time as we know it is only a fragment, "eternity broken in space." According to Heschel:

> The craving for unity and coherence is the predominant feature of a mature mind. All science, all philosophy, all art are a search after it. But unity is a task, not a condition. The world lies in strife, in discord, in divergence. Unity is beyond, not within, reality. . . . Yet God has not withdrawn entirely from this world. The spirit of this unity hovers over the face of all plurality, and the major trend of all our thinking and striving is its mighty intimation. The goal of all efforts is to bring about the restitution of the unity of God and world.[20]

> Plurality is incompatible with the sense of the ineffable. You cannot ask in regard to the divine: Which one? There is only one synonym for God: One.
>
> Abraham Joshua Heschel[21]

In traditional Judaism, God is often perceived as a loving Father who is nonetheless infinitely majestic, sometimes revealing divine power when the children need chastising.

Love for God

The essential commandment to humans is to love God. The central prayer in any Jewish religious service and the inscription on the *mezuza* at the doorpost of every traditional Jewish home is the *Shema Israel*:

> Hear, O Israel! The Lord is our God, the Lord alone. You shall love the Lord your God with all your heart and with all your soul and with all your might. Take to heart these instructions with which I charge you this day. Impress them upon your children. Recite them when you stay at home and when you are away, when you lie down and when you get up. Bind them as a sign on your hand and let them serve as a symbol on your forehead; inscribe them on the doorposts of your house and on your gates.
>
> Deuteronomy 6:4–9

Even Maimonides, the great proponent of reason and study, asserted the primacy of love for God. He emphasized that one should not love God from selfish or fearful motivations, such as receiving earthly blessings or avoiding problems in the life after death. One should study Torah and fulfill the commandments out of sheer love of God.

The sacredness of human life

Humans are the pinnacle of creation, created in the "image" of God, according to the account of Creation in Genesis 1. Jews do not take this passage to mean that God literally looks like a human. It is often interpreted in an ethical sense: that humans are so wonderfully endowed that they can mirror God's qualities, such as justice, wisdom, righteousness, and love.

All people are potentially equal; they are said to be common descendants of the first man and woman. But they are also potentially perfectible, and in raising themselves they uplift the world. God limited the divine power by giving humans free will, involving them in the responsibility for the world's condition, and their own. If we are suffering, according to the Talmud, we should examine our own deeds.

Martin Buber describes the relationship between God and humans as reciprocal:

> You know always in your heart that you need God more than everything; but do you not know too that God needs you—in the fulness of His eternity needs you? How would man exist, how would you exist, if God did not need him, did not need you? You need God, in order to be—and God needs you, for the very meaning of your life. . . . There is divine meaning in the life of the world . . . of human persons, of you and of me. . . . We take part in creation, meet the Creator, reach out to him, helpers and companions.[22]

Human life is sacred, rather than lowly and loathsome; Judaism celebrates the body. Sexuality within marriage is holy, and the body is honored as the instrument through which the soul is manifested on earth. Indeed, according to some thinkers, body and soul are an inseparable totality.

I praise You, for I am awesomely, wondrously made.   Psalm 139:14

Law

Because of the great responsibility of humankind, traditional Jews give thanks that God has revealed in the written and oral Torah the laws by which they can be faithful to the divine will and fulfill the purposes of Creation by establishing a Kingdom of God here on earth, in which all creatures can live in peace and fellowship. In the words of the biblical prophet Isaiah, speaking for God,

> The wolf and the lamb shall graze together,
> And the lion shall eat straw like the ox,
> And the serpent's food shall be earth.
> In all my sacred mount
> Nothing evil or vile shall be done.[23]

To the extent that traditional Jews act according to the Torah, they feel they are upholding their part of the ancient covenant with God.

The Torah, as indicated through rabbinic literature, is said to contain 613 commandments, or mitzvot (singular: **mitzvah**). Jewish law does not differentiate between sacred and secular life, so these include general ethical guidelines such as the Ten Commandments and the famous saying in Leviticus 29:18—"Love your fellow as yourself"—plus detailed laws concerning all aspects of life, such as land ownership, civil and criminal procedure, family law, sacred observances, diet, and ritual slaughter. The biblical book of Genesis also sets forth what is called the *Noahide Code* of seven universal principles for a moral and spiritual life: idolatry (worshipping many gods or images of God), blasphemy against God, murder, theft,

sexual behaviors outside of marriage, and cruelty to animals are all prohibited, and the rule of law and justice in society is affirmed as a positive
value. A Sabbath prayer, *Ahavat Olam*, thanks the Lord for all this guidance,
a token of the divine love, because the commandments "are our life and
the length of our days; on them we will meditate day and night."[24]

From the time of its final editing in Babylonia in the mid-sixth century
CE, the Talmud, together with its later commentaries, has served as a blueprint for Jewish social, communal, and religious life. Through the rabbinic
tradition, law became the main category of Orthodox Jewish thought and
practice, and learned study of God's commandments one of the central
expressions of faith.

Suffering and faith

Jewish tradition depicts the universe as being governed by an all-powerful,
personal God who intervenes in history to reward the righteous and
punish the unjust. Within this context, Jews have had considerable diffi-
culty in answering the eternal question: Why must the innocent suffer?
This question has been particularly poignant since the Holocaust.

The Hebrew Bible itself brings up the issue with the challenging parable
of Job, a blameless, God-fearing, and wealthy man. The story involves
Satan, depicted as an angel beneath God, who, in a conversation with God,
predicts that Job will surely drop his faith and blaspheme the Lord if he is
stripped of all his possessions. With God's assent, Satan tests Job by
destroying all that Job has, including his children and his health. On hearing the news of his children's deaths

> *Job arose, tore his robe, cut off his hair, and threw himself on the ground
> and worshipped. He said, "Naked came I out of my mother's womb, and
> naked shall I return there; the Lord has given, and the Lord has taken
> away, blessed be the name of the Lord."[25]*

With an itchy inflammation covering him from head to foot, Job begins
to curse his life and to question God's justice. In the end, Job acknowledges
not only God's power to control the world but also his inscrutable wisdom,
which is beyond human understanding. God then rewards him with long
life and even greater riches than he had before the test.

Debate over the meanings of this story, which came from the esoteric
Wisdom tradition, has continued over the centuries. One rabbinical
interpretation is that Satan was cooperating with God in helping Job grow
from fear of God to love of God. Another is that faith in God will finally
be rewarded in this life, no matter how severe the temporary trials.
Another is that those who truly desire to grow toward God will be asked
to suffer more, that their sins will be expiated in this life so they can enjoy
the divine bliss in the life to come. Such interpretations assume a personal,
all-powerful, loving God doing what is best for the people, even when
they cannot understand God's ways. In such belief, God is seen as always
available, like a shepherd caring for his sheep, no matter how dark the
outer circumstances.

> *Though I walk through a valley of deepest darkness,*
> *I fear no harm, for You are with me;*
> *Your rod and Your staff – they comfort me.*
>
> *Psalm 23:4*

On the other hand, oppression and then the Holocaust have led some Jews to complain to God in anguish. They, too, feel close to God, but in a way that allows them to scream at God, as it were. In questioning the justice of history, they hold God responsible for what is inexplicably monstrous. But even in the Holocaust, there were those who held fast to hope for better times. As they walked to their death in Nazi gas chambers, some were reciting the hymn *Ani maamin*: "I believe with complete faith in the coming of the Messiah, and even though he may delay, nevertheless I anticipate every day that he will come."[26]

Sacred Practices

The ideal is to remember God in everything one does, through prayer and keeping the commandments. These commandments are not other-worldly. Many are rooted in the body, and spiritual practices often engage all the senses in awareness of God.

Boys are ritually circumcised when they are eight days old, to honor the seal of God's commandment to Abraham. Orthodox Jews consider women ritually unclean during their menstrual periods and for seven days afterwards. They are not to have sexual intercourse with their husbands, and at the end of this forbidden period Orthodox Jewish women undertake complete immersion in a **mikva**, a special deep bath structure, symbolizing their altered state. Marital sex is sacred, with the **Sabbath** night the holiest time for making love. By contrast, adultery is strictly forbidden as one of the worst sins against God, for Jewish tradition is extremely concerned with maintaining pure lines of descent.

What one eats is also of cosmic significance, for according to Torah, some foods are definitely unclean. For example, the only ritually acceptable, or **kosher**, meats, are those from warmblooded animals with cloven hoofs who chew their cuds, such as cows, goats, and sheep. Poultry is kosher, except for birds of prey, but shellfish are not. Meat is also kosher only if it has been butchered in the traditional humane way with an extremely sharp, smooth knife by an authorized Jewish slaughterer. Great pains are taken to avoid eating blood; meat must be soaked in water and then drained on a salted board before cooking. Meat and milk cannot be eaten together, and separate dishes are maintained for their preparation and serving.

These dietary instructions are laid out in the biblical book of Leviticus, which quotes God as saying to Moses and Aaron, "For I the Lord am He who brought you up from the land of Egypt to be your God: you shall be holy, for I am holy."[27] The rules of diet, if strictly followed, give Jews a

Living Judaism

Herman Taube is a poet, Professor Emeritus of Jewish Studies and Yiddish Literature, and volunteer chaplain to nursing home patients. He emigrated to the United States in 1947 from Poland with his wife, who had earlier been sent to a concentration camp where her younger sister and mother died. During World War II, Herman was a medic working side by side with Russian Orthodox and Muslim doctors in Uzbekhistan to aid people in a refugee camp. He says,

"If you do charitable work—if you help in clinics, if you help unfortunate children, if you go into the jails to help inmates—this is God's work. It is not the responsibility of the rich only to help the poor. Even the poorest man has to give charity. This is the law in Jewish religion.

Maimonides says, and Jews are saying every morning in their prayers, that a human being has to believe every day in the coming of the Messiah. Messiah does not come with a long beard and a donkey. Messiah can be you. Messiah can be a man on the street who helps a fellow human being. In the Hebrew Bible, in the Talmud, there are quotations indicating that the Messiah will come in a generation which is full of innocence or full of guilt—one of the two. And he will spiritually lead the people away from evil. I think this will become a messianic era.

Look at the fall of communism, the fall of fascism in our generation. Something is changing. You don't have to go far—look at Washington. You see good people living in the streets, with no roof over their head. They cannot make a meal. On the other side, you see those big parties where people spend millions. There is a need for a messianic age, a need for a better world.

A reporter asked me, 'Can you believe in God after the Holocaust?' Belief is not something static. My wife and I sometimes ask, 'Where was God?' A million and a half Jewish children were killed. Little boys and girls who were just learning how to say, 'Mama,' and the grandmother said, 'How big is the baby?' and tried to pick up their hands. And this child was taken and thrown into a lamppost. So yes, there are questions. We have no answers.

Why did Polish people, nuns and plain peasants risk their lives to save Jewish people, when they knew that for saving a Jew's life their house would be burned down? And their children were taken into forced labor. Why did the people of Assisi save sixty Jewish people under the noses of the Nazis? The Vatican wasn't too helpful, didn't speak up, but they, the simple people, risked their lives. So there is goodness in the world, too. There is goodness and Godness in the hearts of those people.

The Talmud says God said, 'You don't believe in me? So you don't believe in me. But keep my commandments. Care for the poor and for the widows.' This is exactly what a lot of those Messiahs are doing.

My wife doesn't like to be interviewed. It's like pulling off a bandage from an open wound. Even after forty-five years, it comes to the holidays and she's missing her mother and her sister. That unbelievable guilt feeling: Why did we survive and they die?

I believe in God. There is a Power above us that rules our life. We do not see it, we cannot comprehend it. But there is something. I do not deny Him—or Her; maybe it's a Her. And I don't deny my roots."

feeling of special sacred identity and link them to the et[e] Torah.

Some contemporary Jews feel that consciousness a[t] can be extended to environmental considerations. To t[.] box in which a cheeseburger is sold at fast-food places is as [in]c lem as the mixing of meat and milk. Nuclear power-generated electr[ic..] used for cooking might itself be non-kosher, so long as there is no safe provision for disposing of nuclear waste.

For traditional Jews, the morning begins with a prayer before opening one's eyes, thanking God for restoring one's soul. The hands must then be washed before reciting blessings and, for all traditional male Jews, putting a special fringed rectangle of cloth around the neck. It is usually worn under the clothes as a reminder of the privilege of being given divine commandments. For weekday morning prayers men also put on **t'fillin**, or phylacteries, small leather boxes containing biblical verses about the covenant with God, on the forehead and on the upper arm, held against the heart, in fulfillment of the Shema commandment, as literally understood: "Bind them [the Shema's words about the primacy of love for God] as a sign on your hand and let them serve as a symbol on your forehead." Traditional Jewish men also wear a fringed prayer shawl (**talit**) whose fringes act as reminders of God's commandments, and keep their heads covered at all times, if possible.

Traditionally, prayers are recited on waking and at bedtime. In addition, three prayer services are chanted daily in a synagogue by men if there is a *minyan* (quorum of ten). Women can say them also, but they are excused from rigid schedules because their household responsibilities are considered important. Jews are also expected to give thanks continually. One should recite a hundred benedictions to God every day.

The Jewish Sabbath runs from sunset Friday night to sunset Saturday night, because the Jewish "day" begins with nightfall. The Friday night service welcomes the Sabbath as a bride and is often considered an opportunity to drop away the cares of the previous week so as to be in a peaceful state for the day of rest. Just as God is said to have created the world in six days and then rested on the seventh, all work is to cease when the Sabbath begins. Ruth Gan Kagan describes the experience:

I am aware of a wave of peace flooding my heart and that transparent veils of tranquility are covering the World around me. A moment before I would probably be rushing around trying to finish all the preparations, . . . but all this tension and rush vanishes when the fixed moment arrives; not a second earlier nor a second later. The moment I light the Sabbath candles and usher in the Sabbath spirit everything undergoes a magical transformation.

The Queen has arrived. In Her presence there are not even talks of weekday matters. The mind quiets down leaving business, plans and worries behind as one quietly walks to the synagogue for services; the sky is aglow with the colours of sunset; the bird-song is suddenly more present; the people of the congregation gather to welcome in the Sabbath in song, prayer and silence.

> *Coming home, the stars are out; in a religious neighborhood, no*
> *travelling cars break the descended peace; children are holding their*
> *parents' hands, walking in the middle of the road without fear of*
> *death.*[28]

The Saturday morning service incorporates public and private prayers, singing, and the reading of passages from the Pentateuch and Prophets sections of the Hebrew Bible. Torah scrolls are kept in a curtained ark on the wall facing Jerusalem. They are hand-lettered in Hebrew and are treated with great reverence. It is a great honor to be "called up" to read from the Torah.

More liberal congregations may place emphasis on an in-depth discussion of the passage read. Often it is examined not only from an abstract philosophical perspective but also from the point of its relevance to political events and everyday attempts to live a just and humane life. Torah study, and study of all Jewish literature, is highly valued as a form of prayer in itself, and synagogues usually have libraries for this purpose, sometimes in the same space that is used for worship.

In Hasidic congregations, the emphasis falls on the intensity of praying, or **davening**, even in saying fixed prayers from the prayer book. Some sway their bodies to induce the self-forgetful state of ecstatic communion with the Loved One. Others quietly shift their attention from earthly concerns to "cleave to God." The rabbinical tradition states the ideal in prayer: "A person should always see himself as if the Shekhinah is confronting him."[29]

In addition to or instead of going to a service welcoming the Sabbath, observant families usually begin the Sabbath eve with a special Friday night dinner. The mother lights candles to bring in the Sabbath light; the father recites a blessing over the wine. Special braided bread, *challah*, is shared as a symbol of the double portions of manna in the desert. The rituals help to set a different tone for the day of rest, as do commandments against working, handling money, traveling except by foot, lighting a fire, cooking, and the like. The Sabbath day is set aside for public prayer, study, thought, friendship, and family closeness, with the hope that this renewed life of the spirit will then carry through the week to come.

It is customary to recognize coming of age, at thirteen, in Jewish boys by the **Bar Mitzvah** ("son of the commandment") ceremony. The boy has presumably undertaken some religious instruction, including learning to pronounce Hebrew, if not always to understand it. He is called up to read a portion from the Torah scroll and recite a passage from one of the books of the prophets, in Hebrew, and then perhaps to give a short teaching about a topic from the reading. Afterwards there may be a simple *kiddush*, a celebration with blessing of wine and sweet bread or cake, but a big party is more likely. This custom of welcoming the boy to adult responsibilities has been extended to girls in non-Orthodox congregations in the **Bat Mitzvah** ("daughter of the commandment").

Holy Days

Judaism follows an ancient lunar calendar of annual holidays and memorials. The spiritual year begins with the High Holy Days of Rosh Hashanah and Yom Kippur. *Rosh Hashanah* (New Year's Day), a time of spiritual renewal, is celebrated on the first two days of the seventh month (around the fall equinox). For thirty days prior to Rosh Hashanah, each morning synagogue service brings blowing of the *shofar* (a ram's horn that produces an eery, unearthly blast) to remind the people that they stand before God. At the service on the eve of Rosh Hashanah, a prayer is recited asking that all humanity will remember what God has done, that there will be honor and joy for God's people, and that righteousness will triumph while "all wickedness vanishes like smoke."[30]

Yom Kippur, ten days after Rosh Hashanah, is the Day of Atonement. Historically, this was the only time when the high priest entered the Holy of Holies in the Temple of Jerusalem, and the only time that he would pronounce the sacred name of the Lord, YHWH, in order to ask for forgiveness of the people's sins. Today, there is an attempt at personal inner cleansing and individuals must ask pardon from everyone they may have wronged during the past year. People fast for twenty-four hours as a sign of self-denial and repentance.

Sukkot is a fall harvest festival. A simple outdoor booth (a *sukkah*) is built and decorated as a dwelling place of sorts for seven days. Usually this is done as a ritual act, but seeking a deeper experience of the meaning of Sukkot, some contemporary Jews are actually attempting to live in the *sukkah* they construct. Michael Lerner, a major figure in contemporary Jewish renewal, relates,

> *Living in a temporary shelter—particularly one with a water-permeable roof made of twigs, reeds, vines, tree branches, and other forms of vegetation arranged in such a way that one can see through them to the stars—has a special effect of reconnecting urban and suburban dwellers to the natural order, and to the transitory nature of our carefully constructed forms of material security.*[31]

The fragile home reminds the faithful that their real home is in God, who sheltered their ancestors on the way from Egypt to the promised land of Canaan. Some contemporary groups also pray for peace amid our vulnerability to nuclear war. Participants hold the *lulav* (a bundle made of a palm branch, myrtle twigs, and willow twigs) in one hand and the *etrog* (a citrus fruit) in the other and wave them together toward the four compass directions, earth and sky, praising God and acknowledging him as the unmoving center of creation. There is an offering of water, precious in the desert lands of the patriarchs, and great merrymaking. During the second Temple days, the ecstatic celebration even included burning of the priests' old underclothes. The last day of the seven-day Sukkot festival is *Simhat Torah* ("Joy in Torah"), ending the yearly cycle of Torah readings, from Creation to the death of Moses, and beginning again.

Near the winter solstice, the darkest time of the year, comes *Hanukkah*, the Feast of Dedication. Each night for eight nights, another candle is lit on a special candle holder. The amount of light gradually increases like the lengthening of sunlight. Historically, Hanukkah was a celebration of the victory of the Maccabean Rebellion against the attempt by Antiochus to force non-Jewish practices on the Jewish people. According to legend, when the Jews regained access to the Temple, they found only one jar of oil left undefiled, still sealed by the high priest. It was only enough to stay alight for one day, but by a miracle, the oil stayed burning for eight days. Many Jewish families also observe the time by nightly gift-giving, as rewards for Torah study. The children have their own special Hanukkah pastimes, such as "gambling" for nuts with the *dreidel*, a spinning top with four letters on its sides as an abbreviation of the sentence "A great miracle happened there."

As the winter rainy season begins to diminish in Israel, Jews everywhere celebrate the reawakening of nature on *Tu B'shvat*. Observances lavish appreciation on a variety of fruits and plants. In Israel, the time is now marked by planting of trees to help restore life to the desert.

On the full moon of the month before spring comes *Purim*. It theoretically commemorates the legend of Esther, queen of Persia, and Mordecai, who saved their fellow Jews from destruction by the evil viceroy Haman. It has been linked to Mesopotamian mythology about the goddess Ishtar, whose spring return brings joy and fertility. Purim is a bawdy time of dressing in costumes and mocking life's seriousness, and the jokes frequently poke fun at sacred Jewish practices. As the story of Esther is read from an ornate scroll, the congregation responds with noisy stomping, rattles, horns, and whistles whenever Haman's name is read.

The next major festival is *Pesach*, or *Passover*, which celebrates the liberation from bondage in Egypt and the spring-time advent of new life. It was the tenth plague, death to all first-born sons of the Egyptians, which finally brought the Pharaoh to relent. The Israelites were warned to slaughter a lamb for each family and mark their doors with its blood so that the angel of death would pass over them. They were to roast the lamb and eat it with unleavened bread and bitter herbs. So quickly did they depart that they didn't even have time to bake the bread, which is said to have baked in the sun as they carried it on their heads. The beginning of Pesach is still marked by a **Seder** dinner, with the eating of unleavened bread (*matzah*) to remember the urgency of the departure, and bitter herbs as a reminder of slavery, so that they would never impose it on other peoples. Also on the table are *charoset* (a sweet fruit and nut mixture, a reminder of the mortar that the enslaved Israelites molded into bricks) and salt water (a reminder of the tears of the slaves) into which parsley or some other plant (a reminder of spring life) is dipped and eaten. Children ask ritual questions about why these things are done, as basic religious instruction. A movement for contemporary liturgical renewal has yielded many new scripts for the Seder—such as special **liturgies** for feminists, for secular Zionists, and for co-celebration of Pesach with Muslims.

Early summer brings *Shavuot*, traditionally identified with the giving of the Torah to Moses at Mount Sinai and the people's hearing of the voice of God. It is likely that Shavuot was initially a summer harvest festival that later was linked with the revelation of the Torah. In Israeli kibbutzim the old practice of bringing the first fruits to God has been revived. Elsewhere, the focus is on reading the Ten Commandments and on presenting the Torah as a marriage contract between God and Israel.

Then come three weeks of mourning for the Temples, both of which were destroyed on the ninth day of the month of Av (July or August), *Tisha Be-Av*. This is traditionally a time of fasting and avoidance of joyous activities. Some feel that there is no longer cause for mourning because even though the Temple has not been rebuilt, the old city of Jerusalem has been recaptured. Others feel that we are all still in exile from the state of perfection.

Contemporary Judaism

Within the extended family of Judaism, there are many groups, many different focuses, and many areas of disagreement. Currently disputed issues include the degree of adherence to Torah and Talmud, requirements for conversion to Judaism, the extent of the use of Hebrew in prayer, and the full participation of women.

Major branches today

Judaism, like all modern religions, has struggled to meet the challenge of secularization: the idealization of science, rationalism, industrialization, and materialism. The response of the *Orthodox* has been to stand by the Hebrew Bible as the revealed word of God and the Talmud as the legitimate oral law. Orthodox Jews feel that they are bound by the traditional rabbinical halakhah, as a way of achieving closeness to God. But within this framework there are great individual differences. Orthodoxy includes mystics and rationalists, Zionists and anti-Zionists. The Orthodox also differ greatly in their tolerance for other Jewish groups and in their degree of accommodation of the surrounding secular environment. Thus, while some Hasidic groups practice complete withdrawal from the secular world and the rest of the Jewish community, others, such as the *Lubavich Hasidim* (originally from Lithuania, with strong communities in many countries), are devoted to extending their message to as many Jews as possible, using all the tools of modern technology for their sacred purpose. The Lubavich, who offer highly structured and nurturing communities in which male–female roles are strictly defined and an all-embracing piety and devotion to a charismatic leader are universally shared, have had considerable success in attracting young Jews to their way of life. They are seen as strong role models, and present themselves as true Jews. This return to a structured practice of Judaism has surprised many observers. When the seventh Lubavich rabbi came to the United States, he was discouraged by other Jewish rabbis from trying to interest people in Torah in a country where so many had abandoned their tradition and were living secular lives. To the contrary, the emphasis on Torah proved to have great appeal and encouraged many to return to their Jewish roots.

Janice Perlman

Brilliant and hardworking, Dr. Janice Perlman is a renowned urban anthropologist and political scientist who has created "Mega-Cities," a global organization seeking to make urban life sustainable and livable by sharing innovative solutions to urban problems, celebrating successes, and supporting grassroots leadership in the world's largest cities. Mega-Cities tries to increase political participation to address urban problems such as severe environmental stress, great gaps between rich and poor, fragmented planning, and budgetary strains in rapidly growing cities. In the 1970s she had gained academic fame as author of *The Myth of Marginality: Urban Poverty and Politics in Rio de Janeiro*. It was based on her own research among Brazilian villagers who had been lured to city life.

Janice identifies her passion for uplifting people at the margins of society as being an outgrowth of her Jewish roots. She is not an observant Jew in the sense of worshiping at a synagogue. But she and her Christian husband Rick Spreyer continue her family traditions, such as lighting candles on Hanukkah. Janice explains,

Rick and I sing the traditional blessing in Hebrew, he having learned it from me, I having learned it from my mother, who now says she doesn't know it, and none of us knowing exactly what it means. Yet it, and the Jewish religion, were absolutely fundamental in shaping the person that I am and the values that I hold dear. Being Jewish has affected my passion for social transformation and social justice; my identification with migrants and so-called "marginal" elements, and

my commitment to and natural solidarity with the struggles of poor and disenfranchised communities around the world.[32]

Janice's paternal grandparents came from Rumania, her mother's mother from a close-knit Jewish community in Kiev, and her mother's father from Poland. Both sets of grandparents escaped from the twentieth-century pogroms in Europe to the United States. All those in their families who did not escape were killed in the pogroms.

Janice's parents were both born in America, and she and her brother were naturally raised within Jewish cultural traditions, if not overtly within the religious traditions. Both parents inculcated in Janice and her brother the Jewish value placed on studying, learning, and knowledge. Her parents met while doing scientific research at the Rockefeller Institute in New York, where the Jewish intellectuals of the time were very excited about the promise of the Russian Revolution and hoped to see a more equitable model of society emerge as a result.

Despite persecution and assimilation, the traditional Jewish ideal of uplifting society still glimmers deep within the hearts of many contemporary Jews, and quite brightly so in Janice's case. Looking ahead to the increasingly urban future, she says,

Given the deeply vested interests in the status quo, how can we find the political will for urban transformation in a non-revolutionary situation? Together— only together—we can do something to alleviate need. I know we will.[33]

The *Reform* movement, at the other end of the religious spectrum from Orthodoxy, began in eighteenth-century Germany as an attempt to help modern Jews appreciate their religion rather than regarding it as antiquated, meaningless, or even repugnant. In imitation of Christian churches, synagogues were redefined as places for spiritual elevation, with choirs added for effect, and the Sabbath service was shortened and translated into the vernacular. Halakhic observances were re-evaluated for their relevance to modern needs, and Judaism was understood as an evolving, open-ended religion rather than one fixed forever by the revealed Torah. Reform congregations are numerous in North America where they are continually engaged in a "creative confrontation with modernity." Rather than exclusivism, Reform rabbis cultivate a sense of the universalism of Jewish values. It is felt that only by making Judaism meaningful to modern tastes and modern minds can it survive.

Given this approach, it is not surprising that Reform Judaism, particularly in North America, has been at the forefront in the establishment of interfaith dialogue and civic cooperation with non-Jewish groups. Reform Judaism is not fully accepted in Israel, where the Israeli Rabbinate, which has considerable civil and political power, does not recognize the authority of non-Orthodox rabbis. For example, Israeli religious officials are reluctant to acknowledge Reform converts as true Jews who can be Israeli citizens.

Conservative Judaism is the largest Jewish movement in the United States. While Conservative Jews feel they are totally dedicated to traditional rabbinical Judaism, at the same time they are restating and restructuring it in modern terms so that it is not perceived as a dead historical religion. To appeal to intelligent would-be believers, Conservative Judaism has sponsored critical studies of Jewish texts from all periods in history. They believe that Jews have always searched and added to their laws, liturgy, midrash, and beliefs to keep them relevant and meaningful in changing times. Some of the recent changes introduced are acceptance of riding to a synagogue for Sabbath services and acceptance of women into rabbinical schools as candidates for ordination as rabbis.

Rabbi Mordecai Kaplan, a highly influential American thinker who died in 1983, branched off from Conservatism (which initially rejected his ideas as too radical), and founded a movement called *Reconstructionism*. Kaplan held that the Enlightenment had changed everything and that strong measures were needed to preserve Judaism in the face of rationalism. Kaplan asserted that "as long as Jews adhered to the traditional conception of Torah as supernaturally revealed, they would not be amenable to any constructive adjustment of Judaism that was needed to render it viable in a non-Jewish environment."[34] He defined Judaism as an "evolving religious civilization," both cultural and spiritual, and asserted that the Jewish people are the heart of Judaism. The traditions exist for the people, and not vice versa, he said. Kaplan denied that the Jewish people were specially chosen by God, an exclusivist idea. Rather, they had chosen to try to become a people of God. Kaplan created a new prayer book, deleting traditional portions he and others found offensive, such as derogatory references to women and Gentiles, references to physical resurrection of the body, and passages describing God as rewarding or punishing Israel by manipulating natural phenomena such as rain. Women were accepted fully into synagogue participation.

In addition to those who affiliate with a religious movement, there are many Jews who identify themselves as secular Jews, affirming their Jewish origins and maintaining various Jewish cultural traditions while eschewing religious practice. There are also significant numbers of people of Jewish birth, particularly in North America and Western Europe, whose Jewish identity is vestigial at best, and unlikely to survive in future generations. The possibilities for total assimilation into Western culture are evident in statistics indicating that over fifty percent of Western Jews marry non-Jews. In most cases, neither spouse in such a marriage converts, and research indicates that it is highly unlikely that their children will identify as Jews. Thus, one of the great ironies of the liberty offered to the Jewish people by democratic secular societies is the freedom to leave Judaism as well as to affirm it.

Jewish feminism

In contrast to the option of leaving Judaism, some feminists are coming back to religious observance, but not in the traditional mold, which they regard as patriarchal and sexist. Women have begun to take an active role in claiming their rights to full religious participation—to be counted as part of a *minyan*, for instance, to sit with the men rather than behind a curtain in the synagogue, to be ordained as rabbis. They are also redefining Judaism from a feminist perspective. Part of this effort involves trying to reconstruct the history of significant Jewish women, for the Torah was written down by men who devoted far more space to the doings of men than of women. There are hints, for instance, that there were powerful prophetesses such as Miriam and Huldah, but very little information is given about them.

Among those who champion the rights of women to participate equally with men in ritual and prayer, there is also an ongoing effort to revise liturgical language in gender-neutral and gender-inclusive ways, both in reference to worshippers, and in reference to God. The Hebrew scriptures describe God as both female and male, validating new translations from the Hebrew which use gender-neutral language. As an example of the shift from male-centered to gender-neutral language, the biblical passage: "And God created man in his own image, in the image of God created He them; male and female created He them"[35] has been re-translated thus: "Thus God created us in the divine image, creating us in the image of God, creating us male and female."[36]

Feminist Susannah Heschel explains that changing God-language has profound implications for one's spirituality:

> Whereas God may be neither male nor female, our language for God is overwhelmingly and decidedly male. The consequences of that exclusivity are theological and practical. For instance, we might assume that if God were imaged as female, it might be difficult to justify women's relegation behind the mehitza as preventing men from being distracted during their prayers. . . . We might also speculate about the impact on our experience at prayer if God were imaged as Mother as well as Father. How would the experience of Yom

*Kippur be different if we asked forgiveness from "Our Mother, Our Queen,"
rather than "Our Father, Our King"?*[37]

There is also a feminist critique of women's position in the state of Israel. Women among the early Zionist settlers envisioned a society in which men and women would work side by side and each apply their full capabilities to the creation of a new society. Even though laws were created that supported gender equality, traditional sexual divisions of labor were perpetuated, especially once the Orthodox parties took a major role in the formation and governance of the state. Judith Plaskow links the discrimination against women in Israel to the disempowerment of other minorities, including Palestinians and non-Ashkenazi Jews. She argues passionately,

> *The recognition of diverse constituencies as parts of larger communities involves an obligation to redefine communal life as the sum of all pieces. When one part has been accustomed to speaking for the whole—male Ashkenazi Jewish Israelis for Israelis, elite male Jews for Jews, middle-class white feminists for women—this definition may mean dislodging long-fixed patterns of dominance with difficult and dramatic results.*[38]

Jewish renewal

Both men and women from varied backgrounds are being attracted to newly revitalized expressions of Jewish spirituality. After the Holocaust, many Jews retreated from religious observance to avoid being conspicuous.

Although anti-semitism continues to flare up here and there, many non-Jews are developing sensitivity against negative stereotyping of Jews. The Evangelical Lutheran Church in America has issued an historic public apology for the anti-Jewish writings of Martin Luther, the father of Protestant Christianity:

> *As did many of Luther's own companions in the sixteenth century, we reject this violent invective, and yet more do we express our deep and abiding sorrow over its tragic effects on subsequent generations. In concert with the Lutheran World Federation, we particularly deplore the appropriation of Luther's words by modern anti-Semites for the teaching of hatred toward Judaism or toward the Jewish people in our day. . . . We recognize in anti-Semitism a contradiction and an affront to the Gospel, a violation of our hope and calling, and we pledge this church to oppose the deadly working of such bigotry.*[39]

In post-Soviet Russia, where under Stalin Jews had been so persecuted that only a few rabbis remained in all of Russia, there are now Jewish seminaries and universities, schools, and kindergartens. Rabbi Dovid Karpov, whose congregation serves one hundred and fifty free hot meals a day in Moscow, says that Judaism has begun to flourish again after years of secrecy and danger:

> *Now we can celebrate holidays such as Hanukkah openly. It is not yet a mass movement, but there are more people than you can count on your*

fingers. We feel that soon we will see the fruit of our work. Judaism survives despite all the persecutions. The new world is coming very soon and it will have a very different form. The Messiah is coming. The time will soon come when we will have the peace that everyone is waiting for. It will happen sooner than anyone can imagine.[40]

Contemporary Jewish renewal is not just an absence of fear. It is an active search for personal meaning in the ancient rituals and scriptures, and the creation of new rituals for our times. There are now numerous small *havurot*, or communities of Jews, who are not affiliated with any formal group but get together on a regular basis to worship and celebrate the traditions. They favor a democratic organization and personal experience, and are often engaged in trying to determine what parts of the traditions to use and how. Some incorporate study groups, continuing the ancient intellectual tradition of grappling with the ethical, philosophical, and spiritual meanings of the texts. Some are bringing fresh ideas to traditional celebrations, so that they are actively transformational rather than simply matters of empty habit.

From highly conservative to highly liberal quarters, there are now attempts to renew the ancient messianic ideal of Judaism, that by its practice the world might be healed. Michael Lerner, a disciple of Abraham Heschel and editor of the magazine *Tikkun* (a Hebrew word that refers to the healing and transformation of the world) explains,

A new generation of teachers, rabbis, community activists, and thinkers has begun to reclaim the central insights of Judaism. It is no wonder that after having faced massive and staggering destruction and dislocations, many Jews feel spiritually and emotionally dead. We sought refuge from pogroms and genocide in societies that were themselves spiritually and emotionally dead, and we did our best to assimilate our Judaism to these societies because we hoped that inconspicuousness would keep us from becoming targets. It has taken many decades for Jews to feel secure enough to begin to renew the spiritual tradition. We are witnessing today the miraculous regeneration of the primary ideals of Judaism that have been part of our tradition since Abraham and Moses. ... In every historical period, there has been a recreation of the tradition through commentary, Midrash, and creative reinterpretation. ...

After reading the Torah on Shabbat morning, Jews return the Torah to its ark or resting point, and in fervent devotion sing a moving prayer: "It is a tree of life to those who hold fast to it, and its precepts are right. Its paths are paths of pleasantness, and all its paths are peace. Return us to thee, Lord, and we shall return."[41]

Suggested Reading

Ariel, David S., *The Mystic Quest: An Introduction to Jewish Mysticism*, Northvale, New Jersey: Jason Aronson, 1988. An accessible introduction to mystical Jewish thinking.

Berger, Alan L., ed., *Judaism in the Modern World*, New York: New York University Press, 1994. Articles by leading contemporary Jewish scholars on facets of the changing identities and paradoxes of modern Jewry.

Cohen, Arthur A. and Mendes-Flohr, Paul, eds., *Contemporary Jewish Religious Thought*, New York: Charles Scribner's Sons, 1987. Brief essays on all aspects of Jewish belief, from aesthetics to Zionism, by writers from all Jewish schools.

Encyclopedia Judaica, Jerusalem: Keter Publishing House Jerusalem Ltd., 1972. The authoritative, multi-volume reference on all aspects of Judaism, as seen from a broad spectrum of points of view.

Glatzer, Nahum N., ed., *The Judaic Tradition*, Boston: Beacon Press, 1969. A useful compilation of writings from all periods of Jewish history.

Heschel, Abraham J., *Between God and Man: An Interpretation of Judaism*, ed. Fritz A. Rothschild, New York: The Free Press, 1959. An intimate exploration of the relevance of traditional Judaism for today's world, by a great twentieth-century theologian.

Holtz, Barry W., ed., *The Schocken Guide to Jewish Books*, New York: Schocken Books, 1992. Fifteen fascinating bibliographical chapters by experts in their fields provide entry to all major historical, literary, philosophical, and mystical areas of Jewish study.

Lerner, Michael, *Jewish Renewal: A Path to Healing and Transformation*, New York: HarperCollins, 1994. Profound and moving analyses of why Jews left Judaism and the revitalization that is drawing them back to faith.

Plaskow, Judith, *Standing Again at Sinai: Judaism from a Feminist Perspective*, San Francisco: HarperCollins, 1991. Studies of all aspects of Jewish feminism, including the reconstruction of women's history, women in Israel, gender-equal God-language, sexuality in feminist religious context, and women's role in the repair of the world.

Scholem, Gershom G., *Major Trends in Jewish Mysticism*, New York: Schocken Books, 1974. The classic scholarly work on the development of mystical Judaism.

Seltzer, Robert, *Jewish People, Jewish Thought: The Jewish Experience in History*, New York: Macmillan, 1980. An excellent comprehensive one-volume history of the Jewish people, with a particular emphasis on philosophy, mysticism, and religious thought.

Tanakh: The Holy Scriptures, The New JPS Translation according to the Traditional Hebrew Text, Philadelphia: The Jewish Publication Society, 1988. The preferred translation of the Hebrew scriptures, in graceful and spiritually sensitive modern English.

Wiesel, Elie, *Night*, New York: Bantam, 1960. Short, searing memoir of a teenage boy's Holocaust experience.

CHAPTER 8

CHRISTIANITY

"Jesus Christ is Lord"

Christianity is a faith based on the life, teachings, death, and resurrection of Jesus. He was born as a Jew about two thousand years ago in Roman-occupied Palestine. He taught for fewer than three years and was executed by the Roman government on charges of sedition. Nothing was written about him at the time; some years after his death attempts were made to record what he had said and done. Yet his birth is now celebrated around the world and since the sixth century has been used as the major point from which public time is measured even by non-Christians. The religion centered around him has more followers than any other.

In studying Christianity we will first examine what can be said about the life and teachings of Jesus, based on accounts in the Bible and historians' knowledge of the period. We will then follow the evolution of the religion as it spread to all continents and became theologically and liturgically more complex. This process continues in the present, in which there are not one but many different versions of Christianity.

The Christian Bible

The Bibles used by various Christian churches consist of the Hebrew Bible (called the "Old Testament"), and in some cases non-canonical Jewish texts called the *Apocrypha*, plus the twenty-seven books of the "New Testament" written after Jesus's earthly mission. What we know about Jesus's life and teachings is derived largely from the first four books of the New Testament. They are called the **gospels** ("good news"). On the whole, they seem to have been originally written about forty to fifty years after Jesus's death. They are based on oral transmission of the stories and discourses, which may have been influenced by the growing split between Christians and Jews. The documents, thought to be pseudonymous, are given the names of Jesus's followers Matthew and John, and the apostle Paul's companions Mark and Luke. The gospels were first written down in Greek and perhaps Aramaic, the everyday language which Jesus spoke, and then copied and translated in many different ways over the centuries. They offer a composite picture of Jesus as seen through the eyes of the Christian community.

How do Christians approach the gospels? Traditionally, the holy scriptures have been reverently regarded as the Word of God, divinely inspired.

Furthermore, in Eastern Orthodox Christianity, "the Gospel is not just Holy Scripture but also a symbol of Divine Wisdom and an image of Christ Himself."[1] Nonetheless, some Christians have attempted to clarify what Jesus taught and how he lived, so that people might truly follow him. In general, interpretations of the stories and sayings of Jesus may be literal, allegorical, mystical, or moral. During the eighteenth century, critical study of the Bible from a strictly historical point of view began in Western Europe. This approach, now accepted by many Roman Catholics and Protestants, is based on the literary method of interpreting ancient writings in their historical context, with their intended audience and desired effect taken into account.

Three of the gospels, Matthew, Mark, and Luke, are so similar that they are called the **synoptic** gospels, referring to the fact that they can be "seen together" as presenting rather similar views of Jesus's career, though they are organized somewhat differently. Most historians think that Matthew and Luke are largely based on Mark and another source called "Q." This hypothesized source would probably be a compilation of oral traditions. It is now thought that the author of Mark put together many fragments of oral tradition in order to develop a connected narrative about Jesus's life and ministry, for the sake of propagating the faith.

The other two synoptic gospels often parallel Mark quite closely but include additional material. The gospel according to Matthew (one of Jesus's original disciples, a tax collector) is sometimes called a Jewish Christian gospel. It represents Jesus as a second Moses as well as the Messiah ushering in the kingdom of heaven, with frequent references to the Old Testament. Matthew's stories emphasize that the Gentiles (non-Jews) accept Jesus, whereas the Jews reject him as savior.

Luke, to whom the third gospel is attributed, is traditionally thought to have been a physician who sometimes accompanied Paul the apostle. The gospel seems to have been written with a Gentile Christian audience in mind. Luke presents Jesus's mission in universal rather than exclusively Jewish terms and accentuates the importance of his ministry to the underprivileged and lower classes.

The Gospel of John, traditionally attributed to "the disciple Jesus loved," is of a very different nature than the other three. It concerns itself less with following the life of Jesus than with seeing Jesus as the eternal Son of God, the incarnation of God on earth.

Other gospels circulating in the early Christian church were not included in the canon of the New Testament. They include magical stories of Jesus's infancy, such as an account of his making clay birds and then bringing them to life. The Gospel of Thomas, one of the long-hidden manuscripts discovered in 1945 by a peasant in a cave near Nag Hammadi, Egypt, is of particular interest. Some scholars feel that its core may have been written even earlier than the canonical gospels. It contains many sayings in common with the other gospels but places the accent on mystical concepts of Jesus:

Jesus said: I am the Light that is above them all. I am the All,

*the All came forth from me and the All
attained to me. Cleave a (piece of) wood, I
am there; lift up the stone and you will
find Me there.[2]*

The Life and Teachings of Jesus

It is not possible to reconstruct from the gospels a single chronology of Jesus's life or to account for much of what happened before he began his ministry. Nevertheless, the stories of the New Testament are important to Christians as the foundation of their faith. And after extensive analysis most scholars have concluded on grounds of linguistics that many of the sayings attributed to Jesus by the gospels may be authentic.

Birth

Most historians think Jesus was probably born a few years before the first year of what is now called the **Common Era**. When sixth-century Christian monks began figuring time in relationship to the life of Jesus, they may have miscalculated slightly. Traditionally, Christians have believed that Jesus was born in Bethlehem. This detail fulfills the rabbinic interpretation of the Old Testament prophecies that the Messiah would be born in Bethlehem, the home of David the great king, and in the lineage of David. Both Matthew and Luke offer genealogies tracing Jesus to David. Some scholars suggest that Jesus was actually born in or near Nazareth, his own home town in Galilee. This region, whose name meant "Ring of the Gentiles" (non-Jews), was not fully Jewish; it was also scorned as somewhat countrified by the rabbinic orthodoxy of Judaea. Both Judaea and Galilee were ruled by Rome at the time.

According to the gospels Jesus's mother was Mary, who was a virgin when she conceived him by the Holy Spirit; her husband was Joseph, a carpenter from Bethlehem. Luke states that they had to go to Bethlehem to satisfy a Roman ruling that everyone should travel to their ancestral cities for a census. When they had made the difficult journey, there was no room for them in the inn, so the baby was born in a stable among the animals. He was named Jesus, which means "God saves." This well-loved birth legend exemplifies the humility that Jesus taught. According to Luke, those who came to pay their respects were poor shepherds to whom angels had appeared with the glad tidings that a Savior had been born to the people. Matthew tells instead of Zoroastrian Magi, sages from "the east" who brought the Christ child symbolic gifts of gold and frankincense and myrrh, confirming his kingship and his adoration by Gentiles.

Preparation

No other stories are told about Jesus's childhood in Nazareth until at twelve he accompanied his parents on their yearly trip to Jerusalem for Passover. Left behind by mistake, he was said to have been discovered by his parents in the Temple discussing the Torah with the rabbis; "all who heard him were amazed at his understanding and his answers." When scolded, he reportedly replied, "Did you not know that I must be in my Father's house?"[3] This story is used to demonstrate his sense of mission even as a boy, his knowledge of Jewish tradition, and the close personal connection between Jesus and God. In later accounts of his prayers, he spoke to God as "Abba," a very familiar word for father.

The New Testament is also silent about the years of Jesus's young manhood. What is described, however, is the ministry of John the Baptist, a prophet citing Isaiah's prophecies of the coming kingdom of God. He was conducting baptism in the Jordan River in preparation for the kingdom of God. **Apocalyptic** expectations were running high at the time, with Israel chafing under Roman taxation and rule.

According to all four gospels, at the age of about thirty Jesus appeared before John to be baptized. John was calling people to repent of their sins and then be spiritually purified and sanctified by immersion in the river. He felt it improper to perform this ceremony for Jesus, whom Christians consider sinless, but Jesus insisted. How can this be interpreted? One explanation is that, for Jesus, this became a ceremony of his consecration to God as the Messiah. The Gospel writer reports,

> When he came up out of the water, immediately he saw the heavens opened and the Spirit descending upon him like a dove; and a voice came from heaven. "Thou art my beloved Son; with thee I am well pleased."[4]

Another interpretation is that Jesus's baptism was the occasion for John's publicly announcing that the Messiah had arrived, beginning his ministry. A third interpretation is that by requesting baptism, Jesus identified himself with sinful humanity. Even though he had no need for repentance and purification, he accepted baptism on behalf of all humans.

After being baptized, Jesus reportedly undertook a forty-day retreat in the desert wilderness, fasting. During his retreat, the gospel writers say he was tempted by Satan to use his spiritual power for secular ends, but he refused.

Ministry

In John's gospel, Jesus's baptism and wilderness sojourn were followed by his gathering of the first disciples, the fisherman Simon (called Peter), Andrew (Peter's brother), James, and John (brother of James), who recognized him as the Messiah. First of all Jesus warned his disciples that they would have to leave all their possessions and human attachments to follow him—to pay more attention to the life of the spirit than to physical comfort and wealth. He said that it was extremely difficult for the wealthy to enter the kingdom of heaven. God, the Protector, takes care of physical needs, which are relatively unimportant anyway:

> Is not life more than food, and the body more than clothing? Look at the birds of the air; they neither sow nor reap nor gather into barns, and yet your heavenly Father feeds them. Are you not of more value than they? And which of you by being anxious can add one cubit to his span of life?[5]

Jesus taught that his followers should concentrate on laying up spiritual treasures in heaven, rather than material treasures on earth.

As Jesus traveled, speaking, he is said to have performed many miracles, such as turning water into wine, healing the sick, restoring the dead to life, walking on water, casting devils out of the possessed, and turning a few loaves and fish into enough food to feed a crowd of thousands, with copious leftovers. Jesus reportedly performed these miracles quietly and compassionately; the gospels interpreted them as signs of the coming kingdom of God.

The stories of the miracles performed by Jesus have symbolic meanings taken from the entire Jewish and early Christian traditions. In the sharing of the loaves and fishes, for instance, it may have been more than physical bread that Luke was talking about when he said, "and all ate and were satisfied."[6] The people came to Jesus out of spiritual hunger, and he fed them all, profligate with his love. Bread often signified life-giving sustenance.

On another level of interpretation, the story may prefigure the Last Supper of Jesus with his disciples, with both stories alluding to the Jewish tradition of the Great Banquet, the heavenly feast of God, as a symbol of the messianic age. The fish were a symbol of Christ to the early Christians; what he fed them was the indiscriminate gift of himself.

Theological interpretations of the biblical stories are based on the evidence of the Bible itself, but people also bring their own experiences to them. To William, a twentieth-century Nicaraguan peasant, the miracle was not the multiplication of the loaves but the sharing: "The miracle was to persuade the owners of the bread to share it, that it was absurd for them to keep it all while the people were going hungry."[7]

Jesus preached and lived by truly radical ethics. In contrast to the prevailing patriarchal society and extensive proscriptions against impurity, he touched lepers and a bleeding woman to heal them; in his "table fellowship," he ate with people of all classes. In a culture in which women's role was strictly circumscribed, he welcomed women as his disciples. His was a radically egalitarian vision. He also extended the application of Jewish laws: "You have heard that it was said to the men of old," Jesus began, "You shall not kill; and whoever kills shall be liable to judgment. But I say to you that every one who is angry with his brother shall be liable to judgment. . . ."[8] Not only should a man not commit adultery; it is wrong even to look at a woman lustfully. Rather than revenging an eye for an eye, a tooth for a tooth, respond with love. If a person strikes you on one cheek, turn the other cheek to be struck also. If anyone tries to rob you of your coat, give him your cloak as well. And not only should you love your neighbor, Jesus says:

> Love your enemies and pray for those who persecute you, so that you may be sons of your Father who is in heaven; for he makes his sun rise on the evil and on the good, and sends rain on the just and on the unjust.[9]

The extremely high ethical standards of the Sermon on the Mount (Matthew 5–7) may seem impossibly challenging. Who can fully follow them? And Jesus said these things to people who had been brought up with the understanding that to incompletely fulfill even one divine commandment is a violation of the Law. But when people recognize their help-

An Interview with David Vandiver

Born into a devout small-town Southern Baptist family, David Vandiver describes the evolution of his practice of Christianity.

"The primary values as I grew up were ones of honesty, fairness, and caring for others. It was not until much later in my life that the vast scope of values held by Christians in differing places in the world came to my attention. I was not aware, for example, that there were Christians who believed God wanted them to influence politics for justice, work for equal rights for all people, protect the natural environment, or make peace with other nations and peoples of differing faiths. Our form of faith did a good job of supporting what was valuable in society, but did little to tear down what was destructive. We had no cause to practice tolerance because we were all so similar, except for the African-Americans in our town—about 20 percent of the population—who were already Christian and from whom we, as Anglo-Americans, wished to stay separated. I grew up with racism all around me.

Nonetheless, as a high school youth in the early 1970s, I joined my friends in dragging my church into the foray of the U.S. Civil Rights Movement because I couldn't see Jesus as one who would keep any group of people powerless and poor. Christianity was a voice for the downtrodden and oppressed of the world, and if I was to follow Jesus, I would have to take up their cause for justice in some way.

The most accessible way for me to take up this cause was a vocation as a Christian minister. It guided me to a Masters of Divinity in Pastoral Counseling at a Baptist seminary. It was here that I began to consider the teachings of Jesus the Christ more deeply. What did it mean to "love my neighbor as myself"? In practical terms, it came to mean that I could not simply spend the rest of my life pursuing a comfortable living while ignoring the fact that millions are living in poverty and oppression.

Early in my seminary days, I was married to a wonderful woman, who lost her life in an automobile accident four months after our wedding. I found myself doubting the existence of a caring God. I was plunged into a dark night of the soul and feared I would never escape it. Slowly it began to dawn on me that my plight was not mine alone; that millions had suffered and were suffering similar losses. It became clear to me that anything good and loving in life was a gift, sent as a precious favor.

I saw that following Jesus would take me out of the mainstream of the world in order to love it fully. On the other hand, I was painfully aware of the impossibility of loving others unconditionally. What as a child was an inherent identity became a life-long journey that I would never fully complete.

Vocationally and geographically, I have found a home as the manager of a wilderness camp for inner-city children from Washington. I am reminded of how I grew up, unaware of the larger world around me. I work to help them find the tools that will assist them in loving those they find difficult to love: their enemies, abusers, oppressors, and those who ignore them. Those who have given me those tools have held up the imperatives of Jesus to love the world, even those whom I find difficult to love."

lessness to fulfill such commandments, they are ready to turn to the divine for help. Jesus pointed out, "With man this is impossible, but not with God; all things are possible with God."[10]

The main thing Jesus taught was love. He stated that to love God and to "love your neighbor as yourself"[11] were the two great commandments in Judaism, upon which everything else rested. To love God means placing God first in one's life, rather than concentrating on the things of the earth. To love one's neighbor means selfless service to everyone, even to those despised by the rest of society. Jesus often horrified the religious authorities by talking to prostitutes, tax-collectors, and the poorest and lowliest of people. He set an example of loving service by washing his disciples' feet. This kind of love, he said, should be the mark of his followers, and at the Last Judgment, when the Son of man judges the people of all time, he will grant eternal life in the kingdom to the humble "sheep" who loved and served him in all:

> Then the righteous will answer him, "Lord, when did we see thee hungry and feed thee, or thirsty and give thee drink? And when did we see thee a stranger and welcome thee, or naked and clothe thee? And when did we see thee sick or in prison and visit thee?" And the King will answer them, "Truly, I say to you, as you did it to one of the least of these my brethren, you did it to me."[12]

Jesus preached that God is forgiving to those who repent. He told a story likening God to the father who welcomed with gifts and celebration his "prodigal son" who had squandered his inheritance and then humbly returned home. He told story after story suggesting that those who considered themselves superior were more at odds with God than those who were aware of their sins. Those who sincerely repent—even if they are the hated toll-collectors, prostitutes, or ignorant common people—are more likely to receive God's merciful forgiveness than are the learned and hypocritically self-righteous. Indeed, Jesus said, it was only in childlikeness that people could enter the kingdom of heaven. In a famous series of statements about supreme happiness called the **Beatitudes**, Jesus is quoted as having promised blessings for the "poor in spirit,"[13] the mourners, the meek, the seekers of righteousness, the pure in heart, the merciful, the peacemakers, and those who are persecuted for the sake of righteousness and of spreading the gospel.

Jesus's stories were typically presented as **parables**, in which earthly situations familiar to people of his time and place were used to make a spiritual point. He spoke of parents and children, of masters and servants, of sowing seeds, of fishing. For example,

> The kingdom of heaven is like a dragnet cast into the sea that brings in a haul of all kinds. When it is full, the fishermen haul it ashore; then, sitting down, they collect the good ones in a basket and throw away those that are no use. This is how it will be at the end of time: the angels will appear and separate the wicked from the just to throw them into the blazing furnace where there will be weeping and grinding of teeth.[14]

CHRISTIANITY

	0 CE	Jesus c.4 BCE–30 CE
	100	Paul organizes early Christians c.50–60 CE
	200	Gospels written down c.70–95 CE
Constantine emperor of Roman Empire 306–337	300	
		Life of Augustine 354–430
Christianity established as state religion 380	400	
	500	Life of Benedict and creation of his monastic rule
	600	c.480–542
	700	
Middle Ages in Europe; centralization of papal power 800–1300	800	
	900	
The Crusades 950–1300	1000	Split between Western and Eastern Orthodox Church 1054
	1100	
	1200	St. Francis of Assisi 1182–1226
Proliferation of monastic orders 1300s	1300	
Church of England separates from Rome 1534	1500	Life of John Calvin 1509–1564 Martin Luther posts 95 Theses 1517 The Council of Trent; Roman Catholic Reformation 1545–1563
	1600	
	1700	Life of John Wesley 1703–1791
The Enlightenment in Europe 1800s	1800	
	1900	
World Council of Churches formed 1948 Churches reopened in Russia 1988		Discovery of the Nag Hammadi manuscripts 1945 The Second Vatican Council 1962–1965
	2000	

As we have seen, messianic expectations were running very high among Jews of that time, oppressed as they were by Roman rule. They looked to a time when the people of Israel would be freed and the authority of Israel's God would be recognized throughout the world. Jesus reportedly spoke to them again and again about the fulfillment of these expectations: "The time is fulfilled, and the kingdom of God is at hand; repent, and believe in the gospel"[15]; "I must preach the good news of the kingdom of God . . . for I was sent for this purpose."[16] He taught them to pray for the advent of this kingdom: "Thy kingdom come, Thy will be done on earth as it is in heaven."[17] However, in contrast to expectations of secular deliverance from the Romans, Jesus seems to refer to the kingdom as manifestation of God's full glory, the consummation of the world.

> *Every one who drinks of this water will thirst again, but whoever drinks of the water that I shall give him will never thirst; the water that I shall give him will become in him a spring of water welling up to eternal life.*
> *(Jesus, as quoted in the Gospel of John, 4:13–14)*

Jesus's references to the kingdom, as reported in the gospels, indicate two seemingly different emphases: one that the kingdom is expected in the future, and the other that the kingdom is already here. In his future references, as in the apocalyptic Jewish writings of the time, Jesus said that things would get much worse right before the end. He seemed to foretell the destruction of Jerusalem by the Romans that began in 70 CE. But:

> *then will appear the sign of the Son of man in heaven, and then all the tribes of the earth will mourn, and they will see the Son of man coming on the clouds of heaven with power and great glory; and he will send out his angels with a loud trumpet call, and they will gather his elect from the four winds, from one end of heaven to the other.[18]*

It was his mission to gather together everyone who could be saved.

Challenges to the authorities

As Jesus traveled through Galilee, many people gathered around him to be healed. Herod Antipas, a Jew who had been appointed by the Romans as ruler of Galilee, had already executed John the Baptist and may have been concerned that Jesus might be a trouble-maker, perhaps one of the Zealots of Galilee who were stirring up support for a political uprising against the Romans. Jesus therefore moved outside Herod's jurisdiction for a while, to carry on his work in Tyre and Sidon (now in Lebanon).

According to the gospels, Jesus was also regarded with suspicion by prominent Jewish groups of his time—the emerging Pharisees (the shapers of rabbinic Judaism), Sadducees (the priests and upper class), and the scribes (specially trained laymen who copied the written law and formulated the oral law of Judaism). Jesus seems not to have challenged Mosaic law, but rather, its interpretations in the evolving rabbinic traditions and the hypocrisy of those who claim to be living by the law. It is written in the gospel of Matthew that the Pharisees and scribes challenged Jesus's disciples for not washing their hands before eating. Jesus responded:

"Hypocrites! It was you Isaiah meant when he so rightly prophesied: 'This people honors me only with lip service / while their hearts are far from me. / The worship they offer me is worthless; / the doctrines they teach are only human regulations.'"[19]

He called the people to him and said, "Listen, and understand. What goes into the mouth does not make a man unclean; it is what comes out of the mouth that makes him unclean. ... For things that come out of the mouth come from the heart, and it is these that make a man unclean. For from the heart come evil intentions. ... But to eat with unwashed hands does not make a man unclean."[20] ...

"Alas for you, scribes and Pharisees, you hypocrites! You who are like whitewashed tombs that look handsome on the outside, but inside are full of dead men's bones and every kind of corruption. In the same way you appear to people from the outside like good honest men, but inside you are full of hypocrisy and lawlessness."[21]

Many seemingly anti-Jewish statements in the New Testament are suspected by some modern scholars as additions or interpretations dating from the period after Jesus's death, when rabbinic Judaism and early Christianity were competing for followers. Nevertheless, more universal teachings are apparent in such stories attributed to Jesus. For instance, in all times and all religions there have been those who do not practice what they preach when claiming to speak with spiritual authority.

Jesus is said to have also confronted those who were making a living by charging a profit when exchanging money for Temple currency and selling animals for sacrificial offerings:

So they reached Jerusalem and he went into the Temple and began driving out those who were selling and buying there; he upset the tables of the money changers and the chairs of those who were selling pigeons. Nor would he allow anyone to carry anything through the Temple. And he taught them and said, "Does not scripture say; 'My house will be called a house of prayer for all the peoples?'[22] But you have turned it into a robbers' den."[23] This came to the ears of the chief priests and the scribes, and they tried to find some way of doing away with him; they were afraid of him because the people were carried away by his teaching.[24]

According to the gospel accounts, Jesus appropriated to himself the messianic prophecies of Second Isaiah. It is written that he privately asked his disciples, "Who do you say that I am?" Peter answered, "You are the Christ."[25] *"Christ"* is Greek for "anointed one," a translation of the Aramaic word *M'shekha* or *Messiah*, which also means "perfected" or "enlightened one." His disciples later spoke of him as the Messiah after he died and was resurrected. And his follower Martha, sister of Lazarus whom Jesus reportedly raised from the dead, is quoted as having said to Jesus, "I now believe that you are the Messiah, the Son of God who was to come into the world."[26] Contemporary biblical scholars have concluded that Jesus rejected the title of Messiah, for it might have been misunderstood.

A spectacular event, the "Transfiguration," was witnessed by three disciples. Jesus had climbed a mountain to pray, and as he did:

> He was transfigured before them, and his face shone like the sun, and his garments became white as light. And behold, there appeared to them Moses and Elijah, talking with him. ... When lo, a bright cloud overshadowed them, and a voice from the cloud said, "This is my beloved Son, with whom I am well pleased; listen to him."[27]

The presence of Moses and Elijah placed Jewish law and prophecy behind the claim that Jesus is the Christ. They were representatives of the old covenant with God; Jesus brought a new dispensation of grace.

Jesus claimed that John the Baptist was Elijah come again. The authorities had killed John the Baptist and, Jesus prophesied, they would attack him, too, not recognizing who he was. John's gospel is particularly intent on portraying him as the Christ. John quotes Jesus as saying things like "My teaching is not mine, but his who sent me"; "I am the light of the world"; "You are from below, I am from above; you are of this world, I am not of this world"; and "Before Abraham was, I am."[28]

Jesus characterized himself as a good shepherd who is willing to lay down his life for his sheep. Foreshadowing the crucifixion, he said he would offer his own flesh and blood as a sacrifice for the sake of humanity. His coming death would mark a "new covenant" in which his blood would be "poured out for many for the forgiveness of sins."[29]

It is possible that such passages defining Jesus's role were later interpolations by the early Christians as they tried to explain the meaning of their Master's life and death in new terms during the decades when the New Testament was in process of formation.

Crucifixion

The anti-institutional tenor of Jesus's teachings did not endear him to those in power. Jesus knew that to return to Jerusalem would be politically dangerous. But eventually he did so, at Passover. He entered the town on a donkey, accompanied by multitudes who cried:

> "Hosanna! Blessed be he who comes in the name of the Lord! Blessed be the kingdom of our father David that is coming! Hosanna in the highest!"[30]

However, Jesus warned his disciples that his end was near. At the "Last Supper," a meal during the Passover season, he is said to have given them instructions for a ceremony with bread and wine to be performed thenceforth to maintain an ongoing communion with him. One of the disciples would betray him, he said. This one, Judas, had already done so, selling information leading to Jesus's arrest for thirty pieces of silver.

Jesus took three of his followers to a garden called Gethsemane, on the Mount of Olives, where he is said to have prayed intensely that the cup of suffering would pass away from him, if it be God's will, "yet not what I will, but what thou wilt."[31] The gospels often speak of Jesus's spending long periods in spontaneous prayer to God. It is possible to interpret Jesus's prayer at Gethsemane as a confirmation of his great faith in God's mercy and power. In the words of New Testament theologian Joachim Jeremias:

> *The Father of Jesus is not the immovable, unchangeable God who in the end can only be described in negations. He is not a God to whom it is pointless to pray. He is a gracious God, who hears prayers and intercessions, and is capable in his mercy of rescinding his own holy will.*[32]

Nevertheless, after this period of prayer Jesus said, according to Mark's gospel, "It is all over. The hour has come."[33] A crowd led by Judas approached with swords and clubs; they led Jesus away to be questioned by the chief priest, elders, and scribes.

All four gospels report a hearing before the high priest, Joseph Caiaphas. The high priest asked Jesus, "Are you the Christ?" Jesus answered:

> *You have said so. But I tell you, hereafter you will see the Son of man seated at the right hand of Power, and coming on the clouds of heaven.*[34]

Caiaphas pronounced this statement blasphemy, punishable by death. They took him to Pontius Pilate, the Roman governor, for sentencing. To Pilate's leading question, "Are you King of the Jews?" Jesus is said to have replied, "You have said so."[35]

To quell the cries of the crowd calling for Jesus to be crucified, Pilate released Jesus to his Roman military guard. They took Jesus to a hill called Golgotha and nailed him to a cross, as was the Roman executionary custom. The accusation—"This is Jesus, King of the Jews"—was set over his head, and two robbers were crucified alongside him. The authorities, the people, and even the robbers mocked him for saying that he could save others when he could not even save himself.

Jesus hung there for hours until, according to the gospels, he cried out, "My God, my God, why hast thou forsaken me?"[36] This is the first line of Psalm 22, which is actually a great proclamation of the faith in God of one who is persecuted. Then Jesus died. This event is thought to have happened on a Friday some time between 27 and 33 CE. A wealthy Jewish disciple named Joseph of Arimathea asked Pilate for Jesus's body, which he wrapped in a linen shroud and placed in his own tomb, with a large stone against the door. A guard was placed at the tomb to make sure that no followers would steal the body and claim that Jesus had risen from the dead.

Resurrection

That seemed to be the end of it. Jesus's disciples were terrified, so some of them hid, mourning and disheartened. The whole religious movement could have died out, as did other messianic cults. However, what happened next, according to varying gospel accounts, seemed to change everything. Some of the women who had been close to Jesus visited the tomb on Sunday to prepare the body for a proper burial, a rite which had been postponed because of the Sabbath. Instead, they found the tomb empty, with the stone rolled away. Angels then appeared and told them that Jesus had risen from death. The women ran and brought two of the male disciples, who witnessed the empty tomb with the shrouds folded.

Then followed numerous reports of appearances of the risen Christ to various disciples. He dispelled their doubts about his resurrection, having them touch his wounds and even eating a fish with them. He said to them, as recounted in the gospel of Matthew:

> All authority in heaven and on earth has been given to me. Go therefore and make disciples of all nations, baptizing them in the name of the Father and of the Son and of the Holy Spirit, teaching them to observe all that I have commanded you; and lo, I am with you always, to the close of the age.[37]

The details of the appearances of the resurrected Jesus differ considerably from gospel to gospel, and the gospel of Mark does not mention any resurrection appearances. However, some scholars think that to have women as the first witnesses to the empty tomb suggests that there must be some historical truth in the claims of Jesus's resurrection, for no one trying to build a case would have rested it on the testimony of women, who had little status in a patriarchal society. Feminist scholar Elisabeth Schüssler Fiorenza finds deep meaning in the presence of women disciples at the time of Jesus's death and resurrection. All four gospels mention a woman who anoints Jesus, a sign that she recognizes him as the Messiah. The reports that it is women who faithfully visit the tomb suggest that, as Schüssler Fiorenza puts it,

> Whereas according to Mark the leading male disciples do not understand this suffering messiahship of Jesus, reject it, and finally abandon him, the women disciples who have followed Jesus from Galilee to Jerusalem suddenly emerge as the true disciples in the passion narrative. They are Jesus' true followers who have understood that his ministry was not rule and kingly glory but diakonia, "service" (Mark 15:41). Thus the women emerge as the true Christian ministers and witnesses. The unnamed woman who names Jesus with a prophetic sign-action in Mark's Gospel is the paradigm for the true disciple. While Peter had confessed, without truly understanding it, "you are the anointed one," the woman anointing Jesus recognizes clearly that Jesus' messiahship means suffering and death.[38]

It was the resurrection that turned defeat into victory for Jesus, and discouragement into powerful action for his followers. As the impact of all they had seen set in, the followers came to believe that Jesus had been God present in a human life, walking among them.

The Early Church

Persecution became the lot of Jesus's followers. But by 380 CE, despite strong opposition, Christianity became the official religion of the vast Roman Empire. As it became the establishment, rather than a tiny, scattered band of dissidents within Judaism, Christianity continued to define and organize itself.

From persecution to empire

The earliest years of what became the mainstream of Christianity are described in the New Testament books that follow the gospel accounts of the life of Jesus. "The Acts of the Apostles" was presumably written by the same person who wrote the gospel of Luke. Acts is followed by letters to some of the early groups of Christians, most of them apparently written by Paul, a major organizer and apostle (missionary), in about 50 to 60 CE.

Like the gospel accounts, the stories in these biblical books are examined by many contemporary scholars as possibly romanticized, idealized documents, used to convert, to increase faith, to teach principles, and to establish Christian theology, rather than to accurately record historical facts.

According to Acts, an event called **Pentecost** galvanized the early Christians into action. At a meeting of the disciples, something that sounded like a great wind came down from the sky, and what looked like tongues of fire swirled around to touch each one's head. The narrative states that they all began speaking in languages they had never studied. Some mocked them, saying they were drunk, but Peter declared that they had been filled with the Spirit of God, as the Old Testament prophet Joel had prophesied would happen in the last days before the onset of the kingdom of God. Reportedly, three thousand people were so convinced that they were baptized that day.

One of the persecutors of Christians was Saul. He was a Pharisee tentmaker who lived during the time of Jesus but never met him. Instead, after Jesus died, he helped to throw many of his followers into prison and sentence them to death. Acts relates that on the way to Damascus in search of more heretics, he saw a light brighter than the sun and heard the voice of Jesus asking why Saul was persecuting him. This resistance was useless, said the vision of Jesus, who then appointed him to do the opposite: to go to both Jews and Gentiles:

> to open their eyes, that they may turn from darkness to light and from the power of Satan to God, that they may receive forgiveness of sins and a place among those who are sanctified by faith in me.[39]

Saul was baptized and immediately began promoting the Christian message under his new name, Paul. His indefatigable work in traveling about the Mediterranean world was of great importance in shaping and expanding the early Christian church. He was shipwrecked, stoned, imprisoned, and beaten, and probably died as a martyr in Rome, but nothing short of death deterred him from his new mission.

Paul tried to convince Jews that Jesus's birth, death, and resurrection had been predicted by the Old Testament prophets. This was the Messiah they had been waiting for, and now, risen from death, he presided as the cosmic Christ, offering God's forgiveness and grace to those who repent and trust in God rather than in themselves. Some Jews were converted to this belief, and the Jewish authorities repeatedly accused Paul of leading people away from Jewish law and tradition. However, a major difference remained between Jews and Christians over the central importance given to Jesus. It is possible that Jesus himself may not have claimed that he was the Messiah, and that it was Paul who developed this claim. To this day, Jews tend to feel that to put heavy emphasis on the person of Jesus takes attention away from Jesus's message and from God.

In Paul's time, those Jews who emphasized that Jews had been especially chosen by God were offended by interpretations of Jesus's life and teachings which saw Christianity as a universal mission of salvation for all peoples. These interpretations made the new sect, Christianity, seem irreconcilable with exclusive versions of Judaism, and the gap between the two became deep and bitter. The New Testament writings reflect the criticisms of the early Christians against the large Jewish majority who did not accept Jesus as their Messiah. These polemics have been echoed through the centuries as anti-Semitism.

Paul also tried to sway Gentiles: worshippers of the old gods whose religion was in decline, supporters of the emperor as deity, ecstatic initiates of mystery cults, and followers of dualistic Greco-Roman philosophers who regarded matter as evil and tried to emancipate the soul from its corrupting influence. He taught them that God did not reside in any idol but yet was not far from them, "For in him we live and move and have our being."[40] For Gentiles embracing Christianity, Paul and others argued that the Jewish tradition of circumcision should not be required of them. As Paul interpreted the gospel, salvation came by repentant faith in the grace of Christ, rather than by observance of a traditional law. In Paul's letter to the church in Rome, he argues that even Abraham was **justified**, or accepted by God in spite of sin, because of his great faith in God rather than by his circumcision.

Christianity spread rapidly and soon became largely non-Jewish in membership. By 200 CE, it had spread throughout the Roman Empire and into Mesopotamia, despite fierce opposition. Many Christians were subjected to imprisonment, torture, and confiscation of property, because they rejected polytheistic beliefs, idols, and emperor worship in the Roman Empire. They themselves were suspected of being revolutionaries, with their talk of a Messiah, and of strange cultic behaviors, such as their secret rituals of symbolically drinking Jesus's blood and eating his flesh. Persecution did not deter the most ardent of Christians; it united them intimately to the passion and death of Christ.

With the rise of Constantine to imperial rule early in the fourth century CE, opposition turned to official embracing of Christianity. Constantine said that God showed him a vision of a cross to be used as a standard in battle. After he used it and won, he instituted tolerance of Christianity alongside the state cult, of which he was the chief priest. Just before his death, Constantine was baptized as a Christian.

By the end of the fourth century CE, people of other religions were stripped of all rights, and ordered into Christian churches to be baptized. By the end of the fifth century CE, Christianity was the faith claimed by the majority of people in the vast Roman Empire. It also spread beyond the empire, from Ireland in the west to India and Ceylon in the east.

Evolving organization and theology

During its phenomenal growth from persecuted sect to state religion throughout much of the ancient world, Christianity was developing organizationally and theologically. By the end of the first century CE it had a bureaucratic structure which carried on the rites of the church and attempted to define true Christianity.

One form that was judged to be outside the mainstream was Gnostic Christianity, which appeared as a movement in the second century CE. **Gnosticism** means mystical perception of knowledge. The Nag Hammadi library found in Egypt presents Jesus as a great Gnostic teacher. His words are interpreted as the secret teachings given only to initiates. "He who is near to me is near to the fire," he says in the Gospel of Thomas.[41] The Gnostics held that only spiritually mature individuals could apprehend Jesus's real teaching: that the kingdom of heaven is a present reality experienced through personal realization of the Light.

When the New Testament canon of twenty-seven officially sanctioned texts was set and translated into Latin in the fourth century, the Gnostic gospels were not included. Instead, the Church treated possession of Gnostic texts as a crime against church law because the Christian faith community felt that Jesus had not taught an elitist view of salvation, and had not discriminated against the material aspect of creation.

What became mainstream Christianity is based not only on the life and teachings of Jesus, as set forth in the gospels selected for the New Testament, but also on the ways that they have been interpreted over the centuries. One of the first and most important interpreters was Paul. His central contribution—which was as influential as the four gospels in shaping Christianity—was his interpretation of Jesus's death and resurrection.

> *Let all that you do be done in love.*
> *The First Letter of Paul to the Corinthians, 16:14*

Paul spoke of *agape*—altruistic, self-giving love—as the center of Christian concern. He placed it above spiritual wisdom, asceticism, faith, and supernatural "gifts of the Spirit," such as the ability to heal, prophesy, or spontaneously speak in unknown tongues. Love was applied not only to one's neighbors but also to one's relationship with the divine. It was love plus *gnosis*—knowledge of God, permeated with love—that became the basis of contemplative Christianity, as it was shaped by the "Fathers" of the first centuries.

The cross, with or without an image of Jesus crucified on it, became a central symbol of Christianity. It marked the path of suffering service, rather than political domination, as the way of conquering evil and experiencing union with a compassionate God. To participate in Jesus's sacrifice, people could repent of their sins, be baptized, and be reborn to new life in Christ. In the early fifth century CE the bishop Augustine, one of the most influential theologians in the history of Christianity, described this spiritual rebirth as "slaying my old man and commencing the purpose of a new life, putting my trust in Thee."[42]

Twentieth-century theologian Rowan Williams explains this repentance and spiritual resurrection as:

the refusal to accept that lostness is the final human truth. Like a growing thing beneath the earth, we protest at the darkness and push blindly up in search of light, truth, home—the place, the relation where we are not lost, where we can live from deep roots in assurance. "Because I live, you will live also."[43]

The feeling of expectation of the coming of God's kingdom, so fervent in the earliest Christianity, began to wane as time went by. The notion of the kingdom of God began to shift to the indefinite future, with emphasis placed on a preliminary judgment at one's death. There was nevertheless the continuing expectation that Christ would return in glory to judge the living and the dead and bring to fulfillment the "new creation." This belief in the "*Second Coming*" of Christ is still an article of faith today.

Another early doctrinal development was the doctrine of the Holy **Trinity**. Christians believed that the transcendent, invisible God—the Father—had become immanent in the person of Jesus, God the Son. Furthermore, after his physical death Jesus promised to send the Holy Spirit to his followers. This makes three aspects of God, or three "persons" within the one divine being: Father, Son, and Holy Spirit. The Father is envisioned as the almighty transcendent creator of heaven and earth. The Son is the incarnation of the Father, the divine in human form, who returned at the ascension to live with the Father in glory, though he remains fully present in and to his "mystical body" on earth—the community of believers. The Holy Spirit or Holy Ghost is the power and presence of God, actively guiding and sustaining the faithful.

Although Jesus had spoken in parables with several levels of meaning, the evolving Church found it necessary to articulate some of its beliefs more openly and systematically. A number of **creeds**, or professions of faith, were composed for use in religious instruction and baptism, to define who Jesus was and his relationship to God, and to provide clear stands against the challenge of various heresies. For example, an important early creed is known as the Old Roman Creed:

I believe in God the Father Almighty,
And in Jesus Christ, his only Son, our Lord,
Who was born by the Holy Ghost, of the Virgin Mary, was crucified under
    Pontius Pilate, and was buried.
The third day he rose from the dead,
He ascended into heaven and sits on the right hand of the Father;
From thence he will come to judge the quick and the dead.
And in the Holy Ghost, the Holy Church, the forgiveness of sins, the
    resurrection of the body.

As theological debates continued, phrases were added to affirm the Church's position in contrast to beliefs that were determined to be heresies. The early creeds were developed by global councils of representatives of all area churches. The first of these gatherings for all areas to discuss church matters together was held in 325 CE in Nicea (in present-day Turkey) as Christianity was just emerging from persecution.

Early monasticism

Alongside the development of doctrine and the consolidation of church structure, another trend was developing. Some Christians were turning away from the world to live in solitary communion with God, as ascetics.

By the fourth century CE, there were Christian monks living simply in caves in the Egyptian desert with little regard for the things of the world. Avoiding emphasis on the supernatural powers that often accompany the ascetic life, they told stories demonstrating the virtues they valued, such as humility, submission, and the sharing of food. For example, an earnest young man was said to have visited one of the desert fathers and asked him how he was faring. The old man sighed and said, "Very badly, my child." Asked why, he said, "I have been here forty years doing nothing other than cursing my own self each day, inasmuch as in the prayers I offer, I say to God, 'Accursed are those who deviate from Your commandments.'"[44] The young seeker was moved by such humility and made it his model.

The desert monks were left to their own devices at first. In Christian humility, they avoided judging or trying to teach each other and attempted to be, at best, harmless. But by the fifth century CE, the monastic life shifted from solitary, unguided practice, to formal spiritual supervision. Group monasteries and structures for encouraging obedience to God through an abbot or abbess were set up, and rules devised to help monks persevere in their calling. The Rule of St. Benedict became a model for all later monastic orders in the West, with its emphasis on poverty, chastity, and obedience to the abbot, and its insistence that each monastery be economically self-sufficient through the labor of the monastics. The Benedictines have been famous over the centuries for their practice of hospitality to pilgrims and travelers, and are today active participants in interreligious monastic dialogue.

The Eastern Orthodox Church

Christianity's history has been marked by internal feuds and divisions. One of the deepest schisms occurred in 1054, when the Roman Catholic Church, whose followers were largely in the West, and the Eastern Orthodox Church split apart.

The history of the Orthodox Church

Late in the third century CE, the Roman Empire had been divided into an eastern and a western section. In the fourth century CE, Constantine established a second imperial seat in the east, in Constantinople (now Istanbul, Turkey). It was considered a "second Rome," especially after the sack of Rome by the Goths in 410. The two halves of the Christian world grew apart from each other, divided by language (Latin in the west, Greek in the east), culture, and religious differences.

In the western half, religious power was becoming more and more centralized in the Roman **pope** and other high officials; after the barbarian invasions, the clergy were often the only educated people. The Byzantine east was more democratic, with less distinction between clergy and laypeople, and the east did not recognize the Roman pope's claim to universal authority in the Church. By the early Middle Ages, there were also doctrinal disagreements. In its version of the Niceno-Constantinopolitan Creed, for example, the western church added a *filioque*, a formula professing that the Holy Spirit came from the Father "*and from the Son*"; the eastern church retained what is considered the more original text, professing that the Holy Spirit proceeds only from the Father.

In 1054, leaders of the eastern and western factions excommunicated each other over the disagreement about the Holy Spirit, and also over the papal claim, celibacy for priests (not required in the eastern church), and whether the Eucharistic bread should be leavened or unleavened. To the eastern church, the last straw was its treatment by Crusaders.

From 950 to 1300, loosely organized waves of Christians poured out of Europe in what were presented as "holy Crusades" to recapture the holy land of Palestine from Muslims, to defend the Byzantine Empire against Muslim Turks, and in general wipe out the enemies of Christianity. It was a tragic and bloody time. One of the many casualties was the already tenuous relationship between the eastern and western churches. When Crusaders entered Constantinople in 1204, they tried to intervene in local politics. Rebuffed, they were so furious that they ravaged the city. They destroyed the altar and sacred icons in Hagia Sophia, the awesome Church of the Holy Wisdom, and placed prostitutes on the throne reserved for the patriarch of the region. Horrified by such profanity, the Orthodox Church ended its dialogue with Rome and proceeded on its own, claiming to be the true descendant of the apostolic church. The eastern and western churches are still separate.

The Russian Orthodox Church

When the Ottoman Turks took Constantinople in the fifteenth century, Russia became more prominent in the Orthodox Church, calling itself the "third Rome." The Orthodox Church had spread throughout the Slavic and eastern Mediterranean countries.

Russian Orthodox Christianity was closely associated with Russian national history since its adoption by the royalty in the tenth century. But it was severely repressed by the Soviet government during the twentieth century. Lenin saw institutionalized religion as a divisive, backward force in society, an apology for oppression which should wither away in the socialist state. With the 1917 Revolution, anti-Church propaganda was broadcast, and many intellectuals who sincerely wanted the good of society left the Church. Lenin proclaimed that all church property belonged to the state, and church properties were seized. Thousands of monasteries and churches were taken over during the Revolution and in the early 1920s thousands of priests, nuns, and lay Christians were killed. During the 1930s more monasteries were disbanded, multitudes of churches were closed, and great numbers of clergy were imprisoned. Bishops who refused to accept Soviet control issued what is called the Solovky Memorandum, which stated in part,

> The Church recognizes spiritual principles of existence; communism rejects them. The Church believes in the living God, the Creator of the world, the leader of its life and destinies; communism denies his existence. Such a deep contradiction in the very basis of their Weltanschauungen [world views] precludes any intrinsic approximation or reconciliation between the Church and state, ... because the very soul of the Church, the condition of her existence and the sense of her being, is that which is categorically denied by communism.[45]

The bishops were imprisoned in the Solovky labor camp; many were killed there. It is estimated that some forty thousand priests were killed from 1918 to 1940. Out of almost eighty thousand churches and chapels in the Russian Empire in 1914, only a few hundred or a thousand remained by the beginning of World War II. Under Krushchev, a new campaign against religion was unleashed, and perhaps two-thirds of the remaining Orthodox churches were closed.

Nevertheless, the Orthodox Church did not die, for it was deeply rooted in the minds and hearts of the people, and was closely linked to national identity.

After decades of severe oppression, the Russian Orthodox Church witnessed a great change in government policy in 1988, the celebration of its first millennium in Russia and Ukraine. Mikhail Gorbachev's government approached the Orthodox Church leaders, asking their help in perestroika, returning some church buildings which had been turned into museums or warehouses. Some seventeen hundred churches were reopened in 1988 and 1989, and each was immediately filled with worshippers again. Seminaries where new clergy are trained report a great increase in enrollment. Late in 1989, Soviet President Mikhail Gorbachev ended seven decades of suppression of religion, pronouncing the right of the Soviet faithful to "satisfy their spiritual needs."[46]

Nevertheless, many people are disillusioned with the contemporary Russian Orthodox Church because of its politics. As in all other institutions in the former Soviet Union, its staff included many KGB agents, and some of these people seem to have remained in their positions after the fall of the Soviet Union. Some church leaders felt that they had to make compromises in order to survive at all as a religion under Soviet rule. Now the Russian Orthodox Church has very powerful influence in government policy.

Since the early days of the Soviet Union, there have also been Orthodox Christians who refused to collaborate or compromise with the government. At the risk of their jobs and lives, some Christian laypeople and priests began to worship secretly in what became known as catacomb churches, just as the early Christians had worshipped in underground catacombs to evade persecution. Father Alexey Vlasov, a catacomb priest, explains: "It was not their intention to oppose the Orthodox Church but to bring Christ's love into society."[47]

Even today, some Orthodox Christians continue to worship in secret rather than subject their congregations to the registration requirements of the state and disapproval of the official Church. Bishop Feodor, bishop of underground Christians in Moscow, Riga, and the Far East, objects to the assertive power of the Russian Orthodox Church:

> *If the Church has pride, it has no holy power. We are all brothers in Adam and in Christ. We are all baptized by God. This is true for each Christian. If you cannot love your brother who is next to you, how can you love one you cannot see, such as Christ, who has not been with us for two thousand years?*[48]

The Orthodox world today

There are now fifteen self-governing Orthodox Churches worldwide, each having its own leader, known as patriarch, metropolitan, or archbishop. The majority of Orthodox Christians now live in Russia, the Balkan states, and eastern Europe, in formerly communist countries. The original and still central Patriarchate of Constantinople is based within Turkey, as a small minority within a Muslim country. This Patriarchate also includes islands in the Aegean and the precipitous Mount Athos peninsula. The latter was historically a great center of Orthodox monasticism, but its population of monks declined considerably in the twentieth century when emigration of monks was prohibited by communist regimes. Now women are agitating to be allowed to enter Mount Athos, where even the presence of female animals is banned. Traditionalists maintain that Mount Athos is the only truly monastic community left in the world and should continue its antique ways unchanged and undistracted; women counter that the ban on women is degrading, a "sexist, anti-democratic decision taken by men, not by God."[49]

The Greek Orthodox Church dominates religious life in Greece and is assisting in the revival of interest in the classical books and arts of Orthodox spirituality. Extensive emigration, particularly from Russia during the first few years of communist rule, has also created large Orthodox populations in western countries.

Distinctive features of Orthodox spirituality

Over the centuries, the individual Orthodox Churches have probably changed less than have the many descendants of the early western Church. There is a strong conservative tradition, attempting to preserve the pattern of early Christianity. Even though the religious leaders can make local adaptations suited to their region and people, they are united in doctrine and sacramental observances. Any change that will affect all churches is decided by a **synod**—a council of officials trying to reach common agreements, as did the early Church.

In addition to the Bible, Orthodox Christians honor the writings of the saints of the Church. Particularly important is a collection called the *Philokalia*. It consists of texts written by Orthodox masters between the fourth and fifteenth centuries. "Philokalia" means love of the exalted, excellent, and beautiful.

The Philokalia is essentially a Christian guide to the contemplative life for monks, but it is also for laypeople. A central practice is called "unceasing prayer"; the continual remembrance of Jesus or God, often through repetition of a verbal formula that gradually impresses itself on the heart. The most common petition is the "Jesus prayer": "Lord Jesus Christ, Son of God, have mercy on me, a sinner." The repetition of the name of Jesus brings purification of heart and singularity of desire. To call upon Jesus is to experience his presence in oneself and in all things.

The Orthodox Church has affirmed that humans can approach God directly. Some may even see the light of God and be utterly transformed.

He who participates in the divine energy, himself becomes, to some extent, light: he is united to the light, and by that light he sees in full awareness all that remains hidden to those who have not this grace; ... for the pure in heart see God ... who, being Light, dwells in them and reveals Himself to those who love Him, to His beloved.[50]

Another distinctive feature of Orthodox Christianity is its veneration of **icons**. These are stylized paintings of Jesus, his mother Mary, and the saints. They are created by artists who prepare for their work by prayer and ascetical training. There is no attempt at earthly realism, for icons are representations of the reality of the divine world. They are beloved as windows to the eternal. In addition to their devotional and instructional functions, some icons are reported to have great spiritual powers, heal illnesses, and transmit the holy presence. Believers enter into the grace of this power by kissing the icon reverently and praying before it.

Some of the major icons in an Orthodox church are placed on an *iconostasis*. This is a screen separating the floor area for the congregation from the Holy of Holies, the sanctuary which can be entered only by the clergy. On either side of the opening to the altar are icons of Jesus and the Virgin Mary.

Orthodox choirs sing the divine liturgy in many-part harmony, producing an ethereal and uplifting effect as the sounds echo and re-echo around each other. Everything strives toward that beauty to which the Philokalia refers. Archimandrite Nathaniel of the Russian Othodox Pskova-Pechorsky Monastery, which has been a place of uninterrupted prayer for almost six hundred years despite eight hundred attacks on its walls and numerous sieges, speaks of the ideal of beauty in Orthodox Christianity:

The understanding of God is the understanding of beauty. Beauty is at the heart of our monastic life. The life of prayer is a constant well of beauty. We have the beauty of music in the Holy Liturgy. The great beauty of monastic life is communal life in Christ. Living together in love, living without enmity, as peaceful with each other as one dead body is peaceful with another dead body, we are dead to enmity.[51]

Medieval Roman Catholicism

In the west, from the sixth to tenth centuries CE, the old Roman Empire gradually fell to non-Christian invaders. Islam also made spectacular advances in areas previously converted to Christianity. Arabs took Palestine, Syria, Mesopotamia, Egypt, North Africa, and part of Spain. However, the Angle and Saxon invaders of England were new converts to Christianity, with whole tribes joining the faith at the behest of their chiefs. By the fourteenth century, most of central and western Europe was claimed for Christianity, and missionaries spread the faith to isolated areas of Asia.

The Holy Roman Empire became politically decentralized into feudal kingdoms, with the Christian Church the major force uniting Europe. The chief factors sustaining Christianity through these chaotic centuries were its centralized organization and the periodic refreshing of its spiritual well-springs through monasticism and mysticism.

Papal power

During the late first and early second centuries CE, some men and women had followed a charismatic Christian life, leaving home to preach, baptize, prophesy, and perhaps die as martyrs; others had moved toward an insti-tutionalized patriarchal Church. By the beginning of the second century CE, a consolidation of spiritual power had begun with the designation of specific people to serve as clergy and bishops (superintendents) to admin-ister the church affairs of each city or region. While some women served as deacons ministering to women, the clergy and bishops had to be male, with wife and children. The bishops of the chief cities of the Roman Empire had the greatest responsibilities and authority, with the greatest prestige being held by the Bishop of Rome, eventually known as the pope. By the fifth century CE, Pope Leo I argued that all popes were apostolic successors to Peter, the "rock" on which Jesus in Matthew's gospel said he would found his church. The Roman emperor passed an edict that all Christians were to recognize the authority of the Bishop of Rome, the successor to Peter.

The strongest of church administrators during these early centuries was Gregory I ("the Great"), who died in 604 CE. Wealthy by birth but ascetic by choice, he devoted his personal fortune to founding monasteries and feeding the poor. Suffering from health problems and longing for the quiet life of a monk, he was reluctantly convinced to be pope at a time of pesti-lence, floods, and military invasions. Even in this setting, he managed to provide for the physical needs of the poor, promote the discipline of the clergy (including the western ideal that priests should be celibate), revamp the liturgy (Gregorian chanting is named after him), and to re-establish the Church as a decent, just institution carrying high spiritual values.

The papacy began to wield tremendous secular power. Beginning in the eighth century, the approval of the papacy was sought as conferring divine sanction on feudal kings. In the ninth century the Church produced docu-ments old and new establishing the hierarchical authority of the papacy over the Church, and the Church over society, as the proper means of transmitting inspiration from the divine to humanity. Those who disagreed could be threatened with **excommunication**. This exclusion from participation in the sacraments was a dread ban cutting a person off from the redemption of the Church (blocking one's entrance to heaven in the afterlife), as well as from the benefits of the Church's secular power. Crusades were launched under the auspices of the Church, with war used ostensibly in defense of the faith, with no humane restraints on treatment of the "infidel."

Late in the eleventh century, Pope Gregory VII set forth unprecedented claims for the papacy. The pope, he asserted, was divinely appointed and therefore could be ruled by no human. The pope had the right to depose emperors; the princes of the world should kiss his feet.

This centralization of power became a major unifying element in Europe of the Middle Ages. Kingdoms broke up between 800 and 1100 as Vikings invaded from the north and Magyars from the east. In the midst of the ensuing chaos, people looked to the pope as an orderly wielder of power.

The papacy could not become hereditary. But it was nonetheless open to intrigue, scandal, and power-mongering. The thirteenth century saw the power of the papacy placed behind the **Inquisition**, an ecclesiastical court set up in 1229 to investigate and suppress heresy. This instrument of terror was based on Augustine's concept that heretics should be controlled for the sake of their own eternal salvation, out of love for their souls. In some cases the medieval Inquisitors had them tortured and burned to deter others from dangerous views.

Though strong, the papacy was often embroiled in its own political strife. During the fourteenth century, the popes left their traditional seat in turbulent Rome for the more peaceful climate of Avignon, France. There they built up an elaborate administrative structure, increasingly involved in worldly affairs. After the papacy was persuaded to return to Rome, a would-be reformer, Pope Urban IV, turned to terror tactics to get his way. At one point he had five cardinals tortured and killed. Many people refused to follow him; for a while they followed an "anti-pope" they established in Avignon.

Intellectual revival and monasticism

Although the papacy was subject to abuses, mirrored on a lesser scale by the clergy, Christian spirituality was vigorously revived in other quarters. During the twelfth and thirteenth centuries great universities developed in Europe, often from cathedral schools. Theology was considered the greatest of the sciences, with church ideals permeating the study of all areas of life.

The yearning for spiritual purity was particularly pronounced in monasticism. It was largely through monks and nuns that Christian spirituality survived and spread. Monasteries also became bulwarks of western civilization. In Ireland, particularly, they were the centers of larger communities of laypeople, and places of learning within illiterate societies.

During the twelfth century many new monastic orders appeared in the midst of a massive popular reinvigoration of spiritual activity. A major influence was a new community in Cluny, France. Its monks specialized in liturgical elaborations and prayer, leaving agricultural work to serfs. An alternative direction was taken by the Cistercians, Gregorians, and Carthusians. They returned to St. Benedict's Rule of combining manual work and prayer; "to labor is to pray," said the monks. The Carthusians lived cloistered lives as hermits, meeting each other only for worship and business matters. Despite such austere practices, people of all classes flocked to monastic life as a pious refuge from decadent society.

> *It is not only prayer that gives God glory but work. . . . He is so great that all things give Him glory if you mean they should.*
> *Gerard Manley Hopkins[52]*

In contrast to monks and nuns living cloistered lives, mendicant friars, or brothers, worked among the people. The Dominican Order was instituted primarily to teach and refute heresies. A famous Dominican scholar, Thomas Aquinas, created a monumental work, *Summa Theologiae*, in which rational sciences and spiritual revelations were joined in an immense, consistent theological system.

Franciscans, following the lead of the beloved St. Francis of Assisi (see below), wandered about without personal property or established buildings, telling people about God's love and accepting charity for their meager needs. The mendicant Dominicans and Franciscans, still noted as missionaries today, became one of the major features of medieval Christianity.

In addition to organized orders of nuns, there was a grassroots movement among thirteenth-century German and Flemish women to take private vows of chastity and voluntary simplicity. These women, who were called "beguines," lived frugally by their own work. They chose their own lifestyles, with their chief intention being simply to live "religiously." At times persecuted because it did not fit into any traditionally sanctioned pattern, the movement persisted, drawing tens of thousands of women. Eventually they built small convents for themselves; by the end of the fourteenth century, there were 169 beguine convents in Cologne, the heart of the movement.

Medieval mysticism

Mysticism also flowered during the Middle Ages, renewing the spiritual heart of the Church. Especially in cloistered settings, monks and nuns sat in contemplation of the meanings of the scriptures for the soul. Biblical stories of battles between heroes and their enemies were, for instance, interpreted as the struggle between the soul and one's baser desires. Beyond this rational thought, some engaged in quiet non-conceptual prayer, simply resting receptively in the presence of God.

In thirteenth-century Italy, there was the endearing figure of St. Francis of Assisi (1182–1226). The carefree, dashing son of a merchant, he underwent a radical spiritual transformation. He traded his fine clothes for simple garb and "left the world"[53] for a life of total poverty, caring for lepers and rebuilding dilapidated churches, since in a vision Jesus spoke to him from the cross, saying: "Repair my Church." Eventually Francis understood that his real mission was to rebuild the Church by re-emphasizing the Gospel and its commands of love and poverty. A band of brothers and then of sisters, led by the saintly Clare, gathered around him. The Friars preached, worked, begged, tended lepers, and lived a simple life of penance and prayer while wandering from town to town. This ascetic life was permeated with mystical joy, one of St. Francis's hallmarks. He was also known for his rapport with wild animals and is often pictured with birds resting lovingly on his shoulders. Two years before his death, Francis received the "stigmata," replicas on his own body of the crucifixion wounds of Jesus. This miracle was interpreted as a sign of the saint's union with Christ by suffering, prayer, holiness, and love.

The flowering of English mysticism during the fourteenth century was exemplified by Julian of Norwich. As a girl, she had prayed that when she reached the age of thirty (the age at which Jesus began his public mission) she would have an illness that would bring her an understanding of his Passion (the sufferings of his final days). As requested, she did indeed become so ill when she was thirty that she almost died. During this crisis, she had visions and conversations with Christ which revealed the boundless love with which he continually offers himself for humanity. Her writings delve into the perennial problem of reconciling the existence of evil with the experience of a loving God, whom she sometimes referred to as "God our Mother."

An anonymous fourteenth-century English writer contributed a volume entitled *The Cloud of Unknowing*. Christianity then and now largely follows what is called the *affirmative way*, with art, liturgy, scriptures, and imagery to aid devotion. But the author of *The Cloud* spoke to those who were prepared to undertake the *negative way* of abiding in sheer love for God, with no thoughts. God cannot be known through ideas or physical images; "a naked intent toward God, a desire for him alone, is enough."[54]

Fourteenth-century Italy witnessed a period of unprecedented degradation among the clergy, while the papacy occupied itself with organizational matters in Avignon. In this spiritual vacuum, laypeople gathered around saintly individuals to imbibe their atmosphere of genuine devotion. One of the most celebrated of these was the young Catherine of Siena. In her persistent efforts to restore spiritual purity and religious discipline to the Church, she gained the ear of Pope Gregory XI, helping to convince him to return to Rome. She was called "mother of thousands of souls," and people were said to be converted just by seeing her face.

The Protestant Reformation

Despite the genuine piety of individuals within the Catholic Church, some who clashed with its authority claimed that those in power seemed often to have lost touch with their own spiritual tradition. With the rise of literacy and printing in the late fifteenth century, many Christians were rediscovering early Christianity and comparing it unfavorably with what the

Roman Catholic Church had made of it. Roman Catholic fund-raising or church-building financial activities were particularly criticized. These included "*indulgences*" (remission of the punishment for sin by the clergy in return for services or payments), the sale of relics, purchases of masses for the dead, spiritual pilgrimages, and the earning of spiritual "merit" by donating to the Church.

Salient among the reformists was Martin Luther. Luther was a monk and priest who lectured at the University of Wittenberg. He struggled personally with the question of how one's sins could ever be totally atoned for by one's own actions. The Roman Catholic Church's position was that to be forgiven of post-baptismal sins, people should repent and then confess their sins to a priest and be pardoned. In addition, the punishment after death due to sins could be remitted either for the performance of prescribed penances or through granting of an indulgence. The Castle Church at Wittenberg housed an immense collection of relics, including hairs from the Virgin Mary and a thorn from the "crown" of thorns placed on Jesus's head before he was crucified. This relic collection was deemed so powerful that those who viewed them on the proper day and contributed sufficiently to the Church could receive indulgences from the pope freeing themselves or their loved ones from almost two million years in **Purgatory** (the intermediate place of purifying suffering).

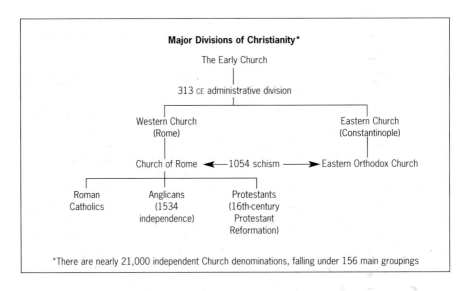

Major Divisions of Christianity*

The Early Church

313 CE administrative division

Western Church (Rome) — Eastern Church (Constantinople)

Church of Rome ◄— 1054 schism —► Eastern Orthodox Church

Roman Catholics — Anglicans (1534 independence) — Protestants (16th-century Protestant Reformation)

*There are nearly 21,000 independent Church denominations, falling under 156 main groupings

By intense study of the Bible, Luther began to emphasize a different approach. Both Paul and Augustine could be interpreted as saying that God, through Jesus, offered salvation to sinners in spite of their sins. This salvation was offered by God's grace alone and received solely by repentant faith. The good works and created graces prescribed by Catholics to earn merit in heaven were not part of original Christianity, Luther argued. Salvation from sin comes from faith in God, which itself comes from God, by grace. Then:

From faith flows love and joy in the Lord, and from love a joyful, willing
and free mind that serves one's neighbor willingly and takes no account of
gratitude or ingratitude, of praise or blame, of gain or loss.[55]

In 1517 Luther invited the university community to debate this issue with
him, by the established custom of nailing his theses to the door of the
church. He apparently had no intention of splitting with the Church. But
a papal bull (decree) of June 15, 1520 excommunicated him.

Luther's evolving theology took him farther and farther from the institutions of the Roman Catholic Church. He did not think that the Bible supported the Roman Catholic tradition that pope, bishops, priests, and monks
should have spiritual authority over laypeople; instead, he asserted that
there is "a priesthood of all believers."

Another major reformer who eventually broke with Rome was the
Swiss priest Ulrich Zwingli (1484–1531). He rejected practices not mentioned in the Bible, such as abstaining from meat during Lent, veneration
of relics and saints, religious pilgrimages, and celibacy for monks and
priests. Zwingli asserted that the Lord's Supper, or mass, should be celebrated only as a memorial of Jesus's sacrifice; he did not believe in the
myserious presence of Jesus's blood and body in the consecrated wine and
bread. He even questioned the spiritual efficacy of rituals such as masses
for the dead and confession of one's sins to a priest:

It is God alone who remits sins and puts the heart at rest, so to Him alone
ought we to ascribe the healing of our wounds, to Him alone display them to
be healed.[56]

The ideals of these reformists were adopted by many Christians. The
freedom of scriptural interpretation which they opened turned out to be a
Pandora's box. *Protestantism*, as the new branch of Christianity came to be
called, was never as monolithic as the Roman Catholic Church had been in
the west. Reform movements branched out in many directions.

A major seat of Protestantism developed in Geneva, under John Calvin
(1509–1564). He shared the reform principles of salvation by faith alone,
the exclusive authority of the Bible, and "the priesthood of all believers."
But Calvin carried the doctrine of salvation by faith to a new conclusion.
To him, the appropriate response to God is a zealous piety and awe-struck
reverence in which one "dreads to offend him more than to die."[57] Human
actions are of no eternal significance because God has already decided the
destiny of each person. By grace, some are to be saved; for God's own
reasons, others are predestined to be damned eternally.

Although there was therefore nothing that people could do about it,
their behavior would reveal which fate awaited them. There are three signs
which humans could recognize: profession of faith, an upright life, and participation in the sacraments. Calvin felt that the Church has the right to chas-
tize and in some extreme situations, excommunicate those who seemed to
violate the sanctity of the Church. Calvin envisioned a holy commonwealth
in which the Church, government, and citizens all cooperate to create a
society dedicated to the glory and mission of God.

Calvin's Christianity made its followers feel that they should fear no one except God. Convinced they were predestined to do God's will, they were impervious to worldly obstacles to the spread of their faith. *Calvinism* became the state religion of Scotland and also had a following in England.

Concurrently, the Church of England separated from the Church of Rome when Henry VIII declared his Church's independence from the Church of Rome. Now called *Anglicanism*, this form of Christianity is in communion with Old Catholics and also shares some similarities to the Protestant churches. One of its thirty-seven autonomous Churches is the Protestant *Episcopal* Church in the United States, a name referring to its being a church with bishops.

As this Protestant Reformation progressed, Spain, France, and Italy remained largely Roman Catholic. Germany was largely Lutheran. Ireland split between Catholicism and Protestantism, leading to wars that continue today. The Calvinist Church of Scotland called itself *Presbyterian*, a reference to its form of organization. Some Polish and Hungarian communities adopted a form of *Unitarianism*, which rejected the ideas of original sin, the Trinity, and Jesus's divinity, in favor of a simple theism and imitation of Jesus.

Some Protestant groups that were outlawed by the Church of England emigrated to new colonies in North America and formed new **denominations** (organized groups of congregations). One of the largest of these groups is the *Baptists*, a denomination which baptizes people as conscious adult believers rather than as infants. *Congregationalists* emphasize the independence of each local church and the "priesthood" of all members. *Quakers* (formally known as the Religious Society of Friends) worship without any liturgy or minister, in the hope that as they sit in worshipful silence, God will speak through any one of their members (although most American Quakers now worship in a more programmed service). *Methodists* are followers of the evangelist John Wesley, who traveled an average of 8000 miles (12,874 km) a year by horseback to promote "vital practical religion and . . . increase the life of God in the souls of men."[58]

During the nineteenth century, yet more Protestant churches sprang up in the United States. *Evangelical* churches—those emphasizing salvation by personal faith in Jesus, personal conversion, the importance of the Bible, and preaching instead of ritual—have proliferated in North America. *Seventh Day Adventists* believe that the Second Coming of Christ will soon occur, and they regard the Bible as an absolute guide to faith and spiritual practice in anticipation of the return of Jesus. *Jehovah's Witnesses* criticize other Christian Churches as having developed false doctrines from the second century onward, and they urge people to leave these "false religions" and prepare for a coming time when all who do not hold true belief will be destroyed. Fundamentalist evangelical sects are also gaining strongholds in South America, which had been largely Roman Catholic since the Spanish conquests of these countries. Protestant missionaries have also carried the gospel to Asia, Africa, and Eastern Europe.

Despite the great diversity among Protestant denominations, most share several characteristics that distinguish them somewhat from Orthodoxy and Roman Catholicism. First, Protestants place their emphasis on the Bible rather than on the authority of the Church, though they differ in how the Bible should be interpreted. Second, they emphasize individual relationship to Jesus and God rather than the mediation of God's grace through the Church. Instead of priests, most Protestant Churches have ministers, whose role emphasizes preaching and building the community rather than acting as vehicles of God's grace. The Quakers have gone even farther in rejecting human spiritual authority. They follow the example of George Fox (1624–1691), who experienced in the inner light the certainty of the divine; these "Children of the Light" utterly rejected any outer religious forms and instead simply sit in the silence, surrendered to God.

The Roman Catholic Reformation

As the Protestant reformers were defining their positions, so was the Roman Catholic Church. Because reform pressures were underway in Catholicism before Luther, Catholics refer to the movement as the Catholic Reformation, rather than the "Counter-Reformation," as Protestants call it. However, the Protestant phenomena provoked the Roman Catholic Church to clarify its own position, largely through the Council of Trent (1545–1563). It attempted to legislate moral reform among the clergy, to tighten the church administration, and to recognize officially the absolute authority of the pope as the earthly vicar of God and Jesus Christ. The Council also took historic stands on a number of issues, emphasizing that its positions were dogmas, or authoritative truths. For example, one of the fundamental doctrines of the Roman Catholic Church is the dogma of *original sin*. All humans are said to be morally defective, or "fallen," having inherited a sinful nature from the first human ancestors. They can be saved from this condition only by the grace of God, as mediated through the death and resurrection of Jesus.

The Council of Trent ruled that salvation requires "good works" as well as faith. These works include acts of mercy, veneration of the saints, relics, and sacred images, and participation in the **sacraments** (sacred rites).

In addition to the actions of the Council of Trent, the Roman Catholic Church gradually chose more virtuous popes than in the past, and several new monastic orders grew out of the desires for reform. The Jesuits offered themselves as an army for God at the service of the pope. The Society of Jesus, as the order was formally called, was begun by Ignatius Loyola in the sixteenth century. His *Spiritual Exercises* is still regarded as an excellent guide to meditation and spiritual discernment. However, it was as activists and educators in the everyday world that Jesuits were highly influential in the Reformation, and they pioneered in carrying Roman Catholicism to Asia.

Roman Catholicism was also carried to the western hemisphere and the Philippines by Spanish conquistadores. At home, Spain was host to a number of outstanding mystics during the sixteenth and seventeenth centuries. St. Teresa of Avila (1515–1582), a Carmelite nun, became at mid-life a dynamo of spiritual activity, in an order of ascetic Reformed (or Discalced) Carmelite nuns and monks. Discalced Carmelites usually pray much, and eat and sleep little. Despite her organizational activity, St. Teresa was able to maintain a calm sense of deep inner communion with God. In her masterpiece entitled *Interior Castle*, she described the state of "spiritual marriage":

> *Here it is like rain falling from the heavens into a river or a spring; there is nothing but water there and it is impossible to divide or separate the water belonging to the river from that which fell from the heavens.*[59]

St. Teresa's great influence fell onto a young friend, now known as St. John of the Cross. He became a member of one of the Carmelite houses for men; when imprisoned by other Carmelites who opposed the reforms, he experienced visions and wrote profound spiritual poetry. For John, the most important step for the soul longing to be filled with God is to surrender all vestiges of the self. This state he called the "dark night of the soul," a relinquishing of human reasoning into a state of not-knowing into which the pure light of God may enter without resistance. St. John of the Cross is still considered one of the great masters of the spiritual life.

The Impact of the Enlightenment

Major potential threats to Christianity arose during the eighteenth-century "Enlightenment" in Europe. Intellectual circles exalted human reason and on this basis rejected faith in biblical miracles and revelations. Some people felt that nineteenth-century scientific advances undermined the biblical story of the creation of the world. However, many nineteenth-century scientists were devout Christians who viewed the truth of science as supporting the truth of faith. There emerged two opposing trends: a liberal one trying to join faith with modern knowledge, versus a conservative one emphasizing the conflict between faith and science. Both views spread rapidly, dividing between them much of Christendom, especially Protestantism. In 1911, "fundamentalists" published as their uncompromising tenets the total inerrancy of the Bible, and Christ's literal virgin birth, substitutionary atonement, bodily resurrection, and anticipated second coming in final glory. Meanwhile, "modernist" theologians were interpreting such concepts in symbolic terms, with an aversion to dogmatism. Individuals were encouraged to judge religious beliefs by their own experience.

Undaunted, and in some cases invigorated, by these challenges to traditional faith, Protestantism developed a strong missionary spirit, joining Roman Catholic efforts to spread Christianity to every country, along with colonialism. John Wesley, the founder of Methodism, explained that it was "my bounden duty to declare unto all that are willing to hear, the glad tidings of salvation."

The "social gospel" movement brought Protestant churches to the forefront of efforts at social and moral reform. Women, long excluded from important positions in the Church, played major roles in church-related missionary and reform efforts, such as the abolition of slavery; they cited certain biblical passages as supporting equality of the sexes. When Sarah Grimke and other women were criticized by their Congregational church for speaking publicly against slavery, Grimke asserted, "All I ask of my brethren is that they will take their feet from off our necks and permit us to stand upright on that ground which God has designed us to occupy."[60]

Liberal trends in Protestant theology led to biblical criticism—that is, to efforts to analyze the Bible as literature. What, for instance, were the earliest texts? Who wrote them? How did they relate to each other? Such questions, unthinkable in earlier generations, continue to enliven Christian theological debate.

The Second Vatican Council

In the meantime, the Roman Catholic and Eastern Orthodox Churches had continued to defend tradition against the changes of modern life. A general council of the Roman Catholic hierarchs was held in 1868. It found itself embroiled chiefly in the question of *papal infallibility*, a doctrine which it upheld. The pope, proclaimed the bishops of the council, can never err when he speaks from the seat of his authority (*ex cathedra*), on matters of faith and morals.

In 1962 Pope John XXIII, known for his holiness and friendliness, convened the Second Vatican Council for the express purposes of updating and energizing the Church and making it serve the people better as a living force in the modern world rather than being an old, embattled citadel. When questioned about his intentions, he demonstrated by opening a window to let in fresh air. With progressives and traditionalists often at odds, the majority nevertheless voted for major shifts in the Church's mission.

Many of the changes involved the liturgy of the mass, or the Eucharist. Rather than celebrate it in Latin, which most people did not understand, the liturgy was to be translated into the local languages. Rites were to be simplified. Greater use of sacred music was encouraged.

For the first time the laity were to be invited to participate actively. After Vatican II thus unleashed creativity and simplicity in public worship, entirely new forms appeared, such as informal folk masses—with spiritual folk songs sung to guitar accompaniment.

Another major change was the new emphasis on **ecumenism**, in the sense of rapprochement among all branches of Christianity. The Roman Catholic Church acknowledged that the Holy Spirit is active in all Christian churches, including Protestant denominations and the Eastern Orthodox churches. It pressed for a restoration of unity among all Christians, while proclaiming that each could preserve its traditions intact. It also extended the concept of revelation, increasing the hope of dialogue with Jews, with whom Christians share "spiritual patrimony"[61] and with Muslims, upon whom the Church "looks with esteem," for they "adore one God" and honor Jesus as a prophet.

Appreciative mention was also made of other world religions as ways of approaching the same One whom Christians call God. Specifically described were Hinduism ("through which men contemplate the divine mystery") and Buddhism ("which acknowledges the radical insufficiency of this shifting world").[62]

Vatican II clearly marked major new directions in Catholicism. Its relatively liberal, pacificistic characteristics are still meeting with some opposition within the Church decades later. In the late twentieth and early twenty-first centuries, conservative elements in the Vatican seemed to be reversing the direction taken by Vatican II, to the dismay of liberal Catholics.

Central Beliefs in Contemporary Christianity

The Church is vast and culturally diverse, and Christian theologies are complex and intricate. Nevertheless there are a few basic motifs on which the majority of faithful Christians would probably agree.

A central belief is the divine Sonship of Jesus—the assertion that Jesus is the incarnation of God. According to the Gospel of John, before Jesus's death he told his disciples that he would be going to "my Father's house ... to prepare a place for you." When they asked how they would find the way to that place, Jesus reportedly said:

> *I am the way, I am the truth and I am life. No one comes to the Father except by me. . . . Anyone who has seen me has seen the Father. . . . It is the Father who dwells in me doing his own work.*[63]

Throughout most of Christian history, there has been the feeling that Jesus was the only incarnation of God. Theologian Paul Knitter is one of the contemporary voices calling for a less exclusive approach which still honors the unique contribution of Jesus:

> *What Christians do know, on the basis of their praxis of following Jesus, is that his message is a sure means for bringing about liberation from injustice and oppression, that it is an effective, hope-filled, universally meaningful way of realizing Soteria [human welfare and liberation of the poor and oppressed] and promoting God's kingdom. . . . Not those who proclaim "only Lord, only Lord," but those who do the will of the Father will enter the kingdom (Matthew 7:21–23).*[64]

For Christians, Jesus is the Savior of the world, the one whom God sent to redeem people from their sins and reconcile them with God. Matthew reports that Jesus said he "did not come to be served, but to serve, and to give up his life as a ransom for many."[65] His own suffering and death are regarded as a substitute sacrifice on behalf of all those who follow and place their faith in him. According to the Gospel of John,

> *God loved the world so much that he gave his only Son, that everyone who has faith in him may not die but have eternal life. It was not to judge the world that God sent his Son into the world, but that through him the world might be saved.*[66]

According to Christian belief, humanity has a sinful character, illustrated metaphorically in the Old Testament by the fall of Adam and Eve. We have lost our original purity. Given free will by God, we have chosen disobedience rather than surrender to the will of God. We cannot save ourselves from our fallen condition; we can only be forgiven by the compassion of a loving God.

Through fully surrendered faith in Jesus, Christians hope to be washed of their egotistical sinfulness, regenerated, adopted by God, sanctified, and glorified in the life to come. These are the blessings of *salvation* which Christians feel Jesus won for them by his sacrifice.

Although Christians worship Jesus as Savior, as the incarnation of a merciful God, they also see him as a human being showing fellow human beings the way to God. His own life is seen as the perfect model for human behavior. Archbishop Desmond Tutu of South Africa emphasizes Jesus's identification with the human condition:

> God does not occupy an Olympian fastness, remote from us. He has this deep, deep solidarity with us. God became a human being, a baby. God was hungry. God was tired, God suffered and died. God is there with us.[67]

This is the central mystery of Christianity: that God became human in order to lead people back to God.

The human virtue most often associated with Jesus is love. Many Christians say they experience Jesus's love even though he is no longer walking the earth in human form. And in turn, they have deep love for Jesus. Those who are experiencing problems in life are comforted to feel that Jesus is a living presence in their lives, standing with them spiritually, supporting them, loving them even in the darkest of times. Reverend Larry Howard, the African–American pastor of Hopps Memorial Christian Methodist Episcopal Church in Syracuse, New York, declares:

> We found a Jesus. A Jesus who came in the midnight hour. A Jesus that was able to rock babies to sleep. A Jesus that stood in the midst and walked the miles when the freedom train rode through the South all the way through Syracuse. Jesus brought us through the mighty trials and tribulations. Why did Jesus do that? Jesus loved us and through that love and because of that love we stand here today. Not because the world has been so good to us. Not because we have been treated fair. Not because we have been able to realize the dream that God has given every man, woman, and child. But we stand here because we love Jesus. We love him more and more and more each day.[68]

In addition to being the paragon of love, Jesus also provides a model of sinlessness. To become like God, humans must constantly be purified of their lower tendencies. This belief has led some Christians to extremes of penance, such as the monks who flogged themselves and wore hairshirts so that their conscience might always be pricked. In a milder form, confession of one's sinfulness is a significant part of Christian tradition. There is an emphasis on self-discipline to guard against temptations, on examination of one's own faults, and on rituals such as baptism that help to remove the contamination that is innate in humanity. Although one must make these efforts at purification, most Christians believe that it is only through the grace of God—as mediated by the saving sacrifice of Jesus—that one can be delivered from sin and rise above ordinary human nature toward a divine state of sinlessness.

Sacred Practices

Imitation of the model set by Jesus in his own life is the primary practice of Christians. In the widely-read fourteenth-century book *The Imitation of Christ*, people are encouraged to aspire to Jesus's own example as well as his teachings:

> *O how powerful is the pure love of Jesus, which is mixed with no self-interest, nor self-love! ... Where shall one be found who is willing to serve God for naught?*[69]

In addition to the inner attempt to become more and more like Jesus, Christians have developed a variety of spiritual practices. Although forms and understandings of the practices vary among the branches of Christendom, they may include public worship services with sermons and offering of the sacraments, celebrations of the liturgical year, private contemplation and prayer, and devotions to Mary and the saints.

Worship services and sacraments

Christian worship typically takes place in a church building which may be revered as a sacred space. The late nineteenth-century Russian Orthodox saint Ioann Kronshtadtsky (d. 1908) explains,

> *Entering the church you enter some special realm which is not like the visible one. In the world you hear and see everything earthly, transient, fragile, liable to decay, sinful. In the church you see and hear the heavenly, the non-transient, the eternal, the holy. A temple is the threshold of heaven. It is like the heaven itself, because here is God's throne, the service of angels, the frequent descent of the Holy Spirit. ... Here everything from icons to censer and the priests' robes fills you with veneration and prayer; everything tells you that you are in God's shrine, face to face with God himself.*[70]

The word sacrament can be translated as "mystery." In Christianity, the sacraments are the sacred rites that are thought capable of transmitting the mystery of Christ to worshippers. Roman Catholic and Eastern Orthodox Churches observe seven sacraments: baptism (initiation and symbolic purification from sin by water), confirmation (of membership in the Church), Eucharist (the ritual meal described below), penance (confession and absolution of sins), extreme unction (anointing of the sick with oil, especially before death), Holy Orders (consecration as a deacon, priest, or bishop), and matrimony. In general, Protestant Churches recognize only baptism and the Eucharist as sacraments.

The ritual of public worship, or liturgy, usually follows a set pattern, though in some Churches the actions of the Holy Spirit are thought to inspire spontaneous expressions of faith.

In most forms of Christianity, the central sacrament is the Holy **Eucharist** (also called Holy Communion). It is a mystery through which the invisible Christ is thought to grant communion with himself. Believers are given a bit of bread to eat, which is received as the body of Christ, and a sip of wine or grape juice, understood as his blood. The priest or minister may consecrate the bread and wine in ritual fashion and share them among the people. In Roman Catholic or Orthodox masses, the cup of wine and the bread are thought to be mystically transformed by the Holy Spirit into the blood and body of Christ. They are treated with profound reverence. In sharing the communion "meal" together, the people are united with each other as well as with Christ.

Jesus is pictured in the Bible as having set the pattern for this sacrament at what is called the Last Supper, the meal he shared with his inner circle before his capture by the authorities in Jerusalem. The body and blood of Christ are seen as the spiritual nourishment of the faithful, that which gives them eternal life in the midst of earthly life.

Mother Julia Gatta, Anglican priest, describes this sacred experience from the point of view of the clergy who preside at the liturgy:

> To be the celebrant of Eucharist is, I think, the most wonderful experience on earth. In a sense, you experience the energy flowing both ways. . . . One experiences the Spirit in them offering their prayer through Christ to the Father. But at the same time, you experience God's love flowing back into them. When I give communion to people, I am aware that I am caught in that circle of love.[71]

The partaking of sacred bread and wine is the climax of a longer liturgy of Holy Communion. The communion service, often called a **mass** in Catholicism, begins with liturgical prayers, praise, and confession of sinfulness. A group confession chanted by some Lutheran congregations enumerates these flaws:

> Most merciful God, we have sinned against you in thought, word, and deed, by what we have done and by what we have left undone. We have not loved you with our whole heart; we have not loved our neighbors as ourselves.[72]

Catholics were traditionally encouraged to confess their sins privately to a priest before taking communion, in the sacrament of *penance*, or "reconciliation." After hearing the confession, the priest pronounces forgiveness and blessing over the penitent, or perhaps prescribes a penance. Orthodox Christians were also traditionally expected to spend several days in contrition and fasting before receiving communion. The reason for the emphasis on purification is that during the service the church itself is perceived as the kingdom of God, in which everything is holy. In Orthodox services, the clergy walk around the church, swinging an incense censer to set apart the area as a sacred space and to lift the prayers of the congregants to God.

In all Christian churches, passages from the Old and New Testaments may be read and the congregation may sing several hymns, songs of praise or thanksgiving to God. The congregation may be asked to recite a credal statement of Christian beliefs, and to make money offerings. There may be an address by the priest or minister (called a sermon or a homily) on the readings for the day. These parts of the liturgy constitute the Liturgy of the Word, in which Christ is thought to be present as the living Word addressing the people through scripture and preaching. In Protestant churches, the Liturgy of the Word is often offered alone, without the communion service.

In both Protestantism and Roman Catholicism, there are now attempts at updating the liturgy to make it more meaningful and personally relevant for contemporary Christians. One innovation that seems to have taken hold everywhere is the "sharing of the peace." Partway through the worship service, congregants turn to everyone around them to hug or shake hands and say, "The Peace of Christ be with you"—"and also with you."

There are also special events treated in sacred ways. The first to be administered is the sacrament of **baptism**. Externally, it involves either immersing the person in water or, more commonly, pouring sanctified water (representing purification) on the candidate's head. The World Council of Churches has defined the general meaning of the practice:

> By baptism, Christians are immersed in the liberating death of Christ where their sins are buried, where the "old Adam" is crucified with Christ, and where the power of sin is broken ... They are raised here and now to a new life in the power of the resurrection of Jesus Christ.[73]

Aside from adult converts to Christianity, the rite is usually performed on infants, with parents taking vows on their behalf. There are arguments that infant baptism has little basis in the Bible and that a baby cannot make the conscious repentance of sin and "conversion of heart" implied in the ceremony. Baptists and several other Protestant groups therefore reserve baptism for adults.

A second ceremony—*confirmation*—is often offered in early adolescence in Roman Catholicism and Protestantism. After a period of religious instruction, a group of young people are allowed to make a conscious and personal commitment to the Christian life.

Some Christians observe special days of fasting. Russian Orthodox Old Believer priest Father Appolinari explains fasting as a way of *soprichiastna*, of becoming part of something very large, the spiritual aura of the Lord. He says,

> When we limit our physicality, as in limiting our food intake, then we grow in our spirituality. I advise my students to notice whether their brain works better when their stomach is full or when it is almost empty. Monks refuse physical things in order to get spiritual benefits. We look at them and see their lives as dark, but for them, it is light.[74]

The liturgical year

The Church every year celebrates a cycle of festivals leading the worshipper through the life of Jesus and the gift of the Spirit. As the faithful repeat this cycle year after year, they hope to enter more deeply into the mystery of God in Christ, and the whole body of believers in Christ theoretically grows toward the kingdom of God.

CHRISTMAS AND EPIPHANY   There are three major events in the church calendar, each associated with a series of preparatory celebrations. The first is the season of light: Christmas and Epiphany. *Christmas* is the celebration of Jesus's birth on earth. **Epiphany** means "manifestation" or "showing forth." It celebrates the recognition of Jesus's spiritual kingship by the three Magi (in the western Church), his acknowledgement as the Messiah and the beloved Son of God when he is baptized by John the Baptist, and his first recognized miracle: the turning of water into wine at the wedding in Cana.

In early Christianity, Epiphany was more important than the celebration of Jesus's birth. The actual birth date is unknown. The setting of the date near the winter solstice allowed Christianity to take over the older rites celebrating the return of longer periods of daylight at the darkest time of year. In the gospel of John, Jesus is "the true light that enlightens every man,"[75] the light of the divine appearing amid the darkness of human ignorance.

Advent, the month preceding Christmas, is supposed to be a time of joyous anticipation. But in industrialized countries, it is more likely a time of frenzied marketing and buying of gifts, symbolizing God's gift to the world in the person of Jesus.

It is traditional to cut or buy an evergreen tree (symbol of eternal life) and erect it in one's house, decorated with lights and ornaments. On Christmas Eve some Christians gather for a candlelit "watch-night" service, welcoming the turn from midnight to a new day in which Christ has come into the world. On Christmas Day, Catholic and Protestant children are sometimes told that presents have been magically brought by St. Nicholas, a fourth-century bishop noted for his great generosity. Exchange of gifts may be followed by a great feast.

EASTER   The second major focus of the liturgical year is *Easter*. This is the commemoration of Jesus's death (on "Good Friday") and resurrection (on Easter Sunday, which falls in the spring but is celebrated at different times by the eastern and western Churches). Like Christmas, Easter is a continuation of earlier rites—those associated with the vernal (spring) equinox, celebrating the regeneration of plant life and the return of warm weather after the cold death of winter. It is also related to Pesach, the Hebrew Passover, the Jewish spring feast of deliverance.

Liturgically, Easter is preceded by a forty-day period of repentance and fasting, called *Lent*. Many Christians perform acts of asceticism, prayer, and charity, to join in Jesus's greater sacrifice. In the Orthodox Church, the last Sunday before Lent is dedicated to asking forgiveness. People request forgiveness from each other, bowing deeply. In the West, Lent begins with Ash Wednesday, when many Christians have ash smudges placed on their foreheads by a priest who says, "Remember, man, thou art dust and unto dust thou shalt return." On the Sunday before Easter, Jesus's triumphal entry into Jerusalem is honored by the waving of palm or willow branches in churches and the proclaiming of Hosannas. His death is mourned on "Good Friday." The mourning is jubilantly ended on Easter Sunday, with shouts of "Christ is risen!"

In Russia, the Great Vigil welcoming Easter morning lasts from midnight until dawn, with the people standing the entire time. Jim Forest describes such a service in a church in Kiev, with two thousand people crowding into the building and as many more standing outside:

> *The dean went out the royal doors into the congregation and sang out,*
> *"Christos Voskresye!" [Christ is risen!] Everyone responded in one voice,*
> *"Veyeastino voskresye!" [Truly he is risen!] It is impossible to put on paper*
> *how this sounds in the dead of night in a church overheated by crowds of*
> *people and hundreds of candles. It is like a shudder in the earth, the*
> *cracking open of the tomb. Then there was an explosion of ringing bells.*[76]

PENTECOST   Fifty days after the Jewish Passover (which Jesus is thought
to have been celebrating at the Last Supper with his disciples) comes the
Jewish celebration Shavuot (which commemorates the giving of the Torah
to Moses, as well as the first fruits of the harvest). Jews nicknamed it
Pentecost, which is Greek for "fiftieth." Christians took over the holiday
season but gave it an entirely different meaning.

In Christianity, Pentecost commemorates the occasion described in Acts
when the Holy Spirit descended upon the disciples after Jesus's death and
resurrection, filling them with the Spirit's own life and power, and enabling
them to speak in foreign tongues they had not known.

THE TRANSFIGURATION AND ASSUMPTION   Some Christian Churches
also emphasize two other special feast days. On August 6, the people honor
the Transfiguration of Jesus on the mountain, revealing his supernatural
radiance. On August 15, they celebrate the Assumption of Mary, known as
"The Falling Asleep of the Mother of God." These feasts are prominent in
the eastern Church, which generally places more emphasis on the ability
of humanity to break out of its earthly bonds and rise into the light, than
on the heaviness and darkness of sin.

Contemplative prayer

The contemplative tradition within Christianity is beginning to re-emerge.
The hectic pace and rapid change of modern life make periods of quietness
essential, if only for stress relief. Many Christians, not aware of a contemplative way within their own Church, have turned to Eastern religions for
instruction in meditation.

One of the most influential twentieth-century Christian contemplatives
was the late Thomas Merton (1915–1968). He was a Trappist monk who
received a special dispensation to live as a hermit in the woods near his
abbey in Kentucky. Merton lived simply in nature, finding joy in the commonplace, experienced attentively in silence. He studied and tried to practice the great contemplative traditions of earlier Christianity and
reintroduced them to a contemporary audience through his writings. In
meditative "prayer of the heart," or "contemplative prayer," he wrote:

> *We seek first of all the deepest ground of our identity in God. We do not*
> *reason about dogmas of faith, or "the mysteries." We seek rather to gain a*
> *direct existential grasp, a personal experience of the deepest truths of life and*
> *faith, finding ourselves in God's truths. ... Prayer then means yearning for*
> *the simple presence of God, for a personal understanding of his word, for*
> *knowledge of his will and for capacity to hear and obey him.*[77]

Before he became a Christian monk, Merton had studied Eastern mysticism, assuming that Christianity had no mystical tradition. He became friends with a Hindu monk who advised him to read St. Augustine's *Confessions* and *The Imitation of Christ*. These classical works led Merton toward a deep appreciation of the potential of the Christian inner life, aligned with a continuing openness to learn from Eastern monasticism. He died in an accident while in Asia visiting Buddhist and Hindu monastics.

Spiritual renewal through inner silence has become an important part of some Christians' practice of their faith. Syrian Orthodox Bishop Paulos Mar Gregorios of India, past-President of the World Council of Churches, concluded from the Bible evidence that Jesus himself was a contemplative:

Christ spent seventy percent of his whole life in meditation. He would sleep rarely. All day he gave himself to healing the sick. At night he would pray, sometimes all night. He was not seeking his own self-realization. His meditation and prayer were not for himself but for the world—for every human being. He held the world in his consciousness through prayer, not with attachment but with compassion. . . . To follow Jesus in the way of the cross means to say, "I lay aside all personal ambition and dedicate myself to God: 'Here I am, God. I belong to you. I have no idea where to go. It matters not what I am, so long as You lead me.' "[78]

A form of Christian meditation that was instituted by the Franciscan monks and is still practiced in many Catholic and Anglican churches is following the Stations of the Cross. These are fourteen plaques or paintings placed on the walls of the church depicting scenes from the death of Jesus. As one sees him taking up the cross, falling three times under its weight, being stripped of his clothes and being nailed to the cross, one becomes painfully and humbly aware of the suffering that God's Son experienced in manifesting as a human redeemer.

In Orthodoxy, the central contemplative practice is repetition of the Jesus Prayer. Eventually its meaning imbeds itself in the heart and one lives in a state of unceasing prayer.

Devotion to Mary

Veneration of Mary, the mother of Jesus, has come more from the grass-roots than from the top. Drawings of her were found in the catacombs in which the early Christians met; explicit devotion to her was well developed by the third or fourth century CE. Despite the absence of detailed historical information, she serves as a potent and much-loved spiritual symbol. She is particularly venerated by Roman Catholics, Eastern Orthodoxy, and Anglicans.

Some researchers feel that devotion to Mary is derived from earlier worship of the Mother Goddess. They see her as representing the feminine aspect of the Godhead. She is associated with the crescent moon, representing the receptive willingness to be filled with the Spirit. In the story of the **Annunciation**—the appearance of an angel who told her she would have a child conceived by the Holy Spirit—her reported response was "Behold, I am the handmaid of the Lord; let it be to me according to your word."[79] Mary, like Christ, embodies the basic Christian paradox: that power is found in "weakness."

Oral Christian traditions have given her many symbolic roles. One links her with Israel, which is referred to as the daughter of Zion or daughter of Jerusalem in Old Testament passages. God comes to her as the overshadowing of the Holy Spirit, and from this love between YHWH and Israel, Jesus is born to save the people of Israel.

Mary is also called the New Eve. The legendary first Eve disobeyed God and was cast out of the garden of Eden; Mary's willing submission to God allows birth of the new creation, in which Christ is in all.

In the Orthodox and Catholic traditions, she is referred to as the Mother of God. In Russia, she is also revered as the protectress of all humanity, and especially of the Russian people. Before he died on the cross, Jesus is said to have told John, the beloved disciple, that thenceforth Mary was to be his Mother. The story is interpreted as meaning that thenceforth all humanity was adopted by Mary.

Another symbolic role ascribed to Mary is that of the immaculate virgin. According to the gospels of Matthew and Luke, she conceived Jesus by heavenly intervention rather than human biology. Virginity is a spiritual sign of being dedicated to God alone, rather than to any temporal attachments.

According to the faithful, Mary is not just a symbol but a living presence, like Christ. She is appealed to in prayer and is honored in countless paintings, statues, shrines, and churches dedicated to her name. Catholics are enjoined to repeat the "Hail Mary" prayer:

> *Hail, Mary, full of grace, the Lord is with thee. Blessed art thou among women, and blessed is the fruit of thy womb, Jesus. Holy Mary, Mother of God, pray for us sinners, now and at the hour of our death.*

Theologians are careful to point out, however, that veneration of Mary is really directed toward God; Mary is not worshipped in herself but as the mother of Christ, reflecting his glory.

Be this as it may, Mary has been said to appear to believers in many places around the world. At Lourdes, in France, it is claimed that she appeared repeatedly to a young peasant girl named Bernadette in the nineteenth century. A spring found where she indicated has been the source of hundreds of medically authenticated healings from seemingly incurable diseases. In 1531, in Guadalupe (within what is now Mexico City), Mary appeared to a converted Aztec, Juan Diego. She asked him to have the bishop build a church on the spot. To convince the skeptical bishop, Juan filled his cloak with the out-of-season roses to which she directed him. When he opened the cloak before the bishop, the petals fell away to reveal a large and vivid image of Mary, with Indian features. The picture is now enshrined in a large new church with moving walkways to handle the crowds who come to see it, and the Virgin of Guadalupe has been declared Celestial Patroness of the New World.

> Each saint is a unique event, a victory over the force of evil. So many
> blessings can pour from God into the world through one life.
> Father Germann, Vladimir, Russia[80]

Veneration of saints and angels

Roman Catholics and Orthodox Christians honor their spiritual heroes as saints. These are men and women who are recognized as so holy that the divine life of Christ is particularly evident in them. After their death, they are carefully judged by the Church for proofs of exalted Christian virtue, such as tolerance under extreme provocation, and of miraculous power. Those who are canonized by this process are subject to great veneration.

Orthodox Christians are given the name of a saint when they are baptized. Each keeps an icon of this patron saint in his or her room and prays to the saint daily. Icons of many saints fill an Orthodox church, helping to make them familiar presences rather than names in history books. Saints are often known as having special areas of concern and power. For instance, St. Anthony of Padua is invoked for help in finding lost things. **Relics**, usually parts of the body or clothes of saints, are felt to radiate the holiness of the saints' communion with God. They are treasured and displayed for veneration in Catholic and Orthodox churches. It is said that saints' physical bodies were so transformed by divine light that they do not decay after death, and that they continue to emit a sweet fragrance.

Roman Catholics and Orthodox Christians also pray to the **angels** for protection. Angels are understood as spiritual beings who serve as messengers from and adoring servants of God. They are usually pictured as humans with wings. In popular piety, each person is thought to have a guardian angel for individual protection and spiritual help.

Contemporary Trends

As the third millennium since the birth of Jesus begins, Christianity is gaining membership and enthusiastic participation in some quarters and losing ground in others. In Egypt, Orthodox Coptic Christians, heirs to the ancient tradition of the Desert Fathers, have long been submerged under Muslim rule, but the monasteries have begun to flourish again. The sixteen million Coptic Christians have their own pope.

Roman Catholicism is experiencing divisions between conservatives and liberals. After the liberal tendencies of Vatican II, Pope John Paul II reaffirmed certain traditional stands and strengthened the position of the right wing of the Church. In a 1995 encyclical, he emphatically insisted upon what he called the fundamental right to human life as opposed to the "culture of death," condemning abortion and euthanasia as "crimes which no human law can claim to legitimize" and condemning the death penalty.[81] Despite his conservative stances, Pope John Paul II uses the latest technologies, including a major Internet website, to spread his messages. He also travels extensively, urging a return to traditional family values. In 1998 the world was stunned to see his tremendous welcome to Cuba, which had been officially atheist for two decades and then neutrally secular since 1991. The Young Communist League encouraged its half a million members to see the pope in Havana, in order to "hear the message of a man of great talent and culture who is concerned about the most pressing problems of modern humanity."[82]

In spite of the public attention paid to the pope as a person, the priesthood is dwindling in some countries, partly because of the requirement that priests be celibate. There is also increased interest in participation by women (who are not allowed by the Vatican to be priests), and widespread disregard of papal prohibitions on effective birth control, abortion, test-tube conception, surrogate motherhood, genetic experimentation, divorce, and homosexuality.

While cautioning against a recreational view of sexuality, Sean McDonagh SSC emphasizes that the environmental and social consequences of unlimited population growth require a rethinking of traditional Catholic proscriptions on birth control:

"Is it pro-life to allow the extinction of hundreds of thousands of living species which will ultimately affect the well-being of all future generations on the planet?"[83]

The Vatican has responded to these trends by insisting on the value of tradition and authority. But many American Catholic leaders are concerned that, in the words of Father Frank McNulty of Newark, New Jersey, "people often do not perceive the church as proclaiming integral truth and divine mercy, but rather as sounding harsh, demanding."[84] Acting as a group, Roman Catholic bishops in the United States have issued statements deploring sexism as a "sin" (recommending that spiritual positions of responsibility and authority be opened to women and that non-sexist language be used in liturgy), supporting peace efforts, and insisting on the morality of economic social justice.

In Protestantism, traditional denominations in Europe and the United States are declining in membership. According to a Gallup poll, only a minority of the "unchurched" actually disagree with their denomination's teachings. They are more likely to drop away because of apathy, a lack of services, or a lack of welcome on the part of the minister. Anglican head Dr. George Carey, the Archbishop of Canterbury, bemoans his impression that Christians are not taking the Church's teachings into consideration in making personal moral choices, and feels that in England God is "being banished to the realm of the private hobby."[85]

Although many traditional Christian churches are losing members, other groups and trends are taking vigorous root. These include evangelical and charismatic groups, non-Western Christian churches, liberation theology, feminist theology, creation-centered Christianity, and the ecumenical movement.

Evangelicalism

To evangelize is to preach the Christian gospel and convert people to Christianity. Evangelical theology, with its emphasis on experiencing the grace of God, has been important throughout the history of American Protestantism. The current evangelical movement has its roots in the fundamentalist–modernist controversy of the early twentieth century.

The fundamentalists were reacting against the liberal or modern movement in Christianity that sought to reconcile science and religion and to use historical and archaeological data to understand the Bible. This movement had an optimistic view of human nature and stressed reason, free will, and self-determination. In response, a group of Christians called for a return to the "fundamentals" which they identified as 1) the inspiration and authority of scripture (and sometimes its inerrancy); 2) an emphasis on the virgin birth of Christ and other miracles; 3) the deity of Christ and the bodily resurrection as a literal historical event; 4) Christ's atoning and substitutionary death; and 5) an emphasis on the literal and imminent second coming of Christ. The controversy between these two groups received its most famous public expression in the Scopes trial in 1925 when John Thomas Scopes, a high school teacher in Tennessee, challenged a state law forbidding the teaching of evolution in schools.

Protestant evangelicalism is making great strides in South America, in areas that were largely Roman Catholic as a result of colonization by Spain centuries ago. In the early 1990s, an average of five evangelical churches were being established each week in Rio de Janeiro, most of them in the slum areas, in an attempt to offer food, job training, day care, and perhaps conversion to the very poor.

Charismatics

Overlapping somewhat with the evangelical surge, there is a rising emphasis on *charismatic* experience—that is, divinely inspired powers—among Christians of all nations and denominations. While Christian fundamentalists stress the historical Jesus, charismatics feel they have also been touched by the "third person" of the Trinity, the Holy Spirit. Many are caught up in a widespread contemporary spiritual renewal which harkens back to the biblical descent of the Holy Spirit upon the disciples of Jesus, firing them with spiritual powers and faith.

Mainstream Christian churches, which have often rejected emotional spiritual experience in favor of a more orderly piety, are gradually becoming more tolerant of it. Among Roman Catholics the movement is often called "Charismatic Renewal," for it claims to bring true life in the Spirit back to Christianity. By broad definition, up to one-fourth of all Christians today could be considered members of this Pentecostal-charismatic movement.[86]

Under the alleged influence of the Spirit, Pentecostalist-charismatics speak in tongues, pray and utter praises, spontaneously heal by the laying on of hands and prayer, and bear witness to spiritual miracles.

Spontaneous spiritual gestures are especially prevalent at large renewal sites.

Speaking of the descent of the Holy Spirit, Roman Bilas, Moscow head of the Union of Pentecostal Christians of Evangelical Faith, says passionately,

This moment when you really feel God's power in yourself brings so much peace and joy within you. It transforms you and society. There comes a sense of total forgiveness for your sins, and the ability in you to forgive others. At that moment, you start to speak in different languages, maybe such that no one can understand.

The main thing is that the person should be filled with God's Power. A nice-looking car will not move unless it is fueled. God's Power will only fill those who are pure. That is why in the early Church people went into the wilderness to fast and repent. Then God could fill them with His Power. Each sermon should have this Power of God; then the people will really listen and repent of their sins.[87]

Cultural broadening

Although contemporary Christianity was largely shaped in Europe and its North American colonies, a large percentage of the Christian Church lies outside these areas. It has great numerical strength and vigor in Africa, Latin America, and parts of Asia.

As missionaries spread Christianity to these regions, they often assumed that European ways were culturally superior to indigenous ways and peoples. But some of these newer Christians have come to different conclusions. Theologians of the African Independent Churches, for instance, reject the historical missionary efforts to divorce them from their traditions of honoring their ancestors. This effort tore apart their social structure, they feel, with no scriptural justification:

As we became more acquainted with the Bible, we began to realise that there was nothing at all in the Bible about the European customs and Western traditions that we had been taught. What, then was so holy and sacred about this culture and this so-called civilisation that had been imposed upon us and was now destroying us? Why could we not maintain our African customs and be perfectly good Christians at the same time? ...

We have learnt to make a very clear distinction between culture and religion. ... [For instance], the natural customs of any particular nation or race must never be confused with the grace of Jesus Christ our Saviour, Redeemer and Liberator.[88]

Contemporary perceptions of Jesus have been deeply enriched by those from the inhabitants of poor Third World countries who have brought personal understanding of Jesus's ministry to the outcasts and downtrodden. In Asia, where Christians are usually in the minority, there is an emphasis on a Christ who is present in the whole cosmos and who calls all people to sit at a common table to partake of his generous love. In Latin America, Jesus is viewed as the liberator of the people from political and social oppression,

Archbishop Desmond Tutu

During the years of struggle against apartheid in South Africa, one voice which refused to be silenced was that of the Anglican Archbishop of Cape Town, Desmond Mpilo Tutu (b. 1931). Afterward, he served his country as Chairperson of the Truth and Reconciliation Commission, "looking a beast in the eye" to investigate abuses from all sides that were perpetrated during the apartheid era. In this capacity, he still refused to mute his criticisms of those wielding power, no matter what their race and stature. In 1995 he proclaimed,

> *The so-called ordinary people, God's favourites, are sick and tired of corruption, repression, injustice, poverty, disease and the violation of their human rights. They are crying out "enough is enough!" It is exhilarating when you are able to say to dictators everywhere: You have had it! You have had it! This is God's world and you will bite the dust! They think it will not happen but it does, and they bite the dust comprehensively and ignominiously.*
>
> *We will want to continue to be the voice of the voiceless. It is the role of the church to be the conscience of society.[89]*

The "Arch's" fearless stance on behalf of truth and justice for the oppressed earned him the Nobel Peace Prize in 1984. He confronted not only those in power but also those who sought change through violence and those in the Church who witnessed the horrors of apartheid but kept silent. He explains, "Our task is to be agents of the Kingdom of God, and this sometimes requires us to say unpopular things."[90]

The former archbishop feels that

> *Faith is a highly political thing. At the centre of all that we believe as Christians is the incarnation—the participation of God in the affairs of this world. As followers of that God we too must be politically engaged. We need inner resources, however, in order to face the political demands of our time.[91]*

How has Mr. Tutu developed his inner resources? Through meditation, prayer, and fasting. He observes the traditional daily devotions of the Anglican Church, always starts meetings with prayer, and annually takes a long spiritual retreat. He regularly prays for others and many are also praying for him; he asserts that intercessory prayer has practical effects. His spiritual confessor, Francis Cull, describes Mr. Tutu's inner life as rooted in the Benedictine monastic discipline which underlies Anglican spirituality. He explains:

> *As I ponder on the prayer life of Desmond Tutu I see the three fundamental Benedictine demands that there shall be: rest, prayer, and work and in that order. It is a remarkable fact, and it is one reason at least why he has been able to sustain the burdens he has carried, that he has within him a stillness and a need for quiet solitude. . . . The "rest" of which St. Benedict speaks is not a mere switching off; it is a positive attempt to fulfill the age-old command to rest in God. . . .[92]*

Desmond Tutu himself insists that spiritual practice is essential in order to know and follow the will of God:

> *God's will has to do with what is right, just, decent and healing of the wounds of society. To know what this means we need to cleanse ourselves of ourselves—of our fears, greed, ambitions and personal desires. . . . We must commit ourselves to tell the truth. We must identify evil wherever we see it.[93]*

from dehumanization, and from sin. In Africa, the African Independent Churches have brought indigenous traditions of drumming, dancing, and singing into community worship of a Jesus who is seen as functioning as the greatest of ancestors—a mediator carrying prayers and offerings between humans and the divine, and watchful caretaker of the people.

Liberation theology

Although many Christians make a distinction between the sacred and the secular, some have involved themselves deeply with social issues as an expression of their Christian faith. For instance, the late Baptist preacher, Martin Luther King Jr., became a great civil rights leader, declaring, "It was Jesus of Nazareth that stirred the Negroes to protest with the creative weapon of love."[94] This trend is now called **liberation theology**—a faith that stresses the need for concrete political action to help the poor. Beginning in the 1960s with Vatican II, and the conference of Latin American bishops in Columbia in 1968, Roman Catholic priests and nuns serving in Latin America began to make conscious, voluntary efforts to understand and side with the poor in their struggles for social justice. Biblical basis for this approach is found in the Acts of the Apostles:

> *The group of believers was one in mind and heart. No one said that any of his belongings was his own, but they all shared with one another everything they had. … There was no one in the group who was in need. Those who owned fields or houses would sell them, bring the money received from the sale and turn it over to the apostles; and the money was distributed to each one according to his need.*[95]

The Peruvian theologian Gustavo Gutierrez, who coined the expression "theology of liberation," explains the choice of voluntary poverty as:

> *a commitment of solidarity with the poor, with those who suffer misery and injustice. … It is not a question of idealizing poverty, but rather of taking it on as it is—an evil—to protest against it and to struggle to abolish it.*[96]

For their sympathetic siding with those who are oppressed, Catholic clergy have been murdered by political authorities in countries such as Guatemala. They have also been strongly criticized by conservatives within the Vatican. Cardinal Ratzinger, who heads the Congregation for the Doctrine of the Faith, has decried liberation theology. He says that it inappropriately emphasizes liberation from material poverty rather than liberation from sin. The movement has nevertheless spread to all areas where there is social injustice. Bakole Wa Ilunga, Archbishop of Kananga, Zaire, explains,

> *Jesus liberates the poor from the feeling that they are somehow less than fully human; he makes them aware of their dignity and gives them motives for struggling against their lot and for taking control of their own lives.*[97]

Feminist theology

The issue of taking control of one's life and defining one's identity has also been taken up by feminists within the Christian Church. The Church institution has historically been dominated by men, although there is strong evidence that Jesus had active women disciples and that there were women leaders in the early churches. The effect of the apostle Paul in shaping attitudes toward women as he guided the developing Christian communities is one area of current scholarship. Some of the statements attributed to him in the biblical letters of the apostles seem oppressive to women; some seem egalitarian. He argues, for example, that men should pray or prophesy with their head uncovered but that women should either wear a veil or have their hair cut off,

> For a man ought not to have his head veiled, since he is the image and reflection of God; but woman is the reflection of man. Indeed, man was not made from woman, but woman from man. Neither was man created for the sake of woman, but woman for the sake of man. ... Nevertheless, in the Lord woman is not independent of man or man independent of woman. For just as woman came from man, so man comes through woman; but all things come from God.[98]

Many contemporary scholars are trying to sort out the cultural and historical as well as the theological contexts of such statements. Elisabeth Schüssler Fiorenza for example, argues that "women were not marginal in the earliest beginnings of Christianity; rather, biblical texts and historical sources produce the marginality of women."[99]

Another area of feminist theological scholarship is the role models for women offered by the Bible. A central female figure in the New Testament is Mary, mother of Jesus. Descriptions of her as a virgin mother present for women ideals of purity and submissiveness. Episcopal Bishop John Shelby Spong offers a radical view of this imagery:

> No female figure in Western history rivals her in setting standards. Since she is known as "the virgin," she has contributed to that peculiarly Christian pattern of viewing women primarily in terms of sexual function. Women may deny their sexuality by becoming virgin nuns, or women may indulge their sexuality by becoming prolific mothers. But in both cases, women are defined not first as persons and second as sexual beings but first and foremost as females whose sexuality determines their identity.[100]

A third major area of Christian feminist theology is the concept of God. The Divine is commonly referred to as "He" or "Father," but scholarship reveals that this patriarchal usage is not absolute; there also existed other models of God as Mother, as Divine Wisdom, as Justice, as Friend, as Lover. Sally McFague points out that to envision God as Mother, for instance, totally changes our understanding of our relationship to the Divine:

> What the father-God gives us is redemption from sins; what the mother-God gives is life itself, ... not primarily judging individuals but calling us back, wanting to be more fully united with us. ... All of us, female and male, have the womb as our first home, all of us are born from the bodies of our mothers, all of us are fed by our mothers. What better imagery could there

be for expressing the most basic reality of existence: that we live and move and have our being in God?[101]

Creation-centered Christianity

Another current trend in Christianity is an attempt to develop and deepen its respect for nature. In the Judeo-Christian tradition, humans are thought to have been given dominion over all the things of the earth. Sometimes this "dominion" was interpreted as the right to exploit, rather than the duty to care for, the earth. This view contrasts with indigenous beliefs that the divine resides everywhere, that everything is sacred, and that humans are only part of the great circle of life. Some Christians now feel that the notion of having a God-given right to control has allowed humans to nearly destroy the planet. In some cases, they are turning to indigenous spiritual leaders for help in extricating the planet from ecological destruction. Historian and passionate earth-advocate Father Thomas Berry feels that "we need to put the Bible on the shelf for twenty years until we learn to read the scripture of life."[102]

A Christianity that would accord greater honor to the created world would also tend to emphasize the miracle that is creation, thus helping to unite science and religion. Creation-centered Christians—such as the late Jesuit priest and paleontologist Teilhard de Chardin—see the mind of God in the perfect, intricate balances of chemistry, biology, and physics that allow life as we know it to exist. This rejoicing in all of life as divine has been advanced by liberal Dominican scholar and workshop leader Matthew Fox. Fox's teachings include appreciation of the feminine aspect of the divine and celebration of the human body as blessed.

Ecumenical movement

The restoration of religious freedom to multitudes of Christians in formerly communist countries increases the great diversity of Christian ways of worshipping. Another contemporary trend is the attempt to unify all Christians around some point of agreement or at least fellowship with each other.

Vatican II asserted that the Roman Catholic Church is the one church of Christ, but opened the way to dialogue with other branches of Christianity by declaring that the Holy Spirit was active in them as well. The Orthodox Church likewise believes that it is the "one, holy, Catholic, and Apostolic Church." Although it desires reunion of all Christians and denies any greed for organizational power, it insists on uniformity in matters of faith. Orthodox and Roman Catholic Churches therefore do not share Holy Communion with those outside their respective disciplines. Some Protestant denominations have branches that also refuse to acknowledge each other's validity.

There are, however, attempts to restore some bonds among all Christian

Churches. In 1995, Pope John Paul issued an encyclical entitled "That They May All Be One" urging Roman Catholics, Protestants, Anglicans, and Orthodox Christians to forgive each other for past mistakes so that the followers of Jesus could be reunified. There are dozens of official ecumenical dialogues going on. *The World Council of Churches*, centered in Geneva, was founded in 1948 as an organizational body allowing Christian Churches to cooperate on service projects even in the midst of their theological disagreements. Its Faith and Order Commission links three hundred culturally, linguistically, and politically, not to mention theologically, different Christian Churches in working out the problems of Christian unity.

At the fiftieth anniversary meeting of the WCC in Harare, Zimbabwe, in 1988, the delegates proclaimed,

We affirm the emphasis of the Gospel on the value of all human beings in the sight of God, on the atoning and redeeming work of Christ that has given every person true dignity, on love as the motive for action, and on love for one's neighbor as the practical expression of active faith in Christ. We are members one of another, and when one suffers all are hurt. . . .[103]

Suggested Reading

Abbott, Walter M., ed., *The Documents of Vatican II*, New York: The America Press, 1966. Landmark conclusions of the Council Fathers, with special emphasis on the poor, religious unity, and social justice.

Borg, Marcus, J., *Meeting Jesus Again for the First Time: The Historical Jesus and the Heart of Contemporary Faith*, San Francisco: HarperSanFrancisco, 1994. An accessible and appreciative discussion of the Jesus of history, as opposed to the Jesus of faith, by a leading figure in the Jesus Seminar.

Braybrooke, Marcus, *Time to Meet: Towards a Deeper Relationship Between Jews and Christians*, London: SCM Press, 1990. Information about both Christianity and Judaism which helps to remove historic ill feelings between them.

Dillenberger, John and Welch, Claude, *Protestant Christianity Interpreted through its Development*, New York: Charles Scribner's Sons, 1954. The classic history and interpretation of Protestantism.

Fosdick, Harry Emerson, ed., *Great Voices of the Reformation*, New York: Random House, 1952. Extensive quotations, with commentary, from major early Protestant leaders.

Jeremias, Joachim, *New Testament Theology: The Proclamation of Jesus*, New York: Charles Scribner's Sons, 1971. Extensive but highly readable analyses of the authenticity and meanings of key biblical passages.

Pope-Levison, Priscilla and Levison, John R., *Jesus in Global Contexts*, Louisville, Kentucky: Westminster/John Knox Press, 1992. Examinations of the question "Who is Jesus?" from poor cultures and feminist perspectives.

Price, James L., *Interpreting the New Testament*, second edition, New York: Holt,

Rinehart and Winston, 1971. Excellent survey of the literature and interpretation of the New Testament.

Robinson, James M., ed., *The Nag Hammadi Library*, San Francisco: Harper and Row, 1977. A fascinating collection of early scriptures that are not included in the Christian canon.

Schüssler Fiorenza, Elisabeth, *In Memory of Her: A Feminist Theological Reconstruction of Christian Origins*, New York: Crossroad, 1983, 1994. Extensive scholarship about the role of women in early Christianity.

Tugwell, Simon, *Ways of Imperfection*, London: Darton, Longman and Todd, 1984, and Springfield, Illinois: Templegate Publishers, 1985. Spirituality as a whole vision of life, as seen by a series of great Christian practitioners.

Walker, Williston, Norris, Richard A., Lotz, David W., and Handy, Robert T., *A History of the Christian Church*, fourth edition, New York: Charles Scribner's Sons, 1985, and Edinburgh: T&T Clark, 1986. A classic history of Christianity.

Ware, Timothy, *The Orthodox Church*, Middlesex, England and Baltimore, Maryland: Penguin Books, 1984. An excellent overview of the history, beliefs, and practices of the Eastern Church.

CHAPTER 9

ISLAM

"There is no god but God"

In about 570 CE, a new prophet was born. This man, Muhammad, is considered by Muslims to be the last of a continuing chain of prophets who have come to restore the true religion. They regard the way revealed to him, Islam, not as a new religion but as the original path of monotheism which also developed into Judaism and Christianity.

After carrying the torch of civilization in the West while Europe was in its Dark Ages, in the twentieth century Islam began a great resurgence. It is now the religion of nearly one-fifth of the world's people. Its monotheistic creed is very simple: "There is no god but God, and Muhammad is his Messenger." Its requirements of the faithful are straightforward, if demanding. But beneath them lie profundities and subtleties of which non-Muslims are largely unaware. Glimmers of appreciation for the faith are just beginning to appear outside Islam, partly as sincere Muslims attempt to counteract negative media portrayals of their religion.

The Prophet Muhammad

Islam, like Christianity and Judaism, traces its ancestry to the patriarch Abraham. Isma'il (Ishmael) was said to be the son of Abraham and an Egyptian slave, Hagar. When Abraham's wife Sarah also bore him a son (Isaac), Abraham took Isma'il and Hagar to the desert valley of Becca (Mecca) in Arabia to spare them Sarah's jealousy.

The sacred book of Islam, the Holy Qur'an, received as a series of revelations to Muhammad, relates that Abraham and Ishmael together built the holiest sanctuary in Islam, the Ka'bah. It was thought to be the site of Adam's original place of worship; part of the cubic stone building is a venerated black meteorite. According to the Qur'an, God told Abraham that the Ka'bah should be a place of pilgrimage. It was regarded as a holy place by the Arabian tribes.

According to Islamic tradition, the region sank into historical oblivion, "the Age of Ignorance," as it turned away from Abraham's monotheism. For many centuries, the events of the rest of the world passed it by, aside from contact through trading caravans. Then into a poor clan of the most powerful of the tribes in the area was born a child named Muhammad ("the praised one"). His father died before he was born. After the death of

ISLAM

	CE	Birth of Muhammad c.570 CE
		Revelation of the Qur'an to
	600	Muhammad begins c.610
Rapid spread of Islam begins 633		The hijrah ("migration") from
		Mecca 622
		Muhammad's triumphant return
		to Mecca 630
		Death of Muhammad, election of
		Abu Bakr as first caliph 632
Umayyad dynasty 661–750		Written text of the Qur'an
Karbala massacre 680		established 650
European advance of Islam		
stopped at Battle of Tours 732	**700**	
Islam reaches its cultural peak		
under Abbasid caliphs 750–1258		
	800	
	900	
		al-Hallaj killed 922
	1000	
		al Ghazali 1058–1111
	1100	
		Salah-al-Din recaptures
		Jerusalem from Crusaders 1187
	1200	
	1400	Turks conquer Constantinople,
Christians take Spain, institute		renaming it Istanbul 1453
Spanish Inquisition 1400s to		Akbar becomes Mughal emperor
1800s		in India 1556
	1600	
	1700	
Muslim areas fall under European		
domination 1800s–1900s		
	1800	
	1900	
Oil-rich Muslim states join OPEC		Partition of Muslim Pakistan from
and Muslim resurgence begins		Hindu India 1947
1970s	**2000**	

his mother and then his grandfather, Muhammad became the ward of his uncle, who put him to work as a shepherd.

Allah (God) is *the* focus in Islam, the sole authority, not Muhammad. But Muhammad's life story is important to Muslims, for his character is considered a model of the teachings in the Qur'an. The stories of Muhammad's life and his sayings are preserved in a vast, not fully authenticated literature called the **Hadith**, which reports on the Prophet's **Sunnah** (sayings and actions). On a trip to Syria with his uncle as a teenager, Muhammad was noticed by a Christian monk who identified marks on his body indicating his status as a prophet. As a young man, Muhammad managed caravans for a beautiful, intelligent, and wealthy woman named Khadijah. When she was forty and Muhammad twenty-five, she offered to marry him. Khadijah became Muhammad's strongest supporter during the difficult years of his early mission.

With Khadijah's understanding of his spiritual propensities, Muhammad began to spend periods of time in solitary retreat. These retreats were not uncommon in his lineage. They were opportunities for contemplation, away from the world.

When Muhammad was forty years old, he made a spiritual retreat during the month called Ramadan. An angel in human-like form, Gabriel, reportedly came to him and insisted that he recite. Three times Muhammad demurred that he could not, for he was unlettered, and three times the angel forcefully commanded him. In desperation, Muhammad at last cried out, "What shall I recite?" and the angel began dictating the first words of what became the Qur'an:

Proclaim! (or Recite!)
In the name
Of thy Lord and Cherisher,
Who created —
Created man, out of
A (mere) clot
Of congealed blood:
Proclaim! And thy Lord
Is Most Bountiful, —
He Who taught
(The use of) the Pen, —
Taught man that
Which he knew not.[1]

Muhammad returned home, deeply shaken. Khadijah comforted him and encouraged him to overcome his fear of the responsibilities and ridicule of prophethood. The revelations continued intermittently, asserting the theme that it was the One God who spoke and who called people to *Islam* (which means complete trusting surrender to God). According to tradition, Muhammad described the form of these revelations thus:

Revelation sometimes comes like the sound of a bell; that is the most painful way. When it ceases I have remembered what was said. Sometimes it is an angel who talks to me like a human, and I remember what he says.[2]

The Prophet shared these revelations with the few people who believed him: his wife Khadijah, his young cousin 'Ali, his friend the trader Abu Bakr, and the freed slave Zayd.

After three years, Muhammad was instructed by the revelations to preach publicly. He was ridiculed and stoned by the Qurayshites, the aristocrats of his tribe who operated the Ka'bah as a pilgrimage center and organized profitable trading caravans through Mecca. Finally, according to some accounts, Muhammad and his followers were banished for three years to a desolate place where they struggled to survive by eating wild foods such as tree leaves.

The band of Muslims were asked to return to Mecca, but their persecution by the Qurayshites continued. Muhammad's fiftieth year, the "Year of Sorrows," was the worst of all: he lost his beloved wife Khadijah and his protective uncle. With his strongest backers gone, persecution of the Prophet increased.

According to tradition, at the height of his trials, Muhammad experienced the Night of Ascension. He is said to have ascended through the seven heavens to the far limits of the cosmos, and thence into the Divine Proximity. There he met former prophets and teachers from Adam to Jesus, saw paradise and hell, and received the great blessings of the Divine Presence.

Pilgrims to Mecca from Yathrib, an oasis to the north, recognized Muhammad as a prophet. They invited him to come to their city to help solve its social and political problems. Still despised in Mecca as a potential threat by the Qurayshites, Muhammad and his followers left Mecca secretly. Their move to Yathrib, later called al-Medina ("The City [of the Prophet]"), was not easy. The Prophet left last, accompanied (according to some traditions) by his old friend Abu Bakr. To hide from the pursuing Meccans, it is said that they took refuge in a cave.

This **hijrah** ("migration") of Muslims from Mecca to Medina took place in 622 CE. The Muslim era is calculated from the beginning of the year in which this event took place, for it marked the change from persecution to appreciation of the Prophet's message.

In Medina, Muhammad drew up a constitution for the city that later served as a model for Islamic social administration. The departure of Muslims from Mecca was viewed with hostility and suspicion by the leaders of Mecca. Their assumption was that Medina had become a rallying point for enemies of the Meccans who, under Muhammad's leadership, would eventually attack and destroy Mecca. To forestall this, Mecca declared war on Medina, and open conflict between the two cities followed.

Muhammad himself directed the first raid against a Meccan caravan. The small group of Muslims was victorious. According to the Qur'anic revelations, God had sent thousands of angels to help Muhammad. Furthermore, Muhammad threw a handful of pebbles at the Meccans and this turned the tide, for it was God who threw, and "He will surely weaken the designs of the unbelievers."[3] After blocking Meccan counter-attacks, Muhammad negotiated a truce between the two cities.

The Qur'anic revelations to Muhammad emphasize the basic religious unity of Jews, Christians, and Muslims, members of the same monotheistic tradition of Abraham. But most of the Jews of Medina refused to accept Islam, because it recognized Jesus and claimed to complete the Torah. The Qur'an taught that the Jews and Christians had distorted the pure monotheism of Abraham; Muhammad had been sent to restore and supplement the teachings of the apostles and prophets. He was instructed to have the people face Mecca rather than Jerusalem during their prayers.

In 630 CE the Prophet returned triumphant to Mecca with such a large band of followers that the Meccans did not resist. The Ka'bah was purged of its idols, and from that time to the present it has been the center of Muslim piety. Acquiescing to Muhammad's political power and the Qur'anic warnings about the dire fate of those who tried to thwart God's prophets, many Meccans converted to Islam. Muhammad declared a general amnesty, and his former opponents were reportedly treated leniently.

The Prophet then returned to Medina, which he kept as the spiritual and political center of Islam. From there, campaigns were undertaken to spread the faith. In addition to northern Africa, the Persian states of Yemen, Oman, and Bahrain came into the fold. As the multi-cultural, multi-racial embrace of Islam evolved, the Prophet declared that the community of the faithful was more important than the older tribal identities that had divided people. The new ideal was a global family, under God. In his "Farewell Sermon," Muhammad stated, "You must know that a Muslim is the brother of a Muslim and the Muslims are one brotherhood."[4]

In the eleventh year of the Muslim era, Muhammad made a final pilgrimage to the Ka'bah. After his return to Medina, he became very ill and died in 632 CE. He left no clear instructions as to who should succeed him. In the circumstances that followed Muhammad's death, his steadfast friend Abu Bakr was elected the first **caliph** (successor to the Prophet). Another possible successor was the trustworthy and courageous 'Ali, the Prophet's cousin and husband of his favorite daughter, Fatima. Tradition has it that the Prophet Muhammad actually transferred his spiritual light to Fatima before his death, but that in the midst of funeral arrangements, neither she nor 'Ali participated in the selection of the first caliph. The Shi'ite faction would later claim 'Ali as the legitimate heir.

Muhammad's own life has continued to be very precious to Muslims, and it is his qualities that a good Muslim tries to emulate. He always denied having any superhuman powers, and the Qur'an called him "a human being like you," just "a servant to whom revelation has come," and "a warner."[5] The only miracle he ever claimed was that, though unlettered, he had received the Qur'anic revelations in extraordinarily eloquent and pure Arabic. He did not even claim to be a teacher—"God guides those whom He will,"[6] he was instructed to say, although Muslims consider the Prophet the greatest of teachers.

Nevertheless, all who saw the Prophet remarked on his touching physical beauty, his nobility of character, the fragrance of his presence, his humility, and his kindness. In his devotion to God, he quietly endured poverty so extreme that he tied a stone over his stomach to suppress the pangs of hunger. He explained, "I eat as a slave eats, and sit as a slave sits, for I am a slave (of God)." Although the Qur'an says that the Prophet is the perfect model for humanity, the purest vehicle for God's message, he himself perpetually prayed for God's forgiveness. When he was asked how best to practice Islam, he said, "The best Islam is that you feed the hungry and spread peace among people you know and those you do not know."[7]

Muhammad's mystical experiences of the divine had not led him to forsake the world as a contemplative. Rather, according to the Qur'an, the mission of Islam is to reform society, to actively combat oppression and corruption, "inviting to all that is good, enjoining what is right, and forbidding all that is wrong."[8] The Prophet's task—which Muslims feel was also undertaken by such earlier prophets as Moses and Abraham—is not only to call people back to faith but also to create a just moral order in the world as the embodiment of God's commandments.

The Qur'an

The heart of Islam is not the Prophet but the revelations he received. Collectively they are called the Qur'an ("reading" or "reciting"). He received the messages over a period of twenty-three years, with some later messages replacing earlier ones. At first they were striking affirmations of the unity of God and the woe of those who did not heed God's message. Later messages also addressed the organizational needs and social lives of the Muslim community.

After the *hijrah*, Muhammad heard the revelations and dictated them to a scribe; many of his companions then memorized them. They are said to have been carefully safeguarded against changes and omissions. Recited, the passages have a lyrical beauty and power that Muslims believe to be unsurpassed; these qualities cannot be translated. The recitation is to be rendered in what is sometimes described as a sad, subdued tone, because the messages concern God's sadness at the waywardness of the people. Muhammad said, "Weep, therefore, when you recite it."[9]

During the life of the Prophet, his followers attempted to preserve the oral tradition in writing as an additional way of safeguarding it from loss. The early caliphs continued this effort until a council was convened by the third caliph around 650 CE to establish a single authoritative written text. This is the one still used. It is divided into 114 **suras** (chapters). The first is the **Fatiha**, the opening sura which reveals the essence of the Qur'an:

In the name of God, Most Gracious, Most Merciful.
Praise be to God,
The Lord of the Worlds;
Most Gracious, Most Merciful;
Master of the Day of Judgment.
Thee do we worship,
And Thine aid we seek.
Show us the straight way,
The way of those on whom
Thou has bestowed Thy Grace

Those whose portion
Is not wrath,
And, who go not astray.

The verses of the Qur'an are terse, but are thought to have multiple levels of meaning. In the mystical early passages there are often three layers: 1 a reference to a particular person or situation, 2 a spiritual lesson, and 3 a deeper mystical significance.

The Qur'an makes frequent mention of figures and stories from Jewish and Christian sacred history, all of which is considered part of the fabric of Islam by Muslims. Islam—surrender to God—is the original religion, according to the Qur'an. Submission has existed as long as there have been humans willing to submit. Adam was the first prophet. Abraham was not exclusively a Jew nor a Christian; he was a monotheistic, upright person who had surrendered to Allah. Jesus was a very great prophet, though different in kind from Muhammad. As Khalid Duran explains:

> *For Muslims, Jesus is an extreme, a heartrending as well as heartwarming example, but one who is to be imitated only under the most extraordinary circumstances—unlike Muhammad, who is for Muslims primarily the good exemplar, for all times and climes.[10]*

Muslims believe that the Jewish prophets and Jesus all brought the same messages from God. However, the Qur'an teaches that God's original messages have been added to and distorted by humans. For instance, Muslims do not accept the idea developed historically in Christianity that Jesus has the authority to pardon or atone for our sins. The belief that this power lies with anyone except God is considered a blasphemous human interpolation into what Muslims understand as the basic and true teachings of all prophets of the Judeo-Christian-Islamic tradition: belief in one God and in our personal moral accountability before God on the Day of Judgment. In the Muslim view, the Qur'an was sent as a final corrective in the continuing monotheistic tradition. Muslims, citing John 14:16, 26 from the Christian New Testament, believe that Jesus prophesied the coming of Muhammad when he promised that the **Paraclete** (advocate) would come to assist humanity after him.

The Qur'an revealed to Muhammad is understood as a final and complete reminder of the prophets' teachings, which all refer to the same God. For example, in Sura 42, Muhammad is told:

> *Say: "I believe in whatever Book Allah has sent down; and I am commanded to judge justly between you. Allah is our Lord and your Lord! For us is the responsibility for our deeds, and for you for your deeds. There is no contention between us and you. Allah will bring us together, and to Him is our final goal."[11]*

The Central Teachings

On the surface, Islam is a very straightforward religion. Its teachings can be summed up very simply, as in this statement by the Islamic Society of North America:

Islam is an Arabic word which means peace, purity, acceptance and commitment. As a religion, Islam calls for complete acceptance of the teachings and guidance of God.

A Muslim is one who freely and willingly accepts the supreme power of God and strives to organize his life in total accord with the teachings of God. He also works for building social institutions which reflect the guidance of God.[12]

This brief statement can be broken down into a number of articles of faith.

The Oneness of God and of humanity

The first sentence chanted in the ear of a traditional Muslim infant is the **Shahadah**—"*La ilaha illa Allah.*" Literally, it means "There is no god but God." Exoterically, the phrase supports absolute monotheism. As the Qur'an reveals in Sura 2:163,

Your God is One God:
There is no god but He,
Most Gracious, Most Merciful.

Esoterically, the Shahadah means that ultimately there is only one Absolute Reality; the underlying essence of life is eternal unity rather than the apparent separateness of things in the physical world. Muslims think that the Oneness of God is the primordial religion taught by all prophets of all faiths. Muhammad merely reminded people of it.

It has been estimated that over ninety percent of Muslim theology deals with the implications of Unity. God, while One, is called by ninety-nine names in the Qur'an. These are each considered attributes of the One Being, such as *al-Ali* ("The Most High") and *ar-Raqib* ("The Watchful"). Allah is the name of God that encompasses all the attributes.

Unity applies not only to the conceptualization of Allah, but also to every aspect of life. In the life of the individual, every thought and action should spring from a heart and mind intimately integrated with the divine. Islam theoretically rejects any divisions within itself; all Muslims around the globe are supposed to embrace as one family. All humans, for that matter, are a global family; there is no one "chosen people," for all are invited into a direct relationship with God. Science, art, and politics are not separate from religion in Islam. Individuals should never forget Allah; the Oneness should permeate their thoughts and actions. Abu Hashim Madani, an Indian Sufi sage, is said to have taught, "There is only one thing to be gained in life, and that is to remember God with each breath; and there is only one loss in life, and that is the breath drawn without the remembrance of God."[13]

"The 'remembrance of God' is like breathing deeply in the solitude of high mountains: here the morning air, filled with purity of the eternal snows, dilates the breast; it becomes space and heaven enters our heart."

Frithjof Schuon[14]

Farid Esack

Farid Esack, one of the world's most brilliant young Muslim scholars, grew up as a victim of apartheid in South Africa. His family was so poor that they had to beg and search through gutters for food. Farid says,

> When you live in poverty and isolation, one of the things you hold on to is religion for your sanity, to keep you going. When you hear people crying in suffering and pain, instead of asking, "Where is God?", this is God crying out to you, "Why are you allowing this?"[15]

Thus it was not only poverty which drove Farid to risk his life again and again to build resistance to apartheid policies. It was also his deep commitment to Islam.

> I was strangely and deeply religious as a child, with a deep concern for the suffering which I experienced and witnessed all around me. I dealt with these two impulses by holding on to an indomitable belief that for God to be God, God had to be just and on the side of the marginalized. More curious was a logic, based on a text in the Qur'an, "If you assist Allah then He will assist you and make your feet firm" (47:7). For me this meant that I had to participate in a struggle for freedom and justice and, if I wanted God's help in this, then I had to assist Him.[16]

In 1984 Farid and three friends founded the Call of Islam which was very active in organizing resistance to apartheid, gender inequality, environmental destruction, and tensions between religions. After years fraught with danger, Farid found himself in a queue of the rural poor, to cast his vote for a freely elected government. He mused,

> I thought of the pain our country had endured in its long march to freedom, the loneliness of exile, of detention without trial, the political murders, the dispossession, the sighs of the tired and the exploited factory and farm workers, the months of living on the run like a fugitive, the attacks by police dogs, the clandestine pamphleteering . . . all for a single mark with a cheap little lead pencil![17]

> Can you imagine that we are the generation responsible for the death of apartheid? . . . Difficult as it was to sustain this belief at times, we did it.[18]

Farid is trying to show through intense Muslim scholarship that if a person of another religion is righteous, just, and God-fearing, he or she should be accepted by Muslims as a mu'min (believer), not a kafir non-believer.

Now serving as a member of South Africa's Gender Equality Commission, Farid concludes:

> In the Last Judgement, I will not be asked whether I succeeded or not. It is not our task to solve the problems of the world. We will only be asked what we did with the gifts He gave us. In Islam and in the Christian Gospels, it is said that God will ask you on the Day of Judgement, "When I was hungry, why did you not feed Me?"[19]

Prophethood and the compass of Islam

Devout Muslims feel that Islam encompasses all religions. Islam honors all prophets as messengers from the one God:

> Say ye: We believe
> In God, and the revelation
> Given to us, and to Abraham,
> Isma'il, Isaac, Jacob,
> And the Tribes, and that given
> To Moses and Jesus, and that given
> To (all) Prophets from their Lord:
> We make no difference
> Between one and another of them:
> And we bow to God in surrender.[20]

Muslims believe that the original religion was monotheism, but that God sent prophets from time to time as religions decayed into polytheism. Each prophet came to renew the message, in a way specifically designed for his culture and time. Muhammad, however, received messages meant for all people, all times. The Qur'anic revelations declared him to be the "Seal of the Prophets," the last and ultimate authority in the continuing prophetic tradition. The prophets are mere humans; none of them are divine, for there is only one Divinity.

All scriptures of all traditions are also honored, but only the Qur'an is considered fully authentic, because it is the direct, unchanged, untranslated word of God. Whatever exists in other religions that agrees with the Qur'an is divine truth.

Human relationship to the divine

> We are nearer to [a person] than his jugular vein.
> The Holy Qur'an, Sura 50:16

In Muslim belief, God is all-knowing and has intelligently created everything for a divine purpose, governed by fixed laws which assure the harmonious and wondrous working of all creation. Humans will find peace only if they know these laws and live by them. They have been revealed by the prophets, but the people often have not believed. As the Qur'an states,

> None believes in Our revelations save those who, when reminded of them,
> prostrate themselves in adoration and give glory to their Lord in all
> humility; who forsake their beds to pray to their Lord in fear and hope; who
> give in charity of that which We have bestowed on them. No mortal knows
> what bliss is in store for these as a reward for their labors.[21]

The Qur'an indicates that human history provides many "signs" of the hand of God at work bestowing mercy and protection on believers. Signs such as the great flood, which was thought to have occurred at the time of

Noah illustrate that non-believers and evil-doers ultimately experience great misfortune in this life or the afterlife. None are punished without first being warned by a messenger of God to mend their ways.

According to Islam, the two major human sins involve one's relationship to God. One is **shirk** (associating anything else with divinity except the one God). The other is **kufr** (ungratefulness to God, atheism). Furthermore, a major human problem is forgetfulness of God.

God has mercifully sent us revelations as reminders. The veils that separate us from God come from us, not from God; Muslims feel that it is ours to remove the veils by seeking God and acknowledging the omnipresence, omniscience, and omnipotence of the Divine. For the orthodox, the appropriate stance is a combination of love and fear of God. Aware that God knows everything and is all-powerful, one wants to do everything one can to please God, out of both love and fear. This paradox was given dramatic expression by the caliph 'Umar ibn al-Khattab:

> If God declared on the Day of Judgment that all people would go to paradise except one unfortunate person, out of His fear I would think that I am that person. And if God declared that all people would go to hell except one fortunate person, out of my hope in His Mercy I would think that I am that fortunate person.[22]

The unseen life

Muslims believe in the angels of God. These are nonphysical beings of light who serve and praise God day and night. They are numerous, and each has a specific responsibility. For instance, certain angels are always with each of us, recording our good and bad deeds. The Qur'an also mentions *archangels,* including Gabriel, highest of the angelic beings, whose main responsibility is to bring revelations to the prophets from God. But neither he nor any other angel is to be worshipped, for the angels are simply utterly submissive servants of God. By contrast, according to Islamic belief, there is a non-submissive being called Satan. He was originally one of the **jinn**—immaterial beings of fire, whose nature is between that of humans and angels—or perhaps even an angel. He proudly refused to bow before Adam and was therefore cursed to live by tempting Adam's descendants— all of humanity—to follow him rather than God. According to the Qur'an, those who fall prey to Satan's devices will ultimately go to hell.

Popular Muslim piety also developed a cult of saints. The tombs of mystics known to have had special spiritual powers have become places of pilgrimage. Many people visit them out of devotion and desire for the blessings of the spirit which is thought to remain in the area. This practice is frowned upon by some reformers, who assert that Muslim tradition clearly forbids worship of any being other than God.

The Last Judgment

In the polytheistic religion practiced by Arabs before Muhammad, the afterlife was only a shadow, without rewards or punishments. People had little religious incentive to be morally accountable. By contrast, the Qur'an emphasizes that after a period of repose in the grave, all humans will be bodily resurrected and assembled for a final accounting of their deeds. At that unknown time of the Final Judgment, the world will end cataclysmically: "The earth will shake and the mountains crumble into heaps of shifting sand" (Sura 73:14). Then comes the confrontation with one's life:

> *The works of each person We have bound about his neck. On the Day of Resurrection, We shall confront him with a book spread wide open, saying, "Read your book."*[23]

Hell is the grievous destiny of unrepentant non-believers—those who have rejected faith in and obedience to Allah and His Messenger, who are unjust and who do not forbid evil. Hell also awaits the hypocrites who even after making a covenant with Allah have turned away from their promise to give in charity and to pray regularly:

> *It is a flaming Fire. It drags them down by their scalps; and it shall call him who turned his back and amassed riches and covetously hoarded them.*[24]

Muslim piety is ever informed by this belief in God's impartial judgment of one's actions, and of one's responsibility to remind others of the fate that may await them.

Basically, Islam says that what we experience in the afterlife is a revealing of our tendencies in this life. Our thoughts, actions, and moral qualities are turned into our outer reality. We awaken to our true nature, for it is displayed before us. For the just and merciful, the state after death is a Garden of Bliss. For them, there will be castles, couches, fruits, sweetmeats, honey, houris (beautiful virgin women), and immortal youths serving from goblets and golden platters. Such delights promised by the Qur'an are interpreted metaphorically to mean that human nature will be transformed in the next life to such an extent that the disturbing factors of this physical existence will no longer have any effect.

By contrast, sinners and non-believers will experience the torments of hell, fire fueled by humans, boiling water, pus, chains, searing winds, food that chokes, and so forth. It is they who condemn themselves; their very bodies turn against them "on the Day when their tongues, their hands, and their feet will bear witness against them as to their actions" (Sura 24:24). The great medieval mystic Al-Ghazzali speaks of spiritual torments of the soul as well: the agony of being separated from worldly desires, burning shame at seeing one's life projected, and terrible regret at being barred from the vision of God. Muslims do not believe that hell can last forever for any believer, though. Only the non-believers will be left there; the others will eventually be lifted to paradise, for God is far more merciful than wrathful.

The Sunni–Shi'ite Split

The preceding pages describe beliefs of all Muslims, although varying interpretations of these beliefs have always existed. Groups within Islam differ somewhat on other issues. After Muhammad's death, resentments over the issue of his succession began to divide the unity of the Muslim community into factions. The two main opposing groups have come to be known as the **Sunni**, who now comprise about eighty percent of all Muslims worldwide, and the **Shi'a** (adj. Shi'ite).

As discussed earlier, a caliph was elected to lead the Muslim community after Muhammad's death. The office of caliph became a lifetime appointment. The first three caliphs, Abu Bakr, Umar, and Uthman, were elected from among the Prophet's closest companions. The fourth caliph was 'Ali, the Prophet's cousin and son-in-law. He was reportedly known for his holy and chivalrous qualities, but the dynasty of Umayyads never accepted him as their leader, and he was assassinated by a fanatic who was a former member of his own party. 'Ali's son Husayn, grandson of the Prophet, challenged the legitimacy of the fifth caliph, the Umayyad Mu'awiyya. When Mu'awiyya designated his son Yazid successor, Husayn rebelled and was massacred by Yazid's troops in the desert of Karbala along with many of his relatives, who were also members of the Prophet's own family. This martyrdom unified Shi'ite opposition to the elected successors and they broke away, claiming a legitimate line of succession through the direct descendants of the Prophet, beginning with 'Ali. The two groups are still separate.

Sunnis

Those who follow the elected caliphs are "the people of the Sunnah" (the sayings and practices of the Prophet, as collected under the Sunni caliphs). They consider themselves traditionalists who emphasize the authority of the Qur'an and the Hadith and Sunnah. They believe that Muhammad died without appointing a successor and left the matter of successors to the **ummah**, the Muslim community. The caliph is not a replacement of the Prophet; he is the leader of worship and the administrator of the **Shari'ah**, the sacred law of Islam.

The Shari'ah consists of teachings and practices for everything in Muslim life, from how to conduct a war to how to pray. Like the Torah for Jews, the Shari'ah sets the pattern for all individual actions and theoretically bonds them into a coherent, divinely regulated, peaceful community.

The Shari'ah is based chiefly on the Qur'an and Sunnah of Muhammad, who was the first to apply the generalizations of the Qur'an to specific life situations. Religion is not a thing apart; all of life is to be integrated into the spiritual unity which is the central principle of Islam. For example, the faithful are enjoined to be kind to their parents and kin, children and strangers, to protect orphans and women, to exercise justice and honesty in their relationships and business interactions, to stop killing infants, to manage their wealth carefully, and to avoid adultery and arrogance.

In the second century of Islam, the Abbasid dynasty replaced the Umayyads, who had placed more emphasis on empire-building and administration than on spirituality. At this point, there was a great concern for purifying and regulating social and political life in accord with Islamic spiritual tradition. Mechanisms for establishing the Shari'ah were developed. Since then, Sunnis have felt that as life circumstances change, laws in the

Qur'an, Hadith, and Sunnah should be continually interpreted by a consensus of opinion and the wisdom of learned men and jurists. For example, a contemporary Muslim faces new ethical questions not specifically addressed in the Qur'an and Hadith, such as whether or not test-tube fertilization is acceptable. Divorce has always been addressed by the Shari'ah, but the conditions under which a wife may petition for divorce have been closely examined in recent years.

Shi'ites

Shi'ites are ardently devoted to the memory of Muhammad's close relatives: 'Ali, Fatima (the Prophet's beloved daughter), and their sons Hasan and Husayn. The martyrdom of Husayn at Karbala in his protest against the alleged tyranny, oppression, and injustice of the Umayyad caliphs is held up as a symbol of the struggle against human oppression. It is commemorated yearly, as 'Ashura. Participants in mourning processions cry and beat their chests or offer cooling drinks to the populace in memory of the martyred Husayn. Shi'ite piety places great emphasis on the touching stories told of 'Ali and Husayn's dedication to truth and integrity, even if it leads to personal suffering, in contrast to the selfish power politics ascribed to their opponents.

Rather than recognize the Sunni caliphs, Shi'ites pay their allegiance to a succession of seven or twelve **Imams** ("leaders," "guides"). The first three were 'Ali, Hasan, and Husayn. According to a saying of the Prophet acknowledged by both Sunni and Shi'a:

> I leave two great and precious things among you: the Book of Allah and my Household. If you keep hold of both of them, you will never go astray after me.[25]

"Twelver" Shi'ites believe that there were a total of twelve Imams, legitimate hereditary successors to Muhammad. The twelfth Imam, they believe, was commanded by God to go into an occult hidden state to continue to guide the people and return publicly at the Day of Resurrection as the Mahdi. A minority of Shi'ites, the Isma'ilis and "Seveners," recognize a different person as the seventh and last Imam, and believe that it is he who is hidden and still living. There must always be an Imam.

Unlike the Sunni caliph, the Imam combines political leadership (if possible) with continuing the transmission of Divine Guidance. This esoteric religious knowledge was given by God to Muhammad, from him to 'Ali, and thence from each Imam to the successor he designated from 'Ali's lineage. It includes both the outer and inner meanings of the Qur'an. The Shari'ah is therefore interpreted for each generation by the Imam, for he is closest to the divine knowledge. When the Imam is not in a position to assert political power, those in positions of authority are expected to carry out his decisions. This assumption of spiritual authority has at times been carried to autocratic, violent extremes by Isma'ilis in power.

Aside from the issue of succession to Muhammad, Sunnis and Shi'ites are in general agreement on most issues of faith. Shi'ites follow the same essential practices as Sunnis, but, as discussed in a later section on spiritual practices, add several that express their ardent commitment to re-establishing what they see as the true spirit of Islam in a corrupt, unjust world.

Sufism

In addition to these two main groups within Islam, there is also an esoteric tradition which is said to date back to the time of the Prophet. He himself was at once a political leader and a contemplative with a deep prayer life. He reportedly said that every verse of the Qur'an has both an outside and an inside. Around him were gathered a group of about seventy people. They lived in his Medina mosque in voluntary poverty, detached from worldly concerns, praying night and day. After the time of the first four caliphs, Muslims of this deep faith and piety, both Sunni and Shi'ite, were distressed by the increasingly secular, dynastic, wealth-oriented characteristics of Muhammad's Umayyad successors. The mystical inner tradition of Islam, called **Sufism** (Arabic: *tasawwuf*), also involved resistance to the legalistic, intellectual trends within Islam in its early development.

Sufis have typically understood their way as a corrective supplement to orthodoxy. For their part, some orthodox Sunnis do not consider Sufis to be Muslims. Sufis consider their way a path to God that is motivated by longing for the One. In addition to studying the Qur'an, Sufis feel that the world is a book filled with "signs"—divine symbols and elements of beauty that speak to those who understand. The intense personal journeys of Sufis and the insights that have resulted from their truth-seeking have periodically refreshed Islam from within.

The early Sufis turned to asceticism as a way of deepening their piety. The Prophet had said: "If ye had trust in God as ye ought He would feed you even as He feeds the birds."[26] Muhammad himself had lived in poverty, reportedly gladly so. Complete trust in and surrender to God became an essential step in the journey. **Dervishes** (poor mendicant mystics) with no possessions, no attachments in the world, were considered holy people like Hindu sannyasins. But Sufi asceticism is based more on inner detachment than on withdrawal from the world; the ideal is to live with feet on the ground, head in the heavens.

To this early asceticism was added fervent, selfless love. Its greatest exponent was Rabi'a, the eighth-century saint. A famous mystic of Iraq, she scorned a very rich man's offer of marriage, saying that she did not want to be distracted for a moment from God. All her attention was placed on her Beloved. Rabi'a emphasized disinterested love, with no selfish motives of hope for paradise or fear of hell. When no veils of self exist, the mystic dissolves into the One she loves.

> *The Beloved is all, the lover just a veil.*
> *The Beloved is living, the lover a dead thing.*   *Jalal al-Din Rumi*[27]

In absolute devotion, the lover desires *fana*, total annihilation in the Beloved. This Sufi ideal was articulated in the ninth century CE by the

Persian Abu Yazid al-Bistami. He is said to have fainted while saying the Muslim call to prayer. When he awoke, he observed that it is a wonder that some people do not die when saying it, overwhelmed by pronouncing the name Allah with the awe that is due to the One. In his desire to be annihilated in God, al-Bistami so lost himself that he is said to have uttered pronouncements such as "Under my garment there is nothing but God,"[28] and "Glory be to Me! How great is My Majesty!"

The authorities were understandably disturbed by such potentially blasphemous statements. Sufis themselves knew the dangers of egotistical delusions inherent in the mystical path. There was strict insistence on testing and training by a sufficiently trained, tested, and illumined **murshid** ("teacher") or **shaykh**. It was through the shaykh that the **barakah** ("blessing," sacred power) was passed down, from the shaykh of the shaykh, and so on, in a chain reaching back to Muhammad, who is said to have transmitted the barakah to 'Ali.

A number of esoteric orders (*tariqas*) evolved, most of which traced their spiritual lineage back to Junayd of Baghdad (who died in 910 CE). He taught the need for constant purification, a continual serious examination of one's motives and actions. He also knew that it was dangerous to speak openly of one's mystical understandings; the exoteric-minded might find them blasphemous, and those who had not had such experiences would only interpret them literally and thus mistakenly. Much Sufi literature after his time is couched in metaphors accessible only to mystics.

Despite such warnings, the God-intoxicated cared little for their physical safety and exposed themselves and Sufism to opposition. The most famous case is that of Mansur al-Hallaj. After undergoing severe ascetic practices, he is said to have visited Junayd. When the master asked, "Who is there?", his disciple answered, "*ana'l-Haqq*" ("I am the Absolute Truth," i.e., "I am God"). After Junayd denounced him, al-Hallaj traveled to India and throughout the Middle East, trying to open hearts to God. He wrote of the greatness of the Prophet Muhammad, and introduced into the poetry of divine love the simile of the moth that flies ecstatic into the flame and, as it is burned up, realizes Reality.

Political maneuverings made a possible spiritual revival a threat to authorities back home, and they imprisoned and finally killed al-Hallaj in 922 CE for his "*ana'l-Haqq*." Now, however, al-Hallaj is considered by many to be one of the greatest Muslim saints, for it is understood that he was not speaking in his limited person. Like the Prophet, who had reportedly said, "Die before ye die,"[29] al-Hallaj had already died to himself so that nothing remained but the One.

What's in your head—toss it away! What's in your hand—give it up! Whatever happens—don't turn away from it. . . . Sufism is the heart standing with God, with nothing in between.

Abu Sa'id Abu al-Khayr[30]

Although Sufi teachings and practices have been somewhat systematized over time, they resist doctrinal, linear specification. They come from the heart of mystical experiences which defy ordinary logic. Paradox, metaphor, the world of creative imagination, of an expanded sense of reality—these characteristics of Sufi thought are better expressed through poetry and stories.

Poetry has been used by Sufis as a vehicle for expressing the profundities and perplexities of relationship with the divine. The thirteenth-century Turkish dervish Jalal al-Din Rumi, by whose inspiration was founded the Mevlevi Dervish Order in Turkey (famous for its "Whirling Dervishes" whose dances lead to transcendent rapture), was a master of mystical poetry. He tells the story of a devotee whose cries of "O Allah!" were finally answered by God:

Was it not I that summoned thee to service?
Did not I make thee busy with My name?
Thy calling "Allah!" was My "Here am I,"
Thy yearning pain My messenger to thee.
Of all those tears and cries and supplications
I was the magnet, and I gave them wings.[31]

The aim of Sufism is to become so purified of self that one is a perfect mirror for the divine attributes. The central practice is called *dhikr*, or "remembrance." It consists of stirring the heart and piercing the solar plexus, seat of the ego, by movements of the head, while continually repeating *la ilaha illa Allah*, which Sufis understand in its esoteric sense: "There is nothing except God." Nothing in this ephemeral world is real except the Creator; nothing else will last. As the seventy thousand veils of self—illusion, expectation, attachment, resentment, egocentrism, discontent, arrogance—drop away over the years, this becomes one's truth, and only God is left to experience it.

The Five Pillars and Jihad

While Sufism carries the inner practice of Islam, the outer practice is set forth in the Shari'ah, the straight path of the Divine Law. It specifies patterns for worship (known as the *Five Pillars of Islam*) as well as detailed prescriptions for social conduct, to bring remembrance of God into every aspect of daily life and practical ethics into the fabric of society. These prescriptions include injunctions against drinking intoxicating beverages, eating certain meats (including pork and improperly slaughtered animals), gambling and vain sports, sexual relations outside of marriage, and sexually provocative dress, talk, or actions. They also include positive measures, commanding justice, kindness, and charity. Women are given many legal rights, including the right to own property, to divorce (according to certain schools of law), to inherit, and to make a will. These rights divinely decreed during the time of the Prophet, fourteen hundred years ago, were not available to Western women until the nineteenth century. Polygyny is allowed for men who have the means to support several wives, to bring all women under the protection of a

Living Islam

Trained as a doctor of pharmacy, Khaled aly Khaled of Egypt did not appreciate his Muslim heritage when he was a child. He explains that his faith grew slowly as he became aware of the scientific accuracy and literary genius of the Qur'an.

"For a very long time in Egypt, we had the idea that it is better for you not to stick to a religion. If you stuck to a religion, people looked at you as just a fool. They thought there is a correlation between the success in the real life and the religion. If you have success in the real world, you didn't have to do these things that were religious. If you pray and fast and talk about Qur'an, the people start to think that you are not having any success.

Ten years ago I could not even read Qur'an. So I started from the very end, very far from religion, but I am getting back to it. For me, maybe the most important thing is scientific interpretation of the Qur'an. I can just believe what I can see, what I can feel, and just try to make interpretation of what I can collect from data. I started to read about the planets and their movement, from the scientific point of view. It is hard to believe these kind of things come just from blind nature. But a Big Mind behind this system? I could not believe that. That's against the science. But it cannot come as an accident. If you change one part out of one hundred million parts, the whole universe will collapse. So you cannot be accurate unless you have some mind or some knowledge to control the whole thing.

Now I'm sure that someone is behind the universe, is creating it, is creating me. You cannot feel the miracle of the universe unless you work in science. The human body cannot come from a primary cell reacting to another primary cell to create a creature from two cells and construct the body. It is beyond probability. Some supreme power created everything.

Some of the statements in the Qur'an had no scientific verification at that time, fourteen hundred years ago, but now they have meaning. For example, 'We have created this universe and we have made it expanding.' 'We have made the earth look like an egg.' Such statements cannot come from just an average person living fourteen hundred years ago. Among ancient Egyptians, ancient Syrians, we cannot find this information. I started to believe that someone was giving the knowledge to Muhammad. I'm not a very good believer—don't ask me to believe just because there is a book. But this information cannot come from any source except One Source.

As for the language of the Qur'an, scholars who speak Arabic have tried to write just one statement similar to this book in beauty. They could not. One computer scientist did a computer analysis of the Qur'an. He found that the number of chapters, the number of statements, and the number of times each letter is used are all multiples of nineteen (which is the number of angels in the Hellfire). Then he tried to see if he could write a book about any subject, using multiple numbers of any figure. No one could do it. The beauty of the Qur'an is pure, supreme.

If you compare the speech of Muhammad to the Qur'an, there is a big difference in beauty. He himself cannot make even one statement like that. He cannot write, he doesn't have knowledge, he just was taking care for the sheep. From this, I started to believe that there is a God."

husband. Women are allowed to inherit only half as much as men because men have the obligation to support women financially.

The Shari'ah is said to have had a transformative effect on Muhammad's community. Before Muhammad, the people's highest loyalty was to their tribe. Tribes made war on each other with no restraints. Women were possessions like animals. Children were often killed at birth either because of poverty or because they were females in a male-dominated culture. People differed widely in wealth. Drunkenness and gambling were commonplace. Within a short time, Islam made great inroads into these traditions, shaping tribes into a spiritual and political unity with a high sense of ethics.

Belief and witness

The first pillar of Islam (the Shahadah) is believing and professing the unity of God and the messengership of Muhammad: "There is no god but God, and Muhammad is his Messenger." The Qur'an requires the faithful to tell others of Islam, so that they will have the information to make an intelligent choice. However, it rules out coercion in spreading the message:

> Let there be [or: There is] no compulsion
> In religion: Truth stands out
> Clear from Error: whoever
> Rejects Evil and believes
> In God hath grasped
> The most trustworthy
> Hand-hold, that never breaks.[32]

The Qur'an insists on respect for all prophets and all revealed scriptures.

Daily prayers

The second pillar is the performance of a continual round of prayers. Five times a day, the faithful are to perform ritual ablutions with water (or sand or dirt if necessary), face Mecca, and recite a series of prayers and passages from the Qur'an, bowing and kneeling. Around the world, this joint facing of Mecca for prayer unites all Muslims into a single world family. When the prayers are recited by a congregation, all stand and bow shoulder to shoulder, with no social distinctions. In a mosque, women and men usually pray in separate groups, with the women in rows behind the men, to avoid sexually distracting the men. There may be an imam, or prayer-leader, but no priest stands between the worshipper and Allah. On Friday noon, there is usually a special prayer service in the mosque, but Muslims observe no sabbath day. Remembrance of God is an everyday obligation.

Repeating the prayers is thought to strengthen one's belief in God's existence and goodness and to carry this belief into the depths of the heart and every aspect of external life. Praying thus is also expected to purify the heart, develop the mind and the conscience, comfort the soul, encourage the good and suppress the evil in the person, and awaken in the believer the innate sense of higher morality and higher aspirations. The words of praise and the bowing express continual gratefulness and submission to the One. At the end, one turns to the two guardian angels on one's shoulders to say the traditional Muslim greeting—"*Assalamu Alaykum*" ("Peace be on you")—and another phrase adding the blessing, "and mercy of God."

While mouthing the words and performing the outer actions, one should be concentrating on the inner prayer of the heart. The Prophet reportedly said, "Prayer without the Presence of the Lord in the heart is not prayer at all."[33]

Zakat

The third pillar is **zakat**, or spiritual tithing and almsgiving. At the end of the year, all Muslims must donate at least two and a half percent of their income (after basic expenses) to needy Muslims. This provision is designed to help decrease inequalities in wealth and to prevent personal greed. Its literal meaning is "purity," for it purifies the distribution of money, helping to keep it in healthy circulation.

Saudi Arabia devotes fifteen percent of its kingdom's GDP to development and relief projects throughout the world. The Islamic Relief Organization which it funds makes a point of helping people of all religions, without discrimination, where there is great need following disasters. Many stories from the life of the Prophet Muhammad teach that one should help others whether or not they are Muslims. For example, the Prophet's neighbor was Jewish. The Prophet reportedly gave him a gift every day, even though the neighbor daily left garbage at his door. Once the neighbor was sick, and the Prophet visited him. The neighbor asked, "Who are you to help me?" The Prophet replied, "You are my brother. I must help you."

In addition to zakat, Shi'ites are obligated to give one-fifth of their disposable income to the Imam. Because the Imam is now hidden, half of this now goes to the deputy of the Imam to be used however he thinks appropriate; the other half goes to descendants of the Prophet to spare them the humiliation of poverty.

Fasting

The fourth pillar is fasting. Frequent fasts are recommended to Muslims, but the only one that is obligatory is the fast during Ramadan, commemorating the first revelations of the Qur'an to Muhammad. For all who are beyond puberty, but not infirm or sick or menstruating or nursing children, a dawn-to-sunset abstention from food, drink, sexual intercourse, and smoking is required for the whole month of Ramadan.

Because Muslims use a lunar calendar of 354 days, the month of Ramadan gradually moves through all the seasons. When it falls in the summer, the period of fasting is much longer than in the shortest days of winter. The hardship of abstaining even from drinking water during these long and hot days is an unselfish surrender to God's commandment and an assertion of control over the lower desires. The knowledge that Muslims all over the world are making these sacrifices at the same time builds a special bond between haves and have-nots, helping the haves to experience what it is to be hungry, to share in the condition of the poor. Those who have are encouraged to be especially generous in their almsgiving during Ramadan. Fasting is expected to allow the body to burn up impurities and provide one with "a Transparent Soul to transcend, a Clear Mind to think and a Light Body to move and act."[34]

Hajj

The fifth pillar is **hajj**, the pilgrimage to Mecca. All Muslims who can possibly do so are expected to make the pilgrimage at least once in their lifetime. It involves a series of symbolic rituals designed to bring the faithful as close as possible to God. Male pilgrims wrap themselves in a special garment of unsewn cloths, rendering them all alike, with no class distinctions. The garment is like a burial shroud, for by dying to their earthly life they can devote all their attention to God. It is a time for *dhikr*, the constant repetition of the Shahadah, the remembrance that there is no god but God.

Pilgrims walk around the ancient Ka'bah seven times, like the continual rotation around the One by the angels and all of creation, to the seventh heaven. Their hearts should be filled only with remembrance of Allah.

Another sacred site on the pilgrimage is the field of 'Arafat. It is said to be the place where Adam and Eve were taught that humans are created solely for the worship of God. Here pilgrims pray from noon to sunset to be forgiven of anything that has separated them from the Beloved. In addition, pilgrims carry out other symbolic gestures, such as sacrificing an animal and throwing stones at the devil, represented by pillars. The animal sacrifice reminds the hajjis of Abraham's willingness to surrender to God that which was most dear to him, his own son, even though in God's mercy he was allowed to substitute a ram for the sacrifice. Most of the meat is distributed to the needy, a service for which Saudi Arabia has had to develop huge preservation and distribution facilities. Hajjis also perform symbolic acts at the holy well of Zum-Zum, the spring which God is said to have provided for Hagar when she and Ishmael were left alone in the desert.

Hajj draws together Muslims from all corners of the earth for this intense spiritual experience. Because Islam is practiced on every continent, it is truly an international gathering. The crowds are enormous. During the month of the pilgrimage, over two million pilgrims converge upon Mecca. To help handle the crowds, the Saudi government has built the immense King Abdul Aziz International Airport near Jedda. The journey was once so hazardous that many people and camels died trying to cross the desert in fulfillment of their sacred obligation.

Though considerably modernized now, hajj is still the vibrant core of the global Muslim community. To be a hajji is as much as ever a badge of pride. Throughout Muslim history, hajj has brought widely diverse people together, consolidating the center of Islam, spreading information and ideas across cultures, and sending pilgrims back into their communities with fresh inspiration.

Jihad

In addition to these Five Pillars of Islam, there is another important injunction: **jihad**. Commonly mistranslated as "holy war," it means "striving." The Greater Jihad, Muhammad is reported to have said, is the struggle against the lower self. It is the internal fight between wrong and right, error and truth, selfishness and selflessness, hardness of heart and all-embracing love. This inner struggle to maintain peaceful equilibrium is then reflected in outer attempts to keep society in a state of harmonious order, as the earthly manifestation of Divine Justice.

On the external level, the Lesser Jihad is exerting effort to protect the Way of God against the forces of evil. This jihad is the safeguarding of one's life, faith, livelihood, honor, and the integrity of the Muslim community. The Prophet Muhammad reportedly said that "the preferred jihad is a truth spoken in the presence of a tyrant."[35]

Jihad is not to be undertaken for personal gain. The Qur'anic revelations that apparently date from the Medina period when the faithful were being attacked by Meccans make it clear that

To those against whom
War is made, permission
Is given (to fight), because
They are wronged;—and verily,
God is Most Powerful
For their aid;

(They are) those who have
Been expelled from their homes
In defiance of right,
(For no cause) except
That they say, "Our Lord
Is God."[36]

The Qur'an gives permission to fight back under such circumstances, but also gives detailed limitations on the conduct of war and the treatment of captives, to prevent atrocities.

Muhammad is the prototype of the true **mujahid**, or fighter in the Path of God, one who values the Path of God more than life, wealth, or family. He is thought to have had no desire for worldly power, wealth, or prestige. By fasting and prayer, he continually exerted himself toward the One, in the Greater Jihad. In defending the Medina community of the faithful against the attacking Meccans, he was acting from the purest of motives. It is believed that a true mujahid who dies in defense of the faith goes straight to paradise, for he has already fought the Greater Jihad, killing his ego.

The absolute conviction which characterizes jihad derives from recognition of the vast disparity between evil and the spiritual ideal, both in oneself and in society. Continual exertion is thought necessary in order to maintain a peaceful equilibrium in the midst of changing circumstances. Traditionalists and radicals have differed in how this exertion should be exercised in society.

The Qur'an asserts that believers have the responsibility to defend their own faith as well as to remind unbelievers of the truth of God and of the necessity of moral behavior. In some passages, Muslims are enjoined simply to stand firm against aggression. For example, "Fight for the sake of Allah those that fight against you, but do not be aggressive. Allah does not love the aggressors."[37] In other passages, the Qur'an suggests active opposition to people who do not believe in the supremacy of the one God:

> *Fight them on*
> *Until there is no more tumult or oppression*
> *And there prevail justice and faith in God.*[38]

The ultimate goal and meaning of Islam, and of jihad, is peace through devoted surrender to God. A peaceful society is like paradise. Sri Lankan Sufi Shayk M. R. Bawa Muhaiyaddeen observes:

> *If one knows the true meaning of Islam, there will be no wars. All that will be heard are the sounds of prayer and the greetings of peace. Only the resonance of God will be heard. That is the ocean of Islam. That is unity. That is our wealth and our true weapon.*[39]

The Spread of Islam

In the time of Muhammad, Islam combined spiritual and secular power under one ruler. This tradition, which helped to unify the warring tribes of the area, was continued under his successors. Islam expanded phenomenally during the centuries after the Prophet's death, contributing to the rise of many great civilizations. The ummah became a community that spread from Africa to Indonesia. Islam spread mostly by personal contacts: trade, attraction to charismatic Sufi saints, appeals to Muslims from those feeling oppressed by Byzantine and Persian rule, unforced conversions. There were some military battles conducted by Muslims over the centuries, but they were not necessarily for the purpose of spreading Islam, and many Muslims feel that wars of aggression violate Muslim principles.

Muhammad's non-violent takeover of Mecca occurred only two years before he died. Under his successors, newly Islamic Arab armies quickly swept through the elegant Sassanian Persian Empire, which had stood for twelve centuries. Within ten years of the Prophet's death, a mere four thousand horsemen commanded by Amr ibn al-As took the major cities of Egypt, centers of the brilliant Byzantine Empire. Another wave of Islamization soon penetrated into Turkey and Central Asia, North Africa, and north through Spain, to be stopped in 732 CE in France at the battle of Tours. At this point, only a hundred years after Muhammad died, the Muslim ummah under the Umayyad caliphs was larger than the Roman Empire had ever been.

Muslims cite the power of the divine will to establish a peaceful, God-conscious society as the reason why this happened. By contrast with their strong convictions, the populations they approached were often demoralized by border fighting among themselves and by grievances against their rulers. Many welcomed them without a fight. Both Christians and Jews often converted to Islam.

Monotheistic followers of revealed traditions, Christians and Jews, who like Muslims were "people of the book," were treated as **dhimmis**, or protected people. They were allowed to maintain their own faith, but not to try to convert others to it. The Dome of the Rock was built on the site of the old Temple of the Jews in Jerusalem, honoring Abraham as well as Muhammad in the city that is still sacred to three faiths: Judaism, Christianity, and Islam.

The Umayyad caliphs had their hands full administering this huge ummah from Damascus, which they had made its capital. They tended to focus more on organizational matters than on the spiritual life. Some were also quite worldly, such as Walid II, who is said to have enjoyed a pool filled with wine so that he could swim and drink at the same time.

Islamic culture

Under the Abbasids, who took over the caliphate in 750 CE, Muslim rule became more Persian and cosmopolitan and Islamic civilization reached its peak. The capital was moved to the new city of Baghdad and merchants, scholars, and artists became the cultural heroes. A great House of Wisdom was built, with an observatory, a famous library, and an educational institution where Greek and Syriac manuscripts on subjects such as medicine, astronomy, logic, mathematics, and philosophy were translated into Arabic. In Cairo, Muslims built in 972 CE a great university and mosque, Al-Azhar, which still plays an important role in Muslim scholarship. In its great cities, Islam went through a period of intense intellectual and artistic activity, absorbing, transmitting, and expanding upon the highest traditions of other cultures.

The pivotal institution of Islamic society was the **ulama**, whose primacy and influence was unchallenged. The ulama were not only guardians of the faith but were also the pervasive force holding together Islamic society. They were *qadis* (judges), *muftis* (jurisconsultants), guides and pastors of the artisans' guilds, spiritual leaders, mosque imams, the sole teachers of the civil and military schools, state scribes, and market inspectors.

Although Baghdad was the capital of the Abbasids, independent caliphates were declared in Spain and Egypt. Muslim Spain became a great cultural center. Cordoba, the capital, had seven hundred mosques, seventy libraries, three hundred public baths, and paved streets. Europe, by contrast, was in its Dark Ages; Paris and London were only mazes of muddy alleys.

Tunisia and Egypt comprised a third center of Islamic power: the Shi'ite Fatimid imamate. Under the deranged Fatimid caliph Al-Hakim, the Fatimids broke with Islamic tradition and persecuted dhimmis; they also destroyed the Church of the Holy Sepulcher in Jerusalem, provoking European Christian crusades to try to recapture the Holy Lands.

Crusading Christians fought their way down to Jerusalem, which they placed under a month-long siege in 1099. When the small Fatimid garrison surrendered, the Crusaders slaughtered the inhabitants of the holy city. Severed hands and feet were piled everywhere. Anti-Crusading Muslims led by the famous Salah-al-Din (known in the West as Saladin) retook Jerusalem in 1187 and treated its Christian population with the generous leniency of Islam's highest ideals for the conduct of war. But widespread destruction remained in the wake of the Crusaders, and a reservoir of ill-will against Christians lingered.

During the thirteenth century, Christians took Spain and later instituted the dread Inquisition against those not practicing Christianity. By the beginning of the sixteenth century, an estimated three million Spanish Muslims had either been killed or had left the country.

Eastward expansion

Its westward advance stopped at Europe, Islam carried its vitality to the north, east, and south. Although Mongolian invasions threatened from Central Asia, the Mongols were converted to Islam; so were the Turks. While Uzbek Khan, Mongol leader from 1313 to 1340, zealously desired to spread Islam throughout Russia, he nonetheless maintained tolerance toward the Christians in the conquered lands, ruling: "Their laws, their Churches; their monasteries and chapels shall be respected; whoever condemns or blames this religion, shall not be allowed to excuse himself under any pretext but shall be punished with death."[40]

Similar tolerance toward other religions was practiced by the Muslim Turks, but in 1453 the Turks conquered Constantinople, the heart of the old Byzantine Empire, and renamed it Istanbul. At its height, the Turkish Ottoman Empire dominated the eastern Mediterranean as well as the area around the Black Sea.

Farther east, Islam was carried into northern India, where Muslims destroyed many Hindu idols and temples but allowed the Hindu majority a protected dhimmi status. The Chishti Sufi saints drew people to Islam by their great love for God. "The heart of a mystic is a blazing furnace of love which burns and destroys everything that comes into it because no fire is stronger than the fire of love," declared Khwaja Muinuddin Chishti.[41]

Under the Muslim Mughals, the arts and learning flourished in India. In the ecumenical spiritual curiosity of the Emperor Akbar, he created a house of worship where representatives from many traditions were invited to the world's first interfaith dialogues.

Under British colonization of India, tensions between Hindus and Muslims were inflamed, partly to help Britain divide and rule. India gained its independence under Gandhi, who was unable to end the enmity between the two faiths. In 1947, West and East Pakistan (now the independent nation of Bangladesh) were partitioned off to be Muslim-ruled and predominantly populated by Muslims, while India was to be run by Hindus. Millions lost their lives trying to cross the borders, and the strife between the two faiths continues. In December 1992, militant Hindus set off renewed communal violence by destroying a mosque in Ayodhya, India, in the belief that it had been built by the Mughals on the site of an ancient temple to Lord Rama.

The greatest concentration of Muslims developed even farther east, in Indonesia. About ninety percent of the people are now Muslim, but the government refuses to establish Islam as a state religion. China and the former Soviet Union encompass tens of millions of Muslims.

To the south, Islam spread into Africa along lines of trade. In competition with Christianity, Islam sought the hearts of Africans and eventually won in many areas. Many converted to Islam; many others maintained some of their indigenous ways in combination with Islam. As the spread of Islam encompassed an increasing diversity of cultures, hajj held its center in Mecca in the midst of worldwide variations.

Relationships with the West

Although Islam honors the prophets of all traditions, its own religion and prophet were denounced by medieval Christian Europe. Christianity had considered itself the ultimate religion and had launched its efforts to bring the whole world under its wings. Islam felt the same way about its own mission. In the struggle for souls, the Church depicted Muhammad as an idol-worshipper, an anti-Christ, the Prince of Darkness. Islam was falsely portrayed as a religion of many deities, in which Muhammad himself was worshipped as a god (thus the inaccurate label "Muhammadanism"). Europeans watched in horror as the Holy Lands became Muslim and the "infidel" advanced into Spain. Even though it was Muslim scholars and artists who preserved, shared, and advanced the classic civilizations, the wealth of Arabic culture was interpreted in a negative light.

By the nineteenth century, Western scholars began to study the Arabic classics, but the ingrained fear and loathing of Muhammad and Muslims remained. The ignorance about, and negative stereotyping of, Muslims continues today. Western cartoonists, for instance, had inevitably drawn Muslims as wild-eyed radicals dressed in desert robes and brandishing scimitars. Annemarie Schimmel, Professor of Indo-Muslim Culture, Harvard University, explains:

> The idea that the Muslims conquered everything with fire and sword was unfortunately deeply ingrained in the medieval mind. All these misconceptions about Islam as a religion and the legends and lies that were told about it are really unbelievable. I have often the feeling that this medieval image of Islam as it was perpetuated in ever so many books and even scholarly works is part of our subconscious. When someone comes and says, "But real Islam is something completely different," people just will not believe it because they have been indoctrinated for almost fourteen hundred years with the image of Islam as something fierce and something immoral. Unfortunately, some of the events of our century have revived this medieval concept of Islam.[42]

Although it had enjoyed great heights of culture and political power, the Muslim world fell into decline. It seems that the Mongol invasions were at least partly responsible, for they eradicated irrigation systems and libraries and killed scholars and scientists, erasing much of the civilization that had been built up over five hundred years. Some Muslims today feel that spiritual laxness was the primary reason that some of the previously glorious civilizations became impoverished Third World countries. Another theory is that Muslim culture was no longer dynamic. As it rigidified and stagnated, it was overwhelmed by cultures both less civilized than itself (the Mongols) and more civilized (the Europeans, who were becoming major world powers on the strength of their industrialization and colonizing navies).

During the late eighteenth and early nineteenth centuries, many Muslim populations fell under European domination. From the mid-twentieth century onward, most gained their independence as states that had adopted certain Western ideals and practices. In many cases, they had let go of some aspects of their Muslim heritage, considering it a relic that prevented them from success in the modern world. Arabic was treated as an unimportant language; Western codes of law had replaced the Shari'ah in social organization. They resumed local rule with little training for self-government in a world economy dominated by industrial nations.

Societies which had been structured along traditional lines fragmented from the mid-nineteenth century onward, as wide-ranging programs of reforms and modernization were unleashed throughout the Muslim world. The local autonomy of the traditional Islamic society was swept away and replaced by centralized regulations of Western origin. Traditional schools, markets, guilds, and courts into which the societies had been organized lost much of their reason for being.

Before the colonial forces moved out, foreign powers led by Britain helped to introduce a Jewish state in the midst of the Middle East. Some historians allege that the chief motive of the countries supporting this claim was to protect European interests as a bulwark against Russian imperialism and as a check against the attempts of Egypt to create a pan-Islamic state encompassing Egypt, Syria, and the Arabian peninsula.

Islam in the United States

Even as Muslims were feeling humiliated by foreign domination elsewhere, they were growing in numbers and self-pride within the United States. Islam is the fastest-growing religion in the United States, and may now be the second largest religion in the country.

Conversion to Islam by African–Americans was encouraged early in the twentieth century as a form of separatism from white oppression. The Christianity espoused by the dominant white population was interpreted as part of the pattern of oppression. Under the leadership of Elijah Muhammad, who proclaimed himself a messenger of Allah, tens of thousands of African–Americans became "Black Muslims," calling themselves the Nation of Islam. However, faith in Elijah Muhammad himself was shaken by allegations about his sexual relationships with his secretaries. Some followers—especially the influential leader Malcolm X and Warith Deen Muhammad, son of Elijah Muhammad—developed contacts with mainstream Muslims in other countries and came to the conclusion that Elijah Muhammad's version of Islam was far removed from Muslim orthodoxy. They steered converts toward what they perceived as the true traditions of the world brotherhood of Islam.

Others of African–American heritage, especially Minister Louis Farrakhan, current leader of the Nation of Islam, maintain a more political focus on unifying against white oppression, despite Islam's strong tradition of non-racism.

However, politicization of Islamic identity is probably not the main aspect of the growth of Islam. Many American Muslims embrace their religion as a bulwark of discipline and faith against the degradations of materialism.

Muslim Resurgence

The Muslim world had lost its own traditional structure and was also generally helpless against manipulations by foreign nations until it found its power in oil. In the 1970s, oil-rich nations found that by banding together they could control the price and availability of oil. OPEC (the Organization of Petroleum Exporting Countries) brought greatly increased revenues into previously impoverished countries and strengthened their self-image as well as their importance in the global balance of power. Most of the oil-rich nations are predominantly Muslim.

As the wealth suddenly poured in, it further disrupted established living patterns. Analysts feel that some people may have turned back to a fundamentalist version of Islam in an effort to restore a personal sense of familiarity and stability amid the chaos of changing modern life; the increase in literacy, urbanization, and communications helped to spread revived interest in Islam. There was also the hope that Islam would provide the blueprint for enlightened rule, bringing spiritual values into community and politics as Muhammad had done in Medina.

With the collapse of colonialism, the world has become divided into autonomous nation-states with strong central governments. In this process, forty-three primarily Islamic nation-states have been created. They differ greatly in culture and in the degree to which each society is ruled by Islamic ethics. But all are now being reconsidered as possible frameworks for dar al-Islam—"the abode of Islam"—within which the Muslim dream of religion-based social transformation might be accomplished.

Return to Shari'ah

The resurgence of Islam takes several forms. One is a call for return to Shari'ah rather than secular law derived from European codes. The feeling of the orthodox is that the world must conform to the divine law, rather than diluting the law to accommodate it to the material world. For example, Egypt has made it illegal for its Muslim citizens to drink alcoholic beverages in public. In Saudi Arabia, morality squads actively enforce the obligatory prayers, and women are not allowed to leave home unless they are accompanied by a close male relative.

Private behaviors are also becoming more traditional. In particular, to honor the Qur'anic encouragement of physical modesty to protect women from being molested, many Muslim women have begun covering their bodies except for hands, face, and feet, as they have not done for decades. In Saudi Arabia, where women have been ordered to be "properly covered" outside their homes, some wear not only head-to-toe black cloaks but also full veils over their faces without even slits for their eyes. Many Muslim women assert that they like dressing more modestly so that men will view them as persons, not as sex objects. Others feel that men are simply treating women as slaves.

In some largely Muslim countries, such as Egypt, it is the possibility of employment which motivates women to adopt **hijab** (veiling for the sake of modesty). Women are allowed to join the work force only if they are veiled. In Iran, the replacement of more Westernized customs with Muslim moral codes, including veiling of women, has allowed women from conservative backgrounds to leave their homes and enter public life without antagonizing their families. This new freedom has been accompanied by a rise in female-initiated divorces.

Women's rights to divorce and to choose their own marriage partners are among the hotly debated issues in contemporary attempts to define Shari'ah. Shari'ah has been locally adapted to various societies over the centuries; to attempt to restore its original form designed for Muhammad's time or any other form from another period is to deny the usefulness of its flexibility. Some customs thought to be Muslim are actually cultural practices not specified in the basic sources; they are the result of Islamic civilization's assimilation of many cultures in many places. Muhammad worked side-by-side with women, and the Qur'an encourages equal participation of women in religion and in society. Veiling and seclusion were practices absorbed from conquered Persian and Byzantine cultures, particularly the upper classes; peasant women could not carry out their physical work under encumbering veils or in seclusion from public view. The authenticity of Hadith relegating women to subordinate status has been questioned in recent years by certain scholars, but cultural determinations of the role of women continue to be practiced and to be commonly considered part of Islam.

Another problem with applying Shari'ah as civil law is that some ethical issues which arise today either did not exist in their present form at the time of Muhammad or were not specifically addressed by the Qur'an or Hadith. Artificial birth control methods, for example, were not available then. However, infanticide and abortion were mentioned by the Qur'an: "Do not kill your children for fear of poverty. We will provide for them and for you." Does this mean that all forms of population control should be considered forbidden by Islam, or should the overpopulation of the earth be a major contemporary consideration? According to Islamic legal reasoning, the accepted method for determining such ambiguous issues is to weigh all the benefits and disadvantages that might result from a course of action and then discourage it if the likely disadvantages outweigh the advantages.

The global family of Islam is not a political unit; its unity under Arab rule broke up long ago. There is as yet no consensus among Muslim states about how to establish a peaceful, just, modern society based on basic Muslim principles. But there is widespread recognition that there are problems associated with modern Western civilization that should be avoided, such as crime, drug abuse, and unstable family life.

> *Today everyone cries for peace but peace is never achieved, precisely because it is metaphysically absurd to expect a civilization that has forgotten God to possess peace.*
>
> *Seyyed Hossein Nasr*[43]

Outreach and education

Another sign of Muslim resurgence is the increase in outreach, as Muslims become more confident of the value of their faith. Islam is the fastest-growing of all world religions, with one billion two hundred million followers. New mosques are going up everywhere, including a $25 million Islamic Cultural Center in the heart of Manhattan. Muslims who constitute a minority in their countries are beginning to assert their rights to practice their religion. They no longer feel they have to be secretive about praying five times a day or apologetic about leaving work to attend Friday congregational prayer at noon.

A third sign of Muslim resurgence is the increasing attention being given to developing educational systems modeled on Islamic thought. Islam is not anti-scientific or anti-intellectual; on the contrary, it has historically bridged reason and faith and placed a high value on developing both in order to tap into the fullness of human potential. Western education has omitted the spiritual aspects of life, so Muslims consider it incomplete and imbalanced. The 1977 First World Conference on Muslim Education defined the goals of education thus:

> *Education should aim at the balanced growth of the total personality of Man through the training of Man's spirit, intellect, his rational self, feelings and bodily senses. Education should cater therefore for the growth of Man in all its aspects: spiritual, intellectual, imaginative, physical, scientific, linguistic, both individually and collectively and motivate all aspects toward goodness and the attainment of perfection.*[44]

Islam in politics

In addition to return to Shari'ah, numerical growth, and Muslim-based education, governments are becoming Islamicized. Some use Islam to support the status quo. Others have used Muslim idealism to rally opposition to ruling elites who are perceived as being corrupt or tied to the West.

In predominantly Shi'ite Iran, the Pahlavi Shahs had tried to rapidly modernize their country, turning it into a major military and industrial power. In the process, they eroded the authority of the ulama. A revolutionary leader emerged from this disempowered group, the Ayatollah Khomeini, and swept the Shah from power in 1979. Once in power, however, the ulama had no clear program for reorganizing society according to Muslim principles. Khomeini made some drastic changes in interpretation of Islam in order to justify violent revolutionary behavior.

The Ayatollah also attempted to export his revolution to other Muslim countries with Shi'ite populations that could carry on the work. He conducted a war against "atheist" Iraq (where the fifty percent of citizens who are Shi'ites are ruled by the forty-five percent who are Sunni), denounced predominantly Sunni Saudi Arabia for its ties to the West, and inspired some Lebanese Shi'ites to see their political struggle against Christians and Jews as part of a great world battle between Islam and the satanic forces of Western imperialism and Zionism. He issued a legal opinion that Indian-born British author Salman Rushdie could be sentenced to death under Islamic law, because his novel, *Satanic Verses*, seemed to defame the Prophet and his wives. In resultant riots over the controversial book, hundreds of people died.

Khomeini's call for governmental change was not heeded, so radicals resorted to sabotage and terrorism as their most powerful weapons. Their surprise attacks on civilians tended to turn world opinion against Islam, rather than promoting its ideals. Little is known of the clandestine radical groups; the Muslim governments they oppose control the media and have portrayed them as mindless fanatics, supporting Western fears and stereo-typing of Islam. More moderate leadership is now in power in Iran, but Khomeini is still revered as a saint.

In Taliban-controlled Afghanistan, all secular laws have been discarded; the Sunni Shari'ah is law. The orthodox Sunni Taliban Islamists claim to be trying to create what they regard as a pure Muslim state. In accordance with their interpretation of Shari'ah, the Taliban government organizes public spectacles to deter crime by amputating the hands of thieves and whipping adulterers, as crowds of thousands watch.

Despite their pious utterances, the Taliban militia have been accused by Amnesty International of conducting racial warfare against civilians of certain ethnic groups, particularly the Hazara of northern Afghanistan. If the alleged massacres of thousands have taken place, they are in direct opposition to the instructions of the Qur'an regarding humane treatment of political opponents even during armed conflict. At Taliban training camps in Afghanistan, militants from many Muslim countries are reportedly taught to mix religion and politics.

Iraq is another Muslim nation which has provoked Western fears of Islam by using Islam as a rallying point for political power. When Saddam Hussein of Iraq tried to unseat the royalty of Kuwait, Islam was again cast as a political football by both sides in the Gulf War. Hussein, an Arab nationalist, resorted to Islam as a means of mass mobilization against what he saw as a foreign Western intrusion in the Gulf. Years of economic sanctions by the United Nations against Iraq over continuing suspicion of its military intentions have created such hardships for the populace that the Iraqis refer to the sanctions as a means of genocide.

In contemporary nationalistic struggles globally, Muslims have often been the losers, to such an extent that some eighty percent of the world's huge refugee population is Muslim. There is as yet no political unity among Muslim states, despite appeals from some Muslims that they should unite in order to advance the Islamization of society. At the turn of the twenty-first century, for instance, tensions were rising between Iran and Afghanistan, and between Sunnis and Shi'ites within Pakistan.

Islam for the future

An unusual side-effect of the negative publicity about Muslim militancy has been a widespread attempt by moderate Muslims to share positive information about their faith. Interest has grown rapidly: Muslim speakers are now in great demand by non-Muslim communities who want to understand and appreciate Islam, rather than remain ignorant about it. Jews are surprised to discover how closely it parallels their own faith; Christians are gradually undoing centuries of sensationalist misinformation about Islam bred by fear.

In Chechnya, where an indigenous movement by the largely Muslim populace was pitted against the power of the central Russian government, joint teams of Christians, Muslims, and Buddhists visited areas of fighting and hospitals to bring help and food supplies. Mufti Magomed-Khaji Albogachiev, Chairman of the Religious Center of Muslims of Ingushetia Republic (which borders Chechnya), said of these efforts: "As Allah taught us, we are to help each other in doing good things."[45]

Mufti Albogachiev speaks of the recent past, in which Muslims, along with people of other religions, were imprisoned and killed by the communist state:

We should remember that there is nothing more horrible, more dangerous, than to live without God. When religious people were considered criminals for their belief, only for the fact that they had religious books in their home, when only seventy mosques survived from a previous count of fourteen thousand mosques in one region of Russia, when tens of thousands of religious leaders were imprisoned and sent to hard labor camps where they died, when hundreds of tons of religious books were burned in Soviet fires, I want to remind you that there is nothing more dangerous than atheism and life without God. But God heard our prayers and this regime was destroyed by itself, because nothing could divide it, except by God's will.[46]

Until recently, Muslims tended to point to their glorious past as proof of the value of their tradition. But the newest thought is forward-looking, exploring how Islam can help to shape a better world. Dr. Ahmad Kamal Abu'l Majd, an ex-Minister of Culture in Egypt, looks toward the future:

I'm glad and proud I'm a Muslim. I carry on my shoulders a scale of values, a code of ethics that I genuinely believe is good for everybody. ... I even venture sometimes to say that Islam was not meant to serve the early days of Islam when life was primitive and when social institutions were still stable and working. It was meant to be put in a freezer and to be taken out when it will be really needed. And I believe that time has come. But the challenge is great because not all Muslims are aware of this fact: That the mission of Islam lies not in the past but in the future.[47]

Suggested Reading

Esack, Farid, *Qur'an, Liberation and Pluralism: An Islamic Perspective of Interreligious Solidarity against Oppression*, Oxford: Oneworld Publications, 1997. A first-person account of the struggle for justice in South Africa from the point of view of a

Muslim scholar and activist, exploring Qur'anic principles which lead to interreligious fraternity.

Esposito, John L., *Islam: The Straight Path*, New York, Oxford: Oxford University Press, 1988. A scholarly, clear introduction to historical and contemporary Islam.

Hefner, Robert W. and Patricia Horvatich, eds., *Islam in an Era of Nation-states: Politics and Religious Renewal in Muslim Southeast Asia*, Honolulu: University of Hawaii Press, 1997. Detailed analyses of Muslim reformist movements in Southeast Asia with reference to modern governmental structures.

The Holy Qur'an. Although the Qur'an is considered untranslatable, numerous translations from the Arabic have been attempted. Many Muslims' favorite English translation is by Abdullah Yusuf Ali (Durban, South Africa: Islamic Propagation Center International, 1946). The King Fahd Holy Qur'an Printing Complex in Medina has published a very helpful revision based on Yusuf Ali's translation, with extensive thematic index. Thomas Ballantine Irving (Al-Hajj Ta'lim'Ali) has prepared "The First American Version" of the Qur'an (translation and commentary, Brattleboro, Vermont: Amana Books, © 1985).

Nasr, Seyyed Hossein, ed., *Islamic Spirituality I: Foundations*, New York: Crossroad Publishing Company, 1987 and London: SCM Press, 1989. Excellent chapters on key features of Muslim spirituality, from fasting to angels, with sections on Sunnism, Shi'ism, and Sufism.

Nasr, Seyyed Hossein, *Traditional Islam in the Modern World*, London and New York: Kegan Paul International, 1990. Religiously sensitive discussions of varied topics to bring forth traditional Muslim values within contemporary social settings.

Nasr, Seyyed Hossein, Dabashi, Hamid, and Nasr, Seyyed Vali Reza, *Shi'ism: Doctrines, Thought, and Spirituality*, Albany, New York: State University of New York Press, 1988. To balance the predominant media attention to Shi'ite politics, a set of thoughtful essays on aspects of Shi'ite spirituality.

Schimmel, Annemarie, *And Muhammad is His Messenger: The Veneration of the Prophet in Islamic Piety*, Chapel Hill, North Carolina: University of North Carolina Press, 1985. Extensive exploration of Muslims' love for the Prophet.

Schimmel, Annemarie, *Mystical Dimensions of Islam*, Chapel Hill, North Carolina: University of North Carolina Press, 1975. A classic survey of Sufi history, teachings, and saints.

Schuon, Frithjof, *Understanding Islam*, London: George Allen and Unwin, 1963. Profound and lyrical observations about the way of Islam.

CHAPTER 10

SIKHISM

"By the guru's grace shalt thou worship Him"

Another great teacher made his appearance in northern India in the fifteenth century CE: Guru Nanak. His followers were called **Sikhs**, meaning "disciples, students, seekers of truth." In time, he was succeeded by a further nine enlightened Gurus, ending with Guru Gobind Singh (1666–1708). Despite the power of these Gurus, the spiritual essence of Sikhism is little known outside India and its diaspora (dispersed communities), even though Sikhism is the fifth largest of all global religions. Although people tend to equate the word "Sikh" with the military and political aspects of the Punjabis' struggle for independence, Sikhs understand their path not as another sectarian religion but as a statement of the universal truth within, and transcending, all religions. Many of their beliefs have been interpreted as a synthesis of the Hindu and Muslim traditions of northern India, but Sikhism has its own unique quality, independent revelation, and history. As awareness of Sikh spirituality spreads, Sikhism is becoming a global religion, although it does not actively seek converts. Instead, it emphasizes the universality of spirituality and the relevance of spirituality in everyday life.

The Sant Tradition

Before Guru Nanak, Hinduism and Islam had already begun to draw closer to one another in northern India. One of the foremost philosophers in this trend was the Hindu saint Ramananda, who held theological arguments with teachers from both religions. But a deeper marriage occurred in the hearts of **sants**, or "holy people," particularly Sufi mystics such as Shaikh Farid and Hindu bhaktas such as Sri Caitanya. They shared a common cause in emphasizing devotion to the Beloved above all else.

The most famous of the bridges between Hindu and Muslim is the fifteenth-century weaver Kabir (1440–1518). He was the son of Muslim parents and the disciple of the Hindu guru Ramananda. Rather than taking the ascetic path, he remained at work at his loom, composing songs about union with the Divine that are at once earthly and sublime. He was opposed to outward forms, preferring ecstatic personal intimacy with God:

Are you looking for Me? I am in the next seat.
My shoulder is against yours.
You will not find Me in stupas, not in Indian shrine rooms, nor in
synagogues, nor in cathedrals:

not in masses, nor kirtans, not in legs winding around your own neck,
  nor in eating nothing but vegetables.
When you really look for Me, you will see Me instantly —
you will find Me in the tiniest house of time.
Kabir says: Student, tell me, what is God?
He is the breath inside the breath.[1]

Guru Nanak

When Guru Nanak was born in 1469, the area of northern India called the Punjab was half-Muslim, half-Hindu, and ruled by a weak Afghan dynasty. For centuries, the Punjab had been the lane through which outer powers had fought their way into India. In 1398, the Mongolian leader Tamerlane had slaughtered and sacked Punjabis on his way both to and from Delhi. Toward the end of Nanak's life, it was the Mughal emperor Babur who invaded and claimed the Punjab. This casting of the Punjab as a perpetual battleground later became a crucial aspect of Sikhism.

Nanak was reportedly little concerned with worldly things. As a child he was of a contemplative nature, resisting the formalities of his Hindu religion. Even after he was married, it is said that he roamed about in nature rather than working and gave away any money he had to the poor. At length he took a job as an accountant, but his heart was not in material gain.

When Nanak was thirty, his life was transformed after immersion in a river, from which it is said he did not emerge for three days. Some people now think he was meditating on the opposite side, but at the time he could not be found until he suddenly appeared in town, radiant. According to one account, he had been taken into the presence of God, who gave him a bowl of milk to drink, saying that it was actually nectar (*amrit*) which would give him "power of prayer, love of worship, truth and contentment."[2] The Almighty charged him to go back into the tainted world to redeem it from Kali Yuga (the darkest of ages).

After his disappearance in the river in 1499, Nanak began traveling through India, the Himalayas, Afghanistan, Sri Lanka, and Arabia, teaching in his own surprising way. When people asked him whether he would follow the Hindu or Muslim path, he replied, "There is neither Hindu nor Mussulman [Muslim], so whose path shall I follow? I shall follow God's path. God is neither Hindu nor Mussulman . . ."[3] Nanak mocked the Hindu tradition of throwing sacred river water east toward the rising sun in worship of their ancestors—he threw water to the west. If Hindus could throw water far enough to reach their ancestors thousands of miles away in heaven, he explained, he could certainly water his parched land several hundred miles distant in Lahore by throwing water in its direction. Another tradition has it that he set his feet toward the Ka'bah when sleeping as a pilgrim in Mecca. Questioned about this rude conduct, he is said to have remarked, "Then kindly turn my feet toward some direction where God is not." He espoused the inner rather than the outer path.

Again and again, Guru Nanak emphasized three central teachings as the straight path to God: working hard in society to earn one's own honest living (rather than withdrawing into asceticism and begging), sharing from one's earnings with those who are needy, and remembering God at all times as the only Doer, the only Giver. To a society which stressed distinctions of caste, class, gender, and religions, Guru Nanak introduced and practiced the idea of a new social order based on equality, justice, and service to all, in devotion to the One God whom Guru Nanak perceived as formless, pervading everywhere.

Nanak's commitment to practical faith, as opposed to external adherence to religious formalities, won him followers from both Hinduism and Islam. Before he died in 1539, they argued over who would bury him. He reportedly told Muslims to place flowers on one side of his body, Hindus on the other; the side whose flowers remained fresh the next day could bury him. The next day they raised the sheet that had covered his body and reportedly found nothing beneath it; all the flowers were still fresh, leaving only the fragrance of his being.

> *Oh my mind, love God as a fish loves water:*
> *The more the water, the happier is the fish,*
> *   the more peaceful his mind and body.*
> *He cannot live without water even for a moment.*
> *God knows the inner pain of that being without water.*   *Guru Nanak[4]*

The Succession of Gurus

Before Nanak's death, he appointed a spiritual successor, his devoted disciple Angad Dev. This Second Guru strengthened the new Sikh tradition and developed a script for setting down its memorized teachings, which had been given orally in the common language.

There were eventually a total of ten Sikh Gurus. The Second Guru, who accepted the Guruship most reluctantly after the death of his beloved master, Guru Nanak, emphasized by his own example the central Sikh virtues of humility and service. The Third and Fourth Gurus developed organizational structures for the growing Sikh church while also setting personal examples of humility. The Fourth Guru founded the holy city of Amritsar, within which the Fifth Guru built the religion's most sacred shrine, the Golden Temple. The Fifth Guru also compiled the sacred scriptures of the Sikhs, the Adi Granth ("original holy book," now known as the **Guru Granth Sahib**), from devotional hymns composed by Guru Nanak, the other Gurus, and Hindu and Muslim saints, including Kabir and many spiritual figures from low social castes. Among the latter are figures like Bhagat Ravi Das, a low-caste Hindu shoemaker who nonetheless achieved the heights of spiritual realization. One of his poems includes these lines:

When I was, You were not.
When You are, I am not.
As huge waves are raised in the wind in the vast ocean,
But are only water in water,

O Lord of Wealth, what should I say about this delusion?
What we deem a thing to be,
It is not, in reality.
It is like a king falling asleep on his throne
And dreaming that he is a beggar.
His kingdom is intact,
But separating from it, he suffers. . . .
Says Ravi Das, the Lord is nearer to us than our hands and feet.[5]

When a copy of the Adi Granth was sent to the emperor Akbar on his demand, he was so pleased with its universalism that he offered a gift of gold to the book. But apparently because of suspicions that the Fifth Guru supported a rival successor to Akbar's throne, the Guru was tortured and executed by Akbar's son and successor, Jehangir, in 1606. It is said that the Fifth Guru remained calmly meditating on God as he was tortured by heat, with his love and faith undismayed:

Merciful, merciful is the Lord.
Merciful is my master.
He blesses all beings with His bounties.
Why waverest thou, Oh mortal? The Creator Himself shall protect you.
He who has created you takes care of you. . . .
Oh mortal, meditate on the Lord as long as there is breath in your body.[6]

From that point on, Sikhism took measures to protect itself and to defend the weak of all religions against tyranny. The Sixth Guru built a Sikh army, carried two swords (one symbolizing temporal power, the other, spiritual power), and taught the people to defend their religion. The tender-hearted Seventh Guru, a pacifist who never used his troops against the Mughals, taught his Sikhs not only to feed anyone who came to their door, but moreover to:

do service in such a way that the poor guest may not feel he is partaking of some charity but as if he had come to the Guru's house which belonged to all in equal measure.[7]

The Eighth Guru became successor to Guru Nanak's seat when he was only five years old and died at the age of eight. When taunted by Hindu pandits the "Child Guru" reportedly touched a lowly deaf and dumb Sikh watercarrier with his cane, whereupon the watercarrier expounded brilliantly on the subtleties of the Hindu scripture, *Bhagavad-Gita*.

The Ninth Guru was martyred in 1675. According to Sikh tradition, he was approached by Hindu pandits who were facing forced conversion to Islam by the Mughal emperor Aurangzeb. The emperor viewed Hinduism as a totally corrupt, idolatrous religion which did not lead people to God; he had ordered the destruction of Hindu temples and mass conversion of Hindus throughout the land, beginning in the north with Kashmir. Reportedly, one of the Kashmiri pandits dreamed that only the Ninth Guru, the savior in Kali Yuga, could save the Hindus. With the firm approval of his young son, Guru Teg Bahadur told the Hindu pandits to inform their oppressors that they would convert to Islam if the Sikh Guru could be persuaded to do so. Imprisoned and forced to witness the torture and murder of his aides, the Ninth Guru staunchly maintained the right of all people to religious freedom. Aurangzeb beheaded him before a crowd of thousands. But as his son later wrote, "He has given his head, but not his determination."[8]

The martyred Ninth Guru was succeeded by his young son, who became the tenth master, Guru Gobind Singh. It was he who turned the intimidated Sikhs into saint-warriors for truth.

In 1699 he reportedly told a specially convened assembly of Sikhs that the times were so dangerous that he had developed a new plan to give the community strength and unity. Total surrender to the master would be necessary, he said, asking for volunteers who would offer their heads for the cause of protecting religious ideals. One at a time, five stepped forward. Each was escorted into the Guru's tent, from which the Tenth Guru emerged alone with a bloody sword. After this scene was repeated five times, the Guru brought all the men out of the tent, alive. Some say the blood was that of a goat, in a test of the people's loyalty; others say that Guru Gobind Singh had actually killed the men and then resurrected them. At any rate, their willingness to serve and bravely to sacrifice themselves was dramatically proven, and the Five Beloved Ones became models for Sikhs. It is noteworthy that those who became the Five Beloved Ones all came from the lowest classes.

Guru Gobind Singh instituted a special baptismal initiation using water stirred with a double-edged sword to turn his followers into heroes, mixed with sugar candies symbolizing that they would also be compassionate. After baptizing the Five Beloved Ones, he established a unique Guru–Sikh relationship by asking that they baptize him—thus underscoring the principle of equality among all Sikhs. The baptized men were given the surname *Singh* ("lion"); the women were all given the name *Kaur* ("princess") and treated as equals. Together, they formed the **Khalsa** ("Pure Ones"), a fraternity pledged to a special code of personal discipline. They were sworn to wear five distinctive symbols of their dedication: long unshorn hair bound under a turban or a veil, a comb to keep it tidy, a steel bracelet as a personal reminder that one is a servant of God, short under-breeches for modesty, and a sword for dignity and the willingness to fight for justice and protection of the weak. All of these innovations were designed to turn the meek into warriors capable of shaking off Mughal oppression and protecting freedom of religion; the distinctive dress made it impossible for the Khalsa to hide from their duty by blending with the general populace. In Sikh history, their bravery was proven again and again. For example, it is reported that the Tenth Guru's own teenage sons were killed as they single-handedly engaged several thousand Mughal soldiers in battle.

In addition to transforming the Sikh faithful into a courageous, unified community, Guru Gobind Singh ended the line of bodily succession to Guruship. As he was dying in 1708, he transferred his authority to the Adi Granth rather than to a human successor. Thenceforth, the Granth Sahib (another name for the Adi Granth, with Sahib an expression of veneration) was to be the Guru Granth Sahib—the living presence of the Guru embodied in the sacred scriptures, to be consulted by the congregation for spiritual guidance and decision-making.

At the end of the eighteenth century and beginning of the nineteenth century under Maharaja Ranjit Singh, Sikhs formed the Sikh Empire—a secular government noted for its generous tolerance toward Muslims, despite the earlier history of oppression by the Muslim rulers. The Sikh Empire attempted to create a pluralistic society, with social equality and full freedom of religion. It also blocked the Khyber Pass against invaders. The Empire lasted only half a century, for the British took over in 1849.

Resistance to oppression became a hallmark of Sikhism, for the times were grim for India's people. Despite heavy losses, Guru Gobind Singh's outnumbered Sikhs began the protection of the country from foreign rule, a process which continued into the twentieth century. High praise of the Guru's military effect has been offered by Dr. S. Radhakrishnan, a highly respected former President of India:

> For one thousand years, after the defeat of Raja Jaipal, India had lain prostrate. The raiders and invaders descended on India and took away the people, to be sold as slaves. ... Guru Gobind Singh raised the Khalsa to defy religious intolerance, religious persecution and political inequality. It was a miracle that heroes appeared out of straws and common clay. Those who grovelled in the dust rose proud, defiant and invincible in the form of the Khalsa. They bore all sufferings and unnamable tortures cheerfully and unflinchingly. ... India is at long last free. This freedom is the crown and climax and a logical corollary to the Sikh Guru's and Khalsa's terrific sacrifices and heroic exploits.[9]

Neither age, nor caste, nor gender is thought to have any relevance in Sikh spirituality. In contrast to the restricted position of women in Indian society, the Sikh Gurus accorded full respect and freedom of participation to women.

> God is like sugar scattered in the sand. An elephant cannot pick it up. Says Kabir, the Guru has given me this sublime secret:
> "Become thou an ant and partake of it."
>
> *Kabir, Guru Granth Sahib 1377*

Central Beliefs

Sikhism's major focus is loving devotion to one God, whom Sikhs recognize as the same One who is worshipped by many different names around the world. God is formless, beyond time and space, the only truth, the only reality. This boundless concept was initially set forth in Guru Nanak's *Mool Mantra* ("basic sacred chant"), which prefaces the Guru Granth Sahib, and **Jap Ji**, the first morning prayer of Sikhs:

> There is One God
> Whose Name is Truth,
> The Creator,

Without fear, without hate,
Eternal Being,
Beyond birth and death,
Self-existent,
Realized by the Guru's grace.[10]

Following Guru Nanak's lead, Sikhs often refer to God as *Sat* ("truth") or as *Ik Onkar*, the One Supreme Being. God is pure being, without form.

Guru Gobind Singh offered a litany of praises of this boundless, formless One. His inspired composition, *Jaap Sahib*, includes 199 verses such as these:

Immortal
Omnipotent
Beyond Time
And Space
Invisible
Beyond name, caste, or creed
Beyond form or figure
The ruthless destroyer
Of all pride and evil
The Salvation of all beings ...
The Eternal Light
The Sweetest Breeze
The Wondrous Figure
The Most Splendid.[11]

The light of God shines fully through the Guru, the perfect master. The light of God is also present in the Guru Granth Sahib, the Holy Word (**shabd**) of God, and in all of creation, in which the Holy Name (**Nam**) of God dwells. God is not separate from this world. God pervades the cosmos and thus can be found within everything. As the Ninth Guru wrote:

Why do you go to the forest to find God? He lives in all and yet remains distinctly detached. He dwells in you as well, as fragrance resides in a flower or the reflection in a mirror. God abides in everything. See him, therefore, in your heart.[12]

Sikhism does not claim to have the only path to God, nor does it try to convert others to its way. It has beliefs in common with Hinduism (such as karma and reincarnation) and also with Islam (such as monotheism). The respected Muslim mystic, Mian Mir, was invited to lay the cornerstone of the Golden Temple in Amritsar. It was constructed with four doors, inviting people from all traditions to come in to worship. When Guru Gobind Singh created an army to resist tyranny, he admonished Sikhs not to feel enmity toward Islam or Hinduism, the religions of the oppressors. The enemy, he emphasized, was oppression and corruption.

Sikh soldier-saints are pledged to protect the freedom of all religions. Sikhism is, however, opposed to empty ritualism, and Guru Nanak and his successors sharply challenged hypocritical religious practices. "It is very difficult to be called a Muslim," sang Guru Nanak. "A Muslim's heart is as soft as wax, very compassionate, and he washes away the inner dirt of egotism."[13] By contrast, said Guru Nanak, "The Qazis [Muslim legal authorities] who sit in the courts to minister justice, rosary in hand and the name of *Khuda* (God) on their lips, commit injustice if their palm is not greased. And if someone challenges them, lo, they quote the scriptures!"[14]

According to the Sikh ideal, the purpose of life is to realize God within the world, through the everyday practices of work, worship, and charity, of sacrificing love. All people are to be treated equally, for God's light dwells in all and ego is a major hindrance to God-realization. From Guru Nanak's time on, Sikhism has refused to acknowledge the traditional Indian caste system.

Like Hinduism, Sikhism conceives a series of lives, with karma (the effects of past actions on one's present life) governing transmigration of the soul into new bodies, be they human or animal. The ultimate goal of life is mystical union with the divine, reflected in one's way of living.

> *I was separated from God for many births, dry as a withered plant,*
> *But by the grace of the Guru, I have become green.*
> *Guru Arjun, the Fifth Guru[15]*

Sacred Practices

To be a true Sikh is to live a very disciplined life of surrender and devotion to God, with hours of daily prayer, continual inner repetition of the Name of God (Nam), and detachment from negative, worldly mind-states. At the same time that one's mind and heart are joined with God, one is to be working hard in the world, earning an honest living, and helping those in need. Of this path, the Third Sikh Guru observes:

> *The way of devotees is unique; they walk a difficult path.*
> *They leave behind attachments, greed, ego, and desires, and do not speak much.*
> *The path they walk is sharper than the edge of a sword and thinner than a hair.*
> *Those who shed their false self by the grace of the Guru are filled with the fragrance of God.[16]*

The standards set by Guru Gobind Singh for the Khalsa are so high that few people can really meet them. In addition to outer disciplines such as abstaining from drugs, alcohol, and tobacco, the person who is Khalsa, said the Guru, will always recite the Name of God. The one who is Khalsa renounces anger and does not criticize anybody. He fights on the front line against injustice and vanquishes the five evils (lust, anger, greed, attachment, and ego) in himself. He burns his karmas and thus becomes egoless. Not only does he not take another person's spouse, he doesn't even look at the things that belong to others. Perpetually reciting Nam is his joy, and he falls in love with the words of the Gurus. He faces difficulties squarely, always attacks evil, and always helps the poor. He joins other people with the Nam, but he is not bound within the forts of narrow-mindedness.[17]

The Sikh Gurus formed several institutions to help create a new social order with no caste distinctions. One is **langar**, the communal kitchen which is freely offered to all who come, regardless of caste. This typically takes place at a **gurdwara**, the building where the Guru Granth Sahib is enshrined and public worship takes place. The congregation is called the **sangat**, in which all are equal; there is no priestly class nor servant class. During communal worship as well as langar, all strata of people sit together, though men and women may sit separately, as in the Indian custom. People of all ethnic origins, ideologies, and castes, including Untouchables, may bathe in the tank of water at Sikh holy places. Baptism into the Khalsa does away with one's former caste and makes a lowly person a chief. At least one-tenth of one's income is to be contributed toward the welfare of the community. In addition, the Sikh Gurus glorified the lowliest forms of manual labor, such as sweeping the floor and cleaning shoes and dirty pots, especially when these are done as voluntary service to God.

The morning and evening prayers take about two hours a day, starting in the very early morning hours. The first morning prayer is Guru Nanak's Jap Ji. *Jap*, meaning "recitation," refers to the use of sound, especially the Name of God (Nam), as the best way of approaching the divine. Like combing the hair, hearing and reciting the sacred words combs all negative thoughts out of the mind.

The second morning prayer is Guru Gobind Singh's universal *Jaap Sahib*. It names no prophet, nor creates any religion. It is sheer homage to God. The Guru addresses God as having no form, no country, and no religion but yet as the seed of seeds, song of songs, sun of suns, the life force pervading everywhere, ever merciful, ever giving, indestructible. Complex in its poetry and profound in its content, *Jaap Sahib* asserts that God is the cause of conflict as well as of peace, of destruction as well as of creation; God pervades in darkness as well as in light. In verse after verse, devotees learn that there is nothing outside of God's presence, nothing outside of God's control.

In addition to recitation of prayers, passages from the Guru Granth Sahib are chanted or sung as melodies, often with musical accompaniment. The Granth is placed on a platform, with a devotee waving a whisk over the sacred book to venerate the royalty of the scripture. Worshippers bow to it, bring offerings, and then sit reverently on the floor before it. Every morning and evening, the spirit of God reveals its guidance to the people as an officiant opens the scripture at random, intuitively guided, and reads a passage that is to be a special spiritual focus for the day.

Some gurdwaras—including the Golden Temple in Amritsar—have previously allowed only men to read publicly from the Guru Granth Sahib, to preach, to officiate at ceremonies, or to sing sacred songs. This has been a cultural custom, however, for nothing in the Sikh scriptures or the Code of Conduct bars women from such privileges. Indeed, Guru Gobind Singh

His Holiness Baba Virsa Singh

For decades, His Holiness Baba Virsa Singh (born c. 1934) has been developing farms and communities in India in which people are trying to live by the teachings of the Sikh Gurus. Not only Sikhs but also Hindus, Muslims, and Christians, literate and illiterate, live and work side by side as brothers and sisters there. Baba Virsa Singh himself is illiterate, the son of a village farmer. He relates,

> From childhood, I kept questioning God, "In order to love Jesus, must one become a Christian or just love?" He told me, "It is not necessary to become a Christian. It is necessary to love him."
>
> I asked, "To believe in Moses, does one have to observe any special discipline, or just love?" The divine command came: "Only love." I asked, "Does one have to become a Muslim in order to please Muhammad, or only love?" He said, "One must love." "To believe in Buddha, must one become a monk or a Buddhist?" He replied, "No. To believe in Buddha is to love." God said, "I created human beings. Afterward, human beings created sectarian religions. But I created only human beings, not religions."[18]

Intense spirituality is the base of Baba Virsa Singh's communities, which are known collectively as "Gobind Sadan" ("The House of God"). Volunteers work hard to raise record crops on previously barren land. The harvests are shared communally and also provide the basis for Gobind Sadan's continual free kitchens (langar) for people of all classes, free medical services, and celebrations of the holy days of all religions. Devotions are carried on around the clock, with everyone from gardeners and pot washers to governors and professors helping to clean the holy areas and maintain perpetual reading of the Sikh scriptures. Everyone is empowered to do useful work, including small children, elderly men and women, mentally disturbed people, and people with physical handicaps. Thus under Baba Virsa Singh's guidance, there is a living example of the power of Guru Nanak's straightforward, nonsectarian spiritual program: Work hard to earn your own honest living, share with others, and wake early to meditate upon and remember God in your everyday life.

Another social effect of the work of Baba Virsa Singh is an easing of the tensions that have arisen between people of different religions in India. Even the most rigid proponents of their own religions come to Babaji and are gently convinced to open their eyes toward the validity of other faiths.

Another area in which Baba Virsa Singh is influencing public life in India and other countries is his effect on government officials. He urges them to attend to the practical needs of the people and to uphold order and justice in society.

Speaking from his prodigious visionary powers, Baba Virsa Singh also gives people spiritual hope for a new world order. To editors of a Russian magazine, he explained,

> Truth is always tested. Who tests it? Evil—evil attacks the truth. But truth never stops shining, and evil keeps falling back. Truth's journey is very powerful, with a very strong base. It never wavers. It is definitely a long journey, full of travails, but evil can never suppress the truth.[19]

initiated women as well as men into the Khalsa and allowed women to fight on the battlefield. In 1996, the central body setting policies for Sikh gurdwaras ruled that women should be allowed to perform sacred services.

Sikhism Today

Sikhism is still a vibrant religion and is becoming a global faith, largely by emigration from India. The center of Sikhism remains the Punjab. The area of this territory, which is under Indian rule, was dramatically shrunk by the partition of India in 1947, for two-thirds of the Punjab was in the area thenceforth called Pakistan. The two million Sikhs living in that part were forced to migrate under conditions of extreme hardship. Some managed to migrate to other countries and parts of India other than the Punjab. Emigration continued, and there are now large Sikh communities in Britain, Canada, the United States, Malaysia, and Singapore.

In India, Sikhs and Hindus have lived side-by-side in mutual tolerance until recent years, when violent clashes have begun between Hindus and Sikhs. Sikh separatists want to establish an independent Sikh state, called Khalistan, with a commitment to strong religious observances. Another purpose of Khalistan would be to protect Sikhs from oppression and exploitation by the much larger Hindu community. In 1984, Prime Minister Indira Gandhi chose to attack the Golden Temple, Sikhism's holiest shrine, for Sikh separatists were thought to be using it as a shelter for their weapons. The attack seemed an outrageous desecration of the holy place, and counter-violence increased. The Prime Minister herself was killed later in 1984 by her Sikh bodyguards. In retribution, terrible killings of Sikhs followed.

Many Sikhs have "disappeared" in the Punjab, allegedly at the hands of both separatists and police terrorists. Guru Gobind Singh himself emphasized that one should resort to the sword only after all other means of effecting change have failed. Sikhs in India generally are going on with their lives now that violence has abated, but tensions are kept alive by Sikhs living outside India who persist in demanding Khalistan. Some three hundred Internet websites seem to have been set up devoted to this purpose and to promoting a militant, rigid version of the religion.

Leadership of gurdwaras is democratic, by elected committees, but this provision has not stopped fractiousness within the organizations. In 1998, factions of a Canadian gurdwara had to be separated by police in their fight over the issue of using chairs and tables in the langar rather than the tradition of sitting in rows on the ground.

There are also tensions between those Sikhs who favor a more spiritual and universal understanding of their religion and those who interpret it more rigidly and exclusively. During the years when Sikhs were asserting their distinct identity, lest they be subsumed under Hinduism, the ecumenical nature of Sikhism was not generally emphasized. There were no forcible attempts to convert anyone else to Sikhism, but Sikhs became proud of their heroic history and tended to turn inward.

AN INTERVIEW WITH G. S. JAUHAL

Living Sikhism

G. S. Jauhal is a Punjabi Sikh, a commandant in the Indian military service and a member of Gobind Sadan established by Baba Virsa Singh. His words illustrate the humility which characterizes those who truly live the teachings of the Sikh Gurus:

"I am not an authority. I'm just a student in the very beginning stage. I want to learn so much. I've been a Sikh since birth and I'm forty-seven now. But I think one needs many births and then the Guru's grace— then only can he learn Sikhism. It is so deep, so vast.

We can only get something if first of all Guru's grace is there. Then we keep on endeavoring sincerely, from the core of our heart, and keep on learning. Again and again reading, reciting Guru Granth Sahib, trying to understand what it means. I myself feel that I am one of those who, without understanding ourselves, we try to teach others. This is a pity. Whatever the Guru has given in the Granth Sahib, we are supposed to practice so that everyone knows that what we say, we do. Otherwise people will not take us as true persons. This is the teaching of Guru Granth Sahib— whatever you do outwardly, the same thing should be in your heart. I do try to recite and follow Gurbani, but I am far, far away from the goal which is desired by the Guru.

There are five things which we should not have—lust, anger, greed, attachment to worldly things, ego. These things take us toward the worldly side and away from the true path. The difficult path is chosen by the Gurus. Once man is trying from his inner being to follow that path, and he prays to his Gurus to help him to achieve that path, the Guru always helps this small being, and there is nothing difficult in the world. As the Guru described, to perfect ourself is a very thin path the Sikh is supposed to walk.

When I was young, I learned from my mother. She was totally uneducated. She knew some hymns from Guru Granth Sahib which she learned verbally from her brother. She used to recite when I was just a small child; she used to put me on her lap and recite the Name. Still I remember today some of the words recited by my mother, so it has gone deep into my mind.

I think Sikhism is a unique religion, and the latest. All the good things of all the religions have been combined in one. It is meant to be spread all over the world. We should understand other religions also; there are so many good things in other religions. But I find that the work toward spreading our religion in other parts of the world has not been done as much as it should have been. That could have been possible if the message of the Gurus had been printed in all the languages and then taken to the doorsteps of the other people. People will not come to you to learn your religion in your language. So it was our duty to make it convenient, to translate our Guru Granth Sahib and Guru's teachings into simple speaking language and take it to the people in their own languages. It is a world religion, and we should not have kept it in our closed doors."

Without going so far as to deny the uniqueness or continuing tradition of Sikhism, many contemporary scholars are appreciating the message of the Sikh Gurus as supporting the underlying unity of people of all religions. His Holiness Baba Virsa Singh expresses this point of view:

> *Guru Nanak prepared a lovely ship, in which all the seats were to be given to those who were doing both manual work and spiritual practice.*
>   *The religion of Guru Gobind Singh, of Guru Nanak was not given to those of one organization, one village, one country. Their enlightened vision was for the whole cosmos. Guru Granth Sahib is not for some handful of people. It is for everyone.[20]*

In the words of Guru Gobind Singh:

> *Same are the temple and the mosque*
> *And same are the forms of worship therein.*
> *All human beings are one though apparently many,*
> *Realize, therefore, the essential unity of mankind.[21]*

Suggested Reading

Cole, W. Owen, and Sambhi, Piara Singh, *The Sikhs: Their Religious Beliefs and Practices*, London: Routledge and Kegan Paul, 1978. A clearly-written survey of the Sikh tradition.

Macauliffe, Max Arthur, *The Sikh Religion: Its Gurus, Sacred Writings, and Authors*, sixteen vols., Oxford: Oxford University Press, reprinted in Delhi: S. Chand and Company, 1963. The most respected general account of Sikhism in English, even though its author was not Sikh.

McLeod, W. H., trans. and ed., *Textual Sources for the Study of Sikhism*, Totowa, New Jersey: Barnes and Noble Books, 1984 and Manchester: Manchester University Press, 1984. Interesting compilation of Sikh literature, from selections from the Adi Granth to rules for the Khalsa initiation ceremony, all with explanatory comments.

Singh, Dharam, *Sikhism: Norm and Form*, New Delhi: Vision and Venture, 1997. Convincing discussion of Sikhism as a vision of a new social order: a classless and casteless brotherhood of enlightened humans.

Singh, Guru Gobind, *Jaap Sahib*, English translation by Surendra Nath, New Delhi: Gobind Sadan Publications, 1997. Powerful praises of the formless, ultimately unknowable God, without reference to any particular religion.

Singh, Dr. Gopal, *A History of the Sikh People 1469–1978*, New Delhi: World Sikh University Press, 1979. Thorough and scholarly history of the Sikhs to modern times.

Singh, Harbans, ed., *The Encyclopedia of Sikhism*, Patiala: Punjabi University, 1992–1999. Four volumes on all aspects of Sikhism prepared by leading scholars.

Singh, Khushwant, trans., *Hymns of Guru Nanak*, New Delhi: Orient Longmans Ltd., 1969. Stories about Guru Nanak's life and selections from his sacred songs.

Singh, Manmohan, trans., *Sri Guru Granth Sahib*, 8 vols., Amritsar: Shiromani Gundwara Parbandhak Committee, 1962. A good English translation of the Sikh sacred scripture.

CHAPTER 11

RELIGION AT THE TURN OF THE CENTURY

As we enter the twenty-first century, the global landscape is a patchwork of faiths. Religious expressions are heading in various directions at the same time. Yet as we conclude this survey of religions as living, changing movements, an overview of religion is necessary to gain a sense of how religion is affecting life now and what impact it may have in the future.

New Religious Movements

The history of religions is one of continual change. Each religion changes over time, new religions appear, and some older traditions disappear. Times of rapid social change are particularly likely to spawn new religious movements, for people seek the security of the spiritual amidst worldly chaos. In Japan, an estimated thirty percent of the population belongs to one of hundreds of new religious movements. Imported versions of ancient traditions, such as Hinduism and Buddhism, have made many new converts in areas such as North America, Europe, and Russia, where they are seen as "new religions."

New religious movements have always met with resistance from previously organized religions. As Hare Krishna devotees or Jain meditation groups move into old Christian church buildings, the newcomers are branded with labels such as "cults" or "sects." These words have specific, neutral meanings: a **cult** is a religion devoted to a single person or deity, often representing a distinct break from the prevailing tradition, while a sect is a splinter group or a subgroup associated with a larger tradition. The word "sect" is often used to indicate a nonmainstream splinter group. Both "cult" and "sect" have sometimes been used imprecisely and pejoratively to distinguish new religions from older ones, each of which already claims to be the best or only way. The word "cult" has often been used to signify a group temporarily gathered around a charismatic leader whose influence may be dangerous to his or her followers.

The label "new religious movement" seems more neutral at this time and is becoming widely used, particularly in academic circles, to avoid such negative connotations. However, the word "new" is itself imprecise, for many of these groups have a rather lengthy history and have survived long after the death of the original founder.

In addition to negative reactions from previously organized religions, new religious movements usually meet with opposition from family members of those who join. In the United States, the "anti-cult" movement has employed special agents who capture and "deprogram" followers of new religions, at the request of their parents. Much of the effort to eliminate or control new religious movements is now taking place in Europe, where governments are struggling with issues of religious freedom versus public safety. France is reportedly home to 172 "sects" and 800 small new religious groups, some of them rather bizarre, including groups who have committed mass suicide. There is concern that some are using a religious front to carry on illegal businesses or extort money from gullible followers. Some are neo-fascist groups in the guise of medieval cults whose intentions seem to involve propagation of white supremacy ideas and hatred of immigrants.

As indicated in Chapter 1 of this book, there are both potential dangers and potential benefits associated with giving power over one's life to any religion, new or old. After members of the Aum Shinrikyo movement were suspected of launching a poison gas attack on a Tokyo subway, Japanese asked themselves how their intelligent countrymen could have been drawn to the movement, which had been associated with meditation training, but after the subway attack, was described in the media as a doomsday cult making chemical weapons. Japanese observers have looked at their modern society and concluded that it creates a susceptibility to blind obedience. Author Reiko Hatsumi writes:

> *I think most of my countrymen are honest and hardworking, yet also gullible, with a childlike naivete and a disinclination to think on their own. . . . By being childlike, we also demand emotional security, a guiding hand. Unfortunately, we no longer have a family system. Fathers have abdicated their position as head of the family. They are too busy working late and commuting. The mothers spur their children to get into good schools. . . . The children don't have much to look forward to, except a struggle to get ahead in a crowded, competitive society.*
>
> *So when someone such as Asahara [leader of Aum Shinrikyo] comes along and takes time to listen and to give advice that seems to resolve dilemmas and solve problems, the young hand over their hearts and follow.[1]*

Nevertheless, in religion, as in other life commitments such as marriage, there are potential benefits in dedication and obedience. Many religions, including the largest world religions, teach self-denial and surrender as cardinal virtues which help to vanquish the ego and allow one to approach Reality. The question for a sincere person is where to place one's faith.

Apocalyptic Expectations

At the beginning of the twenty-first century, according to Christian dating, speculations abound that some major change is about to occur in the world. Some people expect better times ahead; some prophesy forthcoming planetary disaster. The disastrous weather patterns in 1997 and 1998 linked with the worst El Niño in history, unstable political and economic conditions around the world, the sudden collapse of the Asian "dragon" economies, and epidemic exposures of government scandals have given many people the impression that we are experiencing a global crisis of supernatural dimensions.

The expectation of major world changes appears in many religions, including Hinduism, Judaism, Christianity, Islam, and some indigenous religions. In Christianity, for instance, the last book in the Bible, Revelation, predicts a world war between the forces of Satan and the forces of God, with great destruction, followed by the **millennium**, a thousand-year period of special holiness in which Christ rules the earth. Hindus anticipate that Kali Yuga, the worst of times, will be followed by the return of Sat Yuga, when dharma will again prevail over evil. However, when members of less established new religious movements genuinely anticipate a doomsday or a new world order, they tend to be regarded as eccentrics by the rest of their society. To maintain their faith, they may isolate themselves from mainstream society and try to prepare for the coming changes. Alternatively, those who anticipate the end of the present world may accept social scorn and try to share their prophecies with others in order to save them from the anticipated coming destruction. An example of the latter approach—Jehovah's Witnesses—demonstrates ways in which people try to engage others in their expectations.

Jehovah's Witnesses foresee a new world in which people of all races (including many raised from the dead) will join hands in peace. They believe that this will happen only after the majority of humanity is destroyed for not obeying the Bible. In the understanding of Jehovah's Witnesses, God will not let anyone ruin the earth. Those who are of the true religion will be saved from the general destruction, reunited with their dead loved ones in a paradise on earth (except for 144,000 who will live with God in heaven). In the earthly paradise there will be no pain, no food shortages, no sickness, no death, according to the teachings.

The nineteenth-century founder of Jehovah's Witnesses, Charles Taze Russell, supported a prediction that 1873 or 1874 would be the date of this apocalypse. When that period passed uneventfully, the date for the "harvest of believers" was pushed forward again and again. As these dates came and went without any apparent end of the world, Russell developed the idea that Christ had arrived, but was invisibly present. Only the faithful "Jehovah's Witnesses" would recognize his presence. Their mission is to warn the rest of the populace about what is in store. They thus go from door to door, encouraging people to follow their program of studying the Bible as an announcement of the millennium. They encourage people to leave politics and "false religions." The latter include mainstream Christian churches, who, the Witnesses feel, began to deviate from Jesus's message in the second and third centuries by developing untrue doctrines. The movement's statisticians claim that it is continuing to grow rapidly. The magazine which Russell founded, *The Watchtower and Herald of Christ's Presence*, is currently published in 110 languages, and the dedicated Jehovah's Witnesses missionaries around the world sell over fifteen million copies of each issue.

Supernatural Powers and Revelations

Numerous new religious movements operate in the realm of that which is supernatural, beyond the experiences of the senses and therefore mysterious. Those who are interested in penetrating these mysteries may do so to attain personal power, or they may seek to use their presumed contacts with invisible realities to bring healing and insights to those who are suffering.

Many founders of these new religions are women with shamanistic gifts. Miki Nakayama, nineteenth-century Japanese founder of the Tenrikyo movement, was acting as a trance medium for the healing of her son when she was reportedly possessed by ten kami (spirits). They proclaimed through her, "Miki's mind and body will be accepted by us as a divine shrine, and we desire to save this three-thousand-world through this divine body."[2] It is said that she later spontaneously composed 1711 poems under divine inspiration, and that these became the sacred scriptures of a new religion. One of these begins with this revelation:

> Looking all over the world and through all ages, I find no one who has understood My heart. No wonder that you know nothing, for so far I have taught nothing to you. This time I, God, revealing Myself to the fore, teach you all the truth in detail.[3]

Tenrikyo has continued to be popular since Miki's death, and she is revered as the still-living representative of the divine will.

Offshoots and Combinations of Older Religions

In previous chapters we have looked at contemporary versions of ancient religions, such as Hare Krishna in Hinduism. Mixtures of more than one religion also arise in many places. This process is referred to as **syncretism**.

In the Caribbean and Latin America, many mixtures of African and Catholic traditions have evolved, with a prevailing interest in contacting and cooperating with spirits. **Santeria**, which literally means "the way of the saints," blends some of the Yoruba gods of ex-Nigerian slaves in Cuba with images of Catholic saints. The female *orisha* (deity) Oshun is worshipped in Nigeria as the patron of love, marriage, and fertility, and is associated with river water. In Cuba and in areas of the United States with large Cuban populations, devotions to Oshun have merged into reverence of the Virgin Mary as Our Lady of Charity, the patron saint of Cuba. She is said to have appeared to three shipwrecked fishermen at sea. Similarly, *Voodoo*, meaning "spirits," developed in Haiti as a blending of West African and French Catholic teachings. Specialists in these traditions have techniques for "magical" intervention in people's lives to help solve problems that cannot be fixed by ordinary means.

Where remnants of slave populations have coalesced, renewed practice of African traditions has given the people a link with their cultural heritage, a sense of inner integrity, and a means of sheer survival. But these African traditions have been viewed with some suspicion by the dominant societies. For instance, traditional African methods of communicating with the spirits include divination and consecrated slaughter of animals, in the context of a community meal. The latter practice was outlawed in Hialeah, Florida, as "animal sacrifice," but in a landmark judgment in 1993, the United States Supreme Court overruled the ban as an unconstitutional barrier to religious freedom. According to a majority of the Supreme Court Justices, "Religious beliefs need not be acceptable, logical, consistent, or comprehensible to others in order to merit First Amendment protection."[4] Santeria has become so popular in Latin America and the United States that it has an estimated one hundred million practitioners, as well as Internet websites, and pilgrimages to Nigeria.

Some new religions profess certain aspects of older religions but eschew so many other features of those religions, perhaps also adding new elements of their own, that they may no longer be considered within the mainstream of the earlier tradition.

The *Radhasoami* movement is an outgrowth of Sikhism in India. Its leaders often have Sikh backgrounds, but while orthodox Sikhs believe in a succession of masters that stopped with the Tenth Guru and was transferred to the holy scripture, Radhasoamis believe in a continuing succession of living masters. The first of the Radhasoami gurus was Shiv Dayal Singh. In 1861 he offered to serve as a spiritual savior, carrying devotees into "Radhasoami," the ineffable Godhead. Some ten thousand took initiation under him. After his death, the movement eventually split into what are now over thirty branches, each with its own living master, although there is theoretically only one of these at a time on the earth.

Radhasoami is primarily an esoteric path, without exoteric ceremonies. Initiates are taught a secret yoga practice of concentrating on the third eye with attention to the inner sound and inner light in order to commune with the all-pervading power of God, the "Word" or Nam. The faithful are told that the experience must be both initiated and guided by a perfected being. The Perfect Masters feel they are of the same continuing lineage that includes Buddha, Jesus, Muhammad, Kabir, and the Sikh saints.

The Radhasoami movement now claims an estimated 1.7 million initiates. Those in the Agra area of India have created whole spiritual suburbs who live and work as well as worship together. Outside of India, devotees gather in *satsangs* (spiritual congregations), who are supposed to support each other in the path. They are required to be vegetarians, to meditate every day, to forego alcohol and, if possible, tobacco, and to be employed.

Sant Rajinder Singh, the contemporary "god-man" in one Sant Mat lineage which is now called the *Science of Spirituality*, emphasizes universal harmony among people of different religions and different countries. He says his aim is to "take the mystery out of mysticism, to help people put mysticism into action in their own lives. By doing so, they will help themselves as well as those around them attain bliss and universal love."[5]

Nature Spirituality

If religion is defined in the broadest sense as that which ties us back to the sacred, one of the strongest trends in our time is that of the religion of nature.

Some who seek to practice a nature-oriented spirituality look to the past for models. This trend is sometimes called *Neo-Paganism*, with reference to pre-Christian spiritual ways that are thought to have been practiced in Europe. Some, particularly women, are interested in evidence that the divine was once worshipped as a female power. They feel that by worshipping the Goddess they are reviving an ancient tradition, rejecting what they see as the negative aspects of patriarchal religions. Some call their way *Witchcraft* or *"Wicca."* As Starhawk, minister of the Covenant of the Goddess, explains:

> *Modern Witches are thought to be members of a kooky cult, ... lacking the depth, the dignity and seriousness of purpose of a true religion. But Witchcraft is a religion, perhaps the oldest religion extant in the West ... and it is very different from all the so-called great religions. The Old Religion, as we call it, is closer in spirit to Native American traditions or to the shamanism of the Arctic. It is not based on dogma or a set of beliefs, nor on scriptures or a sacred book revealed by a great man. Witchcraft takes its teachings from nature, and reads inspiration in the movements of the sun, moon, and stars, the flight of birds, the slow growth of trees, and the cycles of the seasons.[6]*

Some Neo-Pagans honor pantheons such as the Egyptian gods and goddesses, balancing "masculine" and "feminine" qualities. Some try to reproduce some of the sacred ways of earlier European peoples, such as the Celts in the British Isles or the ancient Scandinavians. Reconstructing these ways is difficult, for they were largely oral rather than written traditions. After religions such as Christianity were firmly established, the remaining practitioners of the old ways were often tortured and killed as witches, and blamed for social ills such as the plague. They were said to be in league with the devil against God, but the pagan pantheons had no devil; he was introduced by the Judeo-Christian-Muslim traditions.

In the absence of sure knowledge of ancient ways of honoring Spirit, Neo-Pagans often make up their own forms of group ritual, attempting to draw on divine inspiration for these new ceremonies. Usually they are held outside, with the trees and rocks and waters, the sun, moon, and stars as the altars of the sacred. Speakers may invoke the pantheistic Spirit within all life or the invisible spirits of the place. At ceremonies dedicated to a phase of the moon or the change of the seasons, worshippers may be reminded of how their lives are interwoven with and affected by the natural rhythms. Prayers and ritual may be offered for the healing of the earth, the creatures, or the people.

Certain spots have traditionally been known as places of high energy, as indicated in Chapter 2, and these are often used for ceremonies and less structured sacred experiences. Ancient ceremonial sites in the British Isles, such as Stonehenge and Glastonbury Tor, draw a new breed of tour groups wanting to experience the atmosphere of the places.

Neo-Pagan festivals—some sixty per year in the United States alone—are popular gatherings where participants shed their usual identities and perhaps their clothes, create temporary "kinship groups," and enjoy activities such as ritual fires, storytelling, dancing, drumming, and workshops on subjects such as astrology and old methods of herbal healing.

Universalist Religions

Efforts are also being made to harmonize the world's religions. To cite some examples, the Theosophical Society begun by the nineteenth-century Russian visionary, Madame Helena Blavatsky encourages study of all religions and maintains interfaith libraries. Many Protestant ministers are trained at interfaith theological seminaries in the United States. A number of temples are being built to honor all religions. In addition, several groups have religious unity as their major focus.

One of these is the *Baha'i* faith. It was foreshadowed in Persia in 1844 when a young man called the Bab ("Gate") announced that a new messenger of God to all the peoples of the world would soon appear. Because he proclaimed this message in a Muslim state, where Muhammad was considered the Seal of the Prophets, he was arrested and executed. Some twenty-two thousand of his followers were reportedly massacred as well. One of his imprisoned followers was Baha'u'llah, a member of an aristocratic Persian family. He was stripped of his worldly goods, tortured, banished to Baghdad, and then finally imprisoned for life in Palestine by the Turks. From prison, he revealed himself as the messenger proclaimed by the Bab. He wrote letters to the rulers of all nations, asserting that humanity was becoming unified and that a single global civilization was emerging.

Despite vigorous initial persecution, this new faith has by now spread to over five million followers in 233 countries and territories around the world, involving people from a great variety of racial and ethnic groups. They have no priesthood but they do have their own sacred scriptures.

The heart of Baha'u'llah's message appears in the *Kitab-i-Iqan* ("The Book of Certitude"). Mere humans cannot understand God's infinite nature with their limited minds, said Baha'u'llah. However, God has become known through divine messengers, the founders of the great world religions. The spiritual education of humans has been a process of "progressive revelation." Humanity has been maturing, like a child growing in the ability to grasp complex ideas. Baha'u'llah proclaimed his own message as the most advanced and the one appropriate for this time. It contains the same eternal truths as the earlier revelations, but with some new features which humanity is now ready to grasp, such as the oneness of all peoples, prophets, and religions, and a program for universal governance for the sake of world peace and social justice. In the unified world which Baha'is envision:

> *The relations between the countries, the mingling, union and friendship of the people ... will reach to such a degree that the human race will be like one family ... The light of heavenly love will shine, and the darkness of enmity and hatred will be dispelled from the world.*[7]

Religious Pluralism

A major feature of religious geography is that no single religion dominates the world. Although authorities from many faiths have historically asserted that theirs is the best and only way, in actuality new religions and new versions of older religions continue to spring up and then divide, subdivide, and provoke reform movements. Christianity claims the most members of any global religion, but Christianity is not a monolithic faith. Thousands of forms of Christianity are now being professed.

With migration, missionary activities, and refugee movements, religions have shifted from their country of origin. It is no longer so easy to show a world map in which each country is assigned to a particular religion. In Russia live not only Russian Orthodox Christians but also Muslims, Catholics, Protestants, Jews, Buddhists, Hindus, shamanists, and members of new religions. At the same time, there are now sizable Russian Orthodox congregations in the United States. Buddhism arose in India but now is most pervasive in East Asia and popular in France, England, and the United States. Islam arose in what is now Saudi Arabia, but there are more Muslims in Indonesia than in any other country. There are large Muslim populations in Central Asia, and growing Muslim populations in the United States, with over fifty mosques in the city of Chicago alone.

Professor Diana Eck, Chairman of the Pluralism Project at Harvard University, describes what she terms the new "geo-religious reality":

> Our religious traditions are not boxes of goods passed intact from generation to generation, but rather rivers of faith—alive, dynamic, ever-changing, diverging, converging, drying up here, and watering new lands there.
>
> We are all neighbors somewhere, minorities somewhere, majorities somewhere. This is our new geo-religious reality. There are mosques in the Bible Belt in Houston, just as there are Christian churches in Muslim Pakistan. There are Cambodian Buddhists in Boston, Hindus in Moscow, Sikhs in London.[8]

Hardening of religious boundaries

As religions proliferate and interpenetrate geographically, one common response has been the attempt to deny the validity of other religions. In many countries there is tension between the religion which has been most closely linked with national history and identity and other religions also practiced or introduced into the country. Protestant congregations are rushing to offer Bibles and religious tracts to citizens of formerly atheistic communist countries, with the idea that they are introducing Christianity there. But Christianity, established more than a thousand years ago in Russia, had continued to exist there despite communist rule, sometimes by collaboration with the oppressive authorities, and sometimes by sheer devotion in the midst of hardship, even though the church structures were limited by the state. People from the more established religions seek to find a balance between freedom of religion for all and the threat they perceive to their traditional values, customs, and sense of national identity.

The issue arises of which religions will receive state funding. In Ontario, Canada, for instance, the government has given funding to Roman Catholic schools for a hundred years, yet such funds have been denied to Jewish, Muslim, and Protestant Christian schools. In some countries, there is resistance to offering such public funds to new groups which are organized and financed from abroad.

Registration requirements are another means used to help control the introduction of religions into countries where they did not originate. Another is outright banning of new or minority religions. In 1994, the Russian Orthodox Church warned that any of its followers who promoted the teachings of new religious movements would be excommunicated. It referred to newly introduced religions and new religious movements as wolves in sheep's clothing who were destroying "the traditional order of life which grew under the influence of the Orthodox Church, our common spiritual and moral ideal, and threaten the integrity of national self-conscience and cultural identity." Then in 1997, the Russian Parliament passed a law prohibiting religions which had not been officially existing in Russia longer than fifteen years from distributing religious materials or running schools. The bill protects the powerful status of the Russian Orthodox Church and provides "respect" only to other long-established religions.

In some previously communist countries, old animosities between people of different ethnic groups resurfaced with great violence once totalitarian regimes toppled. These intense ethnic and political struggles often pit people of different faiths against each other. In former Yugoslavia, horrifying atrocities arose among largely Orthodox Christian Serbs, Roman Catholic Croats, and Muslims living mainly in Bosnia and Hercegovina. Gyorgy Bulanyi, founder of the Hungarian Bokor Movement, charges that religious leaders were instigators of rather than dissuaders from violence:

Neither the cardinal in Zagreb nor the Patriarch of Belgrade nor the Great Mufti of Sarajevo preaches to his people that Serbians—or Croats or Muslims—are also created by God, and that it is therefore a cardinal sin to kill them. This is not the line we hear from them, but rather another one: "It is a human right and duty to defend one's family and nation against attack."[9]

The twentieth-century rush for materialism and secular values also fanned an increase in "fundamentalism." Reactionaries do not want their values and life patterns to be despoiled by contemporary secular culture, which they see as crude and sacrilegious. They may try to withdraw socially from the secular culture or they may actively try to change the culture, using political power to shape social laws or ban textbooks which do not include their religious point of view. As described by the Project on Religion and Human Rights,

Fundamentalists' basic goal is to fight back—culturally, ideologically, and socially—against the assumptions and patterns of life that are taken for granted in contemporary secular society and culture, refusing to celebrate them or to embrace them fully. They keep their distance and refuse to

endorse the legitimacy of any culture that opposes what they perceive as
fundamental truths. Secular culture, in their eyes, is base, barbarous, crude,
and essentially profane. It produces a society that respects no sacred order
and ignores the possibility of redemption.[10]

Although fundamentalism may be based on religious motives, it has often been politicized and turned to violent means. Political leaders have found the religious loyalty and absolutism of some fundamentalists an expedient way to mobilize political loyalties, and fundamentalists have themselves attempted to control the political arena in order to bring the social changes they prefer. Thus, Hindu extremists in India have been encouraged to demolish Muslim mosques built on the foundation of older Hindu temples and to rebuild Hindu temples in their place. The United States, which had prided itself on being a "melting pot" for all cultures, with full freedom of religion and no right of government to promote any specific religion, has witnessed attempts by Christian fundamentalists to control education and politics, and a simultaneous rise in violence against ethnic and religious minorities. Buddhism, long associated with nonviolence, has become involved in violent suppression of the Hindu minority in Sri Lanka. Violence among different branches of the same religion is also raging, with Roman Catholic churches being burned in Northern Ireland by Protestants, and Sunni and Shi'ite Muslims taking up arms against each other in neighboring Arabic countries.

Interfaith Movement

At the same time that boundaries between religions are hardening in some areas, they are softening in other areas around the world as the interfaith movement gains momentum. There has been a rapid acceleration of **interfaith dialogue**—the willingness of people of all religions to meet, explore their differences, and appreciate and find enrichment in each other's ways to the divine. This approach has been historically difficult, for many religions have made exclusive claims to being the best or only way. Professor Ewert Cousins, editor of books on spiritual aspects of religions, comments, "I think all the religions are overwhelmed by the particular revelation they have been given and are thus blinded to other traditions' riches."[11]

Religions are quite different in their external practices and culturally-influenced behaviors. There are doctrinal differences on basic issues, such as the cause of and remedy for evil and suffering in the world, or the question of whether the divine is singular, plural, or nontheistic. And some religions make apparent claims to superiority which are difficult to reconcile with other religions' claims. The Holy Qur'an, for instance, while acknowledging the validity of earlier prophets as messengers of God, refers to the Prophet Muhammad as the "Seal of the Prophets" (Sura 33:40).This description has been interpreted to mean that prophecy was completed with the Prophet Muhammad. If he is believed to be the last prophet, no spiritual figures after he passed away in c. 632—including the Sikh Gurus and Baha'u'llah of the Baha'is—could be considered prophets, though they might be seen as teachers. Similarly, Christians read in John 14:6 that Jesus said, "I am the way, the truth, and the life; no one comes to the Father but by me." But some Christian scholars now feel that it is inappropriate to take this line out of its context (in which Jesus's disciples were asking how to find their way to him after they died). Relationships with other faiths was not the question being answered.

Many people of broad vision have noted that many of the same principles reappear in all traditions. Every religion teaches the importance of setting one's own selfish interests aside, loving others, harkening to the divine, and exercising control over the mind. What is called the "Golden Rule," expressed by Confucius as "Do not do unto others what you do not want others to do unto you," and by the Prophet Muhammad as "None of you truly have faith if you do not desire for your brother that which you desire for yourself," is found in every religion.

The absolute authority of scriptures is being questioned by contemporary scholars who are interpreting them in their historical and cultural context and thus casting some doubt upon their exclusive claims to truth. Some liberal scholars are also proposing that there is an underlying experiential unity among religions. Wilfred Cantwell Smith, for instance, concludes that the revelations of all religions have come from the same divine Source. Christian theologian John Hick suggests that religions are culturally different responses to one and the same Reality. The Muslim scholar Frithjof Schuon feels that there is a common mystical base underlying all religions, but that only the enlightened will experience and understand it, whereas others will see the superficial differences.

Responses to other faiths

With these contrasting views, there are several different ways in which people of different religions may relate to each other.

Diana Eck, Professor of Comparative Religion and Indian Studies of Harvard Divinity School and Chair of the World Council of Churches committee on interfaith dialogue, observes that there are three responses to contact between religions. One is **exclusivism**: "Ours is the only true way." Eck and others have noted that such a point of view has some value, for deep personal commitment to one's faith is a foundation of religious life and also the first essential step in interfaith dialogue.

Eck sees the second response to interfaith contact as *inclusivism*. This may take the form of trying to create a single world religion, such as Baha'i. Or it may appear as the belief that our religion is spacious enough to encompass all the others, that it supersedes all previous religions, as Islam said it was the culmination of all monotheistic traditions. In this approach, the inclusivists do not see other ways as a threat. They feel that all diversity is included in a single world view—their own.

The third way Eck discerns is **pluralism**—to hold one's own faith and at the same time ask people of other faiths about their path, about how they want to be understood. As Eck sees it, this is the only point from which true dialogue and true cooperation can happen. Uniformity and agreement are not the goals—the goal is to collaborate, to combine our differing strengths for the common good. For effective pluralistic dialogue, people must have an openness to the possibility of discovering sacred truth in other religions.

Raimundo Panikkar, a Catholic/Hindu/Buddhist doctor of science, philosophy, and theology, speaks of "concordant discord":

> *Consensus ultimately means to walk in the same direction, not to have just one rational view. ... To reach agreement suggests to be agreeable, to be pleasant, to find pleasure in being together. Concord is to put our hearts together.*[12]

Interfaith initiatives

People of all faiths have begun to put their hearts together. Initially, ecumenical conferences involved pairs of related religions who were trying to agree to disagree, such as Judaism and Christianity. Now a large number of interfaith organizations and interfaith meetings draw people from all religions in a spirit of mutual appreciation.

In 1986 Pope John Paul II invited 160 representatives of all religions to Assisi in honor of the humble St. Francis, to pray together for world peace. "If the world is going to continue, and men and women are to survive in it, it cannot do without prayer. This is the permanent lesson of Assisi," declared the pope.[13]

Two years later, the Assisi idea was extended to include governmental leaders, scientists, artists, business leaders, and media specialists as well as spiritual leaders. Some two hundred of them from around the globe met in Oxford, England, in 1988 at the Global Forum of Spiritual and Parliamentary Leaders on Human Survival. They held their plenary sessions beneath an enormous banner with the image of the earth, concluding that the ecological dangers now threatening the entire human race may be the key that draws us together. But it was spiritual camaraderie rather than shared fear that brought the participants together. Dr. Wangari Maathai, leader of the Green Belt movement in Kenya, observed:

> *All religions meditate on the Source. And yet, strangely, religion is one of our greatest divides. If the Source be the same, as indeed it must be, all of us and all religions meditate on the same Source.*[14]

Throughout 1993, special interfaith meetings were held around the world to celebrate the one hundredth anniversary of the 1893 Parliament of the World's Religions in Chicago. In 1893, the figure who most captured world attention was Swami Vivekananda, a learned disciple of Sri Ramakrishna. He brought appreciation of Eastern religions to the West, and made these concluding remarks:

> *If the Parliament of Religions has shown anything to the world it is this: It has proved to the world that holiness, purity, and charity are not the exclusive possessions of any church in the world, and that every system has produced men and women of the most exalted character. In the face of this*

evidence, if anybody dreams of the exclusive survival of his own religion and the destruction of others, I pity him from the bottom of my heart.[15]

The largest 1993 centenary celebration of the Parliament of the World's Religions was again held in Chicago. It gathered hundreds of well-known teachers from all faiths and thousands of participants to consider the critical issues facing humanity. It included an attempt to define and then use as a global standard for behavior the central ethical principles common to all religions. The provisional conference document signed by many of the leaders—"The Declaration Toward a Global Ethic"—included agreement on what has been called the Golden Rule:

There is a principle which is found and has persisted in many religious and ethical traditions of humankind for thousands of years: What you do not wish done to yourself, do not do to others. Or in positive terms: What you wish done to yourself, do to others! This should be the irrevocable, unconditional norm for all areas of life, for families and communities, for races, nations, and religions.[16]

Many people have had the vision that the United Nations could be home to representatives or leaders from all faiths, jointly advising the United Nations on international policy from a religious perspective. This dream has taken many forms, including the United Religions Initiative, the dream of Episcopal bishop William Swing of California. His aim is to:

bring religions and spiritual traditions to a common table, where, respecting each other's distinctness, they may seek the common ground necessary to make peace among themselves and to work together, in dialogue with local, national, and international organizations, to create a sustainable future for all people on the earth.[17]

Questions arise in such an effort, in addition to the necessity for substantial funding. Which religions should be represented? As we have seen, most major religions have many offshoots and branches who do not fully recognize each other's authority. And which, if any, of the myriad new religious movements should be included? Should indigenous religions be included? If so, could one representative speak for all the varied traditions? Would such an organization reflect the bureaucratic patriarchal structures of existing religions, or would it include women, the poor, and enlightened people rather than managers? If the members of the body were not elected by their respective organizations, but were rather simply interested individuals, what authority would they have? Conferences have not developed clear answers to such organizational questions, but after one United Religions Initiative conference, Reverend Paul Chaffee reported,

We reached the point where we could say, as someone did, that "your faith is as important to me as mine is to you," and we began to grasp what an incredible gift such mutuality represents in a deeply troubled world where religions have locked horns for millennia.[18]

In addition to international projects and international interfaith organizations, there are many local interfaith initiatives. The varied religious groups from Chicago who helped to put together the Parliament of the World's Religions have become an ongoing interfaith body in Chicago, celebrating their harmony amidst diversity. Interreligious groups and projects are quite active in England, with its increasingly multi-cultural population. The Leicester Council of Faiths, for instance, includes representatives from Christianity, Hinduism, Islam, Sikhism, Judaism, Jainism, Buddhism, and the Baha'i faith. Their efforts include developing a multi-faith Welcome Centre, ensuring that there is balanced representation of all faiths at civic events, providing multi-faith counseling and a multi-faith chaplaincy service in some healthcare institutions, informing the various faiths about political matters which affect them, and working with the National Health Service on care that is sensitive to people's specific faiths.

> *"Spirituality is not merely tolerance. . . . It is the absolute recognition of the other's faith in God as one's own."*
>
> *Sri Chinmoy*

Whatever the organizational strategy, Gordon Kaufman, Harvard professor and Mennonite Christian minister, sees interfaith dialogue as crucial in solving the problems of the planet:

> *The problems with which modernity confronts us—extending even to the possibility that we may obliterate mankind completely in a nuclear holocaust—demand that we bring together all the wisdom, devotion, and insight that humanity has accumulated in its long history. . . . We simply cannot afford not to enter into conversation with representatives of other traditions, making available to each other whatever resources each of our traditions has to offer, and learning from each other whatever we can.[19]*

In some places, interfaith efforts are being applied directly to difficult real-life situations, such as the fighting between Protestants and Catholics in Northern Ireland. In Mayfair, a neighborhood of Washington, D.C., people lived in fear of drug dealers armed with semi-automatic weapons. A group of African–American Muslims went into the area and chased out the drug dealers, making Mayfair a safe place to live. Then, rather than consolidating their own power, they invited African–American Baptist ministers to come and help teach the people about the spiritual life.

In India, where communal violence between people of varying religions is daily news, the Sikh-based interfaith work of Gobind Sadan is bringing together volunteers of all religions in practical farm work on behalf of the poor, and in celebrations of the holy days of all religions. Baba Virsa Singh, the spiritual inspiration of Gobind Sadan, continually quotes from the words of all the prophets and says:

> *All the Prophets have come from the same Light; they all give the same basic messages. None have come to change the older revealed scriptures; they have come to remind people of the earlier Prophets' messages which the people have forgotten. We have made separate religions as walled forts, each claiming one of the Prophets as its own. But the Light of God cannot be*

*confined within any manmade structures. It radiates throughout all of
Creation. How can we possess it?[20]*

Where people have seen their relatives tortured and killed by fanatics of
another faith, reconciliation is very difficult but necessary if the cycle of
violence and counter-violent reactions is to be halted. Andreas D'Souza
and Diane D'Souza, who are working to heal hatreds among Muslim victims of violence in India, point out that we tend mentally to divide society
into opposing camps:

*In our world today, particularly in Western countries, we are tending to
demonize the other. It is "us," the sane and balanced, against "them," the
demented, violent, and inhuman. We must resist this attempt to polarize
"the good" and "the bad," for it leads to complacency at best, and to the
rationalization of violence, death, and destruction at worst.[21]*

However, embedded within religions is the basis for harmony, for all teach
messages of love and self-control rather than murderous passions.

Religion and Social Issues

Within every religion, there are contemporary attempts to bring religious
perspectives to bear on the critical issues facing humanity. Today we are
facing new issues which were not directly addressed by older teachings,
such as the ethics of cloning. And some issues have reached critical pro-
portions in our times, such as the deterioration of the natural environment.
Many religious groups including indigenous spiritual traditions sent representatives to the huge 1992 Earth Summit in Rio de Janeiro, lobbying for
careful environmental stewardship. At the 1994 Cairo Conference on
Population and Development, Christian and Muslim delegations took
strong stands on behalf of just economic development and education and
health care for women rather than forced population control or abortion as
means of stabilizing population. Buddhists are spearheading efforts to ban
landmines. Hindus and Muslims are trying to stop the spread of immoral,
violent, and cynical mass media communications, to help protect the minds
of the young. Poverty and injustice in societies are being addressed by
many religious groups. South Africa, long known for oppression and injustice, has become an inspiring example of peace and forgiveness under its
new leadership, with an overtly spiritual basis. The Catholic liberation
theologian Gustavo Gutierrez asserts,

*In the last analysis, poverty means an unjust and early death. Now
everything is subordinated to market economies, without taking into
consideration the social consequences for the weakest. People say, for
example, that in business there are no friends. Solidarity is out of fashion.
We need to build a culture of love, through respect of the human being, of
the whole of creation. We must practice a justice inspired by love. Justice is
the basis of true peace. We must, sisters and brothers, avoid being sorry for
or comforting the poor. We must wish to be friends of the poor in the
world.[22]*

In 1994 and 1995, Buddhists of the Nipponzan Myohoji order sponsored an Interfaith Pilgrimage for Peace and Life, in which approximately one hundred people from many countries and many faiths walked from Auschwitz in Poland to Hiroshima and Nagasaki in Japan to commemorate the fiftieth anniversary of the end of World War II, with personal witness to the need for non-violence and respect for all of life. The group walked and chanted through many areas of conflict, including former Yugoslavia, Israel, Iraq, and Cambodia, with considerable impact both on the participants and those they met along the way. Martha Penzer, a Quaker from Boston who made the pilgrimage, reflects:

> What united us in this was our hunger, our yearning, our searching to find a better way, our acknowledgement that in the fifty years since that war humanity had to face itself and make reckoning with the demonic forces in us ... We should never forget that there are people struggling for reconciliation. The supreme grace of it is when we don't run away and get stuck in our own enmities, when we allow God to enter into those enmities and transform them. I think that is the task of religious people—not that we are perfected, by any means, but that we are willing to say to God, "I am just a work in progress and I need Your help."[23]

Religion and Materialism

All religions teach that one should not hurt others, should not lie, should not steal, should not usurp others' rights, should not be greedy, but rather should be unselfish, considerate and helpful to others, and humble before the Unseen. These universal spiritual principles have been swamped by the expansion of capitalism in the twentieth century, as the profit motive has triumphed as the most important value in economies around the world.

Many people live by material greed alone, with no further meaning to their lives. As Vaclav Havel, President of the Czech Republic, wrote to his wife Olga when he was imprisoned for his courageous human rights work,

> The person who has completely lost all sense of the meaning of life is merely vegetating and doesn't mind it; he lives like a parasite and doesn't mind it; he is entirely absorbed in the problem of his own metabolism and essentially nothing beyond that interests him: other people, society, the world, Being— for him they are all simply things to be either consumed or avoided or turned into a comfortable place to make his bed. Everything meaningful in life, though it may assume the most dramatic form of questioning and doubting, is distinguished by a certain transcendence of individual human existence. Only by looking outward ... does one really become a person, a creator of the "order of the spirit," a being capable of a miracle: the re-creation of the world.[24]

Now, at the turn of the century, many individuals and corporations have stepped back to consider how to reconcile spiritual motives with earning a living. Books on voluntary simplicity are proliferating on the bestseller lists. Typically, they encourage the relatively wealthy to cut back on their breakneck work pace for the sake of their own spiritual peace, and to cut back on unnecessary individual expenditures for the sake of sharing with others. Many people are also taking a second look at the effect of economic systems. Liberal capitalism, for example, is being reinterpreted not as a means of allowing industrious people to climb out of poverty, but as a potentially amoral system. In free market capitalism, as Pope Paul VI commented, "The right to the means of production is absolute. It has no limits. It has no social obligation."[25]

A new social consciousness which reflects religious values is beginning to enter some workplaces. Professor Syed Anwar Kabir, a faithful Muslim on the faculty of the Management Development Institute in New Delhi, India, teaches his managerial students to do mind-stilling meditation daily in order to listen to their own conscience and make ethical choices from a base of inner tranquility. He observes,

> *Businessmen themselves say that the uninhibited, reckless way in which you accumulate wealth will not give you a good name. For a company to survive in a highly competitive world in the long term means creating an image in the mind of the public, creating good will, creating its own impact and niche in the market. . . . If you treat human beings not as means but also as ends, naturally it is reflected in your products and services and creates an impact in the world of consumers so that they also come to respect the company's principles and strategies.[26]*

At the turn of the century, power-mongering, self-interest, and corruption are at the forefront of political activities; honesty, altruism, service, harmony, justice, and the public good are not the primary motivating forces in most government actions. Here and there—in South Africa, for instance—there are glimmers of religious principles in government. But in general, attempts to practice religious principles seem more evident in the common people than in their political leaders.

Individual acts of conscience have emerged as a quiet but potent force on the political scene. The astonishingly fast fall of totalitarian communist regimes seems to have been aided by the courageous actions of great numbers of unsung heroes who decided that they had to put their faith into practice, even if it meant facing torture or death. In Christianity alone, it is speculated that there were more martyrs of faith in the twentieth century than in all preceding centuries.

In Latvia, Ukraine, Poland, Czechoslovakia, East Germany, Russia, throughout the former communist bloc, individual choices to stand up for one's faith led to an informal but extremely powerful network of people whose opposition to totalitarian oppression—including religious repression—brought down massively powerful and entrenched regimes. Journalist Barbara von der Heydt, who interviewed many such people for her book *Candles Behind the Wall*, concludes:

> *When tanks surrounded the Russian parliament building in the attempted coup of August 1991, what gave a young woman the courage to walk up to a tank and speak to its driver, urging him not to fire? Why did a young border*

*guard stationed at the Berlin Wall refuse to shoot at anyone attempting to
escape? What motivated tens of thousands to risk their lives on the streets of
Leipzig in the fall of 1989, armed with nothing but candles? . . . The most
important aspect of the collapse was a moral and spiritual revolution.*[27]

After the initial euphoria over the fall of communism, those countries
which quickly adopted free market capitalism are reeling from economic
and social problems. In the chaos of choices which might be correctives,
perhaps options based on religious principles will be given some consideration. Ultimately, social order and the public welfare depend upon the principles which all religions have taught.

Religion and the Future of Humanity

Freedom of religion does not automatically mean that religion is fully practiced. The worst excesses of materialistic greed, crime, and ethnic hatreds
have erupted wherever repressive governments have fallen. Amorality is
widespread. Many religious "leaders" themselves operate religion as a business, rather than a living spiritual experience.

The negative signs of our times are interpreted by some as the darkness
before the dawn, chaos from which will emerge a new and greater order.
As Yasuhiro Nakasone, former Prime Minister of Japan, optimistically
states, "Perhaps we are undergoing a trial—a test that will facilitate the
rebirth of the human race."[28]

Baba Virsa Singh confidently asserts that sweeping change in the hearts
and actions of humanity is not difficult at all for the One who has created
the entire cosmos. He reminds people of the value of practicing the eternal
spiritual teachings and advises them to ignore religious leaders who do not
practice what they preach and who have led people away from the truth
because they themselves are not connected to it. He says that truth and
love are ultimately very powerful:

*Anticipate that day when God transforms the world, and the Truth, which is
now hidden, comes out and starts working among the people again. That day
is upon us.*[29]

At the turn of the century, the world stage is ready for a true moral and
spiritual revolution, in which people of every faith truly begin to practice
in their own lives what their prophets have taught. The words of the late
French sage Teilhard de Chardin are often quoted in these millennial days:

*Some day, after mastering the winds, the waves, the tides, and gravity, we
shall harness for God the energies of love. And then, for the second time in
the history of the world, man will have discovered fire.*

Suggested Reading

Beversluis, Joel V., ed., *A Sourcebook for Earth's Community of Religions*, second
edition, Grand Rapids, Michigan: 1995. Essays on contemporary issues, reflections
on how religious people might come together in harmony, and resources guides

for religious education, first prepared for the 1993 Chicago Parliament of the World's Religions.

Braybrooke, Marcus, *Faith and Interfaith in a Global Age*, Grand Rapids, Michigan: CoNexus Press and Oxford: Braybrooke Press, 1998. One of the world's central interfaith coordinators surveys the interfaith movement at the turn of the century.

Cenkner, William, *Evil and the Response of World Religion*, St. Paul, Minnesota: Paragon House, 1997. Leading scholars from many religions explore the diversity of religious beliefs about a major spiritual issue: Why is there evil and suffering in the world?

Ellwood, Robert S. and Partin, Harry B., *Religious and Spiritual Groups in Modern America*, Englewood Cliffs, New Jersey: Prentice Hall, 1988. Useful source of information and appreciation of new religions that have flourished in the United States.

Gonzalez-Wippler, Migene, *Santeria: The Religion*, second edition, St. Paul, Minnesota: Llewellyn Publications, 1996. Description of usually hidden practices of this syncretistic faith, by an anthropologist and Santeria initiate.

Kelsay, John and Sumner, B. Twiss, eds., *Religion and Human Rights*, New York: The Project on Religion and Human Rights, 1994. A sensitive introduction to conflicts caused by religious "fundamentalism," with positive suggestions as to the potential of religions for insuring human rights.

Khan, Hazrat Inayat, *The Unity of Religious Ideals*, New Lebanon, New York: Sufi Order Publications, 1927, 1979. A master of Sufi mysticism explores the underlying themes in the religious quest which are common to all religions.

Miller, Timothy, *America's Alternative Religions*, Albany: State University of New York Press, 1995. A lengthy survey of the major alternative traditions in America, with chapters written by scholars specializing in specific groups.

Swidler, Leonard, ed., *Toward a Universal Theology of Religion*, Maryknoll, New York: Orbis Books, 1988. Leaders in the evolving interfaith dialogue grapple with the issues of transcending differences.

World Scripture: A Comparative Anthology of Sacred Texts, New York: Paragon House/International Religious Foundation, 1991. A thematic compendium of appealing excerpts from the scriptures and oral traditions of many religions, in excellent translations selected by major scholars.

NOTES

CHAPTER ONE
THE RELIGIOUS RESPONSE

1 Karl Marx, from "Contribution to the Critique of Hegel's Philosophy of Right," 1884, *Karl Marx, Early Writings*, translated and edited by T. B. Bottomore, London: C. A. Watts and Co., 1963, pp. 43–44; *Capital*, vol. 1, 1867, translated by Samuel Moore and Edward Aveling, ed. F. Engels, London: Lawrence and Wishart, 1961, p. 79; "The Communism of the Paper 'Rheinischer Beobachter'," *On Religion*, London: Lawrence and Wishart, undated, pp. 83–84.
2 Jiddu Krishnamurti, *The Awakening of Intelligence*, New York: Harper and Row, 1973, p. 90.
3 Mahatma Gandhi, quoted in Eknath Easwaran, *Gandhi the Man*, Petaluma, California: Nilgiri Press, 1978, p. 121.
4 *The Bhagavad-Gita*, portions of Chapter 2, translated by Eknath Easwaran, quoted in Easwaran, op. cit., pp. 121–122.
5 Excerpted from Agnes Collard, in "The Face of God," *Life*, December 1990, p. 49.
6 From *The Kabir Book* by Robert Bly, copyright 1971, 1977 by Robert Bly, copyright 1977 by Seventies Press. Reprinted by permission of Beacon Press.
7 John White, "An Interview with Nona Coxhead: The Science of Mysticism—Transcendental Bliss in Everyday Life," *Science of Mind*, September 1986, pp. 14, 70.
8 Albert Einstein, *The World As I See It*, New York: Wisdom Library, 1979; *Ideas and Opinions*, translated by Sonja Bargmann, New York: Crown Publishers, 1954.
9 Sallie McFague, *Models of God: Theology for an Ecological Nuclear Age*, Philadelphia: Fortress Press, 1987, p. 133.
10 Maimonides, "Guide for the Perplexed," 1, 59, as quoted in Louis Jacobs, *Jewish Ethics, Philosophy, and Mysticism*, New York: Behrman House, 1969, p. 80.
11 Guru Gobind Singh, *Jaap Sahib*, English translation by Surendra Nath, New Delhi: Gobind Sadan, 1992, verses 7, 29–31.
12 Antony Fernando, "Outlining the Characteristics of the Ideal Individual," paper for the Inter-Religious Federation for World Peace conference, Seoul, Korea, August 20–27, 1995, p. 9.
13 Joseph Campbell, *The Hero with a Thousand Faces*; second edition, Princeton, New Jersey: Princeton University Press, 1972, p. 29.
14 Rev. Valson Thampu, "Religious Fundamentalisms in India Today," *Indian Currents*, November 2, 1995, p. 3.
15 Dr. Syed Z. Abedin, "Let There be Light," *Saudi Gazette*, Jeddah, June 1992, reprinted in Council for a Parliament of the World's Religions Newsletter, Vol. 4, no. 2, August 1992, p. 2.

CHAPTER TWO
INDIGENOUS SACRED WAYS

1 Lorraine Mafi Williams, personal communication, September 16, 1988.
2 Gerhardus Cornelius Oosthuizen, "The Place of Traditional Religion in Contemporary South Africa," in Jacob K. Olupona, *African Traditional Religions in Contemporary Society*, New York: Paragon House, 1991, p. 36.
3 Quoted by Bob Masla, "The Healing Art of the Huichol Indians," *Many Hands: Resources for Personal and Social Transformation*, Fall 1988, p. 30.
4 Knud Rasmussen, *Across Arctic America*, New York: G. P. Putnam and Sons, 1927, p. 386.
5 Interview with Rev. William Kingsley Opoku, August 1992.
6 Josiah U. Young III, "Out of Africa: African Traditional Religion and African Theology," in *World Religions and Human Liberation*, Dan Cohn-Sherbok, ed., Maryknoll, New York: Orbis Books, 1992, p. 93.
7 Jo Agguisho/Oren R. Lyons, spokesman for the Traditional Elders Circle, Wolf Clan,

Onondaga Nation, Haudenosaunee, Six Nations Iroquois Confederacy, from the speech to the Fourth World Wilderness Conference, September 11, 1987, p. 2.

8 Bill Neidjie, *Speaking for the Earth: Nature's Law and the Aboriginal Way*, Washington: Center for Respect of Life and Environment, 1991, pp. 40–41. Reprinted from Kakadu Man by Big Bill Neidjie, Stephen Davis, and Allan Fox, Northryde, New South Wales, Australia: Angus and Robertson.

9 Kahu Kawai'i, interviewed by Mark Bochrach in *The Source*, as quoted in Hinduism Today, Dec. 1988, p. 18.

10 Quoted in Matthew Fox, "Native teachings: Spirituality with power," *Creation*, January/February 1987, vol. 2, no. 6.

11 Lame Deer with Richard Erdoes, op. cit., p. 116.

12 Tlakaelel, talk at Interface, Watertown, Massachusetts, April 15, 1988.

13 Leonard Crow Dog and Richard Erdoes, *The Eye of the Heart*, unpublished manuscript, quoted by Joan Halifax, *Shamanic Voices: A Survey of Visionary Narratives*, New York: E. P. Dutton, 1979, p. 77.

14 Quoted in John Neihardt, *Black Elk Speaks*, op. cit., pp. 208–209.

15 Lame Deer with Richard Erdoes, op. cit., pp. 145–146.

16 Tsering, in Ian Baker, "Shaman's Quest," *Hinduism Today*, November 1997, p. 23.

17 From an interview conducted for this book by Tatiana Kuznetsova.

18 Ruth M. Underhill, *Papago Woman*, New York: Holt, Rinehart and Winston, 1979, p. 9.

19 Dhyani Ywahoo, *Voices of our Ancestors*, Boston: Shambhala Publications, 1987, p. 89.

20 Leonard Crow Dog and Richard Erdoes, in Joan Halifax, *Shamanic Voices*, op. cit., p. 77.

21 Interview with Wande Abimbola, August 6, 1992.

22 Tlakaelel, op. cit.

23 "Aborigine aiming to be first native woman MP," AFP, *Asian Age*, September 30, 1998, p. 5.

24 Jameson Kurasha, "Plato and the Tortoise: A Case for the death of ideas in favour of peace and life?", paper presented at Assembly of the World's Religions, Seoul, Korea, August 1992, pp. 4–5.

25 Winona LaDuke, *Last Standing Woman*, Stillwater, Minnesota: Voyageur Press, 1997, p. 17.

26 Winona LaDuke, as quoted by Jamie Marks, "A campaignless campaign," *Becker County Record*, September 8, 1996, p. 1A.

27 Winona LaDuke, *Last Standing Woman*, op. cit., p. 299.

28 "Declaration of Vision: Toward the Next 500 Years," from the Gathering of the 1993 United Indigenous Peoples at the Parliament of the World's Religions, Chicago, Illinois, 1993.

29 Rigoberta Menchú, quoted in Art Davidson, *Endangered Peoples*, San Francisco: Sierra Club Books, 1994, p. ix.

CHAPTER THREE
HINDUISM

1 English transliteration of the Sanskrit s as "s" or "sh" varies widely and is by no means consistent. In accordance with the inconsistencies long found, this chapter follows existing usage and does not try to standardize it, to conform with popular though inconsistent English usage.

2 Sri Aurobindo, *The Immortal Fire*, Auroville, India: Auropublications, 1974, pp. 3–4.

3 *The Upanishads*, translated by Swami Prabhavananda and Frederick Manchester, The Vedanta Society of Southern California, New York: Mentor Books, 1957.

4 Chandogya Upanishad, ibid., p. 46.

5 T. M. P. Mahadevan, *Outlines of Hinduism*, second edition, Bombay: Chetana Ltd., 1960, p. 24.

6 A condensation by Heinrich Zimmer of the Vishnu Purana, Book IV, Chapter 24, translated by H. H. Wilson, London, 1840, in Zimmer's *Myths and Symbols in Indian Art and Civilization*, New York: Pantheon Books, 1946, p. 15.

7 Uttara Kandam, *Ramayana*, third edition, as told by Swami Chidbhavananda, Tiriuuparaitturai, India: Tapovanam Printing School, 1978, pp. 198–199.

8 Ibid., III: 30, p. 57.

9 Ibid., IV: 3, p. 64.

10 Ibid., IV: 7–8, pp. 68–69.

11 Ibid., VII: 7–8, 12, pp. 126, 128.

12 Swami Sivananda, *Dhyana Yoga*, fourth edition, Shivanandanagar, India: The Divine Life Society, 1981, p. 67.

13 Ramana Maharshi, *The Spiritual Teaching of Ramana Maharshi*, Boston: Shambhala, 1972, pp. 4, 6.
14 Swami Vivekananda, *Karma-Yoga and Bhakti-Yoga*, New York: Ramakrishna-Vivekananda Center, 1982, p. 32.
15 *Bhagavad-Gita as It Is*, op. cit., Chapter 2:49 (p. 36), Chapter 5:8, p. 12.
16 Saint Nam Dev, as included in Sri Guru Granth Sahib, p. 693, adapted from the translation by Manmohan Singh, Amristsar, India: Shiromani Gurdwara Parbandhak Committee, 1989.
17 Ramakrishna, quoted in Carl Jung's introduction to *The Spiritual Teaching of Ramana Maharshi*, op. cit., p. viii.
18 Leela Arjunwadkar, "Ecological Awareness in Indian Tradition (Specially as Reflected in Sanskrit Literature)," paper presented at Assembly of the World's Religions, Seoul, Korea, August 24–31, 1992, p. 4.
19 Swami Sivasiva Palani, personal communication, October 26, 1989.
20 Robert N. Minor, "Sarvepalli Radhakrishnan and 'Hinduism': Defined and Defended," in Robert D. Baird, ed., *Religion in Modern India*, New Delhi: Manohar Publications, 1981, p. 306.
21 Ramakrishna, as quoted in Swami Vivekananda, *Ramakrishna and His Message*, Howra, India: Swami Abhayananda, Sri Ramakrishna Math, 1971, p. 25.
22 Paraphrased from brochure from Vedanta Centre, Ananda Ashram, Cohasset, Massachusetts.
23 All quotations are from an interview with Dr. Karan Singh, November 17, 1998.
24 Abbreviation of Indian Supreme Court definition of Hinduism, as itemized in "The DNA of Dharma," *Hinduism Today*, December 1996, p. 33.
25 Karan Singh, *Essays on Hinduism*, second edition, New Delhi: Ratna Sagar, 1990, p. 43.

CHAPTER FOUR
BUDDHISM
1 Muhaparinibbana Sutta, Digha Nikaya, 2.99f, 155–156, quoted in *Sources of Indian Tradition*, ed. William Theodore de Bary, New York: Columbia University Press, 1958, pp. 110–111.
2 "A message from Buddhists to the Parliament of the World's Religions," Chicago, September 1993, as quoted in *World Faiths Encounter* no. 7, February 1994, p. 53.
3 Majjhima-Nikaya, "The Lesser Matunkyaputta Sermon," Sutta 63, translated by P. Lal in the introduction to *The Dhammapada*, op. cit., p. 19.
4 Walpola Sri Rahula, *What the Buddha Taught*, revised edition, New York: Grove Press, 1974, p. 17.
5 Sigalovada Sutta, Dighanikaya III, pp. 180–193, quoted in H. Saddhatissa, *The Buddha's Way*, New York: George Braziller, 1971, p. 101.
6 *The Dhammapada*, translated by P. Lal, op. cit., p. 152.
7 Ibid., p. 49.
8 Achaan Chah, *A Still Forest Pool*, eds. Jack Kornfield and Paul Breiter, Wheaton, Illinois: Theosophical Publishing House, 1985.
9 *The Mahavagga* 1.
10 *Suttanipatta* 1093–4.
11 *Majjhima-Nikaya* 1: 161–4.
12 *The Dhammapada*, translated by P. Lal, op. cit., pp. 71–72.
13 Samyutta Nikaya, quoted in the introduction to *The Dhammapada*, translated by P. Lal, op. cit., p. 17.
14 Chatsumarn Kabilsingh, *Thai Women in Buddhism*, Berkeley, California: Parallax Press, 1991, p. 25.
15 Joko Beck, as quoted in Lenore Friedman, *Meetings with Remarkable Women*, Boston: Shambhala, 1987, p. 119.
16 His Holiness the Fourteenth Dalai Lama, speaking on February 15, 1992, in New Delhi, India, Ninth Dharma Celebration of Tushita Meditation Centre.
17 David W. Chappell, personal communication, July 26, 1995.
18 Tarthang Tulku, *Openness Mind*, Berkeley, California: Dharma Publishing, 1978, pp. 52–53.
19 His Holiness the Fourteenth Dalai Lama, *My Land and my People*, New York: McGraw-Hill, 1962; Indian edition, New Delhi: Srishti Publishers, 1997, p. 50.
20 His Holiness the Fourteenth Dalai Lama, evening address after receiving the Nobel Peace Prize, 1989, in Sidney Piburn, ed., *The Dalai Lama: A Policy of Kindness*, second edition, Ithaca, New York: Snow Lion Publications, 1993, p. 114.

21 *Stories and Songs from the Oral Tradition of Jetsun Milarepa,* translated by Lama Kunga Rimpoche and Brian Cutillo in *Drinking the Mountain Stream,* New York: Lotsawa, 1978, pp. 56–57.

22 Platform Scripture of the Sixth Patriarch, Hui-neng, quoted in *World of the Buddha,* ed. Lucien Stryk, New York: Doubleday Anchor Books, 1969, p. 340.

23 From "Hsin hsin ming" by Sengtsan, third Zen patriarch, translated by Richard B. Clarke.

24 Roshi Philip Kapleau, *The Three Pillars of Zen,* New York: Anchor Books, 1980, p. 70.

25 Bunan, quoted in *World of the Buddha,* Stryk, op. cit., p. 343.

26 Genshin, *The Essentials of Salvation,* quoted in ed. William de Bary, *The Buddhist Tradition in India, China, and Japan,* New York: Modern Library, 1969, p. 326.

27 The Most Venerable Nichidatsu Fujii, quoted in a booklet commemorating the dedication for the Peace Pagoda in Leverett, Massachusetts, October 5, 1985.

28 "Introduction to NSA" (Nichiren Shoshu Soka Gakkai of America).

29 Ibid.

30 "Rissho Kosei-kai, Practical Buddhism and Interreligious Cooperation," brochure from Rissho Kosei-kai, Tokyo.

31 Thich Nhat Hanh, *Being Peace,* Indian edition, Delhi: Full Circle, 1997, pp. 53–54.

32 Richard B. Clarke, personal communication, October 2, 1981.

33 Walpola Rahula, "The Social Teachings of the Buddha," in *The Path of Compassion,* ed. Fred Eppsteiner, Berkeley, California: Parallax Press, 1988, pp. 103–104.

34 *Metta Sutta,* as translated by Maha Ghosananda, in "Invocation: A Cambodian Prayer," *The Path of Compassion,* op. cit., p. xix.

35 Sulak Sivaraksa, "Buddhism in a World of Change," in *The Path of Compassion,* op. cit., p. 16.

CHAPTER FIVE
TAOISM AND CONFUCIANISM

1 Excerpt from verse 1 in *Tao-te Ching,* translated by Stephen Mitchell. Translation copyright 1988 by Stephen Mitchell. Reprinted by permission of Harper and Row, Publishers, Inc.

2 *Tao-te Ching,* translated by Lin Yutang, New York: Modern Library, 1948, verse 1, p. 41.

3 Lao-tzu, *Tao-te Ching,* translated by D. C. Lau, London: Penguin Books, 1963, verse 25, p. 82.

4 Chuang-tzu, *Basic Writings,* translated by Burton Watson, op. cit., p. 40.

5 *The Way to Life: At the Heart of the Tao-te Ching,* non-literal translation by Benjamin Hoff, New York/Tokyo: Weatherhill, 1981, p. 52, chapter 78.

6 *The Way to Life,* translated by Benjamin Hoff, op. cit., p. 33, chapter 35.

7 Sun Bu-er, in *Immortal Sisters: Secrets of Taoist Women,* translated by Thomas Cleary, Boston: Shambhala Publications, 1989, p. 50.

8 *Tao-te Ching,* translated by Stephen Mitchell, op. cit., Chapter 15.

9 Chuang-tzu, op. cit., p. 59.

10 Excerpted from Huai-Chin Han, translated by Wen Kuan Chu, *Tao and Longevity: Mind-Body Transformation,* York Beach, Maine: Samuel Weiser, 1984, pp. 4–5.

11 Quoted in *T'ai-chi,* Cheng Man-ch'ing and Robert W. Smith, Rutland, Vermont: Charles E. Tuttle, 1967, p. 106.

12 Ibid., p. 109.

13 Excerpted from Al Chung-liang Huang, *Embrace Tiger, Return to Mountain,* Moab, Utah: Real People Press, 1973, pp. 12, 185.

14 Quoted by Da Liu, *The Tao and Chinese Culture,* London: Routledge and Kegan Paul, 1981, p. 161.

15 Yu Yingshi, "A Difference in Starting Points," *Heaven Earth,* ibid., p. 1.

16 *The Analects,* VII: 1, in *Sources of Chinese Tradition,* vol. 1, eds. William Theodore de Bary, Wing-tsit Chan, Burton Watson, p. 23.

17 Ibid. XIII: 6, p. 32, and Analects II: 1, as translated by Ch'u Chai and Winberg Chai in *Confucianism,* Woodbury, New York: Barron's Educational Series, 1973, p. 52.

18 *The Texts of Confucianism, Sacred Books of the East,* Max Müller, ed., Oxford: Oxford University Press, 1891, vol. 27, pp. 450–451.

19 *The Analects,* XI:11, in Ch'u Chai and Winberg Chai, *The Sacred Books of Confucius and Other Confucian Classics,* New Hyde Park, New York: University Books, 1965, p. 46.

20 Ibid., X:25.

21 Ibid., X:103.

22 The Mencius, in De Bary, op. cit., p. 91.

23 Ibid., p. 89.

24 From the Hsun Tzu, Chapter 17, in de Bary, op. cit., p. 101.

25 Chang Tsai's *Western Inscription*, in William Theodore de Bary et. al., *Sources of Chinese Tradition*, op. cit.

26 A prayer offered by the Ming dynasty emperor in 1538, in James Legge, *The Religions of China*, London, 1880, pp. 43–44.

27 *Quotations from Chairman Mao tse-Tung*, second edition, Peking: Foreign Language Press, 1967, pp. 172–173.

28 *China Daily*, January 30, 1989, p. 1.

29 Xinzhong Yao, "Confucianism and the Twenty-first Century: Confucian Moral, Educational and Spiritual Heritages Revisited," First International Conference on Traditional Culture and Moral Education, Beijing, August 1998, p. 4.

30 Tu Wei-ming, "Confucianism," in Arvind Sharma, ed., *Our Religions*, New York: Harper Collins Publishers, 1993, pp. 221–222.

31 Korean Overseas Information Service, *Religions in Korea*, Seoul, 1986, pp. 55–57.

CHAPTER SIX
SHINTO
1 Yukitaka Yamamoto, *Way of the Kami*, Stockton, California: Tsubaki America Publications, 1987, p. 75.

2 Adapted from the *Nihon Shoki* (Chronicles of Japan), I:3, in Stuart D. B. Picken, *Shinto: Japan's Spiritual Roots*, Tokyo: Kodansha International, 1980, p. 10.

3 Sakamiki Shunzo, "Shinto: Japanese Ethnocentrism," in Charles A. Moore, ed., *The Japanese Mind*, Hawaii: University of Hawaii Press, p. 25.

4 Kishimoto Hideo, "Some Japanese Cultural Traits and Religions," in Charles A. Moore, ed., *The Japanese Mind*, op. cit., pp. 113–114.

5 Ise-Teijo, *Gunshin-Mondo, Onchisosho*, vol. x., quoted in Genchi Kato, p. 185.

6 Yamamoto, op. cit., pp. 73–75.

7 Unidentified quotation, Stuart D. B. Picken, ed., *A Handbook of Shinto*, Stockton, California: The Tsubaki Grand Shrine of America, 1987, p. 14.

8 Ibid.

9 Hitoshi Iwasaki, "Wisdom from the night sky," Tsubaki Newsletter, June 1, 1988, p. 2.

10 Motoori Norinaga (1730–1801), *Naobi no Mitma*, quoted in Tsubaki Newsletter, November 1, 1988, p. 3.

11 *Ofudesaki*, as quoted in *Aizen Newsletter of the Universal Love and Brotherhood Association*, no. 17, September–October 1997, p. 2.

12 Jinja-Honcho (The Association of Shinto Shrines), "The Shinto View of Nature and a Proposal Regarding Environmental Problems," Tokyo.

CHAPTER SEVEN
JUDAISM
1 Genesis 1: 1. *Tanakh—The Holy Scriptures*: The New JPS Translation According to the Traditional Hebrew Text, Philadelphia: The Jewish Publication Society, 1985. This translation is used throughout this chapter.

2 Genesis 1: 28.

3 Genesis 6: 17.

4 Genesis 9: 17.

5 Genesis 22: 12.

6 Personal communication, March 24, 1989.

7 Deuteronomy 7: 7.

8 Exodus 3: 5.

9 Exodus 3: 10.

10 Exodus 3: 12.

11 Exodus 3: 14–15.

12 I Kings 9: 3.

13 Daniel 7: 13–14.

14 From the Talmud and Midrash, quoted in *The Judaic Tradition*, ed. Nahum N. Glatzer, Boston: Beacon Press, 1969, p. 197.

15 Maimonides, *Guide of the Perplexed*.

16 Quoted in S. A. Horodezky, *Leaders of Hasidism*, London: Ha-Sefer Agency for Literature, 1928, p. 11.

17 Elie Wiesel, speech for the UConn Convocation, September 7, 1988, University of Connecticut, Storrs, Connecticut.

18 Maimonides' "First Principles of Faith," as quoted in Louis Jacobs, *Principles of Jewish Faith*, Northvale, New Jersey: Jason Aronson, 1988, p. 33.

19 Ibn Gabirol, *Keter Malkhut*, quoted in Abraham J. Heschel, "One God," *in Between God and Man: An Interpretation of Judaism, from the Writings of Abraham J. Heschel*, ed. Fritz A. Rothschild, New York: Free Press, 1959, p. 106.

20 Abraham Joshua Heschel, *Man is not Alone*, New York: Farrar, Straus and Giroux, 1951, 1976, p. 112.

21 Abraham J. Heschel, "One God," op. cit., p. 104.

22 Martin Buber, in *The Way of Response: Martin Buber—Selections from His Writings*, ed. Nahum N. Glatzer, New York: Schocken Books, 1968, p. 53.

23 Isaiah 65: 25, JPS *Tanakh*.

24 Translated from the Hebrew by Rabbi Sidney Greenberg, *Likrat Shabbat*, Bridgeport, Connecticut: Media Judaica/The Prayer Book Press, 1981, p. 61.

25 Job 1: 20–21.

26 The Jewish Prayer Book, as quoted by Jocelyn Hellig, "A South African Jewish Perspective," in Martin Forward, ed., *Ultimate Visions*, Oxford: Oneworld Publications, 1995, p. 136.

27 Leviticus 11: 45.

28 Excerpted from Ruth Gan Kagan, "The Sabbath: Judaism's Discipline for Inner Peace," paper presented at the Assembly of the World's Religions, Seoul, Korea, August 24–31, 1992, pp. 3, 7.

29 Sanhedrin 22a, quoted in *The Second Jewish Catalog*, eds. Sharon Strassfeld and Michael Strassfeld, Philadelphia: The Jewish Publication Society, 1976.

30 Rabbi Yochanan ben Nuri, Rosh Hashanah prayer quoted by Arthur Waskow, *Seasons of Our Joy*, New York: Bantam Books, 1982, p. 11.

31 Michael Lerner, *Jewish Renewal: A Path to Healing and Transformation*, New York: HarperCollins, 1994, p. 365.

32 Janice Perlman, personal communication, December 16, 1998.

33 Janice Perlman, "A Dual Strategy for Deliberate Social Change in Cities," in *Cities: The International Journal of Urban Policy and Planning*, Butterworth and Co., vol. 7, no. 1, February 1990, p. 15; and Perlman, "A Tale of NGOs," op. cit., p. 1.

34 Mordecai M. Kaplan, "The Way I Have Come," in *Mordecai M. Kaplan: An Evaluation*, eds. I. Eisenstein and E. Kohn, New York, 1952, p. 293.

35 Genesis 1: 26 from *The Torah*, Philadelphia: The Jewish Publication Society, 1962.

36 *The Gates of Repentance*, New York: Central Conference of American Rabbis, p. 197.

37 Susannah Heschel, "The Feminist Confrontation with Judaism," in Alan L. Berger, ed., *Judaism in the Modern World*, New York: New York University Press, 1994, p. 276.

38 Judith Plaskow, *Standing Again at Sinai*, San Francisco: HarperCollins, 1991, p. 120.

39 "Declaration of the ELCA to the Jewish Community," as quoted in Joel Beversluis, *A Sourcebook for Earth's Community of Religions*, revised edition, Grand Rapids, Michigan: CoNexus Press-Sourcebook Project, 1995, p. 170.

40 Rabbi Dovid Karpov, interviewed October 24, 1994.

41 Michael Lerner, op. cit., pp. xvii, xxviii.

CHAPTER EIGHT
CHRISTIANITY

1 Publishing Department of Moscow Patriarchate, *The Russian Orthodox Church*, Moscow, 1980, p. 239 in English translation by Doris Bradbury, Moscow: Progress Publishers, 1982.

2 *The Gospel According to Thomas*, Coptic text established and translated by Guilloaumont et al., Leiden: E. J. Brill; New York: Harper and Row, 1959, verse 77.

3 Luke 2: 47, 49. Most Biblical quotations in this chapter are from the Revised Standard Version of the Bible, copyright 1946, 1952, 1971 by The Division of Christian Education of the National Council of the Churches of Christ in the USA. Used by permission.

4 Mark 1: 10–11.

5 Matthew 6: 25–27.

6 Luke 9: 17.

7 William, quoted in *The Gospel in Art by the Peasants of Solentiname*, eds. Philip and Sally Scharper, Maryknoll, New York: Orbis Books, 1984, p. 42.

8 Matthew 5: 21–22.

9 Matthew 5: 44–45.

10 Mark 10: 27.

11 Matthew 22: 39.

12 Matthew 25: 37–40.

13 Matthew 5: 3.

14 Matthew 13: 47–50, The New English Bible, Cambridge, England: Cambridge University Press, corrected impression, 1972.

15 Mark 1: 15.

16 Luke 4: 43.

17 Matthew 6: 10.

18 Matthew 24: 29–31.

19 Isaiah 29: 13, The New English Bible.

20 Matthew 15: 1–20, The New English Bible.

21 Matthew 23: 1–3, 27–28, The New English Bible.

22 Isaiah 56: 7.

23 Jeremiah 7: 11.

24 Mark 11: 15–18, The New English Bible

25 Mark 8: 29–30.

26 John 11: 27.

27 Matthew 17: 2–5.

28 John 7: 16, 8: 12, 8: 23, 8: 58.

29 Matthew 26: 28.

30 Mark 11: 10.

31 Mark 14: 36.

32 Joachim Jeremias, *New Testament Theology: The Proclamation of Jesus,* translated by John Bowden, New York: Charles Scribner's Sons, 1971, p. 40.

33 Mark 14: 41.

34 Matthew 26: 64.

35 Matthew 27: 11.

36 Matthew 27: 46.

37 Matthew 28: 18–20.

38 Elisabeth Schüssler Fiorenza, *In Memory of Her,* New York: Crossroad, 1983, 1994, p. xliv.

39 Acts 26: 18.

40 Acts 17: 28.

41 *The Gospel According to Thomas,* op. cit., 82.

42 *Confessions of St. Augustine,* translated by Edward Bouverie Pusey, Chicago: Encyclopedia Britannica, vol. 18 of Great Books of the Western World, 1952, p. 64.

43 Rowan Williams, *Resurrection,* New York: The Pilgrim Press, 1984, p. 46 with quotations from John 14:19.

44 Archimandrite Chrysostomos, *The Ancient Fathers of the Desert,* Brookline, Massachusetts: Hellenic College Press, 1980, p. 78.

45 The Solovky Memorandum, as quoted in Barbara von der Heydt, *Candles Behind the Wall,* Grand Rapids, Michigan: William B. Eerdmans Publishing Company, 1993, p. 46.

46 Mikhail S. Gorbachev, quoted in Michael Dobbs, "Soviets, Vatican to Establish Ties," *The Hartford Courant,* December 2, 1989, p. 1.

47 Father Alexey Vlasov, interviewed October 26, 1994.

48 Father Feodor, interviewed October 29, 1994.

49 Fotini Pipili, in Iina Kyriakidou, "Greek women poised to take on all-male monastic community," *Asian Age,* October 14, 1997, p. 7.

50 St. Gregory Palamas, "Homily on the Presentation of the Holy Virgin in the Temple," ed., Sophocles, 22 *Homilies of St. Gr. Palamas,* Athens, 1861, pp. 175–177, quoted in Vladimir Lossky, *The Mystical Theology of the Eastern Church,* New York: St. Vladimir's Seminary Press, 1976, p. 224.

51 Jim Forest, *Pilgrim to the Russian Church,* New York: Crossroad Publishing Company, 1988, p. 50.

52 From *A Hopkins Reader,* ed. John Pick, New York: Oxford University Press, 1953, quoted in D. M. Dooling, ed., *A Way of Working,* New York: Anchor Press/Doubleday, 1979, p. 6.

53 St. Francis, *Testament,* April 1226, p. 3, quoted in eds. Jean Leclerc, Francois Vandenbroucke, and Louis Bouyer, *The Spirituality of the Middle Ages,* vol. 2 of *A History of Christian Spirituality,* New York: Seabury Press, 1982, p. 289.

54 *The Cloud of Unknowing and The Book of Privy Counseling,* Garden City, New York: Image Books, 1973 edition, p. 56.

55 Martin Luther, *A Treatise on Christian Liberty,* quoted in John Oillenberger and Claude Welch, *Protestant Christianity,* New York: Charles Scribner's Sons, 1954, p. 36.

56 Ulrich Zwingli, "On True and False Religion," quoted in ed. Harry Emerson Fosdick, *Great Voices of the Reformation*, New York: Random House, 1952, p. 169.

57 John Calvin, "Instruction in Faith," quoted in Fosdick, op. cit., p. 216.

58 John Wesley, as quoted in F. L. Cross and E. A. Livingstone, eds., *The Oxford Dictionary of the Christian Church*, Oxford: Oxford University Press, 1983, p. 1467.

59 St. Teresa of Avila, *Interior Castle*, translated by E. Allison Peers from the critical edition of P. Silverior de Santa Teresa, Garden City, New York: Image Books, 1961, p. 214.

60 Sarah Grimke, "Letters on the Equality of the Sexes and the Condition of Women" (1836–37), in *Feminism: The Essential Historical Writings*, ed. M. Schneir, New York: Vintage, 1972, p. 38.

61 The Documents of Vatican II, ed. Walter M. Abbott, New York: Guild Press, 1966, p. 665.

62 Ibid., pp. 661–662.

63 John 14: 2–10, The New English Bible.

64 Paul Knitter, in John Hick and Paul F. Knitter, eds., *The Myth of Christian Uniqueness: Toward a Pluralistic Theology of Religions*, Maryknoll, New York: Orbis Books, 1987, pp. 192–193.

65 Matthew 20: 28.

66 John 3: 16–17, The New English Bible.

67 Archbishop Desmond Tutu, "The Face of God," *Life*, December 1990, pp. 49–50.

68 Rev. Larry Howard, interfaith service, Syracuse, New York, October 25, 1992.

69 (Thomas a Kempis), *The Imitation of Christ*, p. 139.

70 F. Ioann Kronshtadtsky, as quoted in F. Veniamin Fedchenkov, *Heaven on Earth*, Moscow: Palmnik, 1994, p. 70.

71 Julia Gatta, personal communication, July 22, 1987.

72 "Brief Order for Confession and Forgiveness," *Lutheran Book of Worship*, prepared by the churches participating in the Inter-Lutheran Commission on Worship, Minneapolis, Minnesota: Augsburg Publishing House, 1978, p. 56.

73 World Council of Churches, *Baptism, Eucharist and Ministry*, Faith and Order Paper No. 111, Geneva, 1982, p. 2.

74 Father Appolinari, interviewed October 28, 1994.

75 John 1: 9.

76 Jim Forest, *Pilgrim to the Russian Church*, op. cit., p. 72.

77 Thomas Merton, *Contemplative Prayer*, Garden City, New York: Image Books, 1969, p. 67.

78 Father Paulos Mar Gregorios, World Congress of Spiritual Concord, Rishikesh, India, December 11, 1993.

79 Luke 1: 38.

80 Quoted in Jim Forest, *Pilgrim to the Russian Church*, New York: Crossroad Publishing Company, 1988, p. 63.

81 *New York Times*, as reprinted in "The Gospel of Life," *Indian Currents*, April 8, 1995, p. 1.

82 Young Communist League, as quoted by Gerardo Tena, "Catholic imagery for papal visit transforms Havana," *Asian Age*, January 20, 1998, p. 6.

83 Sean McDonagh, *The Greening of the Church*, Maryknoll, New York: Orbis Books, p. 65.

84 Quoted in Don A. Schanche and Russell Chandler, Los Angeles Times, "Tensions confront pope in U.S.," *The Hartford Courant*, September 11, 1987, p. 1.

85 "Archbishop says religion reduced to a hobby in UK," *Asian Age*, July 6, 1996, p. 10.

86 Harvey Cox, *Fire from Heaven: The Rise of Pentecostal Spirituality and the Reshaping of Religion in the Twenty-first Century*, Reading, Massachusetts: Addison-Wesley, 1995.

87 Roman I. Bilas, interviewed October 25, 1994.

88 Members of African Independent Churches Report on their Pilot Study of the History and Theology of their Churches, "Speaking for Ourselves," Braamfontein, South Africa: Institute for Contextural Theology, 1985, pp. 23–24.

89 Desmond Tutu, quoted in Charles Vila-Vicencio, "Tough and Compassionate: Desmond Mpilo Tutu," in Leonard Hulley, Louise Kretzschmar, and Luke Lungile Pato, eds., *Archbishop Tutu: Prophetic Witness in South Africa*, Cape Town: Human and Rousseau, 1996, pp. 41–42.

90 Desmond Tutu, in Vila-Vicencio, op. cit., p. 37.

91 Ibid., p. 38.

92 Francis Cull, "Desmond Tutu: Man of Prayer," in Hulley et al., op. cit., pp. 31–32.

93 Desmond Tutu, in Vila-Vicencio, op. cit., pp. 44–45.

94 Martin Luther King, Jr., "An Experiment in Love," in *A Testament of Hope: The Essential*

Writings of Martin Luther King, Jr., ed. James Melvin Washington, San Francisco: Harper and Row, 1986, p. 16.

95 Acts 4: 32–35.

96 Gustavo Gutierrez, quoted in Phillip Berryman, *Liberation Theology*, New York: Pantheon Books, 1987, p. 33.

97 Bakole Wa Ilunga, *Paths of Liberation: A Third World Spirituality*, Maryknoll, New York: Orbis Books, 1984, p. 92.

98 1 Corinthians 11: 7–12.

99 Fiorenza, op. cit., p. xx.

100 John Shelby Spong, *Born of a Woman*, San Francisco: HarperCollins, 1992, p. 2.

101 Sally McFague, *Models of God: Theology for an Ecological, Nuclear Age*, Philadelphia: Fortress Press, 1987, pp. 101, 106.

102 Thomas Berry, remarks at "Seeking the True Meaning of Peace" conference in San Jose, Costa Rica, June 27, 1989.

103 From Document PU3, Second Report of the Public Issues Committee, article 4.4, p. 13, and Document PL 3.1: Report of the Moderator, p. 3, World Council of Churches, Eighth Assembly, 3–14 December 1998, Zimbabwe.

CHAPTER NINE
ISLAM

1 *The Holy Qur'an*, XCVI: 1–5, English translation by Abdullah Yusuf Ali, Durban, R.S.A.: Islamic Propagation Center International, 1946. This translation is used throughout this chapter, by permission. Note that despite the layout of this translation, the Qur'an is not a work of poetry.

2 Abu Abdallah Muhammad Bukhari, *Kitab jami as-sahih*, translated by M. M. Khan as *Sahih al-Bukhari*, Lahore: Ashraf, 1978–80, quoted in Annemarie Schimmel, *And Muhammad is His Messenger*, Chapel Hill, North Carolina: University of North Carolina Press, 1985, p. 11.

3 Sura 8: 18.

4 Maulana M. Ubaidul Akbar, *The Orations of Muhammad*, Lahore: M. Ashraf, 1954, p. 78.

5 Sura 41: 6.

6 Sura 28: 56.

7 Hadith quoted by Annemarie Schimmel, *And Muhammad is His Messenger*, Chapel Hill, North Carolina: University of North Carolina Press, 1985, pp. 48 and 55.

8 *The Holy Qur'an*, III: 104.

9 Quoted by Mahmoud Ayoub, *The Qur'an and its Interpreters*, Albany: State University of New York Press, 1984, vol. 1, p. 14.

10 Khalid Duran, "Interreligious Dialogue and the Islamic 'Original Sin,'" in Leonard Swidler, ed., *Toward a Universal Theology of Religion*, Maryknoll, New York: Orbis Books, 1988, p. 213.

11 Sura 42: 15.

12 Islamic Society of North America, "Islam at a Glance," Plainfield, Indiana: Islamic Teaching Center.

13 Abu Hashim Madani, quoted in Samuel L. Lewis, *In the Garden*, New York: Harmony Books/Lama Foundation, 1975, p. 136.

14 Frithjof Schuon, *Understanding Islam*, translated by D. M. Matheson, London: George Allen and Unwin, 1963, p. 59.

15 Farid Esack, personal communication, March 29, 1998.

16 Farid Esack, *Qur'an, Liberation and Pluralism: An Islamic Perspective of Interreligious Solidarity against Oppression*, Oxford: Oneworld Publications, 1997, p. 4.

17 Ibid., p. 223.

18 Ibid., p. 222.

19 Farid Esack, personal communication, March 29, 1998.

20 Sura 2: 136.

21 Sura 32: 16–17.

22 Quoted by Abdur-Rahman Ibrahim Doi, "Sunnism," *Islamic Spirituality: Foundations*, ed. Seyyed Hossein Nasr, New York: Crossroad, 1987, p. 158.

23 Sura 17: 13–14.

24 Sura 70: 16–18.

25 Quoted by Muhammad Rida al-Muzaffar, *The Faith of Shi'a Islam*, London: The Muhammadi Trust, 1982, p. 35.

26 Hadith # 535 cited in Badi'uz-Zaman Furuzanfar, *Ahadith-i Mathnawi*, Tehran, 1334 sh./1955, in Persian, quoted in Annemarie Schimmel, *Mystical Dimensions of Islam*, Chapel Hill: University of North Carolina Press, 1975, p. 118.

27 Mevlana Jalal al-Din Rumi, opening lines of the *Mathnawi*, as translated by Edmund Helminski, *The Ruins of the Heart: Selected Lyric Poetry of Jelaluddin Rumi*, Putney, Vermont: Threshold Books, 1981, p. 20.

28 Jalal al-Din Rumi, *Mathnawi-i ma'nawi*, ed. and translated by Reynold A. Nicholson, London, 1925–40, vol. 4, line 2102.

29 Hadith of the Prophet, #352 in Zaman Furuzanfar, *Ahadith-i Mathnawi*, op. cit.

30 Quoted in Javad Nurbakhsh, *Sufism: Meaning, Knowledge, and Unity*, New York: Khaniqahi-Nimatullahi Publications, 1981, pp. 19, 21.

31 Rumi, *Mathnawi*, VI, 3220–3246, as translated by Coleman Barks in *Rumi: We are Three*, Athens, Georgia: Maypop Books, 1987, pp. 54–55.

32 Sura 2: 256.

33 Hadith quoted by Syed Ali Ashraf, "The Inner Meaning of the Islamic Rites: Prayer, Pilgrimage, Fasting, Jihad," in *Islamic Spirituality: Foundations*, op. cit., p. 114.

34 Hammudah Abdalati, *Islam in Focus*, Indianapolis, Indiana: American Trust Publications, 1975, p. 88.

35 Hadith of the Prophet, as quoted in Fakhr al-Din Al-Razi, *Tafsir al-Fakhr al-Razi*, 21 vols., Mecca: al-Kaktabah al-Tijariyyah, 1990, vol. 7, p. 232.

36 Sura 22: 39–40.

37 Sura 2: 190.

38 Sura 2: 217, 192.

39 M. R. Bawa Muhaiyaddeen, "Islam's Hidden Beauty: The Sufi Teachings of M. R. Bawa Muhaiyaddeen," tape from New Dimensions Foundation, San Francisco, 1989, side 1.

40 Uzbek Khan, 1313 charter granted to Metropolitan Peter, as quoted in *Al Risala*, June 1994, p. 12.

41 Dalil-ul-Arifin, p. 37, as quoted in W. D. Begg, *The Holy Biography of Hazrat Khwaja Muinuddin Chishti*, Botswana, Africa: G. N. Khan, 1979, p. 41.

42 Annemarie Schimmel, speaking in "Islam's Hidden Beauty," tape from New Dimensions Foundation, San Francisco, 1989, side 1.

43 Seyyed Hossein Nasr, "The Pertinence of Islam to the Modern World," *The World Religions Speak on the Relevance of Religion in the Modern World*, ed. Finley P. Dunne Jr., The Hague: Junk, 1970, p. 133.

44 The First World Conference on Muslim Education, quoted in Syed Ali Ashraf, *New Horizon in Muslim Education*, Cambridge, England: Hodder and Stoughton/The Islamic Academy, 1985, p. 4.

45 Mufti Magomed-Khaji Albogachiev, remarks at The Inter-Religious Federation for World Peace Conference, Seoul, Korea, 1995.

46 Ibid.

47 Dr. A. K. Abu'l Majd, quoted in the video "Islam," Smithsonian World series, Smithsonian Institution and WETA, Washington, D.C., originally broadcast July 22, 1987, transcript pp. 6, 17.

CHAPTER TEN
SIKHISM

1 Kabir, in modern translation by Robert Bly, *The Kabir Book: Forty-four of the Ecstatic Poems of Kabir*, Copyright 1971, 1977 by Robert Bly, copyright 1977 by Seventies Press. Reprinted by permission of Beacon Press, p. 33.

2 Puratan, quoted in Khushwant Singh, *Hymns of Guru Nanak*, New Delhi: Orient Longmans Ltd., 1969, p. 10.

3 Guru Nanak, as quoted in W. Owen Cole and Piara Singh Sambhi, *The Sikhs: Their Religious Beliefs and Practices*, London: Routledge and Kegan Paul, 1978, p. 39.

4 Sri Rag, p. 59, quoted in Trilochan Singh, Jodh Singh, Kapur Singh, Bawa Harkishen Singh, and Kushwant Singh, trans., *The Sacred Writings of the Sikhs*, reproduced by kind permission of Unwin Hyman Ltd., 1973, p. 72.

5 Bhagat Ravi Das, Rag Sorath, *Guru Granth Sahib*, p. 657.

6 *Guru Granth Sahib*, p. 724.

7 Guru Har Rai, as quoted in Dr. Gopal Singh, *A History of the Sikh People*, New Delhi: World Sikh University Press, 1979, p. 257.

8 Guru Gobind Singh, *Bachittar Natak*, autobiography.

9 From Dr. S. Radhakrishnan, letter in the Baisakhi edition of "The Spokesman," 1956, reprinted as introduction to Giani Ishar Singh Nara, *Safarnama and Zafarnama*, New Delhi: Nara Publications, 1985, pp. iv–v.

10 Mool Mantra, quoted in *Hymns of Guru Nanak*, op. cit., p. 25.

11 *Jaap Sahib*, verses 84, 159, English translation by Harjett Singh Gill, New Delhi: Gobind Sadan Institute for Advanced Studies in Comparative Religion.

12 Adi Granth 684, quoted in Cole and Sambhi, op. cit., p. 74.

13 Guru Nanak, *Guru Granth Sahib*, p. 141.

14 Ibid.

15 Guru Arjun, Rag Majh, p. 102, quoted in Singh et al, *Sacred Writings of the Sikhs*, op. cit., p. 180.

16 *Anand Sahib*, verse 14.

17 Excerpted from *Rahitnamas*, op. cit.

18 Baba Virsa Singh, quoted by Juliet Hollister in *News from Gobind Sadan*, August 1997, p. 1.

19 Baba Virsa Singh, in *News from Gobind Sadan*, April 1997, p. 3.

20 Baba Virsa Singh, "News from Gobind Sadan," May 1994, p. 4.

21 Guru Gobind Singh, *Dasam Granth*.

CHAPTER ELEVEN
RELIGION AT THE TURN OF THE CENTURY

1 Reiko Hatsumi, "In a spiritual vacuum anything can flourish, even destruction," *Asian Age*, May 28, 1995, p. 9.

2 *Tenri kyoso den* ("Life of the Founder of the Tenri-kyo Sect") compiled by the Tenri-kyo doshi-kai, Tenri, 1913, quoted in Ichiro Hori, *Folk Religion in Japan*, Chicago: University of Chicago Press, 1968, p. 237.

3 Miki Nakayama, *Ofudesaki: The Tip of the Divine Writing Brush*, Tenri City, Japan: The Headquarters of the Tenrikyo Church, 1971, verses 1–3.

4 Justice Anthony M. Kennedy, United States Supreme Court majority opinion summation in *The Church of the Lucumi vs. The City of Hialeah*, June 11, 1993.

5 "A Brief Biography of Rajinder Singh," Delhi: Sawan Kirpal Publications Spiritual Society, p. 11.

6 Starhawk, *The Spiral Dance: A Rebirth of the Ancient Religion of the Great Goddess*, San Francisco: Harper and Row, 1979, pp. 2–3.

7 'Abdu'l-Baha', as quoted in "One World, One Faith," New Delhi: National Spiritual Assemblies of the Baha'is of India, 1979, p. 3.

8 Diana Eck, "A New Geo-Religious Reality," paper presented at the World Conference on Religion and Peace Sixth World Assembly, Riva del Garda, Italy, November 1994, p. 1.

9 Gyorgy Bulanyi, "Church and Peace: Vision and Reality," address at Overcoming Violence, a Church and Peace Conference in Pecel, Hungary, April 1995, as printed in *Church and Peace*, Spring 1995, p. 4.

10 Charles Strozier et al., "Religious Militancy or 'Fundamentalism,'" *Religion and Human Rights*, New York: The Project on Religion and Human Rights, 1994, p. 19.

11 Ewert Cousins, Speech at North American Interfaith Conference, Buffalo, New York, May 1991.

12 Raimundo Panikkar, "The Invisible Harmony: A Universal Theory of Religion or a Cosmic Confidence in Reality?", *Toward a Universal Theology of Religion*, ed. Leonard Swidler, Maryknoll, New York: Orbis Books, 1987, p. 147.

13 Pope John Paul II, quoted in Richard N. Ostling, "A Summit for Peace in Assisi," *Time*, November 10, 1986, p. 78.

14 Wangari Maathai, speaking at the Oxford Global Survival Conference, quoted in *The Temple of Understanding Newsletter*, Fall 1988, p. 2.

15 Swami Vivekananda, speech for the Parliament of the World's Religions, Chicago, 1893.

16 "Towards a Global Ethic," Assembly of Religious and Spiritual Leaders, at the Parliament of World Religions, Chicago, 1993.

17 The Right Rev. William E. Swing, "United Religions Initiative 2000: An Invitation to Share the Vision, an Invitation to Change the World," July 1996 pamphlet.

18 Paul Chaffee, "Ring of Breath around the World," *United Religions: Journal of the United Religions Initiative*, issue 4, Fall 1997, p. 7.

19 Gordon Kaufman, *The Myth of Christian Uniqueness*, Maryknoll, New York: Orbis Books, 1987.

20 Baba Virsa Singh, in Mary Pat Fisher, ed., *Loving God: The Practical Teachings of Baba Virsa Singh*, New Delhi: Gobind Sadan Institute for Advanced Studies in Comparative Religion, pp. 7–8.

21 Andreas D'Souza and Diane D'Souza, "Reconciliation: A New Paradigm for Missions," Hyderabad, India: Henry Martyn Institute of Islamic Studies, p. 5.
22 Gustavo Gutierrez, address to the World Conference on Religion and Peace, Riva del Garda, Italy, November 1994.
23 Martha Penzer, interviewed March 31, 1995, in New Delhi.
24 Vaclav Havel, *Letters to Olga*, translated by Paul Wilson, London and Boston: Faber and Faber, 1988 edition of 1983 original, pp. 236–237.
25 Pope Paul VI, *Populorum Progressio* Encyclical, 1967.
26 Professor Syed Anwar Kabir, interviewed April 12, 1995.
27 Barbara von der Heydt, *Candles Behind the Wall*, Grand Rapids, Michigan: William B. Eerdmans Publishing Company, 1993, p. xiii.
28 Yasuhiro Nakasone, speech at the Sixth World Conference on Religion and Peace, Riva del Garda, Italy, November 4, 1994, p. 3.
29 Baba Virsa Singh, *Loving God*, New Delhi: Gobind Sadan Institute for Advanced Studies in Comparative Religion, second edition, 1995, p. 60.

GLOSSARY

In the glossary, most words are accompanied by a guide to pronunciation. This guide gives an accepted pronunciation as simply as possible. Syllables are separated by a space and those that are stressed are underlined. Letters are pronounced in the usual manner for English unless they are clarified in the following list.

a *as in* flat
aa   father
aw   saw
ay   pay
ai   there
ee   see
e   let
i   pity
ī   high
o   not
ŏŏ   book
oo   food
oy   boy
ō   no
ow   now
u   but
ă, ĕ, ŏ, ŭ, about (unaccented vowels represented by "ə" in some phonetic
           alphabets)
er, ur, ir fern, fur, fir

ch   church
j   jet
ng   sing
sh   shine
wh   where
y   yes
kh   guttural aspiration (ch in Welsh and German)

absolutism Rigid, literal, exclusive belief in doctrines of one's religion.
Agni (<u>aag</u> nee) The god of fire in Hinduism.
agnosticism (ag <u>nos</u> ti siz ĕm) The belief that if there is anything beyond this life, it is impossible for humans to know it.
Allah (<u>aa</u> lă) The one God, in Islam.
Amida (ă <u>mee</u> dă) (Sanskrit: Amitabha) The Buddha of infinite light, the personification of compassion whom the Pure Land Buddhists revere as the intermediary between humanity and Supreme Reality; esoterically, the Higher Self.
anatta (ă <u>nat</u> ă) In Buddhism, the doctrine that nothing in this transient existence has a permanent self.
angel In the Zoroastrian–Jewish–Christian–Islamic traditions, an invisible servant of God.
anicca (ă <u>ni</u> chă) In Buddhism, the impermanence of all existence.
animism (<u>a</u> nim izĕm) The belief in usually invisible spirits present within things and people.
Annunciation (ă <u>nun</u> see ay shun) In Christianity, the appearance of an angel

to the Virgin Mary to tell her that she would bear Jesus, conceived by the Holy Spirit.

apocalypse (ă paw kă lips) In Judaism and Christianity, the dramatic end of the present age.

arhant (aar haˇnt) (Pali: arhat or arahat) A "Worthy One" who has followed the Buddha's Eightfold Path to liberation, broken the fetters that bind us to the suffering of the Wheel of Birth and Death, and arrived at nirvana; the Theravadan ideal.

Ark of the Covenant In Judaism, the shrine containing God's commandments to Moses.

Aryans (ayr ee ăns) The Indo-European pastoral invaders of many European and Middle Eastern agricultural cultures during the second millennium BCE.

asana (aa să nă) A yogic posture.

ashram (ash ram) In Indian tradition, a usually ascetic spiritual community of those who have gathered around a guru.

atheism (ay thee is em) Non-belief in any deity.

Atman (aat man) In Hinduism, the soul.

avatar In Hinduism, the earthly incarnation of a deity.

baptism A Christian sacrament by which God cleanses all sin and makes one a sharer in the divine life, and a member of Christ's body, the Church.

barakah (bă raa ka) In Islamic mysticism, the spiritual wisdom and blessing transmitted from master to pupil.

Bar Mitzvah (baar mitz vă) The coming-of-age ceremony for a Jewish boy.

Bat Mitzvah (bat mitz vă) The coming-of-age ceremony for a Jewish girl in some modern congregations.

Beatitudes (bee at ĕ toods) Short statements by Jesus about those who are most blessed.

Bhagavad-Gita (ba gă văd gee tă) A portion of the Hindu epic *Mahabharata* in which Lord Krishna specifies ways of spiritual progress.

bhakti (bak tee) In Hinduism, intense devotion to a personal aspect of the Deity.

bhikshu (bi kshoo) (Pali: bhikkhu; feminine: bhikshuni or bhikkhuni). A Buddhist monk or nun who renounces worldliness for the sake of following the path of liberation and whose simple physical needs are met by lay supporters.

Bodhisattva (boŏ dee sat vă) In Mahayana Buddhism, one who has attained enlightenment but renounces nirvana for the sake of helping all sentient beings in their journey to liberation from suffering.

Brahman (braa măn) The impersonal Ultimate Principle in Hinduism.

Brahamanas (braa mă năs) The portion of the Hindu Vedas concerning rituals.

Brahmin (braa min) (brahman) A priest or member of the priestly caste in Hinduism.

Buddha-nature A fully awakened consciousness.

caliph (kay lif) In Sunni Islam, the successor to the Prophet.

canon Authoritative collection of writings, works, etc, applying to a particular religion or author.

caste (kast) Social class distinction on the basis of heredity or occupation.

catholic Universal, all-inclusive. Christian churches referring to themselves as Catholic claim to be the representatives of the ancient undivided Christian church.

chakra (chuk ră) An energy center in the subtle body, recognized in kundalini yoga.

ch'i (chee) (ki) The vital energy in the universe and in our bodies, according to Far Eastern esoteric traditions.

ch'i-kung (chee kung) A Taoist system of harnessing inner energies for spiritual realization.

Common Era Years after the traditional date used for the birth of Jesus, previously referred to in exclusively Christian terms as "AD," and now abbreviated to "CE," as opposed to "BCE" ("before Common Era").

cosmogony (kos <u>mog</u> ŏn ee) Model of the evolution of the universe.

creed A formal statement of the beliefs of a particular religion.

cult Any religion that focuses on worship of a particular person or deity.

darsan (<u>daar</u> shan) Visual contact with the divine through encounters with Hindu images or gurus.

davening (<u>daa</u> vĕn ing) In Hasidic Judaism, prayer.

deity yoga (<u>dee</u> i tee <u>yō</u> gă) In Tibetan Buddhism, the practice of meditative concentration on a specific deity.

denomination (di nom ĕ <u>nay</u> shun) One of the Protestant branches of Christianity.

dervish (<u>der</u> vish) A Sufi ascetic, in the Muslim tradition.

deva (<u>day</u> vă) In Hinduism, a deity.

Dhammapada (<u>dam</u> ă pă dă) A collection of short sayings attributed to Buddha.

dharma (<u>daar</u> mă) (Pali: dhamma) The doctrine or law, as revealed by the Buddha; also the correct conduct for each person according to his or her level of awareness.

dhimmi (dĕ <u>hem</u> ee) A person of a non-Muslim religion whose right to practice that religion is protected within an Islamic society.

dogma (<u>dog</u> mă) A system of beliefs declared to be true by a religion.

Dream Time The timeless time of Creation, according to Australian Aboriginal belief.

dualism The separation of reality into two categories, particularly the concept that spirit and matter are separate realms.

dukkha (dŏŏ kă) According to the Buddha, a central fact of human life, variously translated as discomfort, suffering, frustration, or lack of harmony with the environment.

Durga (<u>dŏŏr</u> ga) The Great Goddess as destroyer of evil, and sometimes as sakti of Siva.

ecumenism (ek <u>yoo</u> mĕ niz ĕm) Rapprochement between branches of Christianity or among all faiths.

Epiphany (ee <u>pi</u> făni) "Manifestation"; in Christianity the recognition of Jesus's spiritual kingship by the three Magi.

eschatology (es kă <u>tol</u> ŏ ji) Beliefs about the end of the world and of humanity.

Essenes (<u>es</u> eenz) Monastic Jews who were living communally, apart from the world, about the time of Jesus.

Eucharist (<u>yoo</u> kă rist) The Christian sacrament by which believers are renewed in the mystical body of Christ by partaking of bread and wine, understood as his body and blood.

evangelism (i <u>van</u> jĕ liz ĕm) Ardent preaching of the Christian gospel.

exclusivism The idea that one's own religion is the only valid way.

excommunication Exclusion from participation in the Christian sacraments (applied particularly to Roman Catholicism), which is a bar to gaining access to heaven.

Fatiha (fat <u>haa</u>) The first sura of the Qur'an.

feng-shui (fĕng <u>shwee</u>)The Taoist practice of determining the most harmonious position for a building according to the natural flows of energy.

fundamentalism (fun dă <u>men</u> tăl iz ĕm) Insistence on what people perceive as the historical form of their religion, in contrast to more contemporary influences. This ideal sometimes takes extreme, rigidly exclusive, or violent forms.

Gentile (<u>jen</u> tīl) Any person who is not of Jewish faith or origin.

ghetto Urban area occupied by those rejected by a society, such as quarters for Jews in some European cities.

Gnosticism (<u>nos</u> ti sizĕm) Mystical perception of spiritual knowledge.

gospel In Christianity, the "good news" that God has raised Jesus from the dead and in so doing has begun the transformation of the world.

gunas (gŏŏ năs) In Yoga, the three states of the Cosmic Substance: sattva, rajas, tamas.

gurdwara (gŏŏr <u>dwa</u> ră) A Sikh temple.

guru (<u>gŏŏ</u> roo) In Hinduism, an enlightened spiritual teacher.

Guru Granth Sahib (goo roo granth <u>sa</u> heeb) The sacred scripture compiled by the Sikh Gurus.

Hadith (<u>haad</u> ith) In Islam, a traditional report about a reputed saying or action of the Prophet Muhammad.

haggadah (hă <u>gaa</u> dă) The non-legal part of the Talmud and midrash.

hajj (haaj) The holy pilgrimage to Mecca, for Muslims.

halakhah (haa laa <u>khaa</u>) Jewish legal decision and the parts of the Talmud dealing with laws.

Hasidism (<u>has</u> īd iz ĕm) Ecstatic Jewish piety, dating from eighteenth-century Poland.

hatha yoga (<u>ha</u> thă <u>yo</u>gă) Body postures, diet, and breathing exercises to help build a suitable physical vehicle for spiritual development.

heretic (<u>hair</u> i tik) A member of an established religion whose views are unacceptable to the orthodoxy.

hijab (<u>hay</u> jab) The veiling of women for the sake of modesty in Islam.

hijrah (<u>hij</u> ră) Muhammad's migration from Mecca to Medina.

Hinayana (<u>hee</u> nă <u>ya</u> nă) In Mahayana Buddhist terminology, the label "lesser vehicle," given to the orthodox Southern tradition now represented by Theravada; in Tibetan terminology, one of the three vehicles for salvation taught by the Buddha.

icon (<u>ī</u> kon) A sacred image, a term used especially for the paintings of Jesus, Mary, and the saints of the Eastern Orthodox Christian Church.

Imam (i <u>maam</u>) A leader of Muslim prayer; in Shi'ism, the title for the person carrying the initiatic tradition of the Prophetic Light.

immanent Present in Creation.

incarnation Physical embodiment of the divine.

indigenous (in <u>dij</u> ĕ nĕs) Native to an area.

infidel (<u>in</u> fid ĕl) The Muslim and Christian term for "non-believer," which each of these traditions often applied to the other.

Inquisition (in kwi <u>zi</u> shun) The use of force and terror to eliminate heresies and non-believers in the Christian Church starting in the thirteenth century.

interfaith dialogue Appreciative communication between people of different religions.

Jap Ji (<u>jap</u> jee) The first morning prayer of Sikhs, written by Guru Nanak.

jen (yen) Humanity, benevolence – the central Confucian virtue.

jihad (ji had) The Muslim's battle against the inner forces that prevent God-realization and the outer barriers to establishment of the divine order.

jinn (jin) In Islam, an invisible being of fire.

jnana yoga (ya na yō gǎ) The use of intellectual effort as a yogic technique.

Juchiao (jee tzǔ yow) The Chinese term for the teachings based on Confucius.

justification In Christianity, being absolved of sin in the eyes of God.

Kabbalah (kǎ baa lǎ) The Jewish mystical tradition.

Kali (kaa lee) Destroying and transforming Mother of the World, in Hinduism.

Kali Yuga (kaa lee yoo gǎ) In Hindu world cycles, an age of chaos and selfishness, including the one in which we are now living.

kami (kaa mee) The Shinto word for that invisible sacred quality which evokes wonder and awe in us, and also for the invisible spirits throughout nature that are born of this essence.

kannagara (kǎ nǎ gǎ rǎ) Harmony with the way of the kami in Shinto.

karma (kaar mā) (Pali: kamra) In Hinduism and Buddhism, our actions and their effects on this life and lives to come.

karma yoga (kaar mǎ yō gǎ) The path of unselfish service in Hinduism.

kensho (ken shō) Sudden enlightenment, in Zen Buddhism.

Khalsa (kal sǎ) The body of the pure, as inspired by the Sikh Guru Gobind Singh.

kosher (kō sher) Ritually acceptable, applied to foods in Jewish Orthodoxy.

kshatriya (ksha tree ǎ) A member of the warrior or ruling caste in traditional Hinduism.

kufr (kŏŏ fer) In Islam, the sin of atheism, of ingratitude to God.

lama (laa mǎ) A Tibetan Buddhist monk, particularly one of the highest in the hierarchy.

langar (lan gǎr) A free communal meal without caste distinctions, in Sikh tradition.

li (lee) Ceremonies, rituals, and rules of proper conduct, in the Confucian tradition.

liberal Flexible in approach to religious tradition; inclined to see it as metaphorical rather than literal truth.

liberation theology Christianity expressed as solidarity with the poor.

lingam (ling ǎm) A cylindrical stone or other similarly shaped natural or sculpted form, representing for Saivite Hindus the unmanifest aspect of Siva.

liturgy (lit ěr jee) In Christianity and Judaism, the rites of public worship.

Mahabharata (mǎ haa baa rǎ tǎ) A long Hindu epic which includes the *Bhagavad-Gita.*

Mahayana (maa hǎ ya nǎ) The "greater vehicle" in Buddhism, the more liberal and mystical Northern School which stressed the virtue of altruistic compassion rather than intellectual efforts at individual salvation.

mandala (man daa lǎ) A symmetrical image, with shapes emerging from a center, used as a meditational focus.

mantra(m) (man trǎ) A sound or phrase chanted to evoke the sound vibration of one aspect of creation or to praise a deity.

mass The Roman Catholic term for the Christian Eucharist.

materialism The tendency to consider material possessions and comforts more important than spiritual matters, or the philosophical position that nothing exists except matter, that there are no supernatural dimensions to life.

maya (mī yă) In Indian thought, the attractive but illusory physical world.

Messiah The "anointed," the expected king and deliverer of the Jews, a term later applied by Christians to Jesus.

metta (met ă) In Buddhist terminology, loving-kindness.

midrash (mid rash) The literature of delving into the Jewish Torah.

mikva (mik vă) A deep bath for ritual cleansing in Judaism.

millennium One thousand years, a term used in Christianity and certain newer religions for a hoped-for period of a thousand years of holiness and happiness, with Christ ruling the earth, as prophesied in the book of Revelation.

Mishnah In Judaism, the systematic summation of the legal teachings of the oral tradition of the Torah.

misogi (mee sō gee) The Shinto waterfall purification ritual.

mitzvah (mitz vă) (plural: mitzvot) In Judaism, a divine commandment or sacred deed in fulfillment of a commandment.

moksha (mōk shă) Liberation of the soul from illusion and suffering, in Hinduism.

monism (mon iz ĕm) The concept of life as a unified whole, without a separate "spiritual" realm.

monotheism (mon ō thee iz ĕm) The concept that there is one God.

mujahid (moo jă hid) In Islam, selfless fighter in the path of Allah.

murshid (moor shid) A spiritual teacher, in esoteric Islam.

mystic One who values inner spiritual experience in preference to external authorities and scriptures.

myth A symbolic story expressing ideas about reality or spiritual history.

Nam (naam) The holy Name of God reverberating throughout all of Creation, as repeated by Sikhs.

nirvana (ner va na) (Pali: nibbana) In Buddhism, the ultimate egoless state of bliss.

nontheistic Perceiving spiritual reality without a personal deity or deities.

occult Involving the mysterious, unseen, supernatural.

oharai Shinto purification ceremony.

OM (ōm) In Hinduism, the primordial sound.

orisa The Yoruba term for a deity, often used in speaking of West African religions in general.

orthodox Adhering to the established tradition of a religion.

Pali (paa lee) The Indian dialect first used for writing down the teachings of the Buddha, which were initially held in memory, and still used today in the Pali Canon of scriptures recognized by the Theravadins.

pantheism (pan thee iz ĕm) The concept that One Absolute Reality is everywhere.

parable (par ă bŭl) An allegorical story.

Paraclete (par ă kleet) The entity that Jesus said would come after his death to help the people.

Parvati (paar vă tee) Siva's spouse, sweet daughter of the Himalayas.

Pentateuch (pen tă took) The five books of Moses at the beginning of the Hebrew Bible.

Pentecost (pen tĕ kost) The occasion when the Holy Spirit descended upon the disciples of Jesus after his death.

Pharisees (fair ĕ seez) In Roman-ruled Judea, liberals who tried to practice Torah in their lives.

phenomenology An approach to the study of religions which involves appreciative investigation of religious phenomena to comprehend their meaning for their practitioners.

pluralism An appreciation of the diversity of religions.

polytheism (pol ĕ thee iz ĕm) Belief in many deities.

pope The Bishop of Rome and head of the Roman Catholic Church.

Prakriti (praak ri tee) In Samkhya Hindu philosophy, the cosmic substance.

prana (praa nă) In Indian thought, the invisible life-force.

pranayama (praa nă ya mă) Yogic breathing exercises.

prasad (pră saad) In Indian traditions, blessed food.

puja (poo jă) Hindu ritual worship.

Puranas (pŏŏ raa năs) Hindu scriptures written to popularize the abstract truths of the Vedas through stories about historical and legendary figures.

Pure Land A Buddhist sect in China and Japan that centers on faith in Amida Buddha, who promised to welcome believers to the paradise of the Pure Land, a metaphor for enlightenment.

Purgatory (pur gă tor ee) In some branches of Christianity, an intermediate after-death state in which souls are purified from sin.

Purusha (poo roo shă) The Cosmic Spirit, soul of the universe in Hinduism; in Samkhya philosophy, the eternal Self.

rabbi (rab ī) Historically, a Jewish teacher; at present, the ordained spiritual leader of a Jewish congregation.

rajas (raa jăs) The active state, one of the three gunas in Hinduism.

Ramayana (raa maa yă nă) The Hindu epic about Prince Rama, defender of good.

reincarnation The transmigration of the soul into a new body after death of the old body.

relic In some forms of Christianity, part of the body or clothing of a saint.

Rig Veda (rig vay dă) Possibly the world's oldest scripture, the foundation of Hinduism.

rishi (rish ee) A Hindu sage.

Sabbath (sab ăth) The day of the week set aside for rest and worship in Judaism and Christianity.

sacrament Outward and visible signs of inward and spiritual grace in Christianity. Almost all churches recognize baptism and the Eucharist as sacraments; some churches recognize five others as well.

sacred The realm of the extraordinary, beyond everyday perceptions, the supernatural, holy.

sacred thread In Hinduism, a cord worn over one shoulder by men who have been initiated into adult upper-caste society.

Sadducees (saj ŭ seez) In Roman-ruled Judea, wealthy and priestly Jews.

sadhana (saad hă nă) In Hinduism, especially yoga, a spiritual practice.

sadhu (sad oo) An ascetic holy man, in Hinduism.

Saivite (sīv īt) A Hindu worshipper of the Divine as Siva.

Sakta (sak ta) A Hindu worshipper of the female aspect of Deity.

sakti (sak tee) The creative, active female aspect of Deity in Hinduism.

samadhi (sa maa dee) In yogic practice, the blissful state of superconscious union with the Absolute.

Samkhya (saam khyă) One of the major Hindu philosophical systems, in which human suffering is characterized as stemming from the confusion of Prakriti with Purusha.

samsara (săm saa ră) The continual round of birth-and-death existence, in Hinduism, Jainism, and Buddhism.

Sanatana Dharma (să na tă nă daar mă) The "eternal religion" of Hinduism.

sangat A Sikh congregation, in which all are ideally considered equal.

sangha (sung ă) In Theravada Buddhism, the monastic community; in Mahayana, the spiritual community of followers of the dharma.

sannyasin (sun yaa sin) In Hinduism, a renunciate spiritual seeker.

Sanskrit (san skrit) The literary language of classic Hindu scriptures.

sant A Sikh holy person.

Santeria The combination of African and Christian practices which developed in Cuba.

sativa (sa tee vă) The state of purity and illumination, one of the three gunas in Hinduism.

satori (să taw ree) Enlightenment, realization of ultimate truth, in Zen Buddhism.

sect A sub-group within a larger tradition.

Seder Ceremonial Jewish meal in remembrance of the Passover.

shabd (shaabd) The Sikh term for a Name of God that is recited or a hymn from the Guru Granth Sahib, considered the Word of God.

Shahadah (shă haa dă) The central Muslim expression of faith: "There is no god but God."

shaman (shaa măn) A "medicine person," a man or woman who has undergone spiritual ordeals and can communicate with the spirit world to help the people in indigenous traditions.

Shari'ah (shă ree ă) The divine law, in Islam.

shayk (shaik) A spiritual master, in the esoteric Muslim tradition.

Shekhinah (she kī nă) God's presence in the world, in Judaism.

Shi'a, Shi'ite (shee īt) The minority branch of Islam which feels that Muhammad's legitimate successors were 'Ali and a series of Imams; a follower of this branch.

shirk (shirk) The sin of believing in any divinity except the one God, in Islam.

shudra (shoo dră) A member of the manual laborer caste in traditional Hinduism.

Sikh (seek) "Student," especially one who practices the teachings of the ten Sikh Gurus.

Siva (shee vă) In Hinduism, the Supreme as lord of yogis, absolute consciousness, creator, preserver, and destroyer of the world; or the destroying aspect of the Supreme.

soma (sō ma) An intoxicating drink used by early Hindu worshippers.

stupa (stoo pă) A rounded monument containing Buddhist relics or commemorative materials.

Sufism (soo fis ĕm) The mystical path in Islam.

Sunnah (soo nă) The behavior of the Prophet Muhammad, used as a model in Islamic law.

Sunni (soo nee) A follower of the majority branch of Islam which feels that successors to Muhammad are to be chosen by the Muslim community.

sunyata (soon yă tă) Voidness, the transcendental ultimate reality in Buddhism.

sura (soō ră) A chapter of the Qur'an.

sutra (soō tră) (Pali: suta) Literally, a thread on which are strung jewels – the discourses of the Buddha; in yoga, sutras are terse sayings.

synagogue (sin ă gog) A meeting place for Jewish study and worship.

syncretism (sing kri tis ĕm) A form of religion in which otherwise differing traditions are blended.

synod In Christianity, a council of church officials called to reach agreement on doctrines and administration.

synoptic (sin op tik) Referring to three similar books of the Christian Bible: Matthew, Mark, and Luke.

T'ai-chi chuan (tī chee hwaan) An ancient Chinese system of physical exercises which uses slow movements to help one become part of the universal flow of energy.

talit (ta lit) A shawl traditionally worn by Jewish men during prayers.

Talmud (tal mŏŏd) Jewish law and lore, as finally compiled in the sixth century CE.

tamas (tam ăs) The dull state, one of the three gunas in Hinduism.

Tanakh (ta nakh) The Jewish scriptures.

Tantras (tan trăs) The ancient Indian texts based on esoteric worship of the Divine as feminine.

Tantrayana (tăn tră ya nă) See Vajrayana.

Tao (Dao) (dow) The way or path, in Far Eastern traditions. The term is also used as a name for the Nameless.

Tao-chia (dow cheeă) The ancient philosophical Taoist tradition.

Tao-chiao (dow cheeow) The newer magically religious Taoist tradition.

t'fillin (tĕ fil in) A small leather box with verses about God's covenant with the Jewish people, bound to the forehead and arm.

thang-ka (tang ka) In Tibetan Buddhism, an elaborate image of a spiritual figure used as a focus for meditation.

theistic (thee is tik) Believing in a God or gods.

Theravada (ter ă vă dă) The remaining orthodox school of Buddhism, which adheres closely to the earliest scriptures and emphasizes individual efforts to liberate the mind from suffering.

third eye The center of spiritual insight thought to reside between and slightly above the physical eyes.

Torah (tō raa) The Pentateuch; also, the whole body of Jewish teaching and law.

transcendent Existing outside the material universe.

transpersonal Referring to an eternal, infinite reality, in contrast to the finite material world.

Trinity The Christian doctrine that in the One God are three divine persons: the Father, the Son, and the Holy Spirit.

Triple Gem The three jewels of Buddhism: Buddha, dharma, sangha.

tsumi (tzoo mee) Impurity or misfortune, a quality that Shinto purification practices are designed to remove.

"twice-born" Upper-caste men who have been initiated into Aryan society in traditional Hinduism.

tzaddik (tzaa dik) An enlightened Jewish mystic.

ulama (oo lă maa) The influential leaders in traditional Muslim society, including spiritual leaders, imams, teachers, state scribes, market inspectors, and judges.

ummah (o maa) The Muslim community.

Upanishads (oo pan i shăds) The philosophical part of the Vedas in Hinduism, intended only for serious seekers.

Vaishnavite (v<u>ish</u> nă vīt) (*Vaishnava*) A Hindu devotee of Vishnu, particularly in his incarnation as Krishna.

vaishya (v<u>ish</u> yă) A member of the merchant and farmer caste in traditional Hinduism.

Vajrayana (văj ră <u>yaa</u> nă) or Tantrayana The ultimate vehicle used in Mahayana, mainly Tibetan, Buddhism, consisting of esoteric tantric practices and concentration on deities.

Varuna (<u>va</u> roo nă) The old thunder god of cosmic order in ancient Hinduism.

Vedanta (vi <u>dan</u> tă) A Hindu philosophy based on the Upanishads.

Vedas Ancient scriptures revered by Hindus.

vipassana (vi <u>pas</u> ă nă) In Buddhism, meditation based on watching one's own thoughts, emotions, and actions.

Vishnu (<u>vish</u> noo) In Hinduism, the preserving aspect of the Supreme or the Supreme Itself, incarnating again and again to save the world.

vision quest In indigenous traditions, a solitary ordeal undertaken to seek spiritual guidance about one's mission in life.

Voodoo (<u>voo</u> doo) Latin American and Caribbean ways of working with the spirit world, a blend of West African and Catholic Christian teachings.

wu-wei (woo way) In Taoism, "not doing," in the sense of taking no action contrary to the natural flow.

yagna (<u>yaj</u> nă) (Persian: yasna) Ancient religious rituals in Hinduism and Zoroastrianism.

yang (yang) In Chinese philosophy, the bright, assertive, "male" energy in the universe.

yantra (<u>yan</u> tră) In Hinduism, a linear cosmic symbol used as an aid to spiritual concentration.

yi (yee) Righteous conduct (as opposed to conduct motivated by desire for personal profit), a Confucian virtue stressed by Mencius.

yin (yin) In Chinese philosophy, the dark, receptive, "female" energy in the universe.

yoga (y<u>ō</u> gă) Ancient techniques for spiritual realization, found in several Eastern religions.

Yoga (y<u>ō</u> gă) A systematic approach to spiritual realization, one of the major Hindu philosophical systems.

yoni (y<u>ō</u> nee) Abstract Hindu representation of the female vulva, cosmic matrix of life.

yuga (<u>yoo</u> gă) One of four recurring world cycles in Hinduism.

zakat (zak at) Spiritual tithing in Islam.

zazen (zaa <u>zen</u>) Zen Buddhist sitting meditation.

Zealots Jewish resistance fighters who fought the Romans and were defeated in the siege of Jerusalem.

Zen (zen) (Chinese: Ch'an) A Chinese and Japanese Buddhist school emphasizing that all things have Buddha-nature, which can only be grasped when one escapes from the intellectual mind.

zendo (<u>zen</u> dō) A Zen meditation hall.

INDEX

	2000 BCE	1500	1000	500	0 CE
Indigenous	←				
Hinduism	← Vedas heard	Vedas first written c.1500		*Ramayana* and Code of Manu com[*Mahabharata* in before 100 CE present form 400+ Pantanjali systematizes *Yoga Sutras* 200	
Judaism	Abraham 1900–1700 BCE?	Moses 1300 BCE?	King David 1010–970 First temple destroyed; Jews exiled 586	Jerusalem falls to Romans 70	
Taoism and Confucianism			Chuang-tzu c.400–300 or earlier Lao-tzu c.600–500 Confucius c.551–479 Educational system based on Confucian Classics from 2(		
Buddhism			Gautama Buddha c.563–483	King Asoka spreads Buddhism c.258 Theravada Buddhism develops 200 BCE–200 (	
Christianity				Jesus c.4 BCE–c.30 c Paul organizes early Christians c.50–60 (Gospels written dov c.70–95 CE	
Islam					
Zoroastrianism	Early elements of Zoroastriansim in Indo-Iranian tribes		Zarathushtra c.1100–550 BCE	State religion of Iranian Empire 131 BCE	
Jainism	Series of 23 Tirthankaras		Mahavira 599–527 BCE Digambaras and Svetambaras diverge from 3rd C. BCE		
Shinto	Shinto begins in pre-history as local nature- and ancestor-based traditions				
Sikhism					
Interfaith					

	600	900	1200	1500	1800	2000 CE

nt ways passed down and adapted over millennia ⟶

Bhaki movement 600–1800 ⟶ Ramakrishna
1836–1886

nical tradition — Maimonides 1135–1204 — The Baal Shem Tov 1700–1760 — 1940–1945 the Holocaust 1948 Israel's independence

ped 1st–
, CE

religion institutionalized — 960–1280 Sung dynasty revived ritualistic Confucianism ("neo-Confucianism") — 1966–1976 Cultural Revolution attacks religions
2nd C. CE

c.500–600 Japan imports Confucianism to unite tribes into empire — 1989 Chinese government limits religious freedoms

yana
nism — Buddhism declared national religion of Tibet 700s — Persecution of Buddhism begins in China 845 — Ch'an Buddhism to Japan as Zen 13th C. — Buddhism spreads in the West 20th C.
ps 1st C. CE

Centralization of papal power 800–1100 — Monastic orders proliferate 1300s — Protestantism begins 1521 — Second Vatican council 1962

Western and Eastern Churches split 1054

Spanish Inquisition established 1478

Muhammad c.570–632
Spread of Islam begins 633
Sunni–Shi'ite split c.682 — Mughal Emperor Akbar 1556 — European dominance 1800s–1900s
Islam's cultural peak 750–1258 — OPEC and Muslim resurgence 1970s

Emigration of Parsis to India 10th C.

Jain monks establish Jain centers outside India 1970s–1980s

name adopted
CE — State Shinto established 1868

Guru Nanak 1469–1504 — At death of Guru Gobind Singh, the scriptures become the guru 1708

Mughal Emperor Akbar initiates interfaith dialogues 1556–1605 — First International Human Unity Conference 1974 Centenary Celebrations 1993